The Eastern Origins of Western Civilisation

John Hobson challenges the ethnocentric bias of mainstream accounts of the rise of the West. It is often assumed that since Ancient Greek times Europeans have pioneered their own development, and that the East has been a passive bystander in the story of progressive world history. Hobson argues that there were two processes that enabled the rise of the 'oriental West'. First, each major developmental turning point in Europe was informed in large part by the assimilation of Eastern inventions (e.g. ideas, technologies and institutions) which through oriental globalisation diffused from the more advanced East across the Eastern-led global economy between 500 and 1800. Second, the construction of European identity after 1453 led to imperialism, through which Europeans appropriated many Eastern resources (land, labour and markets). Hobson's book thus propels the hitherto marginalised Eastern peoples to the forefront of the story of progress in world history.

JOHN M. HOBSON is Professor of Politics and International Relations at the University of Sheffield. He is the co-editor (with Steve Hobden) of *Historical Sociology of International Relations* (2002), author of *The State and International Relations* (2000), *The Wealth of States: a Comparative Sociology of International Economic and Political Change* (1997) and co-author (with Linda Weiss) of *States and Economic Development: a Comparative Historical Analysis* (1995).

The Eastern Origins of
Western Civilisation

JOHN M. HOBSON

CAMBRIDGE
UNIVERSITY PRESS

CAMBRIDGE UNIVERSITY PRESS
Cambridge, New York, Melbourne, Madrid, Cape Town, Singapore, São Paulo

Cambridge University Press
The Edinburgh Building, Cambridge, CB2 8RU, UK

Published in the United States of America by Cambridge University Press, New York

www.cambridge.org
Information on the title: www.cambridge.org/9780521547246

First published 2004
Sixth printing 2007

Printed in the United Kingdom at the University Press, Cambridge

A catalogue record for this publication is available from the British Library

Library of Congress Cataloguing in Publication data
Hobson, John M.
The Eastern origins of Western civilization / John M. Hobson.
   p.   cm.
ISBN 0-521-83835-5 – ISBN 0-521-54724-5 (pbk.)
1. East and West.   2. Civilization, Western – History.   I. Title.
CB251.H63   2004
909′.09821 – dc22   2003063549

ISBN 978-0-521-83835-1 hardback
ISBN 978-0-521-54724-6 paperback

To the indirect influence of my great-grandfather,
John Atkinson Hobson,
whose 'heretical' writings have permeated much of
how I explain the world.
I thank you.
Your lone twilight will never fade away.

To the direct influence of my beloved Cecelia
and to my family,
Evangeline, Michael and Gabriella,
whose loving and empathic actions have permeated much
of what I know, feel and understand of the world.
I thank all of you.
Your bright dawn alone warms me every single day.

Contents

Tables

Preface and acknowledgements

To reassure my potential reader who thinks anxiously, 'not another typical book on the rise of the West', let me say this is not one such book. For unlike almost all the books on this topic this one does not recount all the familiar themes according to the standard European, ethnocentric frame of reference. In place of the usual story, I produce one that brings the East into the limelight. Accordingly, though my purpose differs in certain respects to that of Felipe Fernández-Armesto's *Millennium*, nevertheless I, like him, take delight in surprising the reader. I focus on the many Eastern discoveries, peoples and places that enabled the rise of the West, all of which are ignored in the conventional accounts. If I may be permitted I would like to draw on the phraseology found in the prologue to *Millennium* to convey a sense of what my book is and is not about.

In this book the reader will find nothing about the Investiture Conflict, the Thirty Years War or the Treaty of Westphalia. While the Italian merchant communes are discussed, they are at all times revealed as derivative of the wider innovative developments pioneered in the Eastern-led global economy. The European Renaissance and scientific revolution are considered more from the perspective of the Islamic Middle East and North Africa than Tuscany.[1] Da Vinci, Ficino and Copernicus kneel before the likes of al-Shātir, al-Khwārizmī and al-Tūsī. Vasco da Gama fades into the marginalised shadows cast by the brilliance of Asia. This is the only

---

[1] Note that I have used the term 'Middle East' rather than 'West Asia' only because the former term is more recognisable to the general reader. It is also noteworthy that I have used the Wade-Giles as opposed to the Pinyin system for referencing Chinese names, again only because the former is more clearly recognisable to the general reader than is the latter.

mention of Elizabeth I, Oliver Cromwell and Queen Victoria. Louis XIV and Frederick the Great appear only to beg to be excused. For the majority of the period discussed in this book, Madrid, Lisbon, London and Venice are all provincial backwaters of Baghdad, Cairo, Canton and Calicut. London's Great Exhibition turns out to be hubris, given that Britain's industrialisation is but the final stage of the transmission of the much earlier inventions pioneered in China. And the processes of state-led, militarised industrialisation and protectionism are discussed and applied, but in the context of Britain rather than Meiji Japan. Last but by no means least, in place of Germany's 'late industrialisation' the reader will be treated to a discussion of Tokugawa Japan's 'early development'. In general the reader will learn much more about the East – especially the Islamic Middle East, North Africa, India, South-east Asia, Japan and above all China – though in so doing will learn new things about the West and its origins.

Accordingly the reader who expects to be treated to all the specific details of Western development cast only in a European light, will necessarily be disappointed. Nevertheless my intention is precisely to disappoint such a reader, though simultaneously treat him or her with the lost story of how the East enabled the rise of the modern West. Whether the reader is entirely convinced by this book's particular arguments in a sense concerns me less than whether they are perceived to be fresh, interesting and insightful. And I am more interested in the larger questions and issues that this book's arguments pose than the particular answers that it provides. Thus I can reassure my anxious potential reader that there is indeed not a place for yet another typical book on the rise of the Western world. I, therefore, hope that the intrepid reader who does read on will enjoy this book's counter-intuitive journey into the hitherto dark world of the largely forgotten.

Let me now turn to thank a number of people who have in various ways enabled me to chart these waters more effectively than I might otherwise have done. I thank the following who offered helpful advice: Robert Aldrich, Brett Bowden, Jeff Groom, Steve

Hobden, David Mathieson, Leanne Piggott, Tim Rowse, Ahmad Shboul and Richard White. I thank too the following people who read and commented on substantial parts of the manuscript: Amitav Acharya, Ha-Joon Chang, M. Ramesh, Lily Rahim, Leonard Seabrooke and Vanita Seth. Double thanks to Ha-Joon for inviting me to present my ideas in the Department of Development Studies at the University of Cambridge. Ben Tipton very kindly read the whole manuscript and offered characteristically pertinent advice. I thank Michael Mann from whom I have learned a great deal about world history and remain deeply grateful for his generous support ever since I had the luck to take his Masters sociological theory class at the LSE in 1986. Linda Weiss has been equally as supportive in the last decade. And special thanks too go to Eric Jones, who has also helped me learn so much about world history both through his writings (especially *Growth Recurring*) and our personal conversations over the years.

Thanks to John Haslam at CUP, whose patience and sensitive editorial advice is, as always, much appreciated. I also thank my indexer, Trevor Matthews, for his heroic efforts as well as Hilary Scannell for her copy-editing. And special thanks too must go to the three anonymous reviewers, all of whom offered many positive comments as well as constructive criticisms, and proposed the most substantial revision that I have yet undertaken in my career. In particular, I thank them for enabling me to write a better book; certainly one that I am much happier with. And, of course, the familiar rider stands: that I remain responsible for any errors.

Finally, I want to express my love and deepest gratitude to my fiancée, Cecelia Thomas, who guided, anchored and sacrificed for, me in so many ways in three of the most tumultuous years of life-changing events that I have yet experienced. Her humane strengths of sacrifice, sensitivity and empathy represent the best of all that is good on this troubled planet and shed light and warmth upon my place in it. Here the less familiar rider stands: that I remain responsible for any personal errors.

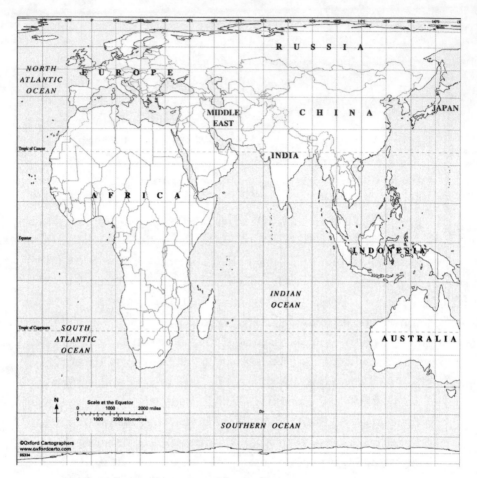

Map 1   Hobo-Dyer projection of the world

ARCTIC OCEAN

C A N A D A

U. S. A.

NORTH
ATLANTIC
OCEAN

Tropic of Cancer

PACIFIC OCEAN

Equator

SOUTH
AMERICA

Tropic of Capricorn

The Hobo-Dyer Equal Area Projection

This new map belongs to the family of Cylindrical Equal Area projections in
which the latitude and longitude lines form a rectangular grid. Other projections
in this family include the Lambert, Gall, Behrmann, Edwards, and Peters
projections. In the present case the "cylinder" is assumed to wrap round the
globe and cut through it at 37½° north and south. In order to preserve the
equal area property the shapes of the landmasses become progressively
flattened towards the poles, but shapes between 45° north and south
are well preserved.

SOUTHERN OCEAN

1 Countering the Eurocentric myth of the pristine West:
discovering the oriental West

> History cannot be written as if it belonged to one group [of people] alone. Civilization has been gradually built up, now out of the contributions of one [group], now of another. When all civilization is ascribed to the [Europeans], the claim is the same one which any anthropologist can hear any day from primitive tribes – only they tell the story of themselves. They too believe that all that is important in the world begins and ends with them . . . We smile when such claims are made [by primitive tribes], but ridicule might just as well be turned against ourselves . . . Provincialism may rewrite history and play up only the achievements of the historian's own group, but it remains provincialism.
>
> Ruth Benedict

> We have been taught, inside the classroom and outside of it, that there exists an entity called the West, and that one can think of this West as a society and civilization independent of and in opposition to other societies and civilizations [i.e. the East]. Many of us even grew up believing that this West has [an autonomous] genealogy, according to which ancient Greece begat Rome, Rome begat Christian Europe, Christian Europe begat the Renaissance, the Renaissance the Enlightenment, the Enlightenment political democracy and the industrial revolution. Industry, crossed with democracy, in turn yielded the United States, embodying the rights to life, liberty and the pursuit of happiness . . . [This is] misleading, first, because it turns history into a moral success story, a race in time in which each [Western] runner of the race passes on the torch of liberty to the next relay. History is thus converted into a tale about the furtherance of virtue, about how the virtuous [i.e. the West] win out over the bad guys [the East].
>
> Eric Wolf

Most of us naturally assume that the East and West are, and always have been, separate and different entities. We also generally believe that it is the 'autonomous' or 'pristine' West that has alone pioneered the creation of the modern world; at least that is what many of us are taught at school, if not at university. We typically assume that the pristine West had emerged at the top of the world by about 1492 (think of Christopher Columbus), owing to its uniquely ingenious scientific rationality, rational restlessness and democratic/progressive properties. From then, the traditional view has it, the Europeans spread outwards conquering the East and Far West while simultaneously laying down the tracks of capitalism along which the whole world could be delivered from the jaws of deprivation and misery into the bright light of modernity. Accordingly, it seems entirely natural or self-evident to most of us to conflate the progressive story of world history with the Rise and Triumph of the West. This traditional view can be called 'Eurocentric'. For at its heart is the notion that the West properly deserves to occupy the centre stage of progressive world history, both past and present. But does it?

The basic claim of this book is that this familiar but deceptively seductive Eurocentric view is false for various reasons, not the least of which is that the West and East have been fundamentally and consistently interlinked through globalisation ever since 500 CE. More importantly, and by way of analogy, Martin Bernal argues that Ancient Greek civilisation was in fact significantly derived from Ancient Egypt.[1] Likewise, the present book argues that the East (which was more advanced than the West between 500 and 1800) provided a crucial role in enabling the rise of modern Western civilisation. It is for this reason that I seek to replace the notion of the autonomous or pristine West with that of the oriental West. The East enabled the rise of the West through two main processes: diffusionism/assimilationism and appropriationism. First, the Easterners created a global economy and global communications network after 500 along which the more advanced Eastern 'resource portfolios' (e.g. Eastern ideas, institutions and technologies) diffused across to the West, where they were subsequently assimilated, through what I call oriental globalisation. And second, Western imperialism after 1492 led the Europeans to appropriate all manner of Eastern economic resources to enable the rise of the West. In short, the West did not autonomously pioneer its own development in the absence of Eastern help, for its rise would have been inconceivable without the contributions of the East. The task of this book, then, is to trace the manifold Eastern contributions that led to the rise of what I call the oriental West.

This book feeds into the debate between Eurocentrism and anti-Eurocentrism. In recent years a small band of scholars have claimed that the standard theories of the rise of the West – Marxism/world-systems theory, liberalism and Weberianism – are all Eurocentric.[2] They all assume that the 'pristine' West 'made it' of its own accord as a result of its innate and superior virtues or properties. This view presumes that Europe autonomously developed through an iron logic of immanence. Accordingly, such theories assume that the rise of the modern world can be told as the story of the rise and triumph of the West. Importantly, the Eurocentric account has enjoyed a new lease of life or fresh reinvigoration, particularly with the 1998 publication of David Landes's *The Wealth and Poverty of Nations*,[3] a book that implicitly harks back to John Roberts's *The Triumph of the West*.[4] Landes's book in particular launches a passionate and pejorative attack against some of the recent anti-Eurocentric analyses (though for all this it is done with verve and wit and is an especially enjoyable read). Perhaps Landes's most significant service is that he has helped transform the old theoretical debate conducted between Marxism/world-systems theory, liberalism and Weberianism into a new one of 'Eurocentrism versus anti-Eurocentrism'. This, it seems to me, is where the real intellectual action lies. For arguably the old debate is something of a non-debate given that all these approaches now appear as but minor or subtle variations on the same Eurocentric theme (see the next section below). Accordingly, the present book enters this new debate and contests each of the major claims made by mainstream Eurocentrism, while simultaneously proposing an alternative account.

It could, however, be replied that the 'Eurocentric versus anti-Eurocentric' framework that this book operationalises is an over-simplification and is itself a 'non-debate'. Presuming a kind of Manichean struggle between two coherent ideologies is problematic mainly because, it could be claimed, there is no coherent paradigm called 'Eurocentrism'. Indeed, I believe it would be wrong to assume that most scholars are fighting to defend an explicitly Eurocentric 'triumphalist' vision of the West. And while there are some who explicitly associate themselves with Eurocentrism (such as Landes and Roberts), most do not. Nevertheless, I firmly believe that Eurocentrism infuses *all* the mainstream accounts of the rise of the West, even if this mostly occurs behind the back of the particular scholar (see the next section below). Accordingly, I believe it to be legitimate to develop my own account by critically evaluating the many claims made by Eurocentrism.

The main argument of this book counters one of Eurocentrism's most basic assumptions – that the East has been a passive bystander in the story of world historical development as well as a victim or bearer of Western power, and that accordingly it can be legitimately marginalised from the progressive story of world history. Although this volume differs in various ways from Felipe Fernández-Armesto's phenomenal book, *Millennium*, nevertheless I share with him his empathic belief that:

> For purposes of world history, the margins sometimes demand more attention than the metropolis. Part of the mission of this book is to rehabilitate the overlooked, including places often ignored as peripheral, peoples marginalized as inferior and individuals relegated to bit-parts and footnotes.[5]

Or in a narrower context, as W. E. B. Du Bois explained in the foreword to his important book, *Africa in World History*:

> there has been a consistent effort to rationalize Negro slavery by omitting Africa from world history, so that today it is almost universally assumed that history can be truly written without reference to Negroid peoples . . . Therefore I am seeking in this book to remind readers . . . of how critical a part Africa has played in human history, past and present.[6]

Likewise, my major claim in this book is that the Eurocentric denial of Eastern agency and its omission of the East in the progressive story of world history is entirely inadequate. For not only do we receive a highly distorted view of the rise of the West, but we simultaneously learn little about the East except as a passive object, or provincial backwater, of mainstream Western world history.

This marginalisation of the East constitutes a highly significant silence because it conceals three major points. First, the East actively pioneered its own substantial economic development after about 500. Second, the East actively created and maintained the global economy after 500. Third, and above all, the East has significantly and actively contributed to the rise of the West by pioneering and delivering many advanced 'resource portfolios' (e.g. technologies, institutions and ideas) to Europe. Accordingly, we need to resuscitate both the history of economic dynamism in the East and the vital role of the East in the rise of the West. Nevertheless, as we shall also see, this does not mean that the West has been a passive recipient of Eastern resources. For the Europeans played an active role in shaping their own fate (especially through the construction of a changing collective identity, which in turn partially informed the direction of Europe's economic and political development). In sum, these two interrelated claims – Eastern agency and the assimilation of advanced Eastern 'resource portfolios' via oriental globalisation on the one hand, entwined with European agency/identity and the appropriation of Eastern resources on the other – constitute the discovery of the lost story of the rise of the oriental West.

In this context it is especially noteworthy that our common perception of the irrelevance of the East and the superiority of Europe is reinforced or 'confirmed' by the Mercator world map. This map is found everywhere – from world atlases to school walls to airline booking agencies and boardrooms. Crucially, the actual landmass of the southern hemisphere is exactly twice that of the northern hemisphere. And yet on the Mercator, the landmass of the North occupies two-thirds of the map while the landmass of the South represents only a third. Thus while Scandinavia is about a third the size of India, they are accorded the same amount of space on the map. Moreover on the Mercator, Greenland appears almost twice the size of China, even though the latter is almost four times the size of the former. To correct for what he saw as the racist privileging of Europe, in 1974 Arno Peters produced the Peters projection (or the Peters–Gall projection), which sought to represent the countries of the world according to their actual surface area. Here the South properly looms much larger, while Europe is considerably downgraded. Although no perfect map of the world exists, his representation is certainly free of the implicit Eurocentric distortion found in the Mercator. Not surprisingly, when the Peters projection first appeared there was a political storm, for as Marshall Hodgson points out, 'Westerners understandably cling to a projection [the Mercator] which so markedly flatters them'.[7]

This present book in effect attempts to correct our perception of world history in the same way that the Peters projection seeks to correct our perception of world geography, by discovering the relative importance of the East *vis-à-vis* the West. More specifically, I have presented a variant of this projection (the 'Hobo-Dyer') at the beginning of this chapter but have reconfigured it so as to place China at the centre, given its pivotal role in the rise of the West. No less importantly, the USA and Europe now properly occupy the diminished peripheral margins of the Far North-east and Far North-west respectively. And while Africa also occupies the Far West, its upgraded size corrects for its downgraded marginalisation in the Eurocentric model.

This chapter proceeds in two sections. The first begins by very briefly tracing the construction of the Eurocentric discourse as it emerged during the eighteenth and nineteenth centuries. It then proceeds to show how the major explanations of the rise of the West, found specifically in the work of Karl Marx and Max Weber, became grounded within this discourse. The second section then briefly fleshes out my own two-prong argument as a remedy to the prevailing Eurocentrism of mainstream accounts.

Constructing the Eurocentric/Orientalist foundations of the mainstream theories of the rise of the West

European identity formation and the invention of Eurocentrism/Orientalism

In 1978 Edward Said famously coined the phrase 'Orientalism', though in fairness a number of other scholars, including Victor Kiernan, Marshall Hodgson and Bryan Turner, were already thinking along such lines.[8] Orientalism or Eurocentrism (I use them interchangeably throughout this book) is a worldview that asserts the inherent superiority of the West over the East. Specifically Orientalism constructs a permanent image of the superior West (the 'Self') which is defined negatively against the no less imaginary 'Other' – the backward and inferior East. As ch. 10 explains in detail, it was mainly during the eighteenth and nineteenth centuries that this polarised and essentialist construct became fully apparent within the European imagination. What then were the specific categories by which the West came to imagine its Self as superior to the Eastern Other?

Between 1700 and 1850 European imagination divided, or more accurately forced, the world into two radically opposed camps: West and East (or the 'West and the Rest'). In this new conception, the West was imagined as superior to the East. The imagined values of the inferior East were set up as the antithesis of rational (Western) values. Specifically, the West was imagined as being inherently blessed with unique virtues: it was rational, hard-working, productive, sacrificial and parsimonious, liberal-democratic, honest, paternal and mature, advanced, ingenious, proactive, independent, progressive and dynamic. The East was then cast as the West's opposite Other: as irrational and arbitrary, lazy, unproductive, indulgent, exotic as well as alluring and promiscuous, despotic, corrupt, childlike and immature, backward, derivative, passive, dependent, stagnant and unchanging. Another way of expressing this is to say that the West was defined by a series of progressive presences, the East by a series of absences.

Particularly important is that this reimagining process stipulated that the West had always been superior (in that this construct

Table 1.1 *The Orientalist and patriarchal construction of the 'West versus the East'*

The dynamic West	The unchanging East
Inventive, ingenious, proactive	Imitative, ignorant, passive
Rational	Irrational
Scientific	Superstitious, ritualistic
Disciplined, ordered, self-controlled, sane, sensible	Lazy, chaotic/erratic, spontaneous, insane, emotional
Mind-oriented	Body-oriented, exotic and alluring
Paternal, independent, functional	Childlike, dependent, dysfunctional
Free, democratic, tolerant, honest	Enslaved, despotic, intolerant, corrupt
Civilised	Savage/barbaric
Morally and economically progressive	Morally regressive and economically stagnant

was extrapolated back in time to Ancient Greece). For the West has allegedly enjoyed dynamically progressive, liberal and democratic values and rational institutions from the outset, which in turn gave birth to the rational individual, whose flourishing life enabled economic progress and the inevitable breakthrough to the blinding light and warmth of capitalist modernity. By contrast, the East was branded as permanently inferior. It has allegedly endured despotic values and irrational institutions, which meant that in the very heart of darkness, a cruel collectivism strangled the rational individual at birth, thereby making economic stagnation and slavery its eternal fate. This argument formed the basis of the theory of oriental despotism and the Peter Pan theory of the East, which conveyed an eternal image of a 'dynamic West' versus an 'unchanging East' (see table 1.1).

It can hardly escape notice that these binary opposites are precisely the same categories that constitute the patriarchally

constructed identity of masculinity and femininity. That is, the modern West is akin to the constructed male, the East the imagined female.
This is no coincidence, because during the post-1700 period Western
identity was constructed as patriarchal and powerful, while the East
was simultaneously imagined as feminine – as weak and helpless.
This led to the Orientalist representation of an Asia 'lying passively
in wait for Bonaparte', for only he could liberate her from her enslaved
existence (an act of liberation, which was subsequently dubbed 'the
white man's burden'). And this theory was vitally important because
branding the East as exotic, enticing, alluring and above all passive
(i.e. as having no initiative to develop of her own accord), thereby
produced an immanent and ingenious legitimating rationale for the
West's imperial penetration and control of the East.

But this was not just a legitimating idea for imperialism and
the subjugation of the East. For by depicting or imagining the East as
the West's passive opposite it was but a short step to make the argument that *only* the West was capable of independently pioneering
progressive development. Indeed, the outcome of the European intellectual revolution was the construction of the 'proactive' European
subject, and the 'passive' Eastern object, of world history. Moreover,
European history was inscribed with a progressive temporal linearity,
while the East was imagined to be governed by regressive cycles of
stagnation. In particular, within the Eurocentric discourse this divide
implied a kind of 'intellectual apartheid regime' because the superior
West was permanently and retrospectively quarantined off from the
inferior East. Or, in Rudyard Kipling's felicitous phrase, 'Oh, East is
East, and West is West, and never the twain shall meet'. This was
crucial precisely because it immunised the West from recognising the
positive influence imparted by the East over many centuries, thereby
implying that the West had pioneered its own development in the
complete absence of Eastern help ever since the time of Ancient
Greece. And from there it was but a short step to proclaiming that the
history of the world can only be told as the story of the pioneering and
triumphant West from the outset. Thus the myth of the pristine West

was born: that the Europeans had, through their own superior ingenuity, rationality and social-democratic properties, pioneered their own development in the complete absence of Eastern help, so that their triumphant breakthrough to modern capitalism was inevitable.

It is no coincidence that the social sciences emerged most fully in the nineteenth century at the time when this process of reimagining Western identity reached its apogee. For by then the Europeans had intellectually divided the whole world into the two antithetical compartments. But rather than critique this Orientalist and essentialist West/East divide, orthodox Western social scientists from the nineteenth century down to the present not only accepted this polarised separation as self-evidently true, but inscribed it into their theories of the rise of the West and the origins of capitalist modernity. How did this occur?

Most generally, as the quote from Eric Wolf (posted at the beginning of this chapter) points out,[9] within the mainstream theories we can detect a latent – though occasionally explicit – triumphalist teleology in which all of human history has ineluctably been leading up to the Western endpoint of capitalist modernity. Thus conventional accounts of world history assume that this all began with Ancient Greece, progressing on to the European agricultural revolution in the low middle ages, then on to the rise of Italian-led commerce at the turn of the millennium. The story continues on into the high middle ages when Europe rediscovered pure Greek ideas in the Renaissance which, when coupled with the scientific revolution, the Enlightenment and the rise of democracy, propelled Europe into industrialisation and capitalist modernity.

Pick up any conventional book on the rise of the modern world. The West is usually represented as the *mainstream civilisation* and is enshrined with a *Promethean* quality (to paraphrase the titles of two prominent books).[10] While Eastern societies are sometimes discussed they clearly lie outside the mainstream story. And it is often the case that if the East is discussed at all, it is discussed in separate sections. Accordingly, one could focus only on the Western sections and get the main story. Thus Eastern societies basically appear as an aside or as an irrelevant footnote. But this aside is important not because it says little about the East but because it describes only the inherent, regressive properties that blocked its progress. Once more, this provides a very powerful confirmation of Western superiority and why the 'triumph of the West' was but a *fait accompli.*

Two main points are of note here. First, this story is one that imagines Western superiority from the outset. And second, the story of the rise and triumph of the West is one that can be told without any discussion of the East or the 'non-West'. Europe is seen as autonomous or self-constituting on the one hand, and rational/democratic on the other, making the breakthrough all by itself. This is what I refer to as the Eurocentric iron logic of immanence. Both these views underpin the triumphalist Eurocentric notion of the 'European miracle' conceived as a 'virgin birth'. Accordingly, the story of the origins of capitalism (and globalisation) is conflated with the rise of the West; the account of the rise of modern capitalism and civilisation *is* the Western story. It is precisely this notion that Ruth Benedict had in mind when she described 'our' conception of world history as 'provincial'.[11] Or as Du Bois put it:

> It has long been the belief of modern men that the history of
> Europe covers the essential history of civilization, with
> unimportant exceptions; that the progress of the white
> [Europeans] has been along the one natural, normal path to
> the highest possible human culture.[12]

Nevertheless, it remains to be ascertained just how the categories of Orientalism became endogenised within the mainstream accounts of the rise of the West. Because other anti-Eurocentric writers have deconstructed a range of modern prominent scholars,[13] I shall concentrate here on revealing the Orientalist foundations of the classical theories of Marx and Weber. This focus is legitimate because most subsequent theories have been derived from Marx and especially Weber in one way or another.

The Orientalist foundations of Marxism

It might be thought that Marxism would *not* fit the Orientalist mould, given that Karl Marx was one of Western capitalism's most strident critics. But the fact is that Marx privileged the West as the active subject of progressive world history and denigrated the East as but its passive object. And in the process Marx's theory demonstrated all the hallmarks of Eurocentric world history. How so?

Karl Marx's theory assumed that the West was unique and enjoyed a developmental history that had been absent in the East. Indeed, he was explicit that the East had had *no* (progressive) history. This was reiterated in numerous pamphlets and newspaper articles. For example, China was a 'rotting semicivilization . . . vegetating in the teeth of time'.[14] Consequently, China's only hope for progressive emancipation or redemption lay with the Opium Wars and the incursion of British capitalists who would 'open up backward' China to the energising impulse of capitalist world trade.[15] India too was painted with the same brush.[16] This formula was most famously advanced in *The Communist Manifesto* where we are told that the Western bourgeoisie,

> draws all, even the most barbarian, nations into civilization . . . It compels all nations, on pain of extinction, to adopt the [Western] bourgeois mode of production; it compels them to introduce what it calls civilization into their midst, i.e., to become [Western] themselves. In one word, it [the Western bourgeoisie] creates a world after its own image.[17]

Marx's dismissal of the East was not confined to his numerous newspaper articles (no fewer than seventy-four between 1848 and 1862) and various pamphlets, but was fundamentally inscribed into the theoretical schema of his historical materialist approach. Crucial here was his concept of the 'Asiatic mode of production' in which 'private property' and hence 'class struggle' – the developmental motor of historical progress – were notably absent. As he explained in *Capital*, in Asia 'the direct producers . . . [are] under direct

subordination to a state which stands over them as their landlord . . .
[Accordingly] no private ownership of land exists.'[18] And it was the
absorption of, and hence failure to produce, a surplus for reinvestment
in the economy that, 'supplie[d] the key to the secret of the *unchange-
ableness* of Asiatic societies'.[19] In short, private property and class
struggle in part failed to emerge because the forces of production were
owned by the despotic state. Thus stagnation was inscribed into this
publicly owned land system because rents were extracted from the
producers, in the form of 'taxes wrung from them – frequently by
means of torture – by a ruthless despotic state'.[20]

This scenario was fundamentally contrasted with the European
situation. In Europe the state did not stand above society but was
fundamentally embedded within, and cooperated with, the dominant
economic class. In turn, being unable to squeeze a surplus through
high taxation the state allowed a space to emerge through which capitalists could accumulate a surplus (i.e. profits) to be reinvested in the
capitalist economy. Accordingly, economic progress was understood
as the unique preserve of the West. Thus what we have in Marx's theoretical understanding of the East and West is the theory of oriental
despotism (which subsequently found its most famous voice in Karl
Wittfogel's neo-Marxist book).[21] It is true that Marx's notion of the
Asiatic mode of production oscillated between the choking powers of
the despotic state on the one hand and the stifling role of rural communal production on the other. But whichever factor was crucial does
not detract from his abiding belief that the East had no prospects for
progressive self-development and could, therefore, only be rescued by
the British capitalist imperialists.

No less importantly, Marx's whole theory of history faithfully
reproduces the Orientalist or Eurocentric teleological story. In *The
German Ideology* Marx traces the origins of capitalist modernity back
to Ancient Greece – the fount of civilisation (and in the *Grundrisse*
he explicitly dismissed the importance of Ancient Egypt).[22] He then
recounts the familiar Eurocentric story of linear/immanent progress
forwards to European feudalism and on to European capitalism, then

socialism before culminating at the terminus of communism.[23] Thus Western man was originally born free under 'primitive communalism' and, having passed through four progressive historical epochs, would eventually emancipate himself as well as the Asian through revolutionary class struggle. For Marx the Western proletariat is humanity's 'Chosen People' no less than the Western bourgeoisie is global capitalism's 'Chosen People'. Marx's inverted Hegelian approach gave rise to a progressive/linear story in which the (Western) species edged closer to freedom through class struggle with each passing historical epoch.

No such progressive 'linearity' was possible in the Orient, where growth-repressive 'cycles' of despotic political regimes and regressive rural production systems did no more than mark time. Underlying this whole approach is a clear denial of Eastern agency. To paraphrase Marx's discussion of the difference between a proletarian 'class-in-itself' (representing inertia and passivity) and a 'class-for-itself' (representing a proactive propensity for emancipation), it is as if Marx saw the East as a 'being-in-itself' that was inherently incapable of becoming a 'being-for-itself'. By contrast, the West was from the outset a 'being-for-itself'. Moreover, it seems no coincidence that the Hegelian influence in Marx's work should have produced this binary 'progressive West/regressive East' couplet, precisely because for Hegel the superior Spirit of the West is progressive freedom, whereas the inferior Spirit of the East is regressive, unchanging despotism.[24] In short, for Marx the West has been the triumphant carrier of historical progress, the East but its passive recipient.

All in all it seems fair to dub Karl Marx's approach as 'Orientalism painted red'.[25] However, none of this is to say that Marxism is moribund, for it undoubtedly remains useful and insightful. But it is to say that as an overall framework it remains embedded firmly within an Orientalist discourse.

The Orientalist foundations of Weberianism
Nowhere is the Orientalist approach clearer than in the works of the German sociologist, Max Weber. Weber's whole approach was founded

on the most poignant Orientalist questions: what was it about the West that made its path to modern capitalism inevitable? And why was the East predestined for economic backwardness? The Orientalist cue in Weber is found both with the initial questions and the subsequent analytical methodology that he deployed in order to answer them. Weber's view was that the essence of modern capital-ism lay with its unique and pronounced degree of 'rationality' and 'predictability', values that were to be found only in the West. From there, as Randall Collins points out,

> the logic of Weber's argument is first to describe these characteristics; then to show the *obstacles to them that were present in virtually all societies of world history until recent centuries in the West;* and finally, by the method of comparative analysis, to show the social conditions responsible for their [unique] emergence [in the West].[26]

This is pristine Orientalist logic, given that Weber selected or imputed a series of progressive features that were allegedly unique to the West. And he simultaneously insisted on their absence in the East, where a series of imaginary blockages ensured its failure to progress. That is, he did not objectively select the key aspects that made the West's rise possible. He in fact imputed them no less than he imputed a series of imaginary blockages that supposedly made the East's failure inevitable (a claim which I demonstrate throughout this book). The Orientalist character of his analytical template is revealed most clearly in his depiction of the East and West (see table 1.2).

The crucial comparison here is between tables 1.1 and 1.2. This comparison confirms that Weber perfectly transposed the Eurocentric categories into his central social scientific concepts. Thus the West was blessed with a unique set of rational institutions which were both liberal and growth permissive. The growth-permissive factors are striking for their presence in the West and for their absence in the East.[27] Here, the division of East and West according to the presence of irrational and rational institutions respectively very much echoes

Table 1.2 *Max Weber's Orientalist view of the 'East' and 'West': the great 'rationality' divide*

Occident (modernity)	Orient (tradition)
Rational (public) law	*Ad hoc* (private) law
Double-entry bookkeeping	Lack of rational accounting
Free and independent cities	Political/administrative camps
Independent urban bourgeoisie	State-controlled merchants
Rational-legal (and democratic) state	Patrimonial (oriental despotic) state
Rational science	Mysticism
Protestant ethic and the emergence of the rational individual	Repressive religions and the predominance of the collectivity
Basic institutional constitution of the West	**Basic institutional constitution of the East**
Fragmented civilisation with a balance of social power between all groups and institutions (i.e. multi-state system or multi-power actor civilisation)	Unified civilisations with no social balance of power between groups and institutions (i.e. single-state systems or empires of domination)
Separation of public and private realms (rational institutions)	Fusion of public and private realms (irrational institutions)

the Peter Pan theory of the East. In particular, the final two categories located at the bottom of the table deserve emphasis. First, the differences in the two civilisations are summarised in Weber's claim that Western capitalist modernity is characterised by a fundamental separation of the public and private realms. In traditional society (as in the East) there was no such separation. Crucially, only when there is such a separation can formal rationality – the *leitmotif* of modernity – prevail. This supposedly infuses all spheres – the political, military, economic, social and cultural.

The second general distinguishing feature between the Orient and Occident was the existence of a 'social balance of power' in the latter and its absence in the former. Taking their cue from Weber, neo-Weberian analyses commonly differentiate 'multi-power actor civilisations' or the European multi-state system from Eastern single-state systems or 'empires of domination'.[28] And they, like some Marxian world-systems theorists as well as a number of non-Marxists,[29] emphasise the vital role that warfare between states played in the rise of Europe (which, 'by definition', did not exist in the single-state empires in the East). It is here where the theory of oriental despotism becomes pivotal. Only the Occident enjoyed a precarious balance of social forces and institutions where none could predominate.[30] European secular rulers could not dominate on a despotic model. They granted 'powers and liberties' to individuals in civil society, initially to the nobles and later on to the bourgeoisie. By 1500 rulers were anxious to promote capitalism in order to enhance tax revenues in the face of constant, and increasingly expensive, military competition between states. By contrast, in the East the predominance of 'single-state systems' led to empires of domination, in large part because a lack of military competition released the state from the pressure of having to nurture the development of society. Thus in contrast to the fief (hereditary land tenure) that Western rulers had granted the nobility before about 1500, Eastern nobles were stifled by the despotic or patrimonial state which imposed prebendal rights (rights which prevented the consolidation of this class's power). Moreover, the Eastern bourgeoisie was thoroughly repressed by the despotic or patrimonial state and was confined to 'administrative camps' as opposed to the 'free cities' that were allegedly found only in the West. In addition, European rulers were also balanced against the power of the Holy Roman empire as well as the papacy, which contrasted with Eastern caesaropapism (where religious and political institutions were fused). Finally, while Western man became imbued with a 'rational restlessness' and a transformative 'ethic of world mastery', in part because of the energising impulse of Protestantism, Eastern man was choked by regressive religions and was thereby marked by a long-term fatalism and passive conformity to the world. Accordingly, the rise of capitalism was as much an inevitability in the West as it was an impossibility in the East.

In sum, although the Weberian argument has a different content from Marx's, both worked within an Orientalist framework. And the obvious link here lies in the centrality that both accord to the absence of oriental despotism in the West on the one hand, and the imputed European logic of immanence on the other. Accordingly, as noted earlier, when seen through an anti-Eurocentric lens these so-called radically opposed perspectives appear as but subtle variations on the exact same Orientalist theme.

Probably the most significant consequence of Max Weber's construction of the Eurocentric theoretical template is that it has permeated almost all Eurocentric accounts of the rise of the West even if, as James Blaut also notes, many of the relevant authors would recognise themselves as neither Weberian nor Orientalist.[31] This should hardly be surprising, given that all mainstream scholars begin their analysis by asking the standard Weberian question: why did *only* the West break through to modern capitalism, while, conversely, the East was doomed to remain in poverty? When expressed in this way, an Orientalist story was made inevitable because the question led the enquirer (often unintentionally) to impute an inevitability to both the rise of the West and the stagnation of the East. How so? Applying the Orientalist conception of the binary 'West–East divide' furnished Western scholars with the inevitable answer: that only the West had the ingenuity and progressive properties to make the breakthrough – values that were deemed to be entirely absent in the East from the outset. Posed in this way, the question begged the answer: how did the ingenious and progressive liberal West advance to capitalist modernity as opposed to the regressive, despotic East, whose eternal fate lay with stagnation and slavery? Thus the essential causal categories had already been assigned in advance of historical enquiry.

But it might be replied that it is reasonable to begin by not-ing the present situation of an advanced West and a backward East and then exploring the past to 'reveal' the factors that made this so. The problem is that in extrapolating retrospectively the notion of a backward East a subtle but erroneous slippage is made: in 'revealing' the various blockages that held the East back, Eurocentrism ends up by imputing to the East a permanent 'iron law of *non*-development'. And above all, because Eurocentrism appraises the East only through the lens of the West's final breakthrough to modern capitalism, any technological or economic developments that were made in the East are immediately dismissed as inconsequential. In contrast, by tak-ing present-day Western superiority as a fact and then extrapolating this conception back through historical time, the enquirer necessarily ends up by imputing to the West a permanent 'iron law of immanent development'. This is rendered problematic by the central argument of this book: that there was nothing inevitable about the West's rise, precisely because the West was nowhere near as ingenious or morally progressive as Eurocentrism assumes. For without the helping hand of the more advanced East in the period from 500 to 1800, the West would in all likelihood never have crossed the line into modernity.

Thus much of our Western thinking is not scientific and objec-tive but is orientated through a one-eyed perspective which reflects the prejudiced values of the West, and which necessarily prevents the enquirer from seeing the full picture. This is equivalent to what Blaut calls 'Eurocentric tunnel history'.[32] What happens, then, when we view the world through a more inclusive two-eyed perspective?

The illusion of Eurocentrism: discovering the oriental West

It is important to note that the Eurocentric and implicit 'triumphal-ist' bias of our mainstream theories does not necessarily make them incorrect. Indeed, as the self-proclaimed Eurocentric scholar, David Landes, has recently argued, there is actually very good reason for Eurocentrism because it *is* the West and *not* the East that has tri-umphed because, he claims, only the Europeans managed to pioneer the breakthrough to capitalist modernity. Accordingly, Landes dismisses the anti-Eurocentric account as 'politically correct goodthink' or 'Europhobic' or simply 'bad history'.[33] But my central argument is that the Eurocentric story is problematic not because it is politically incorrect but because it does not square with what really happened. David Landes, in his self-proclaimed Eurocentric book, forcefully disagrees. As he puts it:

> A third school [in which the present book would be included] would argue that the West–Rest [West–East] dichotomy is simply false. In the large stream of world history, Europe is a latecomer and free rider on the earlier achievements of others. That is patently incorrect. As the historical record shows, for the last thousand years, Europe (the West) has been the prime mover of development and modernity. That still leaves the moral issue. Some would say that Eurocentrism is bad for us, indeed bad for the world, hence to be avoided. Those people should avoid it. As for me, I prefer truth to goodthink. I feel surer of my ground.[34]

But the historical empirical record that I consult reveals that for most of the last thousand years the East has been the prime mover of world development. Conventional scholars assign the leading edge of global power in the last thousand years, without exception, to Western states. But the immediate problem is that Western powers only appear to have been dominant because a Eurocentric view determined from the outset that no Eastern power could be selected in. As this book shows, all the so-called 'leading Western powers' were inferior, economically and politically, to the leading Asian powers (see chs. 2–4 and 7). It was only near the very end of the period (c. 1840) that a Western power finally eclipsed China.

Nevertheless, Landes would still claim that even if all this were true, the fact remains that only the Europeans managed to single-handedly break through to capitalist modernity. Or as Lynn White put it: 'One thing is so certain that it seems stupid to verbalize it: both modern technology and modern science are distinctively

Occidental'.[35] But as I stated earlier, the West only got over the line into modernity because it was helped by the diffusion and appropriation of the more advanced Eastern resource portfolios and resources. Because the success of my account must lie with the empirical evidence that it marshals rather than because it is simply 'goodthink', what then are some of the empirical facts that support my alternative anti-Eurocentric account? Let us take the diffusion and assimilation of Eastern resource portfolios through oriental globalisation first, before turning to the appropriation of Eastern resources through European imperialism.

One revealing example lies with what I call the 'myth of Vasco da Gama' (see ch. 7). We in the West generally pride ourselves on the fact that it was the Portuguese discoverer, Vasco da Gama, who was the first man to have made it round the Cape of Good Hope and sail on to the East Indies where he made first contact with a hitherto isolated and primitive Indian race. But sometime between two and five decades earlier the Islamic navigator, Ahmad ibn-Mājid, had already rounded the Cape and, having sailed up the West African coast, had entered the Mediterranean via the Strait of Gibraltar. Moreover, the Sassanid Persians had been sailing across to India and China from the early centuries of the first millennium CE, as did the Black Ethiopians and, later on, the Muslims (after about 650). And the Javanese, Indians and Chinese had all made it across to the Cape many decades, if not centuries, before Da Gama. It has no less been forgotten that Da Gama only managed to navigate across to India because he was guided by an unnamed Gujarati Muslim pilot. No less irksome is the point that virtually all of the nautical and navigational technologies and techniques that made Da Gama's journey possible were invented (and certainly refined further) in either China or the Islamic Middle East. These were then assimilated by the Europeans, having diffused across the global economy via the Islamic Bridge of the World (see chs. 3, 6–8). And when we add the point that cannon and gunpowder were discovered in China and also diffused across, there is almost nothing left to indicate that the Portuguese had anything to genuinely claim for their own. Finally, as this book argues in detail, the Indians were not primitive barbarians. In fact, they were considerably more advanced than their Portuguese 'discoverers' – itself a misnomer precisely because India had long been in direct trading contact with much of Asia, East Africa and indirectly with Europe, many centuries before Da Gama disingenuously claimed to have discovered it (see chs. 2–4).

More generally it is important to note that Eastern resource portfolios had a significant influence in each of the major European turning points. Most of the major technologies that enabled the European medieval agricultural revolution after 600 CE seem to have come across from the East (chs. 5 and 6). After 1000, the major technologies, ideas and institutions that stimulated the various Western commercial, production, financial, military and navigational revolutions, as well as the Renaissance and the scientific revolution, were first developed in the East but later assimilated by the Europeans (chs. 6–8). After 1700, the major technologies and technological ideas that spurred on the British agricultural and industrial revolutions all diffused across from China (ch. 9). Moreover, Chinese ideas also helped stimulate the European Enlightenment. And it is precisely because the East and West have been linked together in a single global cobweb ever since 500 that we need to dispense with the Eurocentric assumption that these two entities can be represented as entirely separate and antithetical.

It is no less important to note that to each of my points a series of counter-measures are deployed which enable (usually unwittingly) the retention of the Eurocentric vision. Thus when Eurocentric writers concede that a certain idea or technology originated in the East, they often resort to what might be called a specific 'Orientalist clause'. Such clauses dismiss the significance of any particular Eastern achievement, thereby returning us to the Orientalist status quo. This process is rarely undertaken in a conscious way, given that most scholars are not fighting to defend an explicitly Eurocentric vision of the world. More often they deploy Orientalist clauses in order to retain their own theoretical perspective (e.g. Marxist, liberal, Webe-rian, etc.) rather than Eurocentrism *per se*. But whether intended or not, the outcome is still the maintenance of the Eurocentric vision if only because these approaches are inherently Orientalist.

Two examples of how such clauses are employed will suffice to illustrate my point. To my claim made in ch. 3 that China achieved an industrial miracle during the Sung (eleventh century), Eurocentric historians often reply by invoking one of the 'China clauses' (or what Blaut calls the 'China formula').[36] This clause dismisses its signifi-cance by insisting that it was but an 'abortive revolution', with the Chinese economy subsequently reverting back to its normal state of relative stagnation. In this way, such theorists are able to preserve their claim that the British industrial revolution was truly the first (the 'British clause'). Second, to answer the claim that the Middle East transmitted original scientific thoughts and texts to Europe that enabled the Western Renaissance and scientific revolution, the 'Islamic clause' is immediately invoked. This dismisses the Eastern input on the grounds that these texts were in fact pure Greek works and that the Muslims had added nothing of intellectual value – all they did was return the original Greek works to the Europeans. This then overlaps with the 'Greek clause', which stipulates that the Ancient Greeks were the original fount of modern (i.e. Western) civilisation. From these two examples alone it should be clear that there are many Orientalist clauses which all overlap to provide a logically coherent 'Orientalist text'. Thus, to make my case as plausible as possible, it is incumbent upon me – or anyone else who seeks to challenge Euro-centrism – to confront and dismantle every one of these interlinked Orientalist clauses or formulae. It is this task that informs the main narrative of this book. So much for the diffusion process.

The second major way in which the East enabled the rise of the West was through the European imperial appropriation of East-ern resources (land, labour and markets). Here I emphasise the role of European agency or identity. All the major anti-Eurocentric scholars seek to entirely discount the agency of the West. To include it, they reason, would be to fall back into the Eurocentric trap of emphasising European exceptionalism or uniqueness. But by erasing the notion of European agency we risk several dangers. First, we run the risk of representing the European achievement as truly miraculous.[37] Second, given that my main argument comprises the positive contribution of the East to the Western breakthrough, I risk falling into the trap of Occidentalism, in which the East is privileged and the West is denigrated. In the end, this would be no more appropriate than an Orientalist approach. And third, by denying European agency we run the risk of falling into a kind of structural-functionalist trap, in which human agency becomes replaced by the notion of the individual as a 'passive bearer' of material structures. This in effect conceives of humans as receptors of the gift or burden of change rather than as creative directors of change.

My conception of European agency also diverges from the pure materialist approaches of the extant anti-Eurocentric (as well as Eurocentric) literature because it is grounded in the notion of identity, which in turn is a socially constructed phenomenon. And herein lies a link with the first prong of my argument, given that European identity has always been forged in a global context. Thus I pay attention to the various phases in which European identity was constructed and reconstructed in an ever-changing global context, while at all times relating this to the economic progress of the West. Nevertheless, as I explain in the final chapter, this is by no means to say that material factors are unimportant; indeed, they form a major part of my overall argument. Here I merely note that identity is an important aspect of agency. My notion of agency begins from the premise that the way we think of, or imagine, ourselves and our place in the world to a very important extent informs the way that we act in it. How then did the Europeans construct an imperial identity, and how did this in turn enable the later phase of the rise of the West?

During the early medieval period the Europeans came to define themselves negatively against Islam (ch. 5). This was vital to the construction of Christendom, which in turn enabled the consolidation of the feudal economic and political system as it emerged around the end of the first millennium CE. It was also this identity that led on to the Crusades. Subsequently, European Christian identity prompted the so-called 'voyages of discovery' – or what I call the 'second round' of medieval Crusades – led by Vasco da Gama and Christopher Columbus (chs. 7–8). Having arrived in the Americas, various Christian ideas led the Europeans to believe in the inferiority of the American Natives as well as the Negro Africans. This in turn legitimised in their eyes the super-exploitation and repression of the Native Americans and Africans as well as the appropriation of American gold and silver, which in turn assisted European economic development in manifold ways (ch. 8). Then, during the eighteenth century, European identity reconstruction led to the creation of what I refer to as 'implicit racism' which led on to the idea of the moral necessity of the imperial 'civilising mission' (ch. 10). Imagining the East to be backward, passive and childlike in contrast to the West as advanced, proactive and paternal was vital in prompting the Europeans to engage in imperialism. For the European elites sincerely believed that they were civilising the East through imperialism (even if many of their actions belied this noble conception). And in turn, the appropriation of many non-European resources through imperialism underwrote the pivotal British industrial revolution (ch. 11).

All in all, this enables me to reintroduce European agency as part of my anti-Eurocentric account of the rise of the West. Scholars such as Blaut might denounce this aspect of my argument principally because it seems to fall back into a Eurocentric argument that emphasises European exceptionalism. But this would be the case *only* if this formed the linchpin of my explanation. Thus it is vital to appreciate my overall explanatory framework: that European identity constitutes a necessary though not sufficient explanatory variable. For without the diffusion of Eastern material and ideational resources through oriental globalisation, no amount of cupidity and appropriationism exhibited by the Europeans could have got them 'over the line'. This also necessarily means that materialist causes must be factored in alongside the role of identity if we are to craft a satisfactory explanation for the rise of the West.

In sum, when we reveal the larger picture that Eurocentrism obscures, then its pristine picture of Western civilisation – as autonomous, ingenious and morally progressive – appears more like Oscar Wilde's picture of Dorian Gray, whose real image has been hidden away from the viewer. My task, therefore, is to reveal this hidden picture and simultaneously resuscitate the Eastern story. In this way, I seek to undermine the Eurocentric notion of the triumphant West that lies, either latently or explicitly, at the heart of the mainstream accounts of the rise of the West. In the process we necessarily discover the origins of the oriental West. Thus, to use the language of Western positivist social science adopted by Landes and others, it is for these empirical reasons (discussed above) that we should avoid Eurocentrism. For only then can we provide a satisfactory account of the rise of the West.

One final point is noteworthy. I have clearly set myself a very ambitious task, which requires a revisionist history of virtually the whole world in the last fifteen hundred years! Clearly it is not possible to provide all the details in one book. Though desirable, my task must be more circumspect. My central objective is to paint the outlines of an alternative picture and to thereby provide just enough evidence to undermine the major tenets of the Eurocentric approach. Put differently, the 'intellectual success' of the book, I feel, should be appraised not by whether the reader is wholly convinced by the particularities of my own account, but rather by whether (s)he is persuaded by my claim that the Eurocentric explanation and vision of the rise and triumph of the West is a myth that needs to be countered.

Part I
The East as an early developer: the East discovers and leads the world through oriental globalisation, 500–1800

2   Islamic and African pioneers:

building the Bridge of the World and the global economy in the Afro-Asian age of discovery, 500–1500

> If as a philosopher one wishes to instruct oneself about what has taken place on the globe, one must first of all turn one's eyes towards the East, the cradle of all arts, to which the West owes everything.
>
> Voltaire

> Western scholars, at least since the nineteenth century, have tried to find ways of seeing [the] Afro-Eurasian zone of civilization as composed of distinct historical worlds . . . one convenient result [of which] would be to leave Europe . . . with a history that need not be integrated with that of the rest of mankind save on the terms posed by European history itself . . . [But after] 500 AD there was occurring a cumulative improvement in technique, especially in military and even financial [institutions]; the range of commerce expanded, as in sub-Saharan Africa which now effectively entered the Afro-Eurasian area of civilization . . . [Because] the interactions among regions – as a result of Islam, or of the Mongols, or of scientific or artistic borrowing [etc.] – were so frequent, and involved . . . China and . . . Western Europe [this necessarily means] that these developments [in technique] cannot be fully disengaged from each other.
>
> Marshall Hodgson

The standard picture of the world before 1500 presented by Eurocentrism comprises two core features: first, a world mired in so-called stagnant 'tradition'; and second, a fragmented world divided between insulated and backward regional civilisations that were governed by 'irrational' despotic states (mainly in the East). Accordingly, it becomes inconceivable to imagine a globally interdependent world at any point before 1500. In turn, Eurocentrism supposes that it was only by 1500, with the emergence of Europe as advanced civilisation, that the European age of discovery was launched. And this in turn led to the battering down of the walls that had kept apart the major civilisations, thereby paving the way for the future Western age of globalisation that emerged in the nineteenth century and matured after 1945.

This familiar Eurocentric picture is a myth in the first instance because a global economy that broke down civilisational isolationism began as early as the sixth century during the Afro-Asian age of discovery. And as we shall see, the so-called pioneering Europeans entered this pre-existent global circuit very much on terms dictated by the Middle Eastern Arabs, Persians and Africans (see also chs. 4, 6 and 7). Moreover, as this and the following two chapters demonstrate, the period before 1500 witnessed considerable Eastern economic progress, which simultaneously falsifies the Eurocentric theory of oriental despotism. I also show that the 'leading edge of global economic power' in the pre-1800 period belonged to various Eastern societies. There are two generic types of global economic power that may be called, following Michael Mann, 'extensive' and 'intensive'.[1] In the economic realm, extensive power refers to the ability of a state or region to project its economic tentacles outwards into the world, while intensive power refers to a high degree of 'productive' power within its own 'borders'. We need to differentiate these precisely because different regions have enjoyed prominence in one or both of these forms of global power at different times. Thus, for example, between roughly 650 and 1000 the Islamic Middle East/North Africa had the highest levels of extensive and intensive power, though by about 1100 the leading edge of intensive power had passed to China (where it remained until the nineteenth century – see ch. 3). Nevertheless, the Middle East and North Africa maintained the leading edge of extensive power down to about the fifteenth century when China took over, though they continued to enjoy significant levels of intensive and extensive power well into the eighteenth century. This picture was consciously reimagined by Eurocentric intellectuals in the nineteenth century, so that first Venice and later Portugal, Spain, The Netherlands and Britain were (re)presented as the leading global powers in the post-1000 period.

In sum, the purpose of this chapter is to discover the original picture (i.e. the one that existed before it was erased by Eurocentrism). Nevertheless, although I have given over three chapters to discussing the many economic achievements of the East, they can necessarily only provide a sketch. For as Perry Anderson empathically reminds us,

> Asian development cannot in any way be reduced to a uniform category, left over after the canons of European evolution have been established . . . It is merely in the night of our own ignorance that all alien shapes take on the same hue.[2]

As far as possible, therefore, I have sought to disaggregate the East into its major component parts, none of which can be portrayed with the same brush. Thus I hope that readers will forgive the fact that my primary focus in this and the next two chapters will be on the Islamic Middle East, North Africa, China, Japan, India and South-east Asia.

This chapter is in two sections. The first reveals the pioneering role that the Middle Eastern Muslims and North Africans played in creating a global economy after 500 and traces the leading edge of global power. The second section traces the expansion of Islamic extensive power and its shift to Egypt while simultaneously revealing the contours of the global economy between 1000 and 1500.

The Eastern origins of the global economy: the Afro-Asian age of discovery (post-500 CE)

The creation of oriental globalisation after 500

The claim that globalisation began at least as early as the sixth century necessarily counters the Eurocentric insistence that globalisation only emerged after 1500 with the advent of the so-called European age of discovery. Specifically, there are six Eurocentric rebuttals to the claim that globalisation began well before 1500.[3] First, it is assumed that the major regional civilisations were insulated from each other. Second, this claim in turn derives from the assumption that political costs were too high to allow global trade given that oriental despotic rulers sought to stifle all trade and tax profits out of existence. Third, significant global trade could not have existed before 1500 because there was an absence of capitalist institutions (e.g. credit, money-changers, banks, contract law, etc.). Fourth, significant trade on a global level was simply impossible because transport technologies were too crude. And to the extent that there was any global trade at all, it was insignificant because it was in luxury goods which, by definition, were consumed only by a small minority of the world's population (about 10 per cent). Fifth, to the extent that there were any global flows, they were much too slow to be consequential. And sixth, even if there were global processes in operation, they were not robust enough to have a major reorganisational impact on the many societies of the world.

I begin here by presenting my six counter-propositions before elaborating on them throughout this chapter (as well as in chs. 3–9). First, after 500 the Persians, Arabs, Africans, Javanese, Jews, Indians and Chinese created and maintained a global economy down to about 1800, in which the major civilisations of the world were at all times interlinked (hence the term oriental globalisation). Second, the various regions were governed by rulers who provided a pacified environment and kept transit taxes low in order to facilitate global trade. Third, a whole series of sufficiently rational capitalist institutions were created and put in place after 500 to support global trade (these are discussed in detail in ch. 6). As Janet Abu-Lughod noted:

> Distances as measured by time, were calculated in weeks and months at best, but it took years to traverse the entire [global] circuit. And yet goods were transferred, prices set, exchange rates agreed upon, contracts entered into, credit – on funds or on goods located elsewhere – extended, partnerships formed, and, obviously, records kept and agreements honored.[4]

Fourth, while transport technologies were obviously nowhere near as advanced as they are today, they proved to be sufficient for the conduct of global trade. Moreover, the Eurocentric assumption that global trade only affected about 10 per cent of the world's population – and was therefore inconsequential – is challenged in the first instance by Charles Tilly. He defines global connections as consequential to the extent that: 'The actions of powerholders in one region of a network . . . visibly . . . affect the welfare of at least a significant minority (say a tenth) of the population in another region of the network'.[5] Others have suggested that trade in luxuries provided many important effects in the reproduction of states and societies throughout the world.[6] Either way, though, the majority of global trade was actually conducted in mass-based consumer products which affected considerably more than 10 per cent of the world's population (a point that I reiterate in various chapters).

Fifth, while it is undoubtedly true that the velocity of global transmissions was often very slow, global flows nevertheless had a major reorganisational effect on societies across the world. This leads directly on to my sixth claim: that the crucial significance of the global economy lay not in the type or quantity of trade that it supported, but that it provided a ready-made conveyor-belt along which the more advanced Eastern 'resource portfolios' (e.g. ideas, institutions and technologies) diffused across to the West. These global flows ultimately led to a radical reconfiguration of societies across much of the world. Indeed, the major theme of the book seeks to demonstrate this point by showing how the diffusion of best practice (i.e. Eastern) 'resource portfolios' through oriental globalisation was so significant that it underpinned the rise of the West (see chs. 5–9).

Finally, my claim might be objected to on the grounds that not all parts of the globe were completely interconnected. But the assumption that the whole world must be tightly linked before we can declare that it is global is problematic even for the modern period. Again, as Janet Abu-Lughod points out:

> No world system is *global*, in the sense that all parts articulate
> evenly with one another, regardless of whether the role they play
> is central or peripheral. Even today, the world, more globally
> integrated than ever before in history, is broken up into important
> subspheres or subsystems, such as the northern Atlantic
> system . . . the Pacific rim . . . China, still a system unto itself, and
> [so on].[7]

Certainly, globalisation has been a dynamic phenomenon through time and it is undoubtedly the case that its 'extensity' has varied over time. And modern globalisation in the 1800–2000 period is in some crucial respects very different from its oriental predecessor. Nevertheless, globalisation can be said to exist prior to (and indeed after) 1500 insofar as significant flows of goods, resources, currencies, capital, institutions, ideas, technologies and peoples flowed across regions to such an extent that they impacted upon, and led to the transformation of, societies across much of the globe. Even so, Robert Holton maintains that:

> A global history need not take the form of a single uniting process
> (or metanarrative) such as the triumph of reason or western
> civilisation. Nor should it be taken to imply an inexorable process
> of homogenization to a single pattern . . . [T]he *minimum* that is
> required for us to be able to speak of a single global connecting
> thread is that *tangible interconnections exist between distinct
> regions, leading to interchange and interdependency*.[8]

Clearly my definition is less 'minimalist' than that provided by Holton.

I take 500 CE as the approximate starting date of oriental globalisation. As William McNeill explains, although there was a fledgeling set of global linkages going back to the first millennium BCE (or even earlier), nevertheless by about 500 almost all of the interstices that had insulated contact between regions had been filled up.[9] The revival of camel transport between 300 and 500 was especially important.

Camels proved to be far superior 'vehicles' to horses or oxen. They could travel twice as far per day, were far cheaper, could be organised more easily and did not require roads. This meant that the long overland routes across Central Asia could now be relatively easily traversed. So important was this development that McNeill has recently described it as:

> analogous . . . to the far better known opening of the oceans by European [sic] seamen after 1500. Arabia together with the oases and deserts of central Asia, the Steppelands to their north and sub-Saharan Africa were the regions most powerfully affected . . . [and] were all brought into far more intimate contact with the established centers of civilized life – primarily with the Middle East and China – than had been possible before. As a result, between about AD 500 and 1000 an intensified . . . world system [emerged].[10]

But the key development here was the emergence of a series of interlinked world empires that enabled a significantly pacified environment within which overland – as well as seaborne – trade could flourish.[11] The rise of T'ang China (618–907), the Islamic Ummayad/Abbasid empire in the Middle East (661–1258), as well as the Fatimids in North Africa (909–1171) were crucial to the emergence of a sufficiently extensive global trading network. As Philip Curtin notes: 'The simultaneous power of the Abbasids and the T'ang made it comparatively easy for long distance traders to make the whole journey across Asia and North Africa'.[12] And though Jack Goody, André Wink and Nigel Harris see global connections that run as far back as 3500 BCE or earlier still, they agree that the big expansion of global trade occurred during the post-600 period.[13] In short, as McNeill has recently argued, the prosperity and commercialisation of the Arab and Chinese (as well as the South Asian) world acted like a huge bellows that fanned the flames of an emergent global economy.[14] Noteworthy here is that the famous Pirenne thesis – that the Islamic invasions broke the unity of Western Europe from Eastern Europe (Byzantium), and that it was only by the turn of the millennium when trade resumed – needs to be inverted:

> There was a close connection between the Frankish and Arab worlds, and . . . the Carolingian Renaissance, the successes of the Italian city-states, and the growth of the Hanseatic League were all enhanced rather than retarded by contacts with the Muslim East . . . It seems quite certain that trade revived at many places in the late eighth and ninth centuries [in Europe] . . . Contradicting Pirenne, therefore, historians now speak of the economic 'Islamization of early medieval Europe'.[15]

Thus with the birth of the Carolingian empire in 751 in Western Europe and the emergence of various Italian trading city states in the eighth and ninth centuries, the global trading system extended into Europe, thereby linking both extremes of the Eurasian landmass into one continuous network of interlinked world empires. Accordingly, globalisation is not unique to, or consequential only for, the twentieth century. Not only did it begin during Europe's 'Dark Age' but its ultimate significance lay in the fact that oriental globalisation was the midwife, if not the mother, of the medieval and modern West.

The birth of oriental globalisation owes much to the Islamic Middle East/North Africa. The Muslims (and Negroes) of North Africa as well as the Muslims of the Middle East were the real global capitalist pioneers, serving to weave together a global economy of significant scale and importance. For it stretched right across the Afro-Eurasian landmass and sea-lanes from Western Europe across to China and Korea in the east, and Africa, Polynesia (and perhaps Aboriginal Australia) in the south. How then was this achieved?

The Islamic global pioneer: the rise of Islamic extensive and intensive power

The Middle Eastern Arabic Muslims built upon the earlier achievements of the Sassanid Persians, which stem back possibly to the third – and certainly the fourth – century.[16] After 610, the Middle East began its rise to global power with the 'revelation' of Muhammad. Before then the Middle East was highly fragmented and subject to various colonising efforts by Persia, Syria and Byzantine Egypt. One of Muhammad's greatest contributions was to forge a unity through the power of Islam. And one of the most significant aspects of Islam was its penchant for trade and rational capitalist activity. It deserves emphasis that this immediately stands at odds with the Eurocentric assumption that Islam was a regressive religion that blocked the possibility of capitalist, let alone rational capitalist, activity. But it appears to have been forgotten, wittingly or unwittingly, that Muhammad himself had been a *commenda* (or *qirād*) trader. In his twenties he married a rich Qurayshi woman (the Quraysh had grown rich from the caravan trade as well as banking). Interestingly the:

> Meccans – the tribe of Quaraysh – caused their capital to fructify through trade and loans at interest in a way that Weber would call rational . . . The merchants of the Muslim Empire conformed perfectly to Weber's [rational] criteria for capitalist activity. They seized every and any opportunity for profit and calculated their outlays, their encashments and their profits in money terms.[17]

In the light of this, it is interesting to note some of the linkages between Islam and capitalism that can be found in the Qu'rān. According to Maxime Rodinson's detailed examination he asserts that the Qu'rān, 'Does not merely say that one must not forget one's portion of the world, it also says that it is proper to combine the practice of religion and material life, carrying on trade even during pilgrimages and goes so far as to maintain commercial profit under the name of "God's Bounty"'. Islam prescribed that businessmen could more effectively conduct a pilgrimage than those who did only physical labour. Indeed, the Qu'rān states that:

> If thou profit by doing what is permitted, thy deed is a djihād . . . And if thou invest it for thy family and kindred, this will be a Sadaqa [that is, a pious work of charity]; and truly, a dhiram [drachma, silver coin] lawfully gained from trade is worth more than ten dhirams gained in any other way.

And Muhammad's saying that 'Poverty is almost like an apostasy',

> implies that the true servant of God should be affluent or at least
> economically independent. The booths of the money-changers in
> the great mosque of the camp-town Kufa possibly illustrate the
> fact that there was no necessary conflict between business and
> religion in Islam.[18]

It is also significant that the Qu'rān stipulates the importance of
investment. And while we usually consider the *Sharīa* (the Islamic
sacred law) as the root of despotism and economic backwardness, it
was in fact created as a means to prevent the abuse of the rulers' or
caliphs' power and, moreover, it set out clear provisions for contract
law. Not surprisingly, there was a rational reason why the Islamic merchants were strong supporters of the *Sharīa*. Furthermore, there were
clear signs of greater personal freedom within Islam than in medieval
Europe. Offices were determined on the basis of 'egalitarian contractual responsibilities'. These entailed notions of rationality that were,
according to Hodgson, closer to the modern notion of *Gesellschaft*
than to traditional notions of *Gemeinschaft*.[19]

Ultimately Islam's comparative advantage lay in its considerable 'extensive' power. Islam was able to conquer horizontal space,
realised most fully in its ability to spread and diffuse across large parts
of the globe, as well as in its ability to spread capitalism. The centre
of Islam, Mecca, was in turn one of the centres of the global trading
network. Islam's power spread rapidly after the seventh century so
that the Mediterranean became in effect a Muslim lake, and 'Western
Europe' a promontory within the Afro-Asian global economy. Islam
was to have a particularly powerful influence on the development
of Europe (chs. 5–8) especially, though by no means exclusively, via
Islamic Spain. Above all the Islamic world constituted no less than
the Bridge of the World, across which many Eastern 'resource portfolios' as well as trade passed through to the West between 650 and
c. 1800. The growth of towns and the houses that Muslims built are
particularly illustrative of Islam's extensive power. Islam forbade tall

multi-storey houses because to reach up towards God was deemed to be arrogant. In general, for Islam, it was morally reprehensible to conquer vertical space. Thus the most pious sign would be to lower oneself in the eyes of God – to prostrate oneself and to lower one's head to the ground in the face of God's greatness. Similarly, we are told in *The Arabian Nights*, that to show respect for the sovereign is to 'kiss the earth between one's hands'. In short, the notion of *jihad* (*djihād*) preached that Muslims should conquer not vertical but horizontal or extensive space through both religion and trade. Accordingly, towns sprang up throughout the Middle East and rapidly formed the major sinews of the global economic network.

The picture of a dense urban trading network counters the traditional Eurocentric vision of Islam as a desert populated by nomads. As Marshall Hodgson put it, Islam was 'no "monotheism of the desert", born of the Bedouins' awed wonder at the vast openness of sky and land . . . Islam grew out of a long tradition of urban religion and it was as city-oriented as any variant of that tradition'.[20] Maxime Rodinson reinforces the general claim being made here:

> the density of commercial relations within the Muslim world
> constituted a sort of world market . . . of unprecedented
> dimensions. The development of exchange had made possible
> regional specialisation in industry and agriculture . . . Not only did
> the Muslim world know a capitalistic sector, but this sector was
> apparently the most extensive and highly developed in history
> before the [modern period].[21]

Islam spread not only westwards to Europe but also eastwards right across to India, South-east Asia and China, as well as southwards into Africa through either religious or commercial influence (and often both). Its economic reach was extraordinary for the time – so much so that one scholar has aptly stated that, 'the self-evident fact must be accepted that they [the Arabs] were among the pioneers of commerce in those far-away countries and that perhaps, as Tibbets suggests, they acted as middlemen in the trade between China and

South-east Asia'.[22] Certainly, by the ninth century – as various contemporary documents confirm – one long, continuous line of transcontinental trade pioneered by Islamic merchants reached from China to the Mediterranean.[23]

The Middle Eastern Ummayads (661–750), Abbasids (750–1258) and North African Fatimids were especially important, serving to unite various arteries of long-distance trade known in antiquity between the Indian Ocean and the Mediterranean. These included the Red Sea and Persian Gulf routes. The Abbasid capital, Baghdad, was linked to the Persian Gulf route, which in turn fanned out through the Indian Ocean and beyond into the South China Sea as well as the East China Sea. The contemporary, al-Ya'qūbi (c. 875), described Baghdad as the 'water-front to the world', while al-Mansūr proclaimed that 'there is no obstacle to us and China; everything on the sea can come to us on it'.[24] Other Islamic ports were also important, especially Sīrāf on the Persian Gulf (on the coast of Iran south of Shīrāz), which was the major terminus for goods from China and South-east Asia. The Red Sea route (guarded over by Egypt) was also of special importance (see next section). In addition to the sea routes, perhaps the most famous was the overland route to China, along which caravans passed through the Iranian cities of Tabriz, Hamadan and Nishapur to Bukhara and Samarkand in Transoxiana, and then on to either China or India. Marco Polo (the 'Ibn Battūta of Europe'?) was particularly impressed – as was Ibn Battūta himself:

> The people of Tabriz live by trade and industry . . . The city is so favorably situated that it is a market for merchandise from India and Baghdad, from Mosul and Hormuz, and from many other places; and many Latin merchants come here to buy the merchandise imported from foreign lands. It is also a market for precious stones, which are found here in great abundance. It is a city where good profits are made by travelling merchants.[25]

The Muslims were particularly dependent on trade with many parts of Africa (not just North Africa). This was so for a number of reasons including, first, that Egypt presided over one of the vital trade routes that linked the Far East and West (see next section); and second, African markets constituted probably the most profitable branch of Islam's foreign trade. While Eurocentrism dismisses the relevance of Africa to the international trading system before 1500, African trade was far from insignificant and long preceded the European arrival. No less significantly, the Abyssinian Aksumite kingdom boasted Black merchants who conducted significant trade with India even before the Islamic arrival.[26] Abu-Lughod's otherwise masterly description of the global economy is curious only for its omission of south-east Africa.[27] But maritime trade from the south-east coast had been important even before the arrival of the Muslims; its extensity is revealed by the fact that there was regular trade as far east as Polynesia. Moreover, the Indonesians had migrated to East Africa as early as the 2nd–4th centuries CE. Islamic shipping made its way right down the East African coast as far south as Sufālah in Mozambique and Qanbalu (Madagascar). Gold was mined in various places, including Ethiopia and Zimbabwe, while Kilwa (present day southern Tanzania) was the principal entrepôt.[28] The famous Islamic world traveller, Ibn Battūta, described Kilwa as 'one of the most beautiful and best built towns' that he had witnessed on his many travels throughout much of the world.[29] The Africans imported beads, cowries, copper and copper goods, grain, fruit and raisins, wheat and, later on, textiles (almost all of which were mass-based goods, not luxuries). The most intense commercial relations experienced by the East African ports were with India, Aden, Suhār and Sīrāf. And this long-distance trade also helped stimulate trade into the African hinterland.[30]

Moreover, it would be wrong to assume that West Africa was commercially isolated from the east coast and was 'brought to life' by the Europeans after 1492.[31] Indeed, after the much earlier Islamic arrival western entrepôts such as Sijilmassa (in Morocco) and Awdaghast expanded and the eastern and western coasts became interlinked, both in the northern and sub-Saharan regions.[32] Nevertheless, trade links within Africa had begun well before the Islamic arrival (as noted above), as had all manner of forms of production such as gold mining, copper production and iron smelting.[33] Interestingly, the archaeologist Sayce described the iron-production centre, Meroe (capital of the kingdom of Kush at the end of the first millennium BCE), as 'the Birmingham of central Africa'. Moreover, Sufālah (before the arrival of the Muslims) had the best and largest iron mines and its iron was produced in part for export to India.[34]

Noteworthy too is that global trade was also significantly enabled by the Jewish merchants as well as the kingdom of Śrīvijaya in Sumatra. Indeed, the latter acted as a global trading pivot in the so-called 'Far East' much as the Middle East/North Africa did in the West. As Jerry Bentley points out:

> trade linking South China with Ceylon and India grew to such proportions that the kings of Srivijaya, based at Palembang in southeastern Sumatra, organized an island-based empire that for much of the time between the seventh and thirteenth centuries controlled commerce through Southeast Asian waters.[35]

Most authorities agree that Śrīvijaya's rise was significantly assisted by the revival of Chinese trade during the T'ang.[36] And it was a critical meeting point between trade emanating from the Middle East, India and China.[37] Interestingly, the famous Chinese traveller I-Ching counted some thirty five ships arriving from Persia alone during his six-month stay in 671. The Jews (or 'Rhadanite merchants') were also important.[38] Their role was described in detail by the contemporary, Ibn Khurradhbih, as well as in the contemporary Geniza papers (in Cairo).[39] The term 'Rhadanite' seems to have been derived from the Persian term *rha dan* (meaning 'those who know the route'). In particular, these merchants played a very important role within the trade and finance of the Islamic world – in Baghdad down to about the tenth century and subsequently in Cairo in Fatimid Egypt after 969.

Finally, between about 650 and 1000 the leading edge of global intensive power lay in the Islamic Middle East and North Africa. Eric Jones claims that the Abbasid caliphate was the first region to achieve per capita economic growth (supposedly the *leitmotif* of modern capitalism).[40] Fernand Braudel described the economic activity of Islam after 800 in the following terms:

> 'Capitalist' is not too anachronistic a word. From one end of Islam's world connections to the other, speculators unstintingly gambled on trade. One Arab author, Hariri had a merchant declare: 'I want to send Persian saffron to China, where I hear that it fetches a high price, and then ship Chinese porcelain to Greece, Greek brocade to India, Indian iron to Aleppo, Aleppo glass to the Yemen and Yemeni striped material to Persia'. In Basra, settlements between merchants were made by what we would now call a clearing system.[41]

A string of Islamic intensive (productive) innovations and technological/ideational refinements was crucial here. As ch. 6 explains, the possible invention, though certain development, of the lateen sail enabled long-distance sailing, especially in the Indian Ocean. So too did the development of the astrolabe in conjunction with the many breakthroughs in Islamic astronomy and mathematics (see also chs. 7, 8). Paper manufacturing began after 751. Textile manufacturing was especially important: Syria and Iraq were famous for their silk manufactures, while Egypt led the way in linen and woollen fabrics. Muslims also used impressive dyes. Islamic influence is revealed by the many Arabic (and Persian) terms that were imported into European languages. Chemicals known as mordants were needed to make dyes colourfast, especially alkali (from the Arabic word *al-kali*, 'ashes'). Saffron comes from the Arabic *zafaran*. The word *damask* derives from Damascus, *muslin* from the city of Mosul, and *organdy* from the city of Urgench in Central Asia. *Mohair* comes from the Arabic word *mukhayyir* (meaning the best), and *taffeta* from *taftan* (the Persian verb, 'to spin').[42] Notable too is that the Muslims dominated the Europeans in terms of iron production, and in steel production they dominated down to the eighteenth century. Moreover, Islamic production extended to sugar-refinement, construction, furniture manufactures, glass, leather tanning, pottery and stone-cutting.[43] Interestingly, Egyptian sugar-cane production was a leading global industry and refined *sukkar* (hence the term 'sugar') was extensively exported across much of the world. Islam also harnessed energy through windmills and water-mills, which were deployed for industrial production purposes. Notable too is that the Middle East/North Africa long held a comparative advantage over Europe with respect to both scientific knowledge and military technologies (ch. 8). No less important was the creation of a whole series of capitalist institutions (concerning partnerships, contract law, banking, credit and many others), upon which not only Islamic production, investment and commerce rested but also global trade (ch. 6). All in all, as Eric Jones aptly concludes, 'The record of technical and economic advance in the Abbasid . . . demonstrates that the [Islamic] past was by no means changeless'.[44]

Global extensive power and the contours of the global economy, c. 1000–1517

The contours of the global economy in the post-1000 period have most clearly been described by Janet Abu-Lughod in her magisterial book, *Before European Hegemony*. She reveals three principal trade routes that linked up with eight regional subsystems, which I shall discuss in turn.

The northern route and the Mongol empire: the 'benign tribes from Hell'?

A significant boost to oriental globalisation was provided by the emergence of the Mongol empire in the thirteenth century. This empire linked the East and West into a continuous trading space. It is certainly true that by the twelfth century the Seljuk Turks pushed westward and controlled a large area including virtually all of Iraq and the Fertile Crescent. But it was Chingiz (Genghis) Khan and the Mongols who succeeded in conquering much of the Eurasian landmass. Ironically – when viewed through the traditional Eurocentric lens – Chingiz chose not to conquer backward Europe, taking only its eastern parts (mainly Kievan Russia) and instead concentrated on the richest prize, China. By the latter part of the thirteenth century most of the Eurasian landmass was held under Mongol control. The critical point is that this relatively unified territorial empire – the *Pax Mongolica* – provided a pacified region within which capitalism could flourish. It enabled both very long-distance, or global, trade covering the 5000 miles between China and Europe on the one hand, and the diffusion of superior Eastern ideas and technologies across to the West (and elsewhere) on the other.[45] Institutional constraints and political costs were lowered not least because the Mongols proved to be receptive towards the many merchants who traversed the empire. Indeed, the famous contemporary of Marco Polo, Balducci Pegolotti, described the Silk Road as 'perfectly safe by day and night'.

A further irony here is that Eurocentrism views the Mongols or 'Tartars' (as they were called by the Europeans) as fundamentally destructive and inimical to progressive economic activity. As Abu-Lughod explains:

> The Mongols were initially consigned to the same mythological region reserved for the other strange creatures populating the unknown world of Asia. Based on a misinterpretation of the term Tatar (the name for only one of the tribal groups later joining the Mongol confederation), the Mongols were identified as Tartars, that is, coming from the Biblical region of Tartarus or Hell. It is difficult to see how, at the same time, they could have been viewed longingly as potential allies in Christendom's holy war against the Muslims. [Nevertheless] perhaps even those creatures from the lands of Gog and Magog [the harbingers of the apocalypse] (another feeble attempt to identify their provenance) might be mobilized in their struggle [with the Muslims].[46]

The contemporary chronicler, Matthew Paris, characterised the Mongol or 'Tartar invasion' in 1240 as: 'a detestable nation of Satan, to wit the countless armies of the Tartars, broke loose from its mountain-environed home, and piercing the solid rocks [of the Caucausus] poured forth like devils'.[47] He even depicted the 'Tartars' as men with disproportionately sized heads feeding on human flesh. To the medieval Europeans this all seemed natural. For it readily complemented their bizarre images of the Eastern peoples, such as the Blemmyae (who had faces on their chests), the Sciopods (who had one leg and used their huge foot as a sunshade), the Anthropophagi (whose heads grew beneath their shoulders), and last but not least the Cinocephali (dog-headed men).[48]

European perceptions of the Mongols – not to mention the other Eastern peoples – were based on a number of myths. First, the Tatar tribe had been virtually wiped out by Chingiz. Second, the Mongols were highly indifferent to the 'red-haired barbarians' of the backward West. And third, in addition to delivering Eastern goods the Mongol empire indirectly provided highly benign services for Europe insofar as it constituted a transmission belt along which some of the advanced Eastern 'resource portfolios' had passed across to the West (as we shall see in later chapters). Nevertheless, this influential trade circuit was in decline by the mid-fourteenth century. Tamerlane, fighting outwards from Samarkand, helped bring an end to the *Pax Mongolica*, as did the ravages of the Black Death. But this did not mark the end of the Eastern-led global economy. Rather, trade was increasingly channelled through the middle and especially southern routes.

The middle route: the maintenance of Middle Eastern Islamic extensive power

According to Abu-Lughod the Middle route began at the Mediterranean coast of Syria/Palestine, crossed the small desert and then the Mesopotamian plain to Baghdad, before finally breaking up into a land and sea route. The land route continued across Persia to Transoxiana and then either south-eastward to northern India or due eastward to Samarkand and then across the desert to China. The sea route followed the Tigris river down to the Persian Gulf from Baghdad via Basra and then passed the trading kingdoms of Oman, Sīrāf, Hormuz or Qais (guardians of the link between the Gulf and the Indian Ocean beyond). While this route became particularly important after the sixth century, it became extremely influential when Baghdad was the prime Muslim centre of trade after 750. But when Baghdad was plundered by the Mongols in 1258, the route underwent a temporary decline. However, with Iraq being subsequently ruled from Persia, the Gulf route revived. This middle route was also important because it enabled a 'deeply symbiotic' trading relationship between the Crusader kingdoms and the Muslim merchants who brought goods from as far away as the Orient.

The chief Crusader port in the Middle East – Acre – was controlled up to 1291 by the Venetians, and there they excluded their Pisan and Genoese rivals. Nevertheless, although the Venetians dominated the European trading system, they always entered the global system on terms dictated by the Middle Eastern Muslims and especially the North Africans. When Constantinople fell to the Byzantines in 1261, the Genoese were favoured over the Venetians, thereby forcing the latter to focus on the middle and southern routes. But then, with the fall of Acre in 1291, the Venetians had no choice but to rely on the southern route, which was dominated by the Egyptians.

The southern route: Europe's dependence on Egypt's trading hegemony, 1291–1517
This route linked the Alexandria–Cairo–Red Sea complex with the Arabian Sea and then the Indian Ocean and beyond. After the thirteenth century Egypt constituted the major gateway to the East. As Abu-Lughod claims, 'Whoever controlled the sea-route to Asia could set the terms of trade for a Europe now in retreat. From the thirteenth century and up to the sixteenth that power was Egypt.'[49] Indeed, between 1291 and 1517 about 80 per cent of all trade that passed to the East by sea was controlled by the Egyptians. But when Baghdad fell, Al-Qahirah – later Europeanised to Cairo – became the capital of the Islamic world and the pivotal centre of global trade (though this latter process had begun during the Fatimid era in the tenth century).

Eurocentric scholars emphasise that European international trade with the East dried up after 1291 (with the fall of Acre) as Egypt dominated the Red Sea trade to the East at the expense of the Christian Europeans. And it is this that supposedly prompted the Portuguese Vivaldi brothers to search for the more southerly route to the Indies via the Cape in 1291. But this claim is problematic. It is true that the fall of Acre in 1291 prompted Pope Nicholas IV to issue numerous prohibitions on trade with the 'infidel'. But the fact is that the Venetians managed to circumvent the ban and secured new treaties with the Sultan in 1355 and 1361. And right down to 1517, Venice survived because Egypt played such an important role within the global economy. Moreover, Venice and Genoa were not the 'pioneers' of global trade but adaptors, inserting themselves into the interstices of the Afro-Asian-led global economy and trading very much on terms laid down by the Middle Eastern Muslims and especially the Egyptians. In particular, European merchants were blocked from passing through Egypt. When they arrived in Alexandria they were met by customs officials, who stayed on board and supervised the unloading of the goods. Christians, in particular, required a special permit or visa and paid a much higher tax than did their Muslim counterparts. The Europeans then retired to their own quarters which were governed by their own laws. However, they were not allowed to leave their quarters in Alexandria and became wholly dependent upon the Egyptian merchants and government officials. Nevertheless, the Venetians and other Europeans accepted this regime because it was here where they gained access to the many goods produced throughout the East. Indeed, the fortunes of Venice were only made possible by its access to Eastern trade via North Africa.

Finally, it is important to note that Venice and Genoa continued their privileged access to the Afro-Asian-led global economy only through a strong dose of luck (rather than because of their economic strength). The geopolitical challenges posed against Egypt by the Mongols and Crusaders had led to a military reorganisation of Egyptian society. Because Egypt's Mamluke brand of military

organisation was based on the use of slaves, who could not be recruited
from Muslims, Venice and Genoa were permitted to maintain trading relations providing they supplied non-Muslim slaves to Egypt.
After 1261, Genoa provided a crucial role in supplying non-Muslim
Circassian slaves, whom they shipped from the Crimea. But then
in the fourteenth century a series of geopolitical shifts relieved the
Egyptians of the need for non-Muslim slaves. This sealed the fate
of the Genoan slave trade as the Egyptians no longer required their
services. Nevertheless, Venice's favoured connection with Egypt continued – but only because of Egyptian goodwill.

This concludes the description of the contours of the Eastern-led
global economy on the one hand, and West Asia's and North Africa's
trading hegemony over Europe on the other. But it is also important to
note that even after 1517 the Islamic trading hegemony over Europe
was maintained. For the baton of Islamic extensive power was passed
from Egypt to the Ottoman empire, which maintained its hold over
the Portuguese in the Indian Ocean (see ch. 7). Moreover, other centres of Islamic economic power – Mughal India and South-east Asia –
remained strong enough to resist and dominate the European traders
right down to about 1800 (chs. 4 and 7). Nevertheless for all the impres-
siveness of Islamic extensive power and the fact that the Middle East
remained the Bridge of the World for much of the second millennium,
the leading edge of global intensive power was passed not to Italy
after 1000 or Portugal after 1500, but to China in 1100. And there it
remained until the nineteenth century.

3 Chinese pioneers:

the first industrial miracle and the myth of Chinese isolationism, c. 1000–1800

When Marco Polo traveled to the East and reported what he had seen, mixing truth with falsehood but in any event telling something of the truth, the men of the West refused to believe him. In the late Medieval Ages his account of his travels was viewed as a book of fables . . . It was as if occidentals were unable to believe in the reality of the marvels of the Orient.

Jacques Le Goff

European . . . historians [have not] yet realized that the rise of Medieval European civilization after AD 1000 coincided with an eastward shift of the world system's [productive] center from the Middle East to China. That is not surprising given the past pre-occupation of our medievalists with the national histories of England and France – implicitly retrospecting upon the entire human past the circumstances of the late nineteenth century, when the French and British empires did cover most of the globe. It requires a real leap of imagination to recognize China's primacy.

William H. McNeill

By 1100 the leading edge of global intensive power had shifted across to China and remained there until the nineteenth century. China also developed considerable extensive power and came to dominate in this respect after the fifteenth century (even though the Islamic Middle East continued to constitute a vital node of the global economy). All this stands opposed to the Eurocentric depiction. My critique of the standard Eurocentric characterisation of China is made in two stages. The first section reveals that China underwent what I am calling the 'first industrial miracle', where many of the characteristics that we associate with the eighteenth-century British industrial revolution had emerged by 1100. The second section then addresses the common Eurocentric dismissal of the Sung achievement: that subsequent Chinese oriental despotic governments choked the Sung shoots of industrial progress so as to ensure that the economy went into a precipitous decline. This in turn accounts for the alleged Chinese withdrawal from the world after 1434 when the state banned foreign trade and retreated into its imperial tribute system. Here I paint a different picture that reveals, if not a Sinocentric global economy, then certainly one in which China played a major role in the post-1434 period. I also provide further detailed evidence to support the fact of China's lead in chs. 4 and 7.

The first industrial miracle: eleventh-century Sung China

As ch. 9 explains, economic historians conventionally assume that the origins or recipe for industrialisation can be found in eighteenth-century Britain. But what we are not told is that the industrial master-chef was China, not Britain. China's 'industrial miracle' occurred over a period of 1500 years and culminated in the Sung revolution – some six hundred years before Britain entered its industrialisation phase. The Chinese industrial miracle is worth focusing upon in some detail because it was the single most important event in the history of global intensive power between 1100 and 1800. For it was the diffusion of the many Sung Chinese technological and ideational breakthroughs that significantly informed the rise of the West (chs. 6–9).

The iron and steel (r)evolution, 600 BCE to 1100 CE

China's iron and steel miracle goes back to 600 BCE with the first cast-iron object dating from 513 BCE, and steel being produced by the second century BCE.[1] Nevertheless, the industry's staggering growth between 800 and 1100 seems incontrovertible even if the details of the amounts are not precisely clear. In a well-known article Robert Hartwell famously estimated that Chinese per capita iron output rose sixfold between 806 and 1078.[2] In terms of gross annual production, China produced 13,500 tons of iron in 806, some 90,400 tons by 1064 and as much as 125,000 by 1078. Two comparisons are illuminating: first, that Europe as a whole would only produce greater volumes by 1700, and that even as late as 1788 Britain was producing only 76,000 tons. Second, the price ratio (measured as a ratio of the value of iron to rice) stood at 177:100 in Sung Szechwan in 1080 and 135:100 in Shensi, thereby indicating that the price of iron was low. It should also be noted that these provinces were not atypical because prices were even lower in north-east China. But the striking statistic here is that as late as 1700, Britain had an equivalent figure of 160:100, which was perhaps about a third higher than the price found in the north-eastern Chinese markets of the eleventh century. Finally, in 977 the Chinese price ratio had stood as high as 632:100, indicating almost a fourfold reduction in price in the space of just one hundred years. It took Britain over two hundred years, from 1600 to 1822, to achieve a comparable price reduction. Nevertheless, Joseph Needham has suggested that Hartwell's iron output data are a little on the high side for the period (a point I return to below). Even so they would have to be incorrect by a very large margin to invalidate the conclusion that Sung China underwent a massive, if not 'revolutionary', increase in iron production the likes of which would only be matched by the British some seven centuries later.

Eurocentric scholars often dismiss this achievement by arguing that the use of Chinese iron was confined only to weapons and decorative art rather than for tools and production. But the fact is that iron *was* used to make everyday items and tools, as we would expect in an industrial revolution. These included knives, hatchets, chisels, drillbits, hammers and mallets, ploughshares, spades and shovels, wheelbarrow axles, wheels, horseshoes, cooking pots and pans, kettles, bells, chains for suspension bridges, armoured gates and watchtowers, bridges, printing frames and type. These are only a smattering of what was on offer at the time. Hartwell adds to this list saws, hinges, locks, stoves, lamps, nails, needles, pins, boilers, cymbals and drum fittings. More generally, Donald Wagner concludes that, 'mass production of cast-iron implements was extremely important . . . and great fortunes were made by "proto-industrialist" ironmasters', a process which he traces back to the third century BCE.[3]

No less impressive here were the manufacturing techniques that were invented. The Chinese produced a variety of forms of iron, using cast iron for shovels and ploughshares (as well as cannon), while simultaneously producing wrought iron for bladed purposes (e.g. swords and knives). This is especially significant because the Europeans used wrought iron for most of the medieval period. 'It seems in fact that the Chinese world . . . arrived directly at casting iron, without passing, as the European countries did, through the long intermediary stage of forging it.'[4] Cast iron was far superior, given its greater strength. And it was precisely because China could harness the much cheaper cast iron that made the effects of the industrial revolution so widespread throughout the country.

In turn, all this was made possible by the breakthroughs in smelting upon which the production of cast iron was based. Here the use of blast furnaces and piston bellows were especially important (though again, these had already been known for about 1400 years). The bellows delivered the continuous flow of air that was necessary to maintain the required high temperatures (975° C). These were being used in the fourth century BCE and were propelled by water power as early as 31 CE. Moreover, the Chinese were producing steel (which is derived from cast iron), as early as the second century BCE while Europe only developed steel in the modern period. Particularly important here was that Chinese steel was produced in the fifth century CE by a 'co-fusion' process where wrought and cast iron were melded together.

Another striking innovation was the eleventh-century substitution of coke for charcoal (given that wood was in short supply). This is hugely significant precisely because Eurocentrism insists that this was first achieved by the British many centuries later. But Britain was like China in that both countries used coke in order to solve the problem of deforestation. Remarkable achievements in textile manufacturing are yet another feature of the Sung miracle that is usually attributed to the eighteenth-century British. The Chinese silk industry began as early as the fourteenth century BCE. And arguably the most advanced industrial-technological innovation was found in the textile industry with the widespread adoption of the water-powered spinning machine for hemp and silk (see chs. 6 and 9). Though all these achievements in the iron/steel and textiles industry were remarkable, they were but the tip of a large industrial iceberg. For such production presupposed a major infrastructural support network.

The transportation and energy revolutions

While European water-mills were first used to grind grain, with their application to iron production first emerging in south Germany around 1025, the inverse was the case in China. Chinese water-mills were developed in order to propel the bellows in blast furnaces as early as 31 CE. Most significantly, the use of a piston-rod and driving belt in the water bellows bore a remarkable resemblance to the steam engine (see ch. 9 for details). Moreover, the canal and pound-lock were major innovations (the latter having been invented in 984).[5] And the transportation of coal, iron and steel along the canals enabled their distribution to the south of the country, which was vital to the Chinese industrial miracle, not least because it meant that the huge internal demand for these materials could be met. Noteworthy too is that petroleum and natural gas were tapped by the Chinese for fuel, cooking and lighting purposes probably as early as the fourth century BCE.[6] Indeed, the extensity of this innovation is revealed by the fact that permanent asbestos lamps were mass produced for homes some time around the tenth century CE.[7]

Taxation, paper, printing and the rise of a commercialised economy

One particularly significant Sung innovation was the creation of a tax system based on cash. While paper money (fei-ch'ien) was invented around the ninth century for credit purposes, by the early tenth century it evolved into 'true' paper money as a medium of exchange. By 1161 the state was issuing ten million notes a year. Significantly, these pioneering developments were later copied by the Europeans, with the English catching on only as late as 1797.[8] Taxes were increasingly demanded in cash rather than goods in kind. Thus from a figure of 4 per cent in 749, taxes demanded in cash rose rapidly to 52 per cent

by the mid-eleventh century. This was especially important because
it forced peasants to engage in market activity. Market exchange pen-
etrated right down to the lowest levels of society so that even the
poorest had no choice but to produce for the market. As McNeill put it,
'Proliferating market exchanges – local, regional, and trans-regional –
allowed spectacular increases in total productivity, as all the advantages of specialization that Adam Smith later analyzed so persuasively
came into operation.'[9] And he goes on to cite a fourteenth-century
writer who tells us that:

> these days, wherever there is a settlement of ten households, there
> is always a market . . . At the appropriate season, people exchange
> what they have for what they have not, raising or lowering the
> prices in accordance with their estimate of the eagerness or
> diffidence shown by others, so as to obtain the last small measure
> of profit. This is of course the usual way of the world.[10]

In contrast to the Eurocentric depiction of the Chinese state as
an oriental despotism, Eric Jones tells us that the government:

> relinquished its function of allocating and re-allocating land in
> return for labour services and taxes in kind and instead took its
> taxes in cash. This hands-off policy facilitated the growth of the
> private land market . . . [T]he state was neither able to quash
> those economic changes it found socially undesirable, nor, it is
> important to note, did it cream off to the emperor and officials all
> the proceeds of change. Neither the state nor the 'prebends' could
> tax away all the gains . . . Doing so would have destroyed the
> inducement for the supply response we actually observe.[11]

R. Bin Wong similarly notes that Chinese governments, 'believed that
light taxation allowed the people to prosper, and since a prosperous
people was held to be crucial for the maintenance of a powerful state,
tax rates were low'.[12] Indeed, the tax burden imposed by central governments was extremely low – perhaps around 6 per cent of national
income.[13] While Eurocentrism depicts the Chinese economy as an

agrarian subsistence-based system, the fact is that Sung commerce was not only highly developed, but that the state derived most of its tax revenues from the commercial sector. Significant too is that the merchants were taxed at much lower levels than rural producers.[14] The countless reports of the Jesuit missionaries in China are also instructive here; many of them confirm that merchants were left alone by the state to carry on their business.[15]

Striking testimony to the depth of commercialism under the Sung was the rise of towns and large cities. Yoshinobu Shiba points out that estimating urban population sizes is difficult owing to the unevenness of the available data during the Sung period. Estimates for Yin county suggest an urban population of some 13 per cent, 7 per cent for She county and as much as 37 per cent for Tan-t'u county. Even so, urbanisation was not only more pronounced in China than it was in Europe, but China boasted some of the very largest cities in the world. For example, Hang-chou's population lay somewhere between 1.5 and 5 million (owing to divergent estimates).[16]

The development of a money economy was significantly linked to yet another vital innovation: printing and paper-making (the origins of which are traced in chs. 6 and 8). It is worth noting that the widespread use of printed paper money was one of the many aspects of China that had so impressed Marco Polo. No less striking was that paper was employed in a variety of ingenious ways, not least in armour (a tough product that did not rust), wallpaper, articles of clothing, toilet-paper, kites, tissues and many others. The Chinese paper industry was also spurred on by the large demand for books. The National Academy in the capital Khaifeng and later in Hang-chow engaged in large-scale publishing. Nevertheless, book making and selling were not confined to the state – they were also undertaken in the private sphere.

The agricultural or 'Green' revolution

China had in place by the sixth century CE almost all of the aspects that we associate with the British agricultural revolution of the eighteenth and nineteenth centuries (see ch. 9 for a fuller discussion).[17] As Robert Temple puts it:

> It is no exaggeration to say that China was in the position of America and Western Europe today, and Europe was in the position of, say, Morocco [today]. There was simply no comparison between the primitive and hopeless agriculture of Europe before the eighteenth century and the . . . advanced agriculture of China after the fourth century BC.[18]

Indeed, by the Sung period the superiority of Chinese agriculture was such that one Eurocentric historian was even forced to concede that '[f]or Europe as a whole the twelfth century Chinese situation was not achieved until the twentieth century'.[19] Chinese farmers enjoyed much higher yield ratios than their European counterparts.[20] More-over, Chinese agriculture remained impressive over the next seven centuries (see the next section). No less significant was the Sung government initiative known as the 'young shoots policy' (chhing miao fa). The government provided incentives for farmers to invest in agriculture and offered loans at highly favourable interest rates. '[P]erhaps its chief success was the way in which the rural population, alive to the benefits of the new technology, were willing to experiment and improve on their own initiative.'[21]

The navigational revolution

Francis Bacon famously claimed in his *Novum Organum* (1620) that the three most important world discoveries were printing, gunpowder and the compass. Strikingly, all three were invented in China (see below and chs. 6 and 8). Noteworthy too is that it was the Chinese who discovered around 1000 that magnetic north and true north were not one and the same. Later, by the fifteenth century, this knowledge enabled the construction of the most accurate maps then known.

Perhaps the most impressive aspect of the Chinese navigational revolution was the development of ships. These were striking both for their size and their quantity. Thus while as late as 1588 the largest

English ships displaced a mere 400 tons these were dwarfed by the much earlier Chinese junks of over 3000 tons (see also ch. 7). Moreover, the large-scale junks boasted many ingenious features – including the square hull, the sternpost rudder, fore and aft sails and watertight compartments – all of which were assimilated by the Europeans much later (see chs. 6 and 9). In particular the numbers of ships – large and small – bore testimony not just to China's navigational revolution but also to the commercialised nature of its economy. In the eighth century some 2000 boats were working on the Yangtze, which carried a total cargo that was equivalent to about a third of the amount carried by the British merchant fleet one thousand years later. Marco Polo famously estimated there to have been 15,000 ships in the lower Yangtze alone. By the seventeenth century the Jesuit, Alvarez Semedo, counted no fewer than 300 ships sailing upstream on the Yangtze in just one hour![22] Finally, Gang Deng reveals that during the Northern Sung there were about 12,000 grain carrier ships which rose to over 20,000 in the Ch'ing, and some 130,000 private transport ships in the late eighteenth century.[23] All in all, Temple's conclusion seems apt:

> It could probably be safely said that the Chinese were the greatest sailors in history. For nearly two millennia they had ships and sailing techniques so far in advance of the rest of the world that comparisons are embarrassing. When the West finally did catch up with them, it was only by adapting their inventions in one way or another. For most of history, Europeans used ships which were drastically inferior to Chinese ships in every respect imaginable [even as late as 1800].[24]

The first military revolution: China, c. 850–1290
As we shall see in ch. 8, Eurocentrism celebrates the military genius of the Europeans who allegedly pioneered the first major 'military revolution' (1550–1660). The major technological breakthroughs were in gunpowder, the gun and the cannon. But all these were first invented in China during the 'first military revolution' between 850 and 1290.

One of the most common Eurocentric dismissals of this claim is that the Chinese only used gunpowder in fireworks and that it had no military application whatsoever (i.e. the orientalist 'China clause'). Interestingly, in the epic film *The Adventures of Marco Polo* we are told that the first Chinese invention that Polo was introduced to was 'spaghett' (spaghetti), and that the second was exploding gunpowder. Polo is alleged to have said of the latter, 'is this used only for toys?', to which the Chinese reply comes 'Yes, and for fireworks'. Polo then suggests that: 'This might be a valuable weapon in war', to which the Chinese reply comes, 'No, that would be too horrible, too deadly'. This dialogue aptly captures one of the most common Eurocentric myths: that even though the Chinese had invented gunpowder it was left to the more creative Europeans to deploy it in warfare.

While the Chinese had invented gunpowder around 850,[25] by the beginning of the tenth century it was applied in Chinese flame-throwers and by 969 it was used to fire arrows. By 1231 it was used in bombs, grenades and rockets (which took the form of a mortar made in an iron tube). And by the fourteenth century it was used in land- and sea-mines.[26] The Chinese even invented rocket-launchers that could dispatch 320 rockets instantaneously – what Needham describes as a 'medieval equivalent of the bazooka so widely used in the Second World War'.[27] Interestingly, the Chinese also developed in the fourteenth century a rocket with wings and fins which again, according to Needham, 'bore a strong resemblance . . . to the notorious V-1 rockets of the Second World War'.[28] The origins of the gun can be traced back to the 'fire lance' of the mid-tenth century. The first gun that shot iron bullets was invented around 1259 and a metal barrel was used no later than 1275.[29] By about 1288 a crude cannon known as the 'eruptor' had been invented (pre-empting the first European cannon by about thirty-eight years).[30] And there is strong evidence to suggest that the Chinese invention diffused across to Europe (see ch. 8).

Last but not least, one of the most impressive aspects of the Chinese military revolution was its navy. Eventually there were as

many as 20,500 ships in the Sung navy.[31] This Chinese fleet could have
taken out any single European power, and most probably the entirety
of Europe's combined naval power. Importantly, ships' weapons systems were constantly upgraded. In 1129 trebuchets hurled gunpowder bombs and were standard equipment, and by 1203 some ships
were armoured with iron plates. Chinese military shipping had long
enjoyed an impressive lineage. For example, in the late sixth century,
the 'five ensign' battleship had five decks that reached 100 feet in
height and carried some 800 men. It was also equipped with 'striking
arms' or 'holing irons' – 50-feet long poles with heavy pointed iron
spikes on the end – that were fixed to the upper decks. These worked
like giant hammers, crashing downwards to destroy enemy shipping.
And as early as the third century, there were mobile 'square floating
fortresses', which covered no less than 360,000 square feet, had high
towers and hosted more than 2000 men.[32] All in all, Temple's words
once more provide an apt conclusion: 'The Chinese . . . were arms
manufacturers on a scale undreamed of until modern times in the
West.'[33]

An initial Chinese conclusion
Finally, we are now in a position to reappraise one of the central
tenets of Eurocentrism – that only the Western Europeans developed
a 'mechanical outlook'. Frederic Lane's words are typical:

> Necessity explains nothing . . . While the artists of the Far East
> delighted in painting flowers, fish and horses, Leonardo da Vinci
> and Francesco di Giorgio Martini were obsessed with machinery.
> [European] philosophers came to regard the universe as a great
> piece of clockwork, the human body as a piece of machinery, and
> God as an outstanding 'clockmaker'.[34]

But in the light of the extraordinary Chinese mechanical inventions
this view cannot be sustained. In point of fact – as I show in this
book – for much of the period under review, the Europeans invented

very little for themselves. The only genuine innovations that they made before the eighteenth century were the Archimedean screw, the crankshaft or camshaft and alcoholic distillation processes.[35] And while the Europeans showed a strong capacity to assimilate many of China's technological inventions in the ensuing seven hundred years, an assimilationist propensity is not the same thing as an 'innovative' mechanical outlook. For if anyone demonstrated such an outlook it was the Chinese, not the Europeans.

The most common Eurocentric reply is to dismiss the Sung economic achievement as but an 'abortive revolution' where economic progress rapidly washed up on the iceberg of the oriental despotic state and sunk without trace.[36] Apart from the fact that this dismissal cannot explain the striking achievements initiated during the Sung, the Chinese economy did not regress or sink without trace after 1279. Its considerable vibrancy enabled China to stand at or very near the centre of the global economy right down to the nineteenth century.

The myth of Chinese isolationism and economic stagnation: China, first among equals, 1434–1800

For most of the second millennium Chinese trade was so significant that various anti-Eurocentric authors have described the global economy before 1800 as 'Sinocentric'.[37] Actually, while China was indeed the leading power in the world, ultimately it was best characterised as *primus inter pares*. The distribution of economic power in the world under oriental globalisation was 'polycentric', with China, India, the Middle East and Northern Africa, South-east Asia and Japan all being significant players.

Nevertheless, most scholars dismiss Chinese success after the fifteenth century according to two principal arguments contained within the 'China clause'. First, as we noted above, even if it is conceded that there was significant growth during the Sung this is dismissed as an 'abortive revolution', with growth terminating shortly thereafter. And second, the Ming proclamation of an imperial ban on foreign commerce in 1434 ensured that any window of opportunity for China to remake the world immediately slammed shut. And it did so because the Chinese economy was in decline, thereby forcing the authorities to withdraw from international trade. Chinese international trade, they claim, was replaced by the regressive Chinese tribute system that was entirely separate from the global economy. For these two reasons then, Eurocentrism dismisses the possibility that China could have been at the centre of world trade after 1280 and especially 1434. Instead, we are told, China sank back into isolationism.

This so-called withdrawal leads to two of the most important claims in relation to Eurocentric world history. First, it had massive consequences insofar as it allegedly created a power vacuum in the East, which was eagerly filled by the superior Europeans after 1500. In the words of David Landes:

> The abandonment of the program of the great voyages [under Chêng Ho] was part of a larger policy of closure, of retreat from the hazards and temptations of the sea. This deliberate introversion, a major turning point in Chinese history, could not have come at a worse time, for it not only disarmed them in the face of rising European power but set them, complacent and stubborn, against the lessons and novelties that European travellers would soon be bringing.[38]

Second, the ban meant that China became cut off from the mainstream of international trade (which allegedly took off after 1500), so that its economy effectively dried up thereafter. To cite Landes once more: 'Isolationism became China. Round, complete, apparently serene, ineffably harmonious, the Celestial Empire purred along for hundreds of years more, impervious and imperturbable. But the world was passing it by.'[39] Thus the withdrawal allegedly accounts for China's great leap backward while simultaneously enabling Europe's great leap forward after 1500. Clearly then, a very great deal hangs on this issue. In contrast to the standard Eurocentric depiction, I offer four counterpropositions which are discussed in turn.

*The myth of China's withdrawal: the post-1434 continuity
of Chinese international trade*

The conventional picture of a withdrawal errs in the first instance
because Western historians take too literal a view of both the official
ban and the Chinese tribute system. The literal reading of the official ban rests to a certain extent on the problem of misinterpretation.
The official documents are distorted by the Chinese government's
attempt at being seen to maintain a Confucian (i.e. isolationist) ideal.
Moreover, the withdrawal is wrongly confirmed by the existence of
a regressive imperial tribute system, which was supposedly based on
coercion and state-administered forms of tribute rather than commercial trade. But conventional readings misunderstand both the tribute
system and the nature of the ban.

The first rejoinder here is that the tribute system was also a
trading system. As Rodzinski notes, the tribute system

> was often, in effect, only an outward form for very considerable
> foreign trade. In many cases foreign merchants, especially those
> from Central Asia, presented themselves as the bearers of
> fictitious tribute from imaginary states solely for the purpose of
> conducting trade.[40]

Moreover, trade relations in East and South-east Asia expanded as
Chinese tribute relations expanded.[41] This was even at times conceded in official Chinese documents. A number of points can be
added.[42] The tribute system was more voluntary than forced. This
was because gaining access to the Chinese market by paying nom-
inal amounts of tribute was a means by which so-called vassals
could enrich themselves. How else can we explain the fact that the
Portuguese, Spanish and Dutch repeatedly asked to join the system
as vassals? Moreover, vassal states often competed with each other
in order to pay tribute – again, so as to gain access to China's lucrative economy. And a whole variety of rulers, including the sultan of
Melaka, the rulers of Brunei, the Chōla kings of Coromandel and the
princes of Malabar, were anxious to send tribute so that they might

gain Chinese protection against some of their neighbouring enemies. As Anthony Reid points out, some 'states' such as Java, Siam and Melaka were so persistent in conducting tribute missions that they actually managed to irritate the Chinese authorities.[43] It is testimony to the voluntary aspect of the system that when vassals were deprived of their tributary status this often led to a violent reaction by the so-called vassal. For example, at the end of the sixteenth century Japan invaded Korea (a Ming vassal state) in order to force China to resume the tributary relationship and even threatened an invasion of China if it refused! One further strategy frequently deployed by Asian merchants was producing phony credentials, posing as emissaries paying tribute 'as a fig-leaf for humdrum commercial trade';[44] and again, this was well known and even occasionally admitted in Ming documents.

There are three major reasons why the ban was a myth. First, as already noted, the tribute system was in part a disguised trading system. Second, many private Chinese merchants traded by circumnavigating the official ban in a number of ways. Ironically, Eurocentrism's portrayal of the Portuguese *cartaz* system as a sign of European dominance misses the point that for the Chinese, in particular, holding a *cartaz* meant that they could masquerade as Portuguese in order to circumvent the Ming ban. Moreover, much Chinese trade was mixed up with Japanese (but was really Chinese piracy) and was extremely prosperous. But perhaps the most common method for circumventing the ban lay with Cantonese trade practice. As Philip Curtin explains:

> All cargoes in excess of the official tribute were landed with it and labelled 'ballast on board tribute ships' to be held until permission to sell it arrived from Beijing . . . [I]f the foreign ship needed to leave, it had to take on ballast in order to assure safe passage. It therefore brought Chinese goods for ballast on its voyage home. In this way the 'ballast' [i.e. trading goods] ships carried in both directions was more important than the tribute that justified it.[45]

The ruler of the island kingdom of Ryūkyū was particularly creative, encouraging Chinese private merchants from Fujian to settle there from where they could engage in lucrative trade with China. In return all he had to do was send the occasional deferential tribute mission to China. This was part of a more general strategy pursued by private Chinese merchants, who relocated into other parts of the region in order to export products back to China. In the first half of the sixteenth century Chinese merchants spread to all parts of the commercially strategic South China Sea; from Indo-China, Malaysia, Siam and over the arc of islands from Sumatra to Timor to the Philippines. And they dominated this trading network well into the nineteenth century. Moreover, they traded westwards and eastwards and were linked back to Fukien in China.[46] Last, but not least, there was also a thriving smuggling trade. And because government officials often collaborated with the smugglers, the ban obviously became unenforceable. Indeed, so large was the smuggling trade that during the 1560s the Ming government eventually gave in and legalised the smugglers' main port (Port Moon).

The third reason why the ban was a myth lay in the fact that not all private trade was banned. Much of it was officially sanctioned in three key ports: Macao, Chang-chou in Fukien province and Su-chou in western Shensi province. Later in Ch'ing times trade was conducted through Amoy, Ningbo and Shanghai. As Lach and Kley explain:

> The earliest Western observers, such as Mendoza, had been under the impression that Fukienese merchants traded abroad illegally with the connivance of local officials. [But] seventeenth-century writers – Matlief was one of the first – shortly came to recognize that the merchants from the Chang-chou area had official permission to trade beyond the empire's borders.[47]

Various writers have pointed to the significance of the Chinese–Southeast Asian trade link.[48] In particular, Manila was an extremely important entrepôt for the whole global trading system because it was from there that China gained a good deal of its silver (via the Spanish Manila galleon). Indeed, between 1570 and 1642 alone an average of twenty-five Chinese ships were sent to Manila per annum.[49] And this connection not only remained important for much of the period after the 'ban' but in fact intensified at the end of the eighteenth century.[50] But the clincher surely lies with the simple point that most of the world's silver was sucked into China, thereby confirming that the economy was not only fully integrated within the global economy but was robust enough to enjoy a strong trade surplus. Accordingly, it is worth briefly considering this point further.

There are four key reasons why the world's silver tended to gravitate towards China. First, by the mid-fifteenth century the economy was converted to a silver currency. Second, the Chinese economy's strength generated a strong internal demand for silver. Third, China's exports greatly exceeded imports. And fourth, the price of silver relative to gold in China was the highest in the world (the Chinese gold/silver ratio stood at 1:6 compared to 1:14 in Europe).[51] This much was recognised by Adam Smith: 'In China, a country much richer than any part of Europe, the value of the precious metals is much higher than in any part of Europe'.[52] China's economy was pivotal insofar as it constituted a silver sink into which much of the world's silver was channelled. Strikingly, by the 1640s, the Chinese treasury was gaining some 750,000 kg of silver per annum. The level of wealth in China could be gauged from the fact that, 'even a "poor" cloth merchant in Shanghai had a capital of about five tons of silver, and the richest families had [a capital] of several hundred tons of silver'.[53]

Nevertheless, the term 'sink' is misleading only because it conveys the impression that the world's silver ended up in China never to reappear. The fact that the price of Chinese silver relative to gold was very high and that elsewhere the relative price was much lower, gave rise to a global system of arbitrage.[54] As Flynn and Giraldez explain:

> divergent bimetallic ratios imply that one could theoretically use an ounce of gold to buy say eleven ounces of silver in Amsterdam, transport the silver to China and exchange the eleven ounces

there for about two ounces of gold. The two ounces of gold could be brought back to Europe and exchanged for twenty-two ounces of silver, which could again be transported back to China where its value was double again.[55]

This global arbitrage system saw the constant shifting of silver into China, which was then exchanged for gold. This in turn was exported abroad principally to Europe where it was exchanged for silver and then sent back to China where it was exchanged for gold. I call this the 'global silver recycling process': 'global' because it took the form of a continuous loop that went from the Americas, across Eurasia to China and back westwards to Europe. This is why the term 'sink' is problematic. And clearly the Chinese were not hoarders (as I explain in ch. 4). Interestingly, even after the 1640s, when arbitrage profits diminished, silver still poured into China because of the continuing strong demand for its products. This simultaneously refutes the Eurocentric 'China clause' – that after the Sung period the Chinese economy 'just stopped'. Moreover, as Flynn and Giraldez have argued, the fact is that the conversion of the Chinese economy to silver in the mid-fifteenth century was extremely consequential for the fortunes of the Europeans. For as Pomeranz rightly notes, 'had China . . . not had such a dynamic economy [based on a silver monetary base which enabled her to] . . . absorb the staggering quantities of silver mined in the New World over three centuries, those mines might have become unprofitable within a few decades'.[56]

So to sum up, it is clear that one way or another, Chinese merchants continued their extremely lucrative trading with or without official sanction. Many Eurocentric scholars have, therefore, been too easily seduced by the official rhetoric. As Jacques Gernet aptly concluded: 'There was a big gap between the official regulations and the reality of the commercial situation; the [official] restrictions imposed on trade might lead us to suppose that China was isolated at the very time when maritime trade was most intense'.[57] But if the Chinese authorities most certainly turned a blind eye to this extensive illegal private trading system, this begs an immediate question: why then did they insist in officially pretending that the ban was effective? To answer this question we confront yet another common Eurocentric misperception.

The myth of the Chinese 'ban' on international trade: the politics of Chinese identity

Turning to my second major counter-proposition, Eurocentric history emphasises that the official ban on foreign trade was a necessary outcome of Chinese economic decline. And similarly, if the Chinese had any imperial pretensions at this time, its economic decline ensured its withdrawal and isolation. But given the evidence of the continuity of Chinese trade marshalled above it is clear that the ban was but a myth. Here I claim that the myth of the ban was maintained so as to reproduce the legitimacy of the Chinese state (in turn connected to Chinese identity). For the fact is that the tribute system was much more than simply a disguised commercial system. The myth of the ban was maintained through political choice rather than out of economic constraint.

Under the Ming emperor, Hung-hsi, China turned back to its traditional Confucian values which emphasised isolation from the rest of the world. The early Ming dynasty had looked outwards (as represented by Chêng Ho's expeditions), even if it was uninterested in initiating an imperial policy. But when Emperor Hung-hsi took over (in 1424), he set about restoring Confucian practices into the heart of the Chinese state. In 1434 the Ming dynasty officially proclaimed Chinese international trade as dead. But if significant trade continued, why then the pretence of an isolated kingdom in which relations with the outside world were based only on the fictitious suzerain system of tributary vassalage? The tribute system had been a vital means for the Chinese state to maintain its domestic legitimacy. Most importantly, it involved the performance of the kowtow by the ambassadors and emissaries of the vassal states. And the kowtow was the crucial symbol of the emperor's Mandate of Heaven. Thus it was essential that the myth of the tribute system be maintained if only to retain the

domestic legitimacy of the state.[58] Hence the political significance
of the tribute system lay in the fact that the emperor had to demonstrate to his own population that he possessed the allegiance of the
'barbarian' world (hence the tribute system), even though in practice
the tribute system also meant lucrative trade for both the vassals and
the Chinese merchants.

This imperial game of legitimacy construction and trade deception has been aptly captured by Joseph Fletcher, and it is worth quoting
him at length:

> Chinese authorities were happy to be deceived. The emperor's
> prestige [i.e. legitimacy] was not enhanced if his ministers
> exposed the real nature of his 'vassals', and the court had surer
> pick of the merchandise if traders . . . brought them along to the
> capital. As a result, counterfeit embassies bearing counterfeit
> credentials rode back and forth regularly to the Chinese court.
> Merchants and ministers alike were parties to what could have
> been an open secret . . . According to [the contemporary Jesuit
> missionary] Ricci, 'the Chinese themselves (who are by no means
> ignorant of deception) delude their king, fawning with devotion,
> as if truly the whole world paid taxes to the Chinese kingdom,
> whereas on the contrary tribute is more truly paid to those
> kingdoms by China'. And if Ricci was in any way mistaken, it was
> only in believing that the emperor himself was not in on the game
> as well.[59]

Indeed, it was a game of deception that the so-called vassal states
were only too happy to play for, as Bin Wong aptly notes, 'foreign
governments generally allowed the Chinese to promote this view [of
Chinese superiority] without necessarily accepting it themselves'.[60]
For it was clearly in their trading interests to play along.

It is clear, therefore, that it was not economic decline but the
need to maintain legitimacy – connected to Chinese identity – that
prompted the rulers to pretend that the ban worked. However, paradoxically, there was one sense in which the Chinese withdrew. For
they withdrew not from the global economy but 'abstained' from the

imperial power politics that would shortly grip the Iberian states. As Louise Levathes noted,

> During the [early fifteenth century] . . . China extended its sphere . . . of influence throughout the Indian Ocean. Half the world was in China's grasp, and with such a formidable navy the other half was easily within reach, had China wanted it. China could have become the great colonial power, a hundred years before the great age of European exploration [sic] and expansion. But China did not.[61]

The fact is that that the Chinese could have initiated an imperial mission throughout much of the world had they so wished. Why then did they not? It should be clear by now that this was not a function of inadequate material capacity. It was because they *chose* to forgo imperialism, largely as a result of their particular identity. As Felipe Fernández-Armesto noted similarly:

> China's 'manifest destiny' never happened and the world predominance, which, for a time, seemed hers for the taking, was abandoned . . . [China's] forbearance remains one of the most remarkable instances of collective reticence in [world] history.[62]

All in all, therefore, the only problem with this fictitious ban is that Eurocentric scholars have been too easily seduced into believing that it was effective and have simultaneously misunderstood its social function. In turn, this misinterpretation has given rise to one of the greatest fallacies of Eurocentric world history: that it was the withdrawal from the global economy by the Chinese that created the vacuum into which the superior Europeans poured after 1500. For the fact is that there was no vacuum (see also ch. 7).

The myth of the decline of the Chinese economy: China pre-eminent, 1100–1800/1840
After 1100 China's intensive power was second to none in the world. If so, then how are we to deal with the Eurocentric dismissal that

the Sung industrial revolution was in fact an 'abortive revolution'? For Eurocentric scholars, the post-Sung economy dried up mainly as a function of the reimposition of oriental despotism, which was forced into banning trade because of economic weakness and declining output. Ironically, this view is often influenced by Robert Hartwell's iron and steel data, which suggest that production shrank rapidly after 1279. Or as Fernand Braudel typically expressed this standard Eurocentric claim:

> What is so extraordinary is that after this incredible start, Chinese metallurgy progressed no further after the thirteenth century. Chinese foundries and forges made no more discoveries, but simply repeated their old processes. Coke-smelting – if it was known at all – was not developed. It is difficult to ascertain this, let alone explain it.[63]

The first problem with the Eurocentric dismissal is that Chinese international trade remained vibrant (as already explained), as did internal trade.[64] The second problem with the Eurocentric claim lies in the point that Hartwell's estimates are problematic less because they marginally exaggerate the Sung achievement, but mainly because they underestimate *subsequent* iron and steel production levels. Kenneth Pomeranz suggests that contrary to what was once thought, iron production revived after 1420.[65] By the early twentieth century Fang Xing estimates that some 170,000 tons of 'native iron' were produced (compared to 125,000 tons in 1078),[66] Moreover, Peter Golas concludes that iron production probably peaked in the eighteenth century.[67] He also points out that China enjoyed very high levels of coal production in the nineteenth century, that some of it was contained in pits that were as large as anything found in Europe, and that coal was used throughout the economy. Moreover, there is strong evidence that iron production in Guangdong was based on a formal capitalist model.[68] Thus the Sung industrial miracle was not an isolated incident in Chinese history. The economy remained not only vibrant, but one that would have major ramifications for the

developmental prospects of many regions in the world – most especially Europe (see chs. 6–9). What further evidence, therefore, is available to reveal the significant levels of Chinese intensive power after
1280?

One sign of China's high intensive power lay in its productive
agricultural base. By the sixteenth century the economy had recov-
ered from the Black Death. Agricultural yields not only increased by
60 per cent between the late fourteenth century and 1600, but they
also outstripped the rates achieved anywhere in Europe. Moreover,
much of China's agricultural surplus was exported. This was no backward subsistence-based agricultural economy – it was highly commercialised and reliant on international trade.[69] All in all a number
of writers have detailed an impressive picture of Chinese agricultural
development for the eighteenth century.[70] Gernet even labels it an
'era of prosperity' and concludes that Chinese agriculture was still
well ahead of Europe's.[71] Noteworthy too is that between roughly
1700 and 1850 Chinese population growth rates increased at a phenomenal rate that would only be matched by Britain after its industrialisation. This implied an enormous increase in agricultural output
and per capita grain output, which certainly presupposed an enormous
technical potential.[72] Jones concurs, suggesting that there was a substitution of capital for labour that continued into post-Sung times.[73]

China's high intensive power was also reflected in the impres-
siveness of its production and commerce. First, burgeoning silver
imports flowed in from all over the world (which, as already noted,
provides substantial testimony to the superiority of Chinese production capacity). Second, there was a major set of private capitalist infrastructures.[74] In particular, private banking dominated public. Shansi constituted the major centre for private banking, and the
eight largest banks had over thirty branches across China by the early
nineteenth century. Investment in commerce and industry dominated
agriculture, with the power of the merchants increasing considerably.
Third, cotton production was massive, requiring large amounts of raw
cotton. By the late eighteenth century, China was importing more

cotton from India than Britain was importing from America. Added to this are the points made in ch. 4: that China's per capita income was about equal to Britain's as of 1750; that its GNP was as high as Britain's in 1850; and that its share of world manufactures was higher than Britain's right down to 1860. Accordingly, the preoccupation of even many Eurocentric Chinese scholars with linking Chinese economic growth to the incursion of Western influence after 1839 fails to recognise the considerable economic progress that had been achieved well before the advent of the British.

Finally, as ch. 9 explains, the spirit of what I am arguing here was recognised by contemporary Europeans until the eighteenth century. It was only after 1780 that the Europeans revised this view in what probably constitutes one of the more fantastic pieces of social construction initiated by the Europeans in the last millennium. For one minute the Chinese were described as 'an example and a model of advanced civilisation', the next 'a fallen people of eternal standstill'. Unfortunately, the Eurocentric scholars of world history (both Western and Chinese) have mistakenly chosen to endogenise the 'standstill argument',[75] when they should have focused on the notion of China as a dynamic and advanced civilisation for much of the second millennium.

My final counter-proposition asserts that before 1839 China was able to both control those Europeans who were officially allowed access to its markets, and militarily defeat any European challengers who were not granted access. Because I deal with this in some detail in ch. 7 I shall leave it aside for the moment. In sum, it seems fair to conclude that China neither withdrew from the global economy after 1434 nor did its economy dry up. Thus Landes's claim (cited above) that 'isolationism became China' while the outside world was passing it by turns out to be yet another Eurocentric myth. And this conclusion applies no less to India, South-east Asia and Japan, as we shall now see.

4 The East remains dominant:
the twin myths of oriental despotism and isolationism in India, South-east Asia and Japan, 1400–1800

> The assumption that civilization cannot exist at the equator is contradicted by continuous tradition. And God knows better.
>
> Ibn Khaldûn

One of the central Eurocentric propositions asserts that by about 1500 the West had emerged as the dominant region of the world. It is also generally assumed that the leading world powers between 1400 and 1800 were all, without exception, European. But as this chapter shows, none of the major players in the world economy at any point before 1800 was European. Moreover, it was only as late as the nineteenth century that Europe finally caught up, having lagged behind for some fifteen centuries. One of the main reasons why Eurocentric scholars have assumed the long historic economic backwardness of the East derives from their belief that Eastern economies were stifled both by the prevalence of oriental despotism and their isolation from international trade. Falsifying both these assumptions helps reinforce the claim made in the first section below: that the East remained ahead of the West down to the nineteenth century. The second section then reveals as a myth the Eurocentric marginalisation of India and South-east Asia as but isolationist regions, which were held back – in India's case – by an oriental despotic state. The third section does the same for Japan. In particular, I argue that Japan achieved significant economic progress *before* British industrialisation, in turn suggesting that Japan was an 'early developer' rather than a 'late developer'.

The East over the West, 1200–1800

What proof (quantitative or qualitative) is there for the claim that the East was economically more advanced than Europe up to the nineteenth century? Though many of the standard statistical indicators are necessarily crude they are, nevertheless, all we have to go on. And they have in any case been used by Eurocentric authors to support their claims. Let us begin with the national income data. According to Paul Bairoch, future third world (Eastern) income was 220 per cent that of the West in 1750, 124 per cent higher (as of 1830) and 35 per cent higher (as of 1860). Note that Western income refers to Europe, the Americas, Russia and Japan while Eastern income refers to Afro-Asia (a definition which is biased towards the West). Western income only surpassed Eastern levels as late as 1870.[1] According to Angus Maddison, Chinese GDP as of 1820 comprised 29 per cent of world GDP and equalled the whole of Europe's contribution.[2] Not surprisingly, because the East has a much greater population than the West, Eurocentric scholars have tended to focus on the per capita income data. Angus Maddison and David Landes suggest a 2:1 ratio in favour of the West as of 1750.[3] However, on the basis of 1960 US dollars, Bairoch estimates that in 1750 Eastern per capita income was roughly equal to that of Western Europe, and that China was on a par with the leading European economics.[4]

How can we adjudicate between these different estimates and radically different conclusions? As Maddison correctly points out:

> If Bairoch is right, then much more of the backwardness of the [present] third world presumably has to be explained by colonial exploitation and much less of Europe's advantage can be due to scientific precocity, centuries of slow accumulation, and organizational and financial superiority.[5]

Significantly, Maddison concedes that were we to use the methods produced by one of the most sophisticated data sets yet produced, the extrapolations back to 1750 would confirm the Bairoch data.[6] Furthermore in his 1993 book, Bairoch considers a more recent data set produced by Maddison which, when converted into 1960 US dollars, leads to an estimate of $121 for India and Indonesia as of 1830. This is significant because, as Bairoch concludes,

> Taking into consideration the fact that India's level around 1750 was probably at least a third higher than around 1830 and that, at that time (1750), China was richer than India and that Latin America was probably 'richer' than Asia, while Africa was probably 'poorer', a starting level for the future Third World of some $170–190 seems a very conservative estimate. In other words, a figure very close, or at least similar, to my 1981 estimate.[7]

In sum, even as late as 1750, a good case can be made that in terms of per capita income, the West was about equal to the East. Nevertheless, there is consensus on the point that after 1800, Western European per capita income pulled ahead.

What was the comparative situation in terms of the shares of world manufacturing output? Here I have to rely on the 1982 Bairoch data set (which to my knowledge is the only one that exists).[8] According to Bairoch, in 1750 the West contributed about 23 per cent while the East (including Japan) comprised about 77 per cent. Even as late as 1830 the East produced twice that of the West; and the latter probably pipped the former only as late as 1850. But the more important issue concerns the relative positions of the leading countries. As of 1750 China's lead was clear, enjoying 33 per cent of world manufacturing output (which outstrips the resurgent US position today). Strikingly, China's relative share was almost 50 per cent higher than that of the West at that time – which equates with the US share in relation to Europe plus Japan and Canada at its very peak in 1953. Only as late as 1830 did the West just pull ahead of China. What then of the relationship between China and Britain? As of 1750, the Chinese share of world manufacturing output was over 1600 per cent that of Britain's. In 1800 the ratio was 670 per cent in favour of China and 215 per cent as of 1830. Only as late as 1860 did the British share finally equal that of the Chinese. No less important is the fact that the Indian share was higher than the whole of Europe's in 1750 and was 85 per cent higher than Britain's as late as 1830.

How then can we conclude this discussion? If we run with GNP data then the West only rose ahead of the East as late as 1870. If we run with the per capita income data it seems fair to assert that the West only moved ahead after 1800. Nevertheless per capita income does not necessarily indicate strong global economic power. Switzerland and Singapore today enjoy very high per capita income, but no one concludes from this that either of them is a significant global economic power. China's striking lead in the share of world manufacturing output through to the mid-nineteenth century is particularly significant. It seems fair to conclude, then, that the East appears to have been ahead of the West at least down to 1800.

There are also various qualitative measurements that are useful here, including data on life expectancy and calorie intake. Kenneth Pomeranz has recently compiled the relevant data from a wide range of sources and concludes that Asia was at least as well, if not better, off than Europe as late as 1800 (though he focuses mainly on Japan and China).[9] Interestingly, recent research reveals that *contra* the standard Eurocentric claim, the Ottoman Turkish standard of living and real wage rates did not fall behind those of the Europeans at any point before the nineteenth century.[10] Moreover, public health and the provision of clean water were more advanced in China than in Europe. Lee and Feng claim that China's standard of living was certainly comparable to that of the West as of about 1800.[11] And Susan Hanley tells us that even as late as 1850 the Japanese standard of living was higher than that of the British. She also argues that the average Japanese ate far more healthily than did the average Briton.[12]

For all this though, the East was clearly ahead in its trading position within the global economy. As most authorities agree, Europe suffered chronic trade deficits with the major Eastern powers throughout this period – a precedent that was set back in the days of the Roman empire. Because European demand for Asian products was high but Asian demand for European products was very low, Europe made up the difference with bullion exports (a clear sign of Europe's backwardness). Further testimony is provided by the point that the Europeans could not even produce the bullion themselves but plundered it from Africa and the Americas. Or as Andre Gunder Frank puts it:

> In the structure of the world economy, four major regions maintained built in deficits of commodity trade: the Americas, Japan, Africa and Europe. The first two balanced their deficit by producing silver money for export. Africa exported gold money and slaves. In economic terms, these three regions produced 'commodities' for which there was a demand elsewhere in the world economy. The fourth deficitary region, Europe, was hardly able to produce anything of its own for export with which to balance its perpetual trade deficit.[13]

There are, however, two major Eurocentric replies that I shall refute in turn. First, Eurocentric scholars frequently assert that Asians did not buy European goods because Asian consumer tastes were simply not sophisticated enough. But European goods were inferior both in terms of quality and price (which is why the Asians would only accept silver and gold bullion).[14] Moreover, it seems to have escaped notice that Europe was not the only region which endured a deficit with some of the major Eastern powers (in turn suggesting that the problem could not have been due to 'unsophisticated' Eastern consumption patterns).

A second and equally common reply asserts that the Asian preference for bullion is explained by the alleged Asian propensity for hoarding.[15] But the hoarding thesis has three major weaknesses. First, it rests on the incorrect assumption that Asian economies were not monetised. Certainly the Chinese, Japanese and Indian economies were monetised by the 16th/17th centuries. Notable too is that most Asian states insisted in collecting taxes in money rather than in goods 'in kind', which in turn sucked many peasants into the commercial economy. Second, and most importantly, if the Asians were simply hoarding the bullion how can we account for the fact that the Asians resorted to global arbitrage in order to derive further profits? The fact is that while silver bullion was sucked into India and China, in particular, this was then exchanged for gold and exported to Europe where it was exchanged for silver (as we noted in the last chapter). Thus it was not hoarded but was employed in a rational, profit-oriented way. Third, the importation of precious metals provided a major spur to the commercialisation of many Asian economies. In other words, the bullion was not taken out of circulation through hoarding but was used to boost circulation as well as production.[16] For these reasons then it is clear that Europe's export of bullion to pay for the trade deficit was a function of its productive weakness and Asia's relative economic strength.

Thus in sum, there is a good deal of evidence to reveal that in terms of all the key economic indicators the East was ahead of the West until at least the beginning of the nineteenth century. I now turn to disaggregate the East and examine the intensive and extensive capacities of some of its leading powers. Having discussed China in the last chapter, I consider India, South-east Asia and Japan in turn. Note that I briefly consider the Ottoman and Persian empires in ch. 7.

The twin myths of Indian isolationism and oriental despotism

Eurocentrism depicts India as a classic case of an oriental despotism – a brutal, insatiable Leviathan – which in sucking the economy dry of resources, created a backward and static economy that was isolated from the mainstream of international trade.[17] This section advances eight counter-propositions which reveal that before the advent of British imperialism the Indian economy was striking only for its vibrancy.

The Indian state as growth permissive: eight anti-Eurocentric propositions

First, the assumption that the Mughal state crushed all capitalist activity is problematic because the state was at worst indifferent to capitalism, often tolerant of it and sometimes did much to promote it. One notable example of the positive help provided by the state concerns the case of the Gujarati merchants. Thus while royal ships were important up to the early seventeenth century a fundamental change occurred thereafter. The Gujarati merchants managed to persuade the rulers to withdraw the royal marine and to grant them autonomy to ply their trade with their own ships, especially from Surat (a process that was complete by the mid-seventeenth century). And it seems that the accompanying protection to Gujarati merchants offered by the state was an important factor in the massive increase in Indian shipping based in Surat by somewhere between 600 and 1000 per cent. It is also worth noting the philosophy of the Maratha ruler, Shivājī:

> Merchants are the ornaments of the kingdom and the glory of the king. They are the cause of the prosperity of the kingdom. All kinds of goods which are not available come into the kingdom. That kingdom becomes rich. In times of difficulties whatever debt is necessary is available. For this reason the respect due to merchants should be maintained. In the capital markets great merchants should be maintained.[18]

Indeed, it was this attitude that attracted the Gujaratis to migrate into Maharashtra in the seventeenth century. More generally the long-distance traders, the *banjāras*, enjoyed very high levels of prestige. Grover notes that

> On behalf of the state, the Zamindars of the regions were required to ensure their [the *banjāras'*] free passage in their respective Zamindari jurisdictions. As the Banjara class kept up the supply pipeline from one place to another . . . they were well respected in society. Whenever a caravan reached a village . . . it was received with great warmth. The Chief Zamindars . . . often offered robes of honour to Banjara chiefs on their safe arrival in their territories.[19]

Moreover, basing his claims on new primary research, Muzafar Alam shows how Mughal rulers frequently sought to protect Indian merchants. For example, letters were exchanged between the Mughal rulers, the Persian Shah and the Uzbeck khans, in order to promote peace for the sake of maintaining the lucrative trade that linked these regions.[20] And as Van Santen points out, the Mughal rulers engaged in a type of export promotion policy in order to attract precious metals into India.[21] Not surprisingly, Indian traders often saw the rulers as their allies.

A second problem is that the oriental despotism thesis grossly exaggerates the centrality and power of the Mughal state. The central state actually devolved power and control to the localities and was happy to allow (and tolerate) the many provincial authorities that presided over trade. Given that the port and local authorities did much to enable capitalism and commerce, this in itself does much to undermine the Eurocentric argument. This administrative weakness also undermines the Eurocentric notion that trade and prices were administered by the central authority. While there were a few places where the Mughal government sought to influence trade in its own right, nevertheless the private

> shippers were free to run their vessels anywhere they wished; no shipping lines were the monopoly of any man or any group. Occasional attempts at monopoly in particular commodities were known but they were frowned upon and had no lasting effect.[22]

In any case the system was simply too large and the Mughal state too weak to be able to set up a command economy and monopolistic trading system in its own interests.

A third problem is that if the oriental despotism thesis was correct, we would not expect to find significant sources of credit within the Indian economy. But financial institutions were both well developed and extensive. Ahmadabad merchants, for example, made all manner of payments and settled debts in paper. Strikingly, interest rates on the financial markets were equivalent to or lower than those in Britain (varying between a half and 1 per cent per month) in the sixteenth and seventeenth centuries.[23] Moreover local *shroffs* (bankers) offered loans at very low annual interest rates indeed – between 1 and 5 per cent in the rural areas and 1 and 6 per cent in the cities. Furthermore, the rates charged by the *sarrafs* for insuring trade were also very low, which indicates clearly that the roads must have been relatively free of insecurity. Finally, the *sarrafs* engaged in deposit banking, lending out the deposits (mainly to merchants) at higher rates of interest – a clear feature of modern banking finance. Had such capitalists lived in fear of a 'rapacious' state, they would surely not have engaged in such financial activities.

Fourth, if the state had been an oriental despotism how can we explain the fact that many merchants became extremely rich? One seventeenth-century merchant, Abdul Ghafur, conducted a volume of trade that was equivalent to that of the whole of the English East India Company! He was reported to have possessed some twenty ships ranging between 300 and 800 tons each. Another merchant, Virji Vora, had a massive estate worth some 8 million rupees and personally gained such a level of pre-eminence in various sectors of trade that he could even assert control over the Dutch East India Company.[24] Moreover, many Surat merchants were very rich, with some of them worth 5 or 6 million rupees in the mid-seventeenth century. Significant too is the fact that such riches were not confined to the merchants of Surat. As Ashin Das Gupta concludes:

> The Hindu *bania*, trembling in fear of the Mughal, unable to accumulate and retain property due to the [rapaciousness] of the government, is a figure largely conjured up by the ill-informed imagination of a few among India's western [Eurocentric] travellers. Large properties were freely accumulated in maritime trade.[25]

Fifth, if the state was 'all-grasping' how do we explain the fact that tariffs on foreign trade and local transit duties were very low? And if land and commercial taxes had been so crushing how then can we account for the presence of many extremely rich merchant groups (who were not beholden to the state)?

Sixth, Eurocentrism asserts that one of the major signs of Indian oriental despotism lies in the claim that prior to the emergence of the British empire, Indian commerce was insignificant.[26] Moreover, Eurocentric scholars such as Moreland portrayed Indian trade as but a mere appendix or footnote to the European mainstream. There are two specific claims tied in here: first, that the minor extant trade was only in luxury goods and was, therefore, not extensive;[27] and second, that Indian trade was allegedly conducted by small-scale 'pedlars' who were but mere bit-players in the international arena. Let us take each in turn.

One reason why Eurocentrism insists that Indian trade was only marginal comes about through the exotic imagery of Indian luxury textiles which were sold to kings and the wealthy. But this imagery seems to be more the product of an Orientalist mind set in the first place. Thus while luxury textiles *were* produced in places such as Bengal, Gujarat and Coromandel, the majority of the textiles produced in India were aimed at mass markets. What Eurocentric scholars have missed is that a good deal of Indian textiles were of a coarse variety that were suitable only for the poorer consumers. Interesting too is that these mass markets extended far and wide, to Indonesia in the south-east all the way across to Hormuz and Aden in the west. Such markets were, therefore, hardly exceptional. Indeed, the poorer consumer groups in much of the Middle East provided the most demand for the coarse Indian cloth.[28] Mass-based consumer goods also took the form of everyday foods such as rice and pulses, wheat and oil, all of which were traded far and wide throughout the Indian Ocean, and in considerable quantities at that.

The conventional Eurocentric image of Indian trade being conducted by 'pedlars' is also fictitious. This is borne out by the fact that there were many very large-scale merchants plying their trade both inside and outside the Indian economy. Significant here were the *banjāras* (long-distance traders) and *banians* (town merchants). The *banjāras* were certainly not pedlars. Nor were the *banians* not least because they often employed pedlars. The Islamic Gujarati merchants were the largest of all the *banjāras* and their role within the vast Indian Ocean network was extremely impressive.[29] And as noted above, many became extraordinarily wealthy. The *banians* were divided into two groups – the *dallāls* (brokers) and *shroffs* or *sarrafs* (bankers and money-changers). The *banians* were imbued from birth with rational capitalist thinking. As Habib notes:

> Single-minded acquisition of the capacity for acquisition was the cornerstone of the Banyas's traditional outlook . . . In this outlook were married two Calvinistic virtues, namely, thrift and religious spirit. The Banyas would carefully refrain from display of wealth and not spend lavishly on anything, except jewellery for their womenfolk (which was a form of saving).[30]

In particular, the *banians* had access to extraordinary levels of capital. They were key players in financing not just Indian overseas trade but also various European companies, especially the English East India Company. No less significant is that they were able to finance long-distance trade at much higher levels than did the British. Indeed, 'European ships were smaller and less capitalised. The English employed an average capital of 200,000 rupees at the beginning of the seventeenth century, while some Gujarati vessels trading to the Red Sea were worth five times this amount.'[31] Thus although there were many small-scale Indian merchants, the fact is that they (as well as the British) would have been unable to engage in trade without the help of the many larger-scale Indian merchants.

Nevertheless, to retain the Eurocentric picture, it could be claimed that these large-scale capitalists were but mere *compradors* and were subordinate to the superior European traders. In reality, though, the *banians* were more like 'senior partners'.[32] The *banians* were not men of humble origins who were granted wealth and power by the British. They were rich well before the British arrived. And above all, it was their capital that supplied much of the finance for British trade – it was the British who were the junior partners right down to 1800.

It is also important to note that the picture of India as isolated from international trade is clearly wide of the mark. Thus while
the Ottomans and Chinese constituted the most important trading
players in the global economy in the post-1500 period, Indian merchants increasingly came to play a complementary role, especially
within the important Indian Ocean trading system. India was oriented
more towards exports than imports and enjoyed a large trade surplus
with Europe.[33] Not surprisingly, large amounts of silver flowed from
Europe into India. That alone is surely a clincher given the (incorrect) Eurocentric assumption that European trade constituted 'the
mainstream'. Moreover, it would be wrong to assume that the Indian
economy was based on a crude subsistence-based agriculture. Recent
research has shown that the 'typical' Indian village was significantly
connected not just to the vibrant commercial centres within India
but also to the global economy.[34] Significant too was the size of the
internal Indian trade carried by the *banjāras*, which stood at some
821 million metric ton miles per annum. Its considerable size can be
gauged by the fact that as late as 1882, 2,500 million metric-ton miles
were carried by the railways.[35]

Finally, perhaps the clearest problem with the oriental despotism thesis is that the Indian economy displayed impressive levels of intensive (productive) power. It is well known that the two
major industries of the British industrial revolution were cotton and
iron/steel. What is particularly striking here is that in both these
industries, India led the way up to the eighteenth, if not the nineteenth, century. India was well known for its production of Wootz
steel which was exported to Persia, where it provided the foundation
for the famous Damascus (Damask) steel. Blast furnaces were evident during the Mughal period, with some 10,000 in place by the end
of the eighteenth century. Moreover, Indian steel remained not only
superior to that produced in Sheffield but was also cheaper. And even
with the onset of British industrialisation the gap between European
and Indian steel, though closing, remained considerable (see ch. 9).
India was also the foremost cotton-textile producer in the world. Its

production of silk textiles was almost as impressive. The Kasimbazar area alone supplied a total of 2.2 million lb of silk per year. As Braudel concludes:

> In fact all India processed silk and cotton, sending an incredible quantity of fabrics, from the most ordinary to the most luxurious, all over the world, since through the Europeans even America received a large share of Indian textiles . . . There can be no doubt that until the British industrial revolution, the Indian cotton industry was the foremost in the world, both in the quality and quantity of its output and the scale of its exports.[36]

Moreover, the Indian influence was reflected in language itself: chintz, calicoe, dungaree, khaki, pyjama, sash and shawl are all Indian words.[37]

In sum, therefore, given that even as late as the end of the eighteenth century India had greater intensive and extensive power than the major European powers reveals both the myth of Indian oriental despotism and isolationism, and that the dawn of the European age had still not arrived.

A South-east Asian appendix?

Eurocentrism reduces South-east Asia to the Straits of Melaka and then reduces Melaka to an appendix, or minor footnote, in the mainstream Western story. This is in part because the Straits are imagined as but a mere transit point or way station in the so-called 'mainstream trade' between Europe and China and in part because Melaka was allegedly dominated by the Portuguese after 1511 and the Dutch after 1641. But this obscures the fact that the region was involved in trade that stems back to the early years of the common era.[38] It also obscures the vital role that the kingdom of Śrīvijaya in Sumatra played within the global economy between the seventh and thirteenth centuries (as was noted in ch. 2). And tracing Melaka's relevance only to the post-1511 period is problematic not least because it was the voyages of the Chinese (Muslim) admiral, Chêng Ho, about a century earlier, that gave a major boost to Melaka and South-east Asian trade.[39] For it was only then that Melaka replaced Java as the main centre of Indonesian trade, extending its trading links to Gujarat, Dhabol, Bengal and Coromandel in India, to China and the Ryūkyūs, and to the Persian and Ottoman empires as well as the Mediterranean. Ultimately, though, recounting the story of Melaka as a European outpost is problematic because, as we shall see in detail in ch. 7, the Portuguese and Dutch were simply unable to monopolise South-east Asian trade.

The Eurocentric dismissal of South-east Asian trade, like its denunciation of Indian trade, is made on two further grounds. First, trade was allegedly conducted only by small-scale 'pedlars'; and second, trade was conducted only in 'luxury' goods and was, therefore, marginal. The first Eurocentric claim is refuted by the existence of the *nakhodas*, who were large-scale and moderately wealthy junk owners. They were mostly Javanese and were the major carriers of foreign trade. Testimony to this lies in the point that the average South-east Asian cargo ship displaced as much as 500 tons, and the largest – carried by the *nakhodas* – weighed up to 1,000 tons fully laden (all of which exceeded the cargo-carrying capacity of the European ships). Moreover, speaking of the Indonesian trade, Meilink-Roelofsz asserts:

> It is . . . clear that trade on such a [vast] scale . . . cannot be termed peddling trade. On the contrary, it forms a richly variegated pattern in which huge quantities of bulk goods, such as foodstuffs and textiles, alternate with smaller . . . quantities of valuable or even cheap commodities.[40]

This leads on to the rebuttal of the second claim. The familiar Eurocentric claim that South-east Asian trade was dominated only by luxury goods appears to be based on the exaggerated emphasis that is accorded the spice trade – presumably because it was dominated by the Europeans. But spices were in fact only a marginal trading item there.[41] Rather, bulk foods (including rice, salt, pickled and dried fish and palm wine), as well as cheap textiles and metalwares, 'all filled more space in the ships that criss-crossed the calm waters of the Sunda shelf'.[42]

The myth of Japanese oriental despotism and isolationism: Japan as an 'early developer', 1600–1868

It might be thought that Japan – which underwent significant indus-trialisation after 1868 (not to mention an 'economic miracle' after the Second World War) – would surely constitute the exception that even Eurocentric writers would have to concede. But for many such schol-ars, Japan turns out to be the exception that proves the Eurocentric rule.[43] The 'Japan clause' contains two key claims. The first asserts that Meiji Japan only industrialised in the post-1868 period because it was forced out of its policy of international isolation by the Ameri-can, Commodore Perry, in 1853. Western influence was believed to be crucial because if left to its own devices, the backward Japanese econ-omy would have languished as it had done under the oriental despo-tism of the Tokugawa state (1603–1868). And second, Japan proves the Eurocentric rule because its successful industrialisation after 1868 was allegedly achieved by its ability to emulate or copy Western ways (consistent with the strategy of 'late development'). Indeed, the dat-ing of Japanese industrialisation to the post-1868 period is important to the Eurocentric case because such a periodicity would by defini-tion make Japan a 'late developer' (given that all European countries, including Russia, began their industrialisation programmes before 1868). Moreover, Eurocentric scholars often explain Japan's rapid rate of industrial progress after 1868 as a function either of the speed with which Western ideas were absorbed, or the degree to which Japan's social structure was similar to that of Britain's (the 'Britain of the East' thesis).[44]

In these ways, the Japanese case provides reassuring evidence of the superiority of Western ways and thereby confirms the stan-dard Eurocentric assumption made famous by Walt Rostow: that all backward countries can enjoy the fruits of modernity so long as they follow the Western recipe for modernisation.[45] This section critically reviews the Eurocentric perspective and presents a revised picture of Japan as an 'early developer'. In turn this disturbs the Eurocentric assumptions that 'early developers' were found only within Europe and that the East was incapable of pioneering its own development.

How it all really began in Japan: economic dynamism in the Tokugawa era (1603–1868)

In the past little empirical evidence of Japan's development in the pre-Meiji era was available. It was often simply assumed that Tokugawa Japan's economy was backward and stagnant as a function of oriental despotism. Even among Japan specialists, the consensus was that Tokugawa Japan was a backward, feudal or agrarian economy. However, there is one immediate piece of circumstantial evidence that calls this view into question: Japanese economic growth rates experienced in the post-1868 Meiji period exceeded those of almost all the European economies. Such high economic growth rates could not simply have come out of nowhere. It seems inconceivable to assume that the Japanese economy could have been stagnant one moment (just prior to 1853) and then one of the most dynamic economies in the world the next. In recent years research has emerged (often painstakingly conducted) which presents a revised picture of economic dynamism during the Tokugawa era. This has led some to now believe, in Eric Jones's words, that: '[m]uch of the relative ease of the Meiji achievement is now attributed to the start which that history [the Tokugawa] gave it'.[46]

One of the major claims made by Eric Jones in his book *Growth Recurring* is that Tokugawa Japan enjoyed per capita income growth (supposedly the *leitmotif* of modern capitalism). Others have suggested that per capita growth was achieved in the second half of Tokugawa rule.[47] And, as noted earlier, there is evidence that the Japanese enjoyed a comparatively high standard of living with real wages and incomes increasing before 1868.[48] Similarly, the traditional view was that agricultural output grew only slowly under the Tokugawa. But it is now apparent that traditional data on the growth of grain output are subject to a conservative bias. Recent research reveals a significant growth rate in agricultural production for much, if not the whole, of the Tokugawa period.[49] Increases in land productivity were attributable to a number of innovations comprising commercial fertilisers, an increase in the number of plant varieties (especially in rice), the extensive use of irrigation and the conversion of dry fields into paddy fields, the increasing use of specialisation (i.e. freedom from cultivating uneconomic crops), seed selection, multiple cropping and various others.[50]

One conventional argument asserts that it was only during the Meiji period that the old bastions of feudalism – the *daimyo* (aristocracy) and the *samurai* (military vassals) – were undermined. But this was merely the endpoint of a number of policies that had been instigated under the Tokugawa – policies which made this endpoint something of a *fait accompli*. The erosion of the power base of the *daimyo* and *samurai* began back in the first half of the seventeenth century. The *daimyo* were forced to live in the capital (Edo), the ruler's intention being to erode their power by saddling them with high personal debts. Noteworthy here is that this strategy mirrors that of European rulers as they went about their state-centralising policies.[51] These policies were successful in both reducing the local autonomy of the *daimyo* and consequently undermining feudalism.[52] Indeed, so indebted had much of the *daimyo* become by the end of the Tokugawa period that most of them were only too glad to have their lands expropriated by the Meiji state (the condition of which was that they would be absolved of their debts). In short, the Meiji reforms were merely the endpoint of a long process of 'rational' state formation undertaken during the Tokugawa period.

The Tokugawa state also sought to undermine the power of the *samurai* by forcing them to live in castle towns. In turn, the rapid development of these towns had a major commercial multiplier effect, leading to advances in agriculture in order to support these growing urban numbers. By the beginning of the nineteenth century subsistence cropping had almost completely died out, with markets penetrating down to even the smallest village. This was in no small part the result of separating the *samurai* from the peasantry, in turn leading to the full consolidation of the peasant family unit. In the process, the freeing up of the peasants promoted an immediate incentive for them to produce more, particularly as the state was pushing them to do so. They read the emerging agricultural treatises (e.g. the *Nōgyō Zensho* of 1697) to enhance their knowledge, and they began to produce for the market. This was enabled by the extension of the area for cultivating irrigated crops, as well as rising productivity levels. All this fed into the rapid commercialisation of the economy. Testimony to this lies in the fact that by 1800 as much as 22 per cent of the Japanese population lived in towns – a figure which easily exceeds that of Europe.[53] Finally, the instigation of a national currency by the government was helpful in that it forced the major *daimyo* to sell their goods in order to acquire the new currency (before then the *daimyo* had minted their own currency). This provided a further boost to commercialisation and the creation of a unified national market.

In sum, the centralising tendencies of the state and the accompanying rising commercial and production levels means that the conventional image of Japan as a backward feudal society before 1868 is wide of the mark. The end result was of 'A highly elaborate [bureaucratic] power structure . . . [that] proved both cohesive and flexible enough to ensure a swift transition to new strategies of state-building after the second encounter with the West [in 1853]'.[54] Moreover, this increasingly rational, centralised bureaucratic apparatus undermines the Eurocentric depiction of Tokugawa Japan as an oriental despotism. Eric Jones, in particular, details all sorts of 'rational' economic policies instigated by the state which he sees as no less rational than those employed in the West at that time.[55] Let us therefore examine the various rational-capitalist institutions that emerged during the Tokugawa.

To support the rapidly rising commerce of Japan, credit institutions first emerged during the 1630s in Ōsaka. By the 1640s, money-lenders accepted deposits and made loans on these. By 1670 what is known as the Group of Ten (the ten leading Ōsaka financiers), were granted official recognition to act both for the government and take responsibility for the operation of the money market. Moreover, this group of banks possessed some of the characteristics of a central bank, holding final reserves of the banking system and acting as 'lender of last resort', as well as exercising some control over the gold/silver market. And no one could open a banking business without first obtaining their approval and agreeing to observe their regulations.[56] This was a sophisticated financial system which adopted modern methods comprising: deposits, advances, bill discounting, cheques, overdraft facilities, exchange transactions, insurance and life insurance schemes. Both industry and agriculture were financed. Indeed, the traditional assumption that banking institutions did not exist in the rural areas, and the only lenders who did exist there were capricious money-lenders rather than banks, stands wide of the mark. Recent research reveals that a whole network of rural financial or banking entrepreneurs had emerged at least by the 1830s.[57]

Striking testimony to the advanced state of financial institutions in the Tokugawa period lies with the presence of a futures market.[58] Noteworthy too is that the first Japanese futures exchange appeared in Dōjima (in Ōsaka) in 1730. By contrast, the Frankfurt and London futures exchanges only appeared as late as 1867 and 1877 respectively. Also noteworthy here is that the system of commercial law built during the Tokugawa period was particularly sophisticated both for its coverage and its impartiality (the sign of a 'rational' institution). Commercial transactions were understood and the notions of contract, of bankruptcy and the distinction between loans and equity capital were particularly impressive. In sum, as Hanley and Yamamura conclude

> descriptions of these [financial] institutions . . . lead readers to conclude that any economy with such institutions must have been highly commercialized and prosperous. What is important here are the contributions made by these institutions in increasing trade at decreasing transaction costs.[59]

Another area of economic significance lies in the advancement of industry. While the period of more advanced manufacturing had to await the Meiji period there were many signs of 'proto-industrialisation' under the Tokugawa. Such industries included fishing, textiles, paper-making, sake and soy-sauce brewing, iron and other metalworking, agricultural and marine product processing.[60] Once again, the significance of such developments was that when the Meiji state emerged, much of the groundwork had already been laid, thereby easing the drive to full industrialisation.

The myth of Japanese isolationism: the post-1639 continuation of foreign trade

As with their analysis of China after 1434, so Eurocentric scholars place much emphasis on the claim that during the seventeenth century Japan supposedly withdrew and became isolated from international trade as the state implemented the policy known as *sakoku* ('closed country') in 1639. This is used to confirm the presence of oriental despotism on the one hand, and economic backwardness on the other, given that under the Tokugawa the economy allegedly all but dried up. By 1639 only the Dutch and Chinese were officially permitted to reside in Nagasaki, from where they imported foreign products. And such imports and exports were supposedly negligible. The first rejoinder – that the Japanese economy did not dry up during the Tokugawa period – has, of course, been dealt with in some critical detail in the last subsection.

The second problem with this Eurocentric claim is that it misunderstands the policy of *sakoku* and takes the phrase 'closed country' too literally. Like China after 1434, Japan after 1639 was neither closed off from international trade nor was closure the intent of the Japanese state. The state merely sought to regulate or control foreign trade. Most important here is that the Tokugawa was in fact fundamentally committed to maintaining trade. Nevertheless, to the Eurocentric mind set this regulationist or monopolist approach smacks of 'regressive mercantilism' (though notably Eurocentric scholars view European mercantilism as a rational means of creating a national economy). But the main aspect of the system was not to exclude trade *per se*, but to eradicate the foreign influence of Catholic Christian ideas (which is why the Protestant Dutch were favoured over the Catholic Portuguese and Spanish).[61] Either way, though, Eurocentric scholars insist that foreign trade fell off rapidly and was therefore, inconsequential.

The fact is that through most of the seventeenth century – including the period after 1639 – the amounts of silver exported into Asia by the Japanese far surpassed those of the British, Dutch and Portuguese combined (as explained in ch. 7). Interestingly, following Satoshi Ikeda, Frank points out that the Japanese and European positions with regard to Asia and especially to China were analogous. Both Japan and Europe imported manufactures from Asia and exported silver to pay for them. The only difference was that Japan produced its own silver at home while Europe plundered it from its American colonies.[62] Nevertheless, Eurocentric scholars point to the 'fact' that in 1668 the Japanese state banned all silver exports. But according to recent research silver continued to be exported right into the middle of the eighteenth century. Moreover, Japan exported silver and precious metals through the Isle of Tsushima into Korea and China, and the amounts shipped exceeded those that had earlier been transported out of Nagasaki by the Dutch and Chinese. No less significant is that when silver exports dried up in the mid-eighteenth century they were replaced by large and sustained copper exports.[63] As Satoshi Ikeda notes in his summary of the findings of this recent research: 'This cycle of Japanese export items was a result of the [Tokugawa] Bakufu's effort to *maintain the total value of trade.*'[64]

There is further evidence to suggest that Japanese trade continued after the declaration of *sakoku* in 1639.[65] It is usually thought that Japan engaged in a classic mercantilist policy of import substitution in order to build up various domestic industries such as sugar and silk. But in fact, high volumes of silk imports from China were maintained right into the latter part of the eighteenth century. Substantial silk imports also came by way of Korea (which often exceeded the volume that arrived in Nagasaki). And while raw silk imports were restricted in the eighteenth century, Chinese and South-east Asian silk cloth was imported right up to the end of the Tokugawa period. Similarly, while Japanese domestic sugar production became strong in the first half of the nineteenth century, prior to then large volumes were imported, and even after that time, Chinese sugar imports were continued in order to maintain trading relations with China.

The familiar Eurocentric assumption that only the Dutch and Chinese were permitted to trade with Japan is rendered problematic by the fact that significant trade was continued with Siam, Korea and especially the Ryūkyūs (which was in fact authorised by the Japanese state). This was linked to the fact that Japan, having been ejected from the Chinese tribute system in 1557, set up its own rival tribute system. Korea was the only state that was treated as a virtual equal. The Ryūkyūs were considered to be subordinate, the Dutch even more so (see ch. 7). Considerable unofficial private trade as well as smuggling was undertaken by Japanese merchants – a scenario that has echoes of Chinese developments after 1434. Moreover, like their Chinese counterparts after 1434, so after 1639 many Japanese merchants relocated into other parts of South-east Asia in order to continue their trading activities (a process which finds its corollary in the relocation of Japanese multinational companies today). In particular, Japanese and Chinese private merchants enjoyed a vigorous trade with each other in the seaports of the South China Sea. Thus we can now see why the Japanese policy of *sakoku* was designed not to limit trade with the outside world *per se*, but to limit trade only with the Catholic powers of Europe. And in respect of both these aims the policy appears to have been very successful. Overall, then, the standard Eurocentric claim that the American Commodore Perry opened up a closed Japan to world trade after 1853 is problematic only because Japan had been open for global business well before then.

In sum, therefore, it seems clear that Tokugawa Japan was no growth-repressive oriental despotism. The crucial point to note is that the striking economic growth rates achieved after 1868 were not the miraculous result of Western impulses and ideas that suddenly hit Japan in 1853. Considerable groundwork had been laid during the Tokugawa period in terms of state formation, capitalist institution building and capitalist economy formation. The clincher here is ironically provided by Angus Maddison, who reckons that Japanese national income in 1820 was sufficiently large to accord it a respectable position within the European GDP league table.[66]

Finally, I have not considered the Eurocentric proposition that Meiji Japan was successful only because it emulated the West. But it is instructive to note that once again new research suggests that Meiji industrialisation was prompted in large part by Japan's desire to counter the dominance of Chinese rather than Western merchants in the region.[67] If this is the case then it suggests not only an alternative motive that propelled the Meiji industrialisation, but more importantly hints at the possibility that Japan might have undertaken a full industrialisation programme in the absence of the Western incursion. Moreover, there was much about the social development achieved during the Tokugawa to suggest that the economy was capable of spontaneously developing into full capitalism.[68] Either way, though, we can be sure that Japanese development prior to 1853/1868 was not just significant but that with the marginal exception of *rangaku* or *bangaku* ('barbarian learning' from the Dutch), it was achieved independently of Western influence.

Part II
The West was last: oriental globalisation and the invention of Christendom, 500–1498

5 Inventing Christendom and the Eastern origins of European feudalism, c. 500–1000

To the Arabs . . . [Western Europe] was an area of so little interest that, while their geographical knowledge continually improved between AD 700 and 1000, their 'knowledge of Europe did not increase at all'. If Arabian geographers did not bother with Europe, it was not because of a hostile attitude, but rather because Europe at the time 'had little to offer' of any interest.

Carlo Cipolla

[T]he central methodological weakness of my book [*The Rise of the West*] is that . . . it pays inadequate attention to the emergence of the . . . world system . . . Being too much pre-occupied by the notion of civilization, I bungled by not giving the initial emergence of a transcivilizational process the sustained emphasis it deserved.

William H. McNeill

The presence of oriental globalisation before 1500 (as established in part 1 of this book) is confirmed by the claim of this chapter. Not only was the rise of feudal Europe inconceivable without the diffusion of various advanced Eastern 'resource portfolios', but this period witnessed a particularly intense wave of global flows. Nevertheless, Europe was not simply, nor has it ever been, a 'passive beneficiary' of global transmissions of technologies, ideas and resources. To a certain extent 'Europe' made its own history (via its identity formation process). The chapter has three sections. The first examines how the diffusion of Eastern ideas and technologies enabled the medieval agricultural revolution. The second examines the global forces that shaped the political and class system of feudalism (within which the economy was fundamentally embedded). And the third section examines the global context within which European identity was forged. This was important not least because Catholicism enabled the consolidation and reproduction of the feudal economic and political system.

Global and Eastern forces in the rise of the European feudal economy

I aim to move quickly over the economic technologies of the medieval agricultural revolution, largely for two reasons. First, the class, political and moral contexts were more important to the rise of feudal Europe. And second, the progressive history of the rise of the West places far greater emphasis on the rise of commerce and proto-capitalism after 1000 (which I shall deal with in much greater detail in ch. 6).

The basic technological ingredients of the medieval agricultural revolution

Most economic historians agree that there was a series of new agricultural technologies that came together to enable the rise of European feudalism. These comprise the water-mill and windmill, the heavy mouldboard plough, new animal harnesses and the iron horseshoe.[1] The heavy plough was particularly important. Prior to the seventh century, the only plough that was available to the Europeans was the Mediterranean 'scratch plough'. This was effective in the arid conditions of southern Europe, given that its purpose was to pulverise the dry soil and to thereby prevent evaporation. But it was useless in north-western Europe, where wet soils meant that drainage problems went unsolved. Accordingly, this region had remained agriculturally undeveloped. The advent of the heavy 'mouldboard plough' changed all this because it created drainage furrows.

However, this new plough brought with it a set of further problems that had to be solved before its usage could properly 'take off'. First, because it generated very high levels of traction owing to the inefficiency of the wooden mouldboard and the wheels, large teams of oxen were required (usually four at a time). But the oxen were slow, not especially efficient and were very expensive. Over time, peasants acquired horses, which were stronger and therefore required much smaller teams to pull the plough. But there were two initial obstacles to using the horse: the problem of harnessing and the need to protect the horses' hooves from rotting (in the wet soils). The traditional ox-harness (or the 'throat and girth' harness) that was strapped to the belly and the neck was extremely inefficient because it strangled the animal if the load was too heavy. The solution lay with the new 'horse collar harness' which was strapped to the body of the horse avoiding the neck. Most historians agree that this enabled a four- or fivefold increase in traction power. However, the horse could not be used in the wet soils unless its feet were protected, given that the moisture led to hoof rot. Only with the introduction of the nailed iron horseshoe was this solved. Thus, by about the tenth or eleventh centuries, the new horse collar and nailed horseshoe enabled the spread of the heavy plough across Europe. Finally, the last piece that completes this jigsaw is the role of water-mills and windmills (the origins of which I consider in ch. 6).

The Eastern origins of the European feudal economy
In contrast to the general Eurocentric proposition that Europe entirely pioneered its own development, the claim made here is that some of the major instances of technological breakthrough occurred outside Europe and were then passed on through oriental globalisation. What Europe did then was to assimilate these inventions. How did this occur? As already noted, the most significant breakthrough was that of the heavy plough. We know that scratch ploughs were used throughout Asia and parts of Africa well before the turn of the first millennium CE. But these bore little relation to the heavy turn plough. Unfortunately no one knows for sure where its origins lie, as becomes immediately apparent when one scans through the many books on the medieval agricultural revolution. Phrases to the effect that 'the plough probably [or perhaps] first appeared in' abound. More often, historians merely assert that the plough played an 'important role' and then brush over its place of origin. To the extent that Eurocentric historians have been interested in this issue it is often assumed that

it was the Slavs who first developed the plough around 568. However, Lynn White provides a clue here: that the plough was not invented by them but reached the Slavs from an 'unknown source'.[2] What we do know is that the Slavs only began to use the heavy plough immediately after the Avar invasion of 567 (the Avars were 'refugees' who spilled out of the Steppe after the formation of the Turkish confederacy in Mongolia and the Altaic region between 552 and 565). It seems improbable that this was simply a coincidence. Unfortunately, a scan of a vast array of literature on the subject, does not provide any conclusions about the Eastern or Western origins of the plough.

What then of the iron horseshoe and the collar harness? While it is unclear exactly when the horseshoe was invented, circumstantial evidence suggests that it was used by the Huns at least as early as the fifth century.[3] Significantly, it was not used by the Romans. It appears to have entered Eastern Europe from the East (probably Siberia) in the late ninth century, reaching Byzantium by the end of the century, from where it diffused into the backward half of Europe.[4] The collar harness was clearly pioneered by the Chinese in the third century CE, perhaps being derived from the earlier breast-strap harness (or 'trace harness') which had been invented in Han China in 100 BCE. Even the trace harness was much more effective than the Western 'throat and girth', leading one writer to claim that: 'A Han chariot was a bus compared to a Greek or Roman Chariot'.[5] Thus

> while Egyptian, Greek or Roman chariots always appear of minimal size, fit only for two persons at most . . . and often drawn by four horses, the Chinese chariots frequently show as many as six passengers . . . very frequently too they have heavy upcurving roofs . . . and are usually drawn by only one horse.[6]

And clearly the collar harness was directly transmitted from China.[7]

When we add to this the point that the windmill and water-mill had Eastern origins (see ch. 6), it seems reasonable to conclude that the European medieval agricultural revolution was no 'virgin Western birth' but was significantly assisted by the global transmission of various Eastern technologies. But if we left it here we would end up with an account of European feudalism that exaggerates the importance of economic technology. There was, however, a series of other factors that were more important, to which I now turn.

The military and class dimensions of feudalism: the Eastern context

No economy is ever simply an aggregation of economic technologies. The European feudal economy was deeply embedded within the class and politico-military systems, which in turn were fundamentally embedded within the moral and normative structure. By the eighth century a new mode of warfare had emerged (the mounted shock cavalry), which in turn played an important part in creating the institutional structure of both the feudal state and economy. This was dependent upon the prior invention of the stirrup.[8] Before the stirrup, horses were ineffectual in battle because the rider had nothing with which to hold him securely to the horse. Accordingly, a spear could be delivered only through the strength of the rider himself. But the stirrup enabled the rider to deliver a blow with the full strength of the horse. In this way, frail human-muscle power was replaced with superior animal power, enabling shock cavalry simply to plough like a bus through foot soldiers.

While Eurocentric scholars usually attribute the invention of the stirrup to Charles Martel in 733, it seems clear that the basic idea of the stirrup, in which the rider placed only his big toe, first appeared in India (in the late second century BCE). By 100 CE in Northern India (where the climate was colder and therefore prevented the rider from riding barefoot) hooks held the booted feet, though these would have been extremely dangerous since they would have dragged a fallen rider. The crucial development here was the invention of the Chinese bronze and cast-iron stirrup in the third century CE. By 477 it was in common use throughout China.[9] From there it spread via the Silk Road to the Central Asian peoples and seems to have reached Persia by the late seventh century. In particular, the Juan-Juan tribe (known as the Avars) transmitted it, as they were driven westwards settling between the

Danube and the Theiss. By 694, the Arabs were making iron stirrups before this innovation finally spread westwards via the Vikings and the Lombards.[10] Thus the common assumption that Charles Martel invented the all-important stirrup around 733 cannot hold.

However, one reply might be that even if Martel had not invented the stirrup, he was surely the pioneer of the 'new' shock cavalry. That Martel was the principal innovator within the 'European' context seems fair. But the fact is that it was the Persians (as well as the Byzantines) who initiated the mounted shock cavalry. The Arabic Muslims soon learned of the shock cavalry during their battles with the Persians. And during the period after about 640 (almost a century before Martel's 'innovation'), the shock cavalry became a fundamental aspect of Islamic armies. It is notable that cavalry warfare was first introduced by the Assyrians some time in the early first millennium BCE (though the cavalrymen shot arrows and had no stirrups). It is also interesting, if not significant, to note that many of the weapons that we associate with medieval Europe – the long bow, mace and lance – all first appeared in the Middle East.[11] Moreover, Islamic armies deployed superior military technologies for many centuries, many of which were copied or assimilated by the Europeans (see ch. 8). Clearly then Martel invented neither the stirrup nor the shock cavalry.

How then did the shock cavalry enable the rise of the feudal political system? The major problem with the new cavalry-based mode of warfare was its sheer expense. It was therefore necessary to create an economy in which the agricultural surplus could be siphoned off or expropriated from the peasants. Thus monarchs gave out their peasant-populated land to the knights (or vassals), who were free to exploit the peasants. In this way, a powerful noble class emerged and consolidated its power, both over the peasantry and, ironically, over the rulers. Hence the social and political system of feudalism was born. But was all this a response to military problems that emerged within Europe, or was there a global dimension that was important?

Intense waves of Asian migrations presented Europe with numerous military challenges. Moreover, while there were manifold intra-European migrations, these in turn were the result of a displacement caused by the arrival of various Eastern peoples. First in 370, the Huns advanced out of Asia as a result of military disturbances as far afield as China. Their penetration into Europe was dramatic, causing a massive displacement of the Germanic people across Europe and beyond. The Ostrogoths took over Italy; the Visigoths, Spain (until 711); the Franks, Gaul; the Angles and Saxons, England. The Avars invaded Europe in 567 and sought to plunder as much of the territory as they could. They especially targeted Hungary and, having annihilated the Gepid tribe, forced the Lombards to flee south. Their raids continued into the next century. As McNeill tells us:

> These raids provoked two lasting ethnic changes: the occupation of Italy by the Lombards (568), who in turn drove the Byzantines from the interior of that peninsula; and the retreat of the Latin- and Greek-speaking peasantries of the Balkan peninsula to refuge areas in the mountains or along the coasts. Slavs took their places, supporting themselves by a primitive migratory type of agriculture.[12]

During the ninth century the Holy Roman empire (which began in 800 with the crowning of Charlemagne as Holy Roman emperor) began to disintegrate. This fragmentation occurred around the time when another wave of global migrations flowed into Europe. The Muslims attacked from the south from their base in North Africa and set up in Sicily and Sardinia, and even sacked Rome in 846. More importantly (though less significant from a cultural viewpoint), the Magyars invaded from the east, occupying present-day Hungary and wreaking havoc across much of Europe. They also struck present-day Holland, southern France and Germany. This was complemented by the various intra-European Viking (Northmen) raids. As a result of all these migrations (most of which were Eastern), the ethnic composition of Europe was remodelled along new lines.

How does all this relate to the creation of the feudal political system? We can now see that the creation of a feudal political system was not just the result of new technologies (mainly the stirrup) that diffused across from the East. It was also a response to the manifold global military challenges that washed through Europe from the East between 370 and about 1000. But it is also important to note that the political and military institutions were entwined within the feudal class structure. For the nobles and aristocrats were in part granted their control over the peasants so that they could extract a surplus to pay for warfare. And it did not take long for the nobles to consolidate their control over both the peasants and rulers. The social contract known as the *fief* was particularly important. Unlike the earlier *benefice*, which was a lifelong contract between rulers and nobles, the *fief* was hereditary and thereby guaranteed the lineage of the nobility on the one hand, and gave them considerable power over the rulers on the other. Accordingly, sovereignty was effectively 'parcelised' at the level of the feudal locality (the manor or the village), with the nobles enjoying considerable political power.[13]

So to sum up. The feudal system was created by a complex amalgamation of technological, ethnic, class, military and political forces. And in each case there was a significant global or Eastern dimension. But there is a further factor that needs to be discussed before we can finish our discussion of the rise of the Western European medieval agricultural economy. For once the military challenges had begun to subside by about 1000, the central problem revolved around the need to make the economy appear legitimate, given that it comprised a highly unequal social relationship between noble and peasant. Accordingly, once peace had returned and the nobles could no longer justify the exploitation of the peasants on the grounds that they provided them with military protection, so the system would inevitably lose its legitimacy. Thus the exploitation of the peasantry had to be made to appear 'natural'. This was intimately connected with the process by which European identity was constructed or invented. How was this achieved?

Inventing the identity of Christendom in the global context

Constructing or inventing the 'Islamic threat'

It is vital to understand that the identity formation process is at once both simple and complex. Its simplicity derives from the fact that the 'self' (i.e. that which is to be defined as 'us') does not actually exist. Europe was not a harmonious entity but was riven with deep internal conflicts: between peasants and nobles, nobles and rulers, rulers and priests, rulers and popes, popes and Holy Roman emperors.[14] There was, therefore, no intrinsic homogeneity. The only way to forge a single identity was to construct an external 'other' against which a homogeneous 'self' could be constructed. That is, given that there was no single 'self', it was easier to define the 'self' by that which it was not. It is vital to note that the self and other are mere representations or constructions based on how we would like to see 'us' and 'them'. In the medieval context the 'self' represented all that was good and righteous while the 'other' was constructed as its evil or undesirable opposite. Thus the first task was to find and construct an imaginary other. But who to select? Given that the Christian prelates became the key players in the construction of European identity, they selected Islam as the suitable candidate. But Islam had to be constructed not just as evil but also as a threat, so that the Europeans could unite against it. For as Maxime Rodinson originally pointed out, 'The Muslims were a threat to Western Christendom long before they became a problem'.[15]

How then was Islam invented as an evil threat? First of all, despite all the rhetoric, the rise of Islam proved to be a boon for European myth-makers. Islam was immediately condemned by the Christians as an idolatrous pagan religion (even though the two religions shared many vital similarities). This was legitimised by invoking the Genesis story of Noah and his three sons. Crucially, Japheth was given 'Christian Europe' that was 'destined for enlargement', while Shem was given Asia that was 'populated by Pagans' (i.e. infidels) who were destined for absorption by Japheth. This was especially useful for enabling the key Christian power-brokers to represent

Islam in general, and Muhammad in particular, as the embodiment of pagan evil. Indeed, Pope Innocent III described him as the 'Beast of the Apocalypse'.[16]

The denunciation of Muhammad reached its apogee in Dante's *Inferno*, where the author explores the depths of Hell (which comprises nine ever-deeper circles). The more evil a character had been in life, the deeper the circle to which he was condemned. Strikingly, it was in the eighth circle, almost at the bottom, that Dante came across Muhammad. The only people below Muhammad were the most treacherous the world had ever known – most notably Judas Iscariot and Brutus, who were the penultimate figures before Dante reached the bottom, where Satan resided. Moreover, as Edward Said notes of the relevant passage in the book:

> Mohammed's punishment, which is also his eternal fate, is a peculiarly disgusting one: he is endlessly being cleft in two from his chin down to his anus like, Dante says, a cask whose staves are ripped apart. Dante's verse at this point spares the reader none of the eschatological detail that so vivid a punishment entails: Mohammed's entrails and his excrement are described with unflinching accuracy.[17]

Interestingly, though, Dante resisted consigning the Islamic philosophers to the Inferno, given that he was significantly influenced by their writings,[18] and instead consigned them to the border region of 'limbo'. More generally, as Rana Kabbani notes: 'Islam was seen as the negation of Christianity; Muhammad as an imposter, an evil sensualist, an Antichrist in alliance with the Devil. The Islamic world was seen as Anti-Europe.'[19]

This invention process required considerable ingenuity for various reasons. First, the fact is that Islam and Christianity share much in common. Muslims and Christians believe in one and the same God. And while Muslims see Muhammad rather than Jesus as God's major prophet they nevertheless recognise Jesus as an important prophet and, crucially, were happy to tolerate the presence of Christians in their midst. It is also the case that both religions draw on Judaeo-Hellenic traditions: 'Arabic and Hebrew are Semitic languages, and together they dispose and redispose of material that is urgently important to Christianity'.[20] Moreover, both religions trace their origins back to Abraham. The conclusion here is that the profound similarities between these two religions could have served as a bridge to produce a harmonious relationship between Christendom and the Middle East. But in the end the European elites preferred to travel down an avenue that led them to repress the Muslims in order to artificially generate a homogeneous European Self.

The second way in which Islam was portrayed as an immanent threat was the construction of a kind of Islamic 'domino theory'. This was both simple and complex: simple because Islam adhered to the universalistic notion of *jihad* (though this was purposefully misinterpreted). And ironically, it was complex – and required considerable finesse – because had they so wished, the Muslims probably *could* have overrun the backward half of Europe. But they chose not to. This point, of course, clashes with the general Eurocentric claim that had it not been for the defeat of a Muslim 'invasion' in 733 (not 732) at Tours and Poitiers at the hands of the heroic Charles Martel, Europe would have been overrun. And as Edward Gibbon tells us, had this occurred:

> Perhaps the interpretation of the Koran would now be taught in the schools of Oxford, and her pulpits might demonstrate to a circumcised people the sanctity and truth of the revelation of Mohammed. From such calamities was Christendom delivered by the genius and fortune of one man.[21]

But in the Muslim histories of the period, the battle of Tours, Poitiers and the figure of Charles Martel go largely unmentioned. Far greater emphasis is accorded the Arab defeat at Constantinople (718). Indeed, it was not the power of Martel's shock cavalry that defeated the Muslims, but the fact that he managed to lure the so-called invaders to a fort from where his army showered the attackers with a barrage of arrows and javelins. Most significantly though, this was no 'Islamic invasion', but was rather a small band of raiders embarking on a minor raiding mission (the target of which was the wealthy shrine of St Martin). As Bernard Lewis explains:

> There can be little doubt that in disregarding Poitiers [and Tours] and stressing Constantinople, the Muslim historians saw events in a truer perspective than the later Western historians. The Frankish victors at Poitiers encountered little more than a band of [Islamic] raiders operating beyond their most distant frontiers, thousands of miles from home . . . It was the failure of the Arab army to conquer Constantinople, not the defeat of the Arab raiding party at Tours and Poitiers, which enabled both Eastern and Western Christendom to survive.[22]

Thus while the Muslims had taken various parts of 'Western Europe' – most notably Spain and Sicily – the reality was that they were not interested in going any further. The reason was simple: the Western part of Europe was backward and of little interest to them. Byzantium was both more powerful and more attractive. As Marc Bloch originally noted, of all the 'enemies of Western Europe, Islam was certainly the least dangerous . . . For a long period neither Gaul nor Italy, among their poor cities, had anything to offer which approached the splendour of Baghdad or Cordova.'[23] In fact the many waves of migrations that had flooded into Europe had caused far more havoc than did the sporadic Islamic raiding parties. But critically, European myth-makers chose to exaggerate the 'universal threat' of Islam so as to cement a new European identity as 'Defender of the One True Faith' (i.e. Christianity).

The Christian prelates sought to construct a kind of 'Islamic domino theory'. Just as the construction of the domino theory by the United States after 1947 was tied in with the invention of the 'Soviet threat' that had to be contained, so the medieval Christian prelates saw it as vital that Europe be consolidated and strengthened as a 'containing bulwark' against the so-called universalistic 'Islamic threat'. Thus statements such as that proclaimed by the bishops of Rheims (at Trosly in 909) were consistently issued:

> You see before you the wrath of the Lord breaking forth . . . There is naught but towns emptied of their folk, monasteries razed to the ground or given to the flames, fields desolated . . . Everywhere the strong oppresseth the weak and men are like fish of the sea that blindly devour each other.[24]

The containment strategy found its clearest expression in the 'first round' of Crusades between 1095 and 1291. Indeed, as Maxime Rodinson notes, the

> image of Islam was not drawn simply from the Crusades, as some have maintained, but rather from the Latin Christian world's gradually developing ideological unity. This produced a sharper image of the enemy's features and focused the energies of the West on the Crusades.[25]

And ironically the nobles responded to Pope Urban II's rallying cry as the 'Knights of Christ' (milites Christi), galvanised by the knowledge that if they fell they would become Christian martyrs and would be richly rewarded by a passport into heaven.[26]

Inventing Christendom

Having thus constructed Islam as an 'evil threat', it remained to forge an identity for the backward half of Europe. It is important to note that there is no such thing as Europe, if we assume that such an entity exists in a well-defined geographical space. There is nothing natural about Europe. Europe has always been an idea – something which has been constructed and reconstructed over time (as we shall see throughout this book). And it was defined and redefined not as a scientific or objective function of changing geographical circumstances or borders, but according to a moral definition that reassigns the geographical boundaries of what constitutes 'Europe' at any point in time. Ultimately, such a moral definition is founded on how 'Europeans' like to imagine themselves. So how then did Europe construct itself against the Islamic other?

The first point to note here is that the self was forged in a global context. Europe came to be known as 'Christendom' because its identity was imagined or invented as Catholic Christian in contradistinction to the Islamic Middle East. This marked the first phase of European identity formation that would last right down to the sixteenth century (although it is possible to find references to the *respublica christiana* as late as the eighteenth century). That Europe-as-Christendom was an 'idea' was reflected in the fact that Christianity was originally an oriental religion. Inevitably, presenting Europe as the representational birthplace or 'defender' of the Christian faith required some major intellectual acrobatics to make the linking of Europe and Christianity appear a seamless and natural fit. Reinvoking the Genesis story of Noah's three sons was important here because Islam was represented as a pagan religion while Japheth (Europe) was presented as Christian. Moreover, as Mudimbe notes, 'one must not forget that since its birth [European] Christianity has appropriated for itself both the only way to true communication with the divine and the only correct image of God and God's magnificence'.[27] And as Robert Holton notes:

> Christianity originated in the Middle East not Europe, but was subsequently Westernised and Europeanised. This was so successful that it became the bulwark of 'Western civilisation' against Islam in the Crusades. Once again, a non-Western development is appropriated by powerful elements within the emerging West, as part of its own distinctive way of life.[28]

Thus Europe was (re)presented as the source of Christianity, whose mission would be to spread its universal message across the world in order to bring the 'pagan infidel' to heel. In turn, constructing Europe as Christendom was the vital prerequisite for creating order and bringing legitimacy to a highly unequal economic and political feudal system. How was this achieved?

Forging order and legitimacy

The new Christian moral code that would bring legitimacy to the unjust economic and political feudal structure was known as the 'decree of the three orders', or what Georges Duby called 'trifunctionality'.[29] This complemented but extended the extant notion of the 'Peace and truce of God' that Marc Bloch and others have spoken about.[30] The decree was sketched out by a powerful group of prelates in the eleventh century. It stated that God had assigned three separate tasks to mankind. These were, in descending order, to pray for salvation for all (priests and bishops); to fight to protect all (the knights or nobles); and to labour in order to provide the resources necessary to support the first two groups (the peasants). And it was vital that the peasants serve the nobles because the latter were instructed to defend the clergy. This was governed by the belief that,

> it is the will of the Creator in Heaven and in earth [that] the higher
> shall always rule over the lower. Each individual and each class
> should stay in its place, perform its tasks and enjoy the favours and
> rights proper to it . . . To rebel against this rule is a grievous sin.[31]

In short, it was but 'God's Will' that the peasants serve the nobles and priests. In this way, Catholicism and the construction of Christendom served two vital social functions: first to produce a coherent sense of self against the other (deemed to be Islam) so as to enable relative unity and harmony within Europe. And second, without the Decree of the Three Orders, the feudal economic system would almost certainly have imploded.

In this way the celestial hierarchy was transposed on to the feudal social hierarchy. Moreover, the military activities and coercive identity of the knight were prescribed as legitimate, given that neither the Church nor the masses could protect themselves. These new moral principles were the single most important resource that enabled the nobility to sustain itself in a position of power over the peasantry on the one hand and secular rulers on the other. We noted earlier how the institution of the *fief* ensured not only the lineage of the noble families, but also served to consolidate the power of this class over the rulers. The crucial point here is that one of the factors that legitimised the *fief* was the Decree of the Three Orders. Moreover, the new decree established the reimposition of feudal rights over the peasantry (who had fled throughout the continent during the chaos of the centuries when various Asian migrations had washed over Europe). This was achieved by imposing the damning images of Hell that would await them should they fail to comply with the 'will of God'.

Ultimately, this was all made possible by the fact that the Catholic Church held a monopoly of the means of grace or salvation. It could deliver the believer to Heaven, or equally, by excommunicating a believer, it could deliver him or her to the gates of Hell. By the end of the thirteenth century, the images of Hell as described by Dante were so terrible that breaking the Christian code carried with it in the eyes of the masses, a fate worse than death (i.e. eternal damnation). Moreover, in an age where there were no formal states this proved to be an effective means to ensure compliance and relative order. Indeed, the belief that there was no salvation outside of the Church (*extra ecclesiam nulla salus*) was pretty much universally accepted.[32] The major means by which the Church reached into the hearts and minds of the peasants was through the regular administering of the sacraments by the priest. And through the Decree of the Three Orders Christianity was able to present the highly unequal social relationship between peasants and nobles as entirely 'natural'. So successful was this that it would have been extremely difficult for the peasants to have even imagined an alternative social order (and to do so would have been by definition sacrilegious). In this way then, the construction of European identity, forged in a global crucible, was vital in enabling the consolidation and reproduction of medieval feudalism.

Conclusion

This chapter has shown that most of the crucial ingredients that made up European feudal society by the beginning of the second millennium were significantly shaped by Eastern forces. Moreover, the construction of a European collective identity was forged in a global context. Indeed, 'it was out of the [diffusional and imaginary] encounter between the European barbarians and the great civilizations of the East that Western civilization was born'.[33] Nevertheless, the impression conveyed thus far is that Europe was dominated by a feudal or rural 'subsistence-based' economy. More important to the progressive story of the rise of the West was the revival of commerce after about 750. And no less important was a whole series of 'proto-capitalist' mini-revolutions. This side of the story is usually attributed to the 'genius' of the Italian pioneers. But as ch. 6 argues, the Italians were not the ingenious pioneers of capitalism that Eurocentric scholars assume. For behind Italy lay the more advanced East.

6 The myth of the Italian pioneer, 1000–1492

The Venetians, the Pisans, and the Genoese all used to come, sometimes as raiders . . . sometimes as travelers trying to prevail over Islam with the goods they bring . . . and now there is not one of them but brings to our lands his weapons of war and battle and bestows upon us the choicest of what he makes and inherits. . . . [For we have now established communications and arranged terms with them] such that we desire and they deplore, such as we prefer and they do not.

Salah al-din al-Ayyubi [Saladin], 1174

Whoever is lord of Malacca has his hands on the throat of Venice.

Tomé Pires

The rise of a massive market economy in China during the eleventh century may have sufficed to change the world balance [against] command and [towards] market behavior in a critically significant way . . . and as Chinese technical secrets spread abroad, new possibilities opened in other parts of the Old World, most conspicuously in western Europe.

William H. McNeill

Eurocentric scholars place particular emphasis on the 'post-1000' commercial revolution (though as we saw in ch. 2, this revival in fact began in the post-750 period), as well as the navigational and financial revolutions. And we are told that behind all these breakthroughs was the genius of the pioneering Italians. As one scholar put it: 'Even today, it is impossible to find anything – income tax for instance – which did not have some precedent in the genius of one of the Italian republics'.[1] Likewise, Eurocentric accounts of the 'leading powers' in the world in the post-1000 period often begin with Venice.[2]

This chapter argues that the image of the 'Italian pioneer' is but a myth. Italy derived its economic strength by locating itself within a pre-existent global economy that had been pioneered, and maintained, by the major Eastern powers (chs. 2–4). It was not that Italy found the world and then transformed it; rather that the more advanced

Eastern world found Italy and enabled its rise and development. My central claim is that virtually all the major innovations that lay behind the development of Italian capitalism were derived from the more advanced East, especially the Middle East and China, and diffused across the Islamic Bridge of the World through Oriental globalisation. Moreover, while Italy indeed led the inferior or backward European subcontinent it was none the less a mere bit-player in the larger global arena, at all times playing second fiddle to the more advanced Islamic polities and merchants of the Middle East and especially North Africa.

Eastern trade as the fifth element in the high medieval European institutional and technological 'revolutions'

Eurocentric historians typically view the rise of Europe after 1000 in terms of a self-contained or autonomous regional economy or civilisation. Towns in particular were deemed to be 'autocephalous': 'it was the medieval city . . . which, like the yeast in a mighty dough, brought about the rise of Europe'.[3] In the conventional account the proliferation of towns is granted almost 'magic-like' qualities. For it is assumed that with the end of the internal disruptions that had ravaged Europe between 370 and 1000, the ensuing internal order inevitably ensured the development of towns and commerce. Underlying such a claim is the assumption that 'European man' is inherently economically rational, and that under the right conditions (i.e. peace and minimalist, *laissez-faire* governments), so he would naturally get on and do what he does best – i.e. trade. For, as Adam Smith tells us, it is human nature to 'truck, barter and exchange one thing for another'.[4] Here then is one of the classic Eurocentric assumptions: that 'Western freedom' enabled capitalist or commercial development, no better signified than in the common medieval phrase *Stadt luft Macht Frei* (town air makes you free), or *Westen Stadt luft Macht Frei* (Western town air makes you free).

Particularly puzzling within the Eurocentric context is the much used concept of 'long-distance trade': puzzling because while

Europe lay at one end of this nexus, it is not always clear what lay at the other end. And what has been generally missed is that it was the East that not only lay at the other end but played a crucial role in the rise of European trade itself. For European trade was ultimately made possible only by the flow of Eastern goods which entered Europe via Italy. And second, the flow of various Eastern 'resource portfolios' – ideas, institutions and technologies – from the Middle East and China all diffused into Italy and Europe primarily along the commercial arteries of the global economy (though equally some were learned of during the Crusades). Nevertheless, this is not to say that Italy was unimportant to the fortunes of European commerce, finance and production. For it was in fact central. But it only was so because Italy was one of the major conduits through which Eastern 'resources' (not just trade) entered and reshaped Europe.

As we saw in ch. 2, from the late eighth century Italy was linked into various subsystems of the global economy, straddling Europe, Africa and Asia. This conferred upon Italy a unique privilege. Because I discussed this in some detail in ch. 2, I shall merely note the point that it was Italy's direct entry point into the lucrative Afro-Asian-led global economy that secured its destiny. As Abu-Lughod notes:

> This direct entrée to the riches of the East changed the role of the
> Italian merchant mariner cities from passive to active. The revival
> of the Champagne Fairs in the twelfth century can be explained
> convincingly by both the enhanced demand for Eastern goods
> stimulated by the crusades and, because of the strategic position
> of the Italians in coastal enclaves of the Levant, the increased
> supplies of such goods they could now deliver.[5]

Venice ultimately prevailed over its rival Genoa not because of its so-called ingenuity but because of its lucrative access to the East via Egypt and the Middle East. Braudel confirms this through a rhetorical question:

Can [Venice's lead within Europe] be explained by her preferred (and traditional) links with the Orient, whereas the other Italian cities were more concerned with the Western world, then slowly taking shape? . . . The lifeblood of Venetian trade was the Levant connection. So if Venice appears to be a special case, is it because her entire commercial activity from A to Z was dictated by the Levant?[6]

In short, while the Italians played a vitally important role in spreading commercialisation throughout Christendom, they were not the great commercial pioneers that Eurocentrism portrays them. And as noted in ch. 2, they were at all times dependent upon the terms and conditions laid down by the Middle Eastern Muslims down to about 1291 and Egypt thereafter. But in the end the most important function of Italy's trading links with the Middle East and later Egypt lay in the fact that these commercial routes were one of the avenues along which many of the vital Eastern 'resource portfolios' diffused across to fertilise the backward West. And these resource portfolios enabled the various 'Italian' economic and navigational revolutions for which they have been unjustifiably famous.

Eastern origins of the financial revolution
It is generally assumed that a whole series of financial institutions were pioneered by the Italians. The most important innovation we are told was the *commenda* (or *collegantia*), allegedly invented by the Italians around the eleventh century.[7] This was a contractual agreement in which an investor financed the trip of a merchant. Not only did it support international trade through the bringing together of capital and 'trading labour', but it had similar effects to a stock exchange in that it provided a market for savings which thereby fanned the flames of economic development. Nevertheless, the *commenda* was invented in the Middle East. And although its roots stem back to pre-Islamic times,[8] it was developed furthest by the early Islamic

merchants.[9] Indeed, as Abraham Udovitch notes, 'it is the Islamic form of this contract (*qirād, muqārada, mudāraba*) which is the earliest example of a commercial arrangement identical with that economic and legal institution which [much later] became known in Europe as the *commenda*'.[10] This should hardly be a 'revelation' given that Muhammad himself had been a *commenda* merchant. Nor should it be altogether surprising that the Italians came to use this institution given that Italy was directly linked into the Arabic trading system. It is also noteworthy that from the eighth century the *qirād* was applied in Islam to credit and manufacturing, not just trade.[11]

The Italians are also wrongly accredited with the discovery of a range of other financial institutions including the bill of exchange, credit institutions, insurance and banking. For the fact is that all these institutions were derived from either the Islamic Middle East, or the pre-Islamic Middle East given that 'many of the business techniques had been firmly established before the Qu'rān had codified them'.[12] The Sumerians and Sassanids were using banks, bills of exchange and cheques before the advent of Islam, although it was the Muslims who took these early beginnings furthest. Ironically one reason for this lay with the need for Islamic capitalists to circumvent the ban on usury. For example, payment was often delayed by up to two months or more so as to conceal usury by the payment of a higher price (thereby requiring such institutions).[13] Islamic bankers were common, as were international currency changers, and the banks themselves entered into *commenda* agreements for advancing money or credit in return for profits. The banks were a vital conduit for international trade, transferring funds from one place to another. The bankers issued notes – the 'demand note' or bill of exchange at a distant location (*suftaja*) and the 'order to pay' (*hawāla*) which was identical to a modern cheque. As Abu-Lughod notes of the *hawāla*: 'At the upper left corner was the amount to be paid (in numbers), and in the lower left corner was the date and then the name of the payer'.[14] And as she points out on the same page, the demand note was in fact of Persian origin and preceded its use in Europe by many centuries.

Finally, the Italians are usually attributed with the discovery of advanced accounting systems. But various Eastern accounting systems were also well developed, especially in the Middle East, India and most notably in China.[15] Indeed, some of these were probably as efficient as Weber's celebrated occidental 'double-entry' method. Nevertheless it is noteworthy that in the West, single entry bookkeeping was the most widespread method used right down to the end of the nineteenth century.[16] And as we shall see in ch. 8, the Italian traders only began to use mathematics to replace the old abacus system once the Pisan merchant, Leonardo Fibonacci, relayed the Eastern knowledge in 1202. All in all, we can conclude here with the apt words of Jack Goody:

> What we find in Italy was in essence a rebirth, recovery or re-creation of [institutions] that had existed in various forms in the Near East . . . While the sequence of exchequer accounts, commercial accounts, market finance from the fairs of Champagne to more stable banking, of commercial documents and of commercial associations such as the *commenda* and joint stock company, was important to the [future] development of industrial capitalism, it was a sequence that had already taken place in other parts of the world.[17]

The Eastern origins of the navigational revolution
The navigational revolution rested upon the astrolabe and mariner's compass, the lateen sail, the sternpost rudder and square hull (as well as triple-mast systems and new nautical methods, which I deal with in ch. 7). The lateen sail, which was triangular in shape and was suspended by a long yard at an angle of 45 degrees to the mast, could be moved according to the direction of the wind. It was a vital innovation because, unlike the square sail, it enabled ships to tack into an oncoming wind. A major problem confronting European sea-trading was that of ship size, which posed limits to the transportation of bulk cargoes. Here the vital technological breakthrough was the sternpost rudder

(thirteenth century). Because it was mounted on a flat or square stern it enabled the construction of much larger ships, thereby multiplying the cargo space. Navigational constraints were posed by the Portolan charts which, though sufficient for intra-European sailing, were far too crude to allow for oceanic navigation. This was solved by the astrolabe (a device that allows the plotting of position against the stars). And the invention of the compass was no less important because it could be used even in cloudy weather (i.e. when the stars were covered). This directly enabled an extension of the six-month voyage season to the whole year, thereby doubling the number of voyages. These break-throughs enabled the Europeans to take to the oceans. But however successful these innovations were in the European context, the fact is that most of them were invented, and all were refined, in the East.

The astrolabe first emerged in Ancient Greece, though its details were never clear and the references to it are few and far between. It was, however, the Muslims who undertook all the major innovations which can be traced back probably to al-Fazārī in the mid-eighth century (and not Māshā'allāh, as has been sometimes claimed). By the ninth century the astrolabe was in regular production and had diffused into Europe via Islamic Spain by the mid-tenth century.[18] Interestingly, the apparently oldest Latin text on the astrolabe, *Sententie astrolabi* (from late tenth century northern Spain) is heavily reliant on various Islamic texts, including al-Khwārizmī's treatise on the astrolabe.[19] But what was equally as impressive were the many refinements that were pioneered by various Islamic astronomers, which enabled the regular use of the astrolabe by later Europeans (see ch. 8).

The mariner's compass was first used in the European context in 1185. But it could not have been invented by the Italians, or any other European for that matter, for the simple reason that it was clearly deployed on Chinese ships around 1090.[20] Even so, this was merely the culmination of a series of Chinese innovations that stemmed back to 83 CE when crude compasses were invented, and even as far back as the fourth century BCE when even cruder 'lodestone' compasses were discovered. The Italians merely borrowed the compass, which had diffused across to backward Europe via the Muslims, from the Chinese.[21] While I shall deal with the development of navigational techniques in ch. 7, here I shall examine the origins of the new shipping technologies, beginning with Lynn White's claim that the lateen sail originated in Europe.

First of all, despite the fact that we might never know who first invented the lateen sail, Lynn White (drawing on Lionel Casson) insists that it was invented by the Romans. This claim is based on two pictures of boats with a lateen sail (one depicted on a second-century tombstone and the other on a fourth-century mosaic).[22] Second, although White concedes that no large European ship deployed a large lateen sail before the sixth century, nevertheless he justifies this by correctly noting that using a lateen sail on large ships requires considerable experimentation in, and refinement of, design. The implication then is that the Europeans were busy refining the lateen sail further in the four centuries before about 533. Then White points to two pieces of evidence that suggest its use on European ships in the sixth century. The first is the short reference in the biography of St Caesarus of Arles; the second is Jules Sottas's interpretation of Procopius' statement which supposedly provides strong confirmation that the lateen sail was deployed on three large eastern Roman ships in 533.[20] Third, along with many others White claims that the next example appears in the Mediterranean in c. 880. Fourth and finally, White concludes that it was the Portuguese *caravel* that was the vehicle which relayed the invention to the Muslims (who in turn used it first only in the sixteenth century).[24] Let me reply to these claims in turn (though I shall deal with the first point last).

First, the reference in the biography of St Caesarus of Arles (which was cited originally by Jal in 1848) to prove the use of the lateen by the Europeans in the sixth century has been brought into doubt by H. H. Brindley.[25] The original passage cited from Caesarus is, according to Brindley, no more than an allusion: 'tres naves, quas Latenas vocant, majores, plenas tritico direxerunt'. The assumption is that labelling these three wheat ships 'latines' means that they had lateen sails. There is also reason to doubt Sottas's interpretation of Procopius' claim – that three ships of Justinian's fleet in 533 deployed lateen sails. Procopius actually stated that the admiral of the fleet, 'gave an order that the three ships carrying the officers in chief command should have as much as a third of the upper angle of their sails painted red'. As Richard Bowen points out, 'Sottas immediately infers from the word "angle" that the three ships were lateen-rigged'.[26] Apart from the obvious fact that it is anomalous that the whole fleet was not rigged in this way, Bowen concludes on the same page that, 'it seems more logical . . . that the triangular sails refer to triangular top sails, which were standard gear on Roman square-rigged ships after 50 AD'. Note that the triangular top sails were horizontally, not vertically, mounted and did not function as a lateen.

Second, White's claim that the lateen sail was deployed on a European ship in 880 is problematic. This famous sketch, which was originally revealed by Jal in 1848 is, according to Brindley, 'so finished that its accuracy is doubtful; it is too unlike ninth century work in this respect'.[27] More importantly, though unsurprisingly, Brindley proves that the date is wrong (given that the original reference displayed in the Bibliothèque Nationale, though of the ninth century, is in fact to an ancient king rather than a ship bearing a lateen sail).

Third, White's claim that it was ultimately the Portuguese at the very end of the fifteenth century who transmitted the lateen sail to the Muslims cannot be correct. We know (as discussed in ch. 2) that the Persians were sailing to India and beyond via the Persian Gulf from the third and fourth centuries. And by the mid-seventh century the Muslims were sailing the length of the Indian Ocean. But it would have been impossible for the Persian and Arab ships to have returned home with a square sail because of the Gulf's prevailing northerly winds. Without the lateen sail, then, there would have been no Middle Eastern ships plying the Indian Ocean that we actually observe. And certainly there is no trace of a square sail on any Persian or Arab ship at any point in time.

Let me now turn to the discussion of Casson's pictures upon which White exclusively relies. The picture of a Roman ship with a lateen sail depicted on a tombstone of the second century is questioned by Needham, who suggests that it could in fact have been a square sail.[28] And Casson's only other picture (dated to the fourth century) does not provide conclusive evidence of a Roman invention. But even if the Romans had invented the lateen sail, it is important to note that after 50 CE there is no evidence of refinement or further development of sails and rigging.[29] Certainly neither Casson nor White provide such evidence; it is merely implied or assumed. Particularly important here is that the two depictions of Roman boats that supposedly bore a lateen portray only a very small sail. By contrast, the Middle Easterners deployed it on much larger ships and crucially, they were using huge lateen mainsails. The contemporary, ibn-Shahriyā, even mentions one Arabic sail as tall as 76 feet in the mid-tenth century (which would have been roughly commensurate with the masts of the largest European ships of the early sixteenth century).[30] Moreover, Gerald Tibbetts tells us that the Arab ships of the fifteenth century – i.e. before Vasco da Gama in 1498 – were certainly as big as modern dhows (such ships are 100 feet in length with masts of 75 feet).[31] Above all, the use of large lateen sails demonstrates a clear 'adaptive capacity'. That is, to deploy a large lateen sail on a large vessel requires many refinements and a long period of experimentation (as White himself recognises). In sum, it is not possible to conclude that the Persians or Arabs definitively invented the lateen sail – though equally it would be wrong to dismiss the possibility. Nevertheless, it is highly probable that it was the Muslims, and not the Europeans, who, having refined it over a long period of time, passed it on to the latter, thereby enabling Vasco da Gama to set sail in 1498.

As for the sternpost rudder and square hull, these were undoubtedly Chinese inventions. They appeared as early as 400 CE and diffused westwards to arrive in Europe by about 1180 via the Islamic Bridge of the World.[32] Finally, it is instructive to note that although the

Venetian warships were the most advanced in Europe in the early fifteenth century, they paled by comparison with their contemporary Chinese counterparts. Thus the biggest Venetian galleys, which reached 150 feet in length and 20 feet in width, were dwarfed by the largest Chinese ships of 500 by 180 feet. Moreover, 'Venetian galleys were protected by archers; Chinese ships were armed with gunpowder weapons, brass and [cast] iron cannon, mortars, flaming arrows and exploding shells'.[33]

The Eastern origins of the European 'energy' and 'proto-industrial' revolutions

With respect to the medieval energy revolution, Carlo Cipolla conventionally asserts that the invention of water-mills was a strictly European innovation, given their absence in the East.[34] But as Arnold Pacey notes:

> It used to be thought that [the water-mill] was a distinctively European development. But it is now known that there were numerous water mills in the vicinity of Baghdad, and that water power was applied to paper-making in that region for two or more centuries earlier than in Europe.[35]

Actually, Pacey understates the case. A fuller picture is provided by al-Hassan and Hill:

> Muslims were obviously very keen to exploit every possible water supply as a potential source of power for milling. They even gauged the flow of a stream by the number of mills it would turn – the stream was, as it were, so many 'mill-power' . . . There were mills in every province of the Muslim world from Spain and North Africa to Transoxiana.[36]

Strikingly, throughout the Middle East waterwheels and water-mills proliferated along the rivers, being deployed for irrigation, grinding grain and crushing materials for industrial processes. There were also massive *norias* on the Orontes River at Hama in Syria (wooden water-raising machines that stood over 60 feet tall). Crucially, the *norias* and water-mills were also built in Islamic Spain. Moreover, since the second millennium BCE the Middle East had developed all sorts of impressive water-managing schemes, including above-ground aqueducts to transport water to the towns and villages, and especially the underground aqueducts (the *qanat* in Iran or the *khattara* in Morocco).[37] And the irrigation systems could not be seen as a sign of oriental despotism (as Eurocentrics might reply) because in the Middle East these systems were far too decentralised to fit the mould of a hydraulic and centralised despotic state.

Nevertheless, Eurocentrism effectively circumnavigates these Islamic achievements by claiming that the mill originated much earlier, during the Roman empire. But it seems that mills were first developed in Ancient Egypt and spread to the Roman empire later – even if these were not water-mills.[38] The first water-mills (the decisive innovation) emerged in China in the first century BCE. This is sometimes circumvented by asserting that it was the Roman mill that influenced the later European medieval mill, given that the Romans, unlike the Chinese, used vertical wheels that formed the basis of the later medieval water-mills. But the Chinese influence was revealed by the fact that the European medieval water-mill was critically dependent upon the 'trip hammer'. And this had been clearly invented in China in the fourth century BCE.

Finally, was the windmill a unique European invention pioneered during the thirteenth century? This cannot be the case given that the earliest reference to the windmill is in Persia in 644. Nevertheless, as Needham notes, 'more certain perhaps, is the mention of windmills in the works of the Banū Mūsā brothers (850 to 870), while a century later several reliable authors are speaking of the remarkable windmills of Seistan (e.g. Abū Ishāq al-Istakhrī and Abū al-Qāsim ibn Hauqal)'.[39] The Persian windmill subsequently diffused not only to Europe but also to Afghanistan and China.[40] A common reply dismisses the Persian origins on the lines that the Middle Eastern windmill was horizontally mounted in contrast to the vertically mounted

European mill. That the actual design did not diffuse across to Europe seems fair; that there was no Persian input at all seems unfair. For it is clear that the idea of the windmill diffused. And it is surely no coincidence that the European Crusaders, who would undoubtedly have come across the Persian windmill during their 'adventures' – particularly given that many stayed on and settled in the Middle East – deployed it in Europe not long afterwards.

Textile manufacturing

We know that the two most significant industries in Europe after 1000 were textile manufacturing and paper-making, though iron production was also becoming important. It seems clear that a series of textile technologies diffused into Europe from the East, most notably the spinning wheel, filatures, the loom and foot-pedals. The spinning wheel originated in China and diffused across to Italy again via Islamic Spain, arriving in the thirteenth century.[41] It was no coincidence that the thirteenth-century Italian silk-machines so closely resembled the earlier Chinese model. As Hugh Honour points out:

> While the *pax tartarica* established by Kublai Khan reigned over Asia, bales of [Chinese textiles] were carried from China to the Middle East and to Europe along the caravan route which Balducci Pegoletti declared to be perfectly safe whether by night or day. That this great influx of brocades and embroideries, so much finer in quality and richer in colour and design than any Europe could produce, should have aroused admiration and stimulated emulation is hardly surprising.[42]

And given that we find in various Italian cities 'silk filatures using machinery closely similar to that of China [the] presumption is that one or other of the European merchants who travelled East in those days brought back the designs in his saddle-bags'.[43] Crucially, the invention of the silk filatures (reeling machines) had been made in China in 1090. The Chinese machines comprised a treadle-operated silk-reeling frame with a ramping board and a roller system. The

Italian model resembled the Chinese right down to the smallest detail such as the lever joined to the crank.[44] And significantly, the Italian machines more or less replicated the Chinese right down to the eighteenth century.[45] Finally, it was hardly surprising that the machines ultimately entered Europe via Islamic Spain, for all the major aspects of the loom were deployed in full there. And this itself was hardly surprising given that Islamic textiles had dominated the European markets for many centuries.

Paper-making manufacturing

One of the most important medieval European industries was paper-making. Nevertheless, paper was manufactured in Islamic Spain in 1150 thereafter diffusing across Europe. However, paper was invented by Ts'ai Lun in China in 105 CE (see ch. 8) and paper manufacturing began not long after.[46] How then did it diffuse across to Europe? As Thomas Carter originally explained, paper diffused westward very gradually. It arrived in Turkestan between the fourth and sixth centuries, but was only occasionally used. While paper was found in Transoxiana and Persia well before the Battle of Talas in 751,[47] the fact is that it was after that particular battle that Chinese prisoners passed on the vital techniques of paper-making. As al-Qazwīnī noted,

> Prisoners of war were brought from China. Among these was someone who knew [about] the manufacture of paper and so he practised it. Then it spread until it became a main product for the people of Samarqand, whence it was exported to all countries.[48]

Indeed, paper-making spread from Samarkand to Baghdad by 794, and Arabian paper produced in Damascus – suitably known in Europe as *charta damascena* (Damascus paper) – became the main supplier of paper to Europe until the fifteenth century. To sum up then: 'Trade and other contacts between Arabs and Chinese furnished opportunities for the Arabs to know paper quite early, and such Arabic words as *kagaz* for paper and its equivalent *qirtas*, which is found in the Koran, are of Chinese origin.'[49]

Nevertheless, although the original breakthrough was undoubt-edly made by the Chinese, the Arabs did have an independent input. In particular, the Arabs had to starch the paper in order to suit scribes using pens (rather than the brushes that the Chinese used). Paper-making production subsequently diffused into Islamic Spain by 1150 and then across Europe to France by 1157 and Italy by 1276 (well over 1000 years after the Chinese discovery).[50] And Islamic influence is revealed by the fact that the English use the term 'ream' while the Italians use the term 'risma'. The earlier Arabic term was *rismah*.[51]

The early European iron industry

As we saw in ch. 3, while iron production began well before the com-mon era, it was the Chinese who had taken this further than anyone else during the eleventh-century 'Sung miracle'. Here I shall merely note that the diffusional time lags from China to Europe are striking only for their size: eleven centuries for metallurgical blowing engines operated by water power, and fourteen centuries for piston bellows.[52] It has also been suggested that the European *Flussofen*, which replaced the Styrian or Austrian *Stuckofen* (blast furnace) in the fourteenth century, was the final stage in the transfer of Chinese technology that had come via Central Asia, Siberia, Turkey and Russia.[53] Notable too is that the Indians and Muslims were significant producers in their own right. Iron was a vital industry in Islam. It was even given an important place in the Qu'rān: 'God sent iron down to earth, wherein is mighty power and many uses for mankind' (ch. 57). It seems that the Eastern iron production techniques diffused into Europe probably via the Islamic Bridge of the World.

European clock-making

'The clock was the greatest achievement of [European] medieval mechanical ingenuity', says the avowed Eurocentric scholar, David Landes.[54] Allegedly the first public clock was erected on the tower of St Eustorgio's church in Milan in 1309. And the first portable clock supposedly appeared at the Visconti palace in Milan in 1335. Tellingly, though, even Eurocentric scholars concede that no one knows who actually invented it.[55] That the Chinese did not come to rely on the clock is a reasonable proposition. That the Chinese were not interested in, or were unable to make, a mechanical clock is an unreasonable claim. The fact is that at the end of the eleventh century, Su Tzu-Jung built an astronomical clock. In 1086 he was instructed by the Chinese emperor to reconstruct the earlier armillary clock (invented by Han Kung-Lien). Speaking of Su's description of his clock Needham concludes: 'With all its vividness of detail, this passage [concerns] the organisation of one of the greatest technical achievements of the medieval time in any civilisation'.[56] The greatest challenge in making a clock lay with the invention of the escapement mechanism (a device which regulates the movement of the shafts and dials to ensure accurate timekeeping). Cardwell noted that, 'we are left completely in the dark about the steps by which some unknown genius or geniuses invented the escapement mechanism which . . . constituted perhaps the greatest single human invention since the appearance of the wheel'.[57] The riddle is solved by the clear fact that it was the Chinese (probably I-Hsing in 725) who had invented the escapement mechanism and, moreover, there is evidence of its transmission across to the West. Indeed, the idea seems to have spread to the Islamic Middle East. Then in 1277 (some sixty years before the Visconti clock) an Arabic text on time-keeping – which included the idea of the weight-driven clock with a mercury escapement – was translated in Toledo.[58] Notable too is that virtually all the techniques and mechanisms of the European clock, including the automata, complex gear-trains and segmental gears as well as the weight-drive and audible signals, were present in Andalusian (i.e. Islamic Spanish) horology.[59] Interestingly, Lynn White suggests that the six perpetual machines appear to have been inspired by the twelfth-century Indian, Bhāskarā.[60] Either way, though, many of the European clocks had design features that bore a very close resemblance to Su's clock.[61] There is then good circumstantial evidence to suggest that the Chinese (and perhaps the Indians) via the Muslims might well have influenced the European clock-makers.

But if nothing else, this refutes the standard Eurocentric refrain that the Chinese were not technologically advanced enough to produce a clock.

Conclusion

That Italy was important for the development of Europe during much of the medieval era seems an entirely reasonable proposition. But the notion that the Italians pioneered all manner of innovations that propelled European capitalism forward is, however, a myth. Eastern influence on Italy was as profound as it was widespread. Finally, when we think of Italy, we often think of its unique food and many of its cultural artefacts. But the pizza base was first invented in Ancient Egypt. The Arabs introduced the cultivation of rice and saffron into Sicily and Spain (which enabled the making of *paella*). And coffee came from Ethiopia (derived from the Arabic term *kahwa*).[62] Nevertheless, pasta or spaghetti did not come from China (*contra* Marco Polo) but the ancient Etruscans who had resided in the western part of Italy.

One of the greatest signs of Italian ingenuity and refinement we are told lies with the Ponte Vecchio bridge. But as Michael Edwardes points out:

> Those responsible for the first segmental arch bridges in Europe – such as the Ponte Vecchio, spanning the Arno at Florence (1345) – must have been influenced by pioneering Chinese expertise. Indeed, the fame of China's technicians persisted [for many centuries], and Peter the Great of Russia, in process of modernizing his country, called in Chinese engineers in 1675 for his bridge-building projects.[63]

Indeed, with respect to the Ponte Vecchio, Needham notes that 'a comparable bridge of even more advanced character . . . was built by about 610 [CE] by a Chinese engineer of outstanding quality, Li Chhun'.[64] Moreover, there were nearly twenty others like it in China before the fourteenth century. And given that many Westerners visited and marvelled at such bridges (including Marco Polo), it is highly possible that this relayed knowledge directly spurred on the Italian engineers.

For all this, though, what we usually think of when we 'imagine Italy' is the Renaissance, which supposedly set off the European dynamic that would culminate with the West's breakthrough to capitalist modernity. Here we often think of Leonardo da Vinci, who insisted that painting should be based on mathematics – especially geometry and optics (a *leitmotif* of 'advanced Europe'). But the geometry and optics upon which Da Vinci relied were developed, and passed on, by the Middle Eastern and North African Muslims. Indeed, as ch. 8 explains, behind the Western Renaissance lay the East. Finally, the traditional assumption of Eurocentric history – that the baton of global power was subsequently passed from Italy to the Iberians who then launched the European age of discovery – is yet another myth. Chapter 7 explains why.

7 The myth of the Vasco da Gama epoch, 1498–c. 1800

If I remain with those who follow not in my steps
It is more bitter than the dangers of a stormy sea.
Give me a ship and I will take it through danger,
For this is better than having friends who can be insincere . . .
This [ship] is a wonder of God, my mount, my escort.
(Oh Lord be generous) In travel, 'tis the house of God itself . . .
I have exhausted my life for science and have been famous for it.
My honour has been increased by [scientific] knowledge in my old age.
Had I not been worthy of this, kings would not have
Paid attention to me.

Ahmad Ibn Mājid, Islamic navigator, c. 1475

If my claim made in part I of this book is correct – that Asia was ahead of Europe right down to the nineteenth century – how then are we to confront the Eurocentric claim that after 1500 the Europeans conquered Asia? And how are we to deal with the familiar claim that the post-1492 era constituted the European age of discovery that ushered in Western-led proto-globalisation? Or, in an Asian context, how are we to deal with the familiar Eurocentric depiction of Asian history between 1498 and 1800 as but the 'Vasco da Gama epoch'? More specifically, how are we to deal with the familiar Eurocentric depiction so vividly articulated by John Roberts in his book *The Triumph of the West*?

> One fact . . . is so obvious that it is easily overlooked: the exploring was done exclusively by Europeans. What is more, the voyages of discovery were the beginning of a new era, one of world-wide expansion by Europeans . . . [L]ike Luther in the next century, Henry [the Navigator] helped to launch modern history without any intention of doing so . . . It was only a comparatively small boast that the Portuguese king [Manuel] soon called himself 'Lord of Ethiopia, Arabia, Persia and India' . . . The conquest of the

high seas was the first and greatest of all the triumphs over natural forces which were to lead to the domination by western civilization of the whole globe.[1]

And Roberts goes on to argue that:

Nowadays, people have come to use a specially minted word to summarise this state of mind – 'Eurocentrism'. It means 'putting Europe at the centre of things', and its usual implication is that to do so is wrong. But, of course, if we are merely talking about facts, about what happened, and not about the value that we place on them, then it is quite correct to put Europe at the centre of the story in modern times.[2]

My reply is that the 'facts' that Roberts appeals to are merely those which have been selected in by the Eurocentric discourse, precisely so as to 'put Europe at the centre of the story' in the first place. This becomes apparent when we review an alternative set of facts. Here I present six main counter-propositions to the familiar Eurocentric story, which in aggregate paint an altogether different picture and which simultaneously confirm the arguments set out in part I of this book.

The myth of the modern European age of discovery in Asia

The Portuguese voyages were not the embodiment of a pioneering modern European age of discovery that demonstrated the signs of a unique 'rational restlessness' or an impulsive curiosity. They were in fact the 'last gasp', or the 'second round', of the medieval age of Crusades – the 'first round' having occurred between 1095 and 1291. That is, these voyages were informed by the old Crusader mentality rather than a set of modern ideas. The immediate backdrop to the voyages lay with the Ottoman seizure of Constantinople in 1453, which triggered a major crisis in Christendom. This Christian identity crisis was exacerbated by the Muslims taking Athens (the Holy City of the Renaissance thinkers) in 1456. Accordingly, 'a great chorus of lamentation went up . . . The sacred soil of Hellas had been profaned.'[3] This led to a desire to reach out to Christians in the East (most notably the fictitious Black Catholic king, Prester John). Indeed,

> in the second half of the fifteenth century, forming and directing a great Crusade became part of plans for Papal reform of the Church . . . A strong reforming Pope would work for peace within Christendom, inspire a Crusade, and rejuvenate the Faith.[4]

The Islamic 'threat', coupled with the disunity of Christendom, stimulated the Catholic Church to issue a number of papal bulls. For the Church, it was very much a matter of religious life or death: that is, the very survival of Christendom was at stake. As Pope Pius II proclaimed, 'An unavoidable war with the Turks threatens us. Unless we take up arms and go to war to meet the enemy, we think all is over with religion.'[5]

The first papal bull (*Dum Diversas*), issued in 1452 by Pope Nicholas V, asserted that, 'The Pope authorises the King of Portugal to attack, conquer and subdue Saracens [Muslims] . . . to capture their goods and their territories; to reduce their persons to perpetual slavery, and to transfer their lands and properties to the King of Portugal'.[6] This was followed by a second bull (*Romanus Pontifex*) issued by the same pope in 1455, which has been aptly labelled the 'Charter of Portuguese Imperialism'. Here, Prince Henry the Navigator is lavished with praise as a soldier of Christ and defender of the Faith. He is praised for his desire to spread the name of Christ and to compel the 'infidel' to enter the fold of the Catholic Church. And it specifically credits him with the intention of circumnavigating the Cape and making connections with the 'Catholic' inhabitants of the Indies (who were allegedly ruled over by the priest king Prester John). The belief was that these inhabitants, 'honour the name of Christ', and that by forging an alliance with them the Portuguese could carry the struggle against the Saracens and other 'infidels'. Having granted legitimacy to Portuguese imperialism in the Indies, this was followed later by a further crucial papal bull, *Inter Caetera* (1456). This confirmed the *Romanus Pontifex* by granting, 'spiritual jurisdiction of all the regions conquered by the Portuguese now or in the future, "from Capes Bojador [on the North-West coast of Africa] and Nun, by way of Guinea and beyond, southwards to the Indies"'.[7] In particular, they were specifically instructed to find Prester John with whom, it was hoped, the Portuguese could ally and defeat the Muslims (he was sought because it was believed that he lived in the rear of the Islamic empire).

The presumptuous pronouncement made by the Church that the Indian Ocean was a *nullius diocesis* (which was to an extent a medieval Christian pre-emption of the later concept of *terra nullius*), was echoed by the claim that this ocean was a *mare librum*. This led the Portuguese to believe from the outset that it was entirely appropriate that all Asian ships should carry Portuguese permits if they wished to trade in what was now believed to be a 'Portuguese ocean'.[8] Put differently, Christianity was not invoked purely as a justificatory principle for Portuguese 'imperialism' in the Indies after the event: rather, it fundamentally informed their belief from the outset that this course of action was morally appropriate. None of this is to say that economic motivations were unimportant. But economic riches would also be an important means to carry the war to the 'infidel'. Telling here is that in 1457 the Lisbon mint issued a gold coinage with the striking of the *cruzado* (Crusade); and no less crucially, the gold came from Guinea.

The twin myths of the Portuguese age of discovery and the Western age of proto-globalisation

The Portuguese neither 'discovered' Asia and the Cape of Storms, nor were the post-1497/8 'explorations' the first sign of Western proto-globalisation. Rather they were part and parcel of Afro-Asian-led (oriental) globalisation. It is conventionally thought that it was the Portuguese navigator, Bartholomeu Dias, who discovered the Cape of Storms in 1487–8 (subsequently renamed the Cape of Good Hope), and that it was Vasco da Gama who successfully pushed all the way across to India via the Cape a decade later. But in fact, the Portuguese were the last to discover the Cape – various Eastern peoples had already reached, if not circumnavigated, it many centuries earlier. In the mid-fifteenth century the famous Arab navigator Shihāb al-Dīn Ahmad Ibn Mājid, sailed westwards to the Cape and then up the west coast of Africa before entering the Mediterranean via the Strait of Gibraltar.[9] And the coastline 'is described in such detail in the manuals that one cannot doubt the prior circumnavigation of Africa by Arab/Persian sailors'.[10] Also of note is that around 1420 an Indian (or maybe Chinese) vessel sailed past the Cape and continued on for some 2000 miles into the Atlantic ocean.[11] Moreover, the Chinese (Islamic) admiral, Chêng Ho, sailed up the east coast of Africa at the very beginning of the fifteenth century, though it is also possible that Chinese sailors had rounded the Cape as early as the eighth century, if not earlier.[12] There is also evidence that the Javanese made it across to the Cape. In 1645, Diogo do Couto said of the Javanese:

> [they are] all men very experienced in the art of navigation, to the point that they claim to be the most ancient of all . . . [I]t is certain that they formerly navigated to the Cape of Good Hope, and were in communication with . . . [Madagascar], where there are many brown and Javanised natives, who say they are descended from them.[13]

And this migratory pattern certainly began in the early centuries of the first millennium CE.[14] In sum, a whole variety of Eastern traders had already made their way across to the Cape and up the east, if not the west, coast of Africa well before Henry the Navigator had begun to fumble his way down it.

A further Eurocentric myth concerns the claim that Da Gama's arrival in India represented a kind of first contact with a hitherto isolated people. But as we saw in chs. 2–4, India, and the rest of Asia for that matter, had played a crucial role within the Afro-Asian-led global economy for many centuries before Vasco da Gama set off. The reality was that Columbus and Da Gama were pre-empted by the

Afro-Asian age of discovery by about a millennium. Testimony to this point is revealed by the fact that:

> When Da Gama sailed up the East African coast in 1498 he sailed into a familiar world, and one already linked to the Mediterranean and Europe. Arab traders had penetrated, converted, settled and intermarried as far south as Sofala [on the south-east African coast], and linked all littoral East Africa north of here with other parts of the Indian Ocean as well as the Red Sea and Europe.[15]

Another interrelated myth concerns the Eurocentric assumption that Da Gama made first contact with a primitive people. As we saw in some detail in ch. 4 the Indians were more advanced than their European 'discoverers'. Circumstantial testimony to this claim lies in the initial meeting between Da Gama and the Indian Zamorin of Calicut. Far from being overawed or overwhelmed by the arrival of the Portuguese, the Indian Zamorin (ruler) was completely underwhelmed. When Vasco da Gama was graciously granted an audience with the Zamorin, he presented some of the most advanced European products available. But the Indians could scarcely contain their amusement at the inferiority of the goods. As Needham put it:

> The technological gap between the [East] and the West is well evidenced by Vasco da Gama's first visit in 1498 to Calicut. He presented various goods – cloths, hats, sugar, oil . . . The king laughed at them and advised the Admiral rather to offer gold. At the same time, the Muslim merchants already on the spot affirmed to the Indians that the Portuguese were essentially pirates, possessed of nothing that the Indians could ever want.[16]

In point of fact, it was the ruler's advisers who laughed. The ruler took great offence at the offerings, which he dismissed as unworthy of even the poorest merchant.

The notion that the Indians were completely overawed by the Portuguese in fact needs to be inverted. Interestingly, the Portuguese

King John II had sent Pedro de Covilhão to explore India in 1487. When Covilhão returned he reported that he,

> was astonished at what he saw in the Indian ports: the lively commerce . . . and-above-all the lots of cinnamon and cassia bunches in the storehouses of the Arab merchants, the pepper climbing the trees, and the immense quantity of spices which grow in the fields just as wheat grows in Europe.[17]

A few years later Cabral returned home not only with similarly glowing reports but even brought back some Indian produce. The Portuguese in general were as much astonished at the wealth of the population as they were by the wealth displayed in the palaces.[18] Thus if the Portuguese appeared to be motivated by an intense curiosity that the Asians supposedly lacked, it was only because the Portuguese, unlike the Asians, knew very little of the world on the one hand, and that the Asians had a great deal more to offer on the other.

In sum, neither the rounding of the Cape nor the Portuguese arrival in India constituted the label of a pioneering discovery. Though it was undoubtedly a revelation to the Europeans, it was merely yesteryear's news to the Africans and Asians. All that was really happening was that the Europeans were directly joining the Afro-Asian-led global economy that had been created in the post-500 period. In short, the Europeans did not 'discover' Asia and Africa, for the peoples of the latter had already long been in contact with Europe.

The myth of European ingenuity in the Portuguese voyages

The Portuguese arrival in Asia was not the sign of a unique European ingenuity, but was only made possible by Europe's assimilation of superior Asian nautical technologies and scientific ideas. Europe did not remake Asia between 1500 and 1800 – Asia helped remake Europe between 500 and 1800. The fact is that had it not been for the diffusion and assimilation of Eastern science as well as navigational and nautical technologies, Vasco da Gama would not even have got as far as the Cape let alone India. The Portuguese borrowing of Islamic science began in the twelfth century, and was to an extent initiated by the royal family. The Portuguese monarchy employed various Jewish scientists who directly relayed, via their translations, the original Islamic knowledge (which was in the context of the Crusades a more 'politically feasible' method than working directly with the Muslims). Moreover, the Portuguese benefited more generally from the immigration of Jewish scientists who had fled Spain at the end of the fourteenth century at the height of the pogroms.

Oceanic sailing provided new challenges to the Iberians both in terms of shipping design and navigation. But as Patricia Seed points out, they turned to the Easterners – especially the Muslims via the Jews – to solve these numerous challenges.[19] The first challenge was the need to tack into the strong headwinds that blew up south of Cape Bojador on the west coast of Africa. This was solved in the 1440s by the construction of *caravels* that had a sternpost rudder and were rigged with three masts, one of which bore a lateen sail. Nevertheless the origins of the *caravel* date back to the thirteenth century, when the Portuguese built small fishing boats that were based on the Islamic *qārib*.[20] And as we saw in ch. 6, the important sternpost rudder was a Chinese invention. There we also noted that the lateen sail most likely had Middle Eastern origins, though it had become a firm feature of Islamic shipping well before the fifteenth century. And certainly the Middle Easterners had refined it further before passing it on to the Europeans. Also of note is that it was only in the mid-fifteenth century that the all-important triple-mast system (combining square and lateen sails) was introduced to European shipping. Without this innovation the 'voyages of discovery' would never have occurred. Nevertheless, this aspect had long been a staple feature of Chinese shipping, the knowledge of which could have been transmitted by any of the European visitors to China in the thirteenth century, or by the Europeans or Muslims who had long observed Chinese ships sailing to Africa or the Middle East.[21]

In turn, the lateen sail threw up a second challenge. Because the lateen sail led to a zigzagging (or triangular) sailing path, this necessarily made it much harder to calculate the linear distance travelled. This was solved by the use of geometry and trigonometry, which had been developed by, and were borrowed from, the Muslim mathematicians (see ch. 8). A third challenge was posed by the strong tides south of Cape Bojador, which could beach a ship or simply destroy it. To solve this required knowledge of the lunar cycles (since the moon governs the tides). At the end of the fourteenth century this knowledge was developed by the Jewish cartographer resident in Portugal – Jacob ben Abraham Cresques. The fourth challenge was the need for more accurate navigational charts than those already available (such as the Portolan). The answer lay in Islamic astronomy, which was able to calculate the size of the earth and, by using degrees, could record the distance travelled.

The astrolabe was especially important. Again, as we saw in ch. 6, this had been perfected by Muslim astronomers and had passed into Europe via Islamic Spain in the mid-tenth century. But the Portuguese also needed to establish precise location in daytime hours. Here they relied on the suggestions made by the prominent Córdovan Muslim astronomer, Ibn as-Saffār (whose treatise had been translated into Latin). They no less borrowed Islamic innovations in mathematics in order to work out latitude and longitude, relying on the Islamic tables developed by an eleventh-century Muslim astronomer. Moreover, calculating latitude also required knowledge of the solar year (since the sun's declination was pivotal to such calculations). Once again, they turned to the sophisticated Islamic and Jewish solar calendars that had already been developed in the eleventh century. All in all, the contemporary, Pedro Nunes, boasted in 1537 that: 'it is evident that the discoveries of coasts, islands, continents has not occurred by chance, but to the contrary, our sailors have departed very well informed, provided with instruments and rules of astronomy and geometry'.[22] Indeed they were very well informed. But they only were so because of the breakthroughs in Jewish, though mainly Islamic, science upon which the so-called Portuguese voyages of discovery were based.

But Islamic influence did not end here. First, it is possible, though not certain, that Da Gama was shown a remarkably detailed map of India by a Gujarati Muslim, Malemo Cana, at Malindi before he set sail to cross the Arabian Sea. More certain is that Da Gama was only able to cross to the Indies with the help of an unnamed Islamic-Gujarati pilot (who was picked up at Malindi on the East African coast). Interestingly, it is often assumed that this navigator was the famous Ahmad Ibn-Mājid, though Gerald Tibbetts has produced a number of convincing arguments that cast considerable doubt on this assertion.[23] That the influence of the Islamic navigator had indeed been extremely important was revealed by the fact that on the return journey his absence meant that Da Gama was extremely lucky to have made it back at all. As the record in the *Journal of the First Voyage of Vasco da Gama* explains:

> Owing to frequent calms and foul winds it took us three months less three days to cross this gulf [i.e. the Arabian Sea], and all our people . . . suffered from their gums, which grew over their teeth, so that they could not eat. Their legs also swelled, and other parts of the body, and these swellings spread until the sufferer died . . . Thirty of our men died in this manner . . . and those able to navigate each ship were only seven or eight, and even these were not as well as they ought to have been. I assure you that if this state of affairs had continued for another fortnight, there would have been no men at all to navigate the ships.[24]

Later on they were forced to burn one of the ships as there were simply not enough sailors to man them all. Even so, within the European context this experience proved to be far from atypical. Antonio Pigafetta, the young Italian adventurer who accompanied Magellan (some twenty years after Da Gama's voyage), informs us that:

> We ate only old biscuit turned to powder, all full of worms and
> stinking of the urine which the rats had made on it . . . And we
> drank water impure and yellow. We also ate ox hides . . . And of
> the rats . . . [we] could not get enough . . . twenty nine of us
> died . . . twenty-five or thirty fell sick.[25]

Finally, when reading the quotation cited at the beginning of the
chapter, one could be entirely forgiven for assuming that these words
might have been penned by Vasco da Gama. But they were issued by
the famous Islamic navigator, Ahmad ibn-Mājid.[26] Indeed, for about
a millennium, Persian and Arab sailors and navigators had been far
more advanced than their European counterparts. And the irony here
was that while Da Gama sought a Crusade against Islam, it was
the passing of Eastern – especially Islamic – 'resource portfolios' via
the Islamic Bridge of the World that had enabled him to undertake his
journey in the first place.

The myth of European military superiority in Asia

At the heart of the Eurocentric account is Europe's superior military
power. This assumption is certainly a myth. It is instructive to begin
by considering Vasco da Gama in relation to the Chinese (Islamic)
admiral, Chêng Ho, who traversed the Indian Ocean and landed on
the east coast of Africa many decades before Da Gama did the same
albeit in reverse. Would it be appropriate to label Vasco as the 'Chêng
Ho of Europe' or Chêng as the 'Vasco da Gama' of China? Such a comparison can only cause embarrassment for the Europeans. Thus while
the longest of Da Gama's ships was approximately 85 feet in length,
the largest of Chêng's ships was near 500 feet long and 180 feet wide
(each carried some 1000 men).[27] Even the rudder of Chêng's capital
ships (36 feet) was about half as long as Columbus's flagship, the *Nina*.
And the *Nina*'s maximum load displacement of 100 tons again paled
by comparison with the 3100 tons of Chêng's largest ships. Even the
load displacement of the 'huge' Portuguese *carracks* was only a fifth
that of Chêng's largest ships. Furthermore the Portuguese three-mast

ships compared to Chêng's nine- or ten-mast ships that were equipped with multiple bulkheads and twelve watertight compartments. And Da Gama's four ships and 170 men paled by comparison with the several hundred ships and 27,550 men of Chêng's 1431/3 voyage.

Striking too is the point that the number of men carried on some of these Chinese voyages exceeded the size of even the largest armies of the European powers at the time. And, moreover, the number of ships deployed on several of the Chinese voyages exceeded the size of the Royal Navy as late as the end of the sixteenth century by a ratio of 10:1. Striking too was the size of the Chinese navy (as noted in ch. 3). Even after the so-called 'withdrawal' in 1434, the Ming navy remained the largest in the world and probably exceeded the total of what Western Europe had to offer.[28] By contrast, the scale of the Portuguese shipping presence in Asia was feeble. Throughout the sixteenth century the Portuguese sent on average only seven ships a year to the East, and moreover, only four ships per year made the return journey; a story that would continue into the seventeenth century. A similar story is found in the Dutch and English contexts. Between 1581 and 1630 the total number of ships sent by the Dutch, Portuguese and English combined averaged a mere eight ships per annum.

The crucial point though is that Asian ships were militarily sufficient to hold their own against the European ships. Indeed a 'battle between [Chêng Ho's] armada and the other navies of the world combined would have resembled one between a pack of sharks and a shoal of sprats'.[29] But even after 1434 the superiority of the Chinese navy continued. In 1598 the Ming navy defeated an invading Japanese armada of some 500 ships.[30] It also successfully held at bay the Portuguese, Dutch and English fleets whenever they tried to 'open' up China. So, for example, when the Portuguese attempted to expand their beachhead in China by force in 1521 and 1522, they were decisively defeated by the Chinese coastguard fleet. Only as late as 1557 (the year when the Japanese were ejected from the Chinese tribute system) were the Portuguese permitted an officially granted toehold in Macao. Significantly, Macao was a tiny trade depot that was based on a small uninhabited peninsula in the Bay of Canton, which is connected to the mainland by a very narrow isthmus (and whose food supplies could very easily be cut off should Portuguese behaviour prove to be recalcitrant). This 'concession' was due not to Portuguese military superiority, but was a function of the fact that the Chinese were anxious to reduce the trade undertaken by the Japanese and thus 'used' the Portuguese instead. And although the Portuguese were able to acquire a share of the China trade it was conducted on the strictest terms laid down by the Chinese emperor. In any case it would be wrong to exaggerate the impact of Portuguese trade in China given that only one ship per annum was permitted to travel there.

The situation was little different in West Asia. In the Persian Gulf the Portuguese had little impact on the Ottomans who guarded this vital sea-lane. In any case, the Portuguese were hampered from taking this sea-lane because they needed to maintain good relations with Safavid Persia (as a counterweight to the rising Ottoman Turks). Accordingly, they were simply unable to plug the gap in the Persian Gulf (despite the fact that they had taken Hormuz), through which the Turks trafficked huge amounts of spices, the volumes of which vastly outweighed those carried by the Portuguese round the Cape. The Portuguese had no more luck in their efforts to seize the Red Sea route. Their failure to capture Aden was a major blow for their hopes because they were extremely anxious to divert the spice trade away from Ottoman control. Even the Portuguese fleet that had been sent there to block the so-called 'illegal' incoming trade proved to be ineffective. Thus Albuquerque's failure to take Aden in 1513 meant that the Red Sea remained a Muslim lake. This proved particularly deleterious because after 1540 the spice trade via the Red Sea and the Levant took off.

It is true that the Portuguese were not always resisted, but it seems that when they were they usually lost out. For example, they were resisted in Acheh, and with drastic consequences. Acheh maintained its own routes for the spice trade to the Red Sea independently of the Portuguese. Accordingly, the Portuguese remained unable to stop the diversion of increasing amounts of trade from their own routes to the long-established routes via the Red Sea and Egypt. Not only did the Red Sea route remain under Islamic control but so too did the whole route across to India and South-east Asia.[31] Moreover, 'even almost within gunshot of the outlying forts of Goa, the Moplah corsairs of Malabar periodically wrought great havoc on the Portuguese coastal trade by intercepting the *cafilas*'.[32] And at their 'stronghold' in Melaka the Portuguese were often brought virtually to their knees by the Javanese and Achinese fleets. Here it is interesting to note that the image of a militarily impoverished Eastern world was rudely upset as early as 1511 when Albuquerque attacked Melaka, only to find that the Natives were just as well acquainted with the use and deployment of heavy artillery.[33] But this should hardly be surprising given that gunpowder, the gun and cannon were invented in South-east Asia's 'backdoor' – China.

To the extent that the Portuguese enjoyed any success at all it was often more a function of their ability to play off rival Asian factions. There are many cases here but two examples are noteworthy. First, the enmity of the Zamorin (sea-raja) of Calicut and the Raja of Cochin enabled the Portuguese to gain a toehold in Calicut. And second, the rivalry between the three kingdoms in Ceylon enabled the Portuguese to maintain a presence there. That the Portuguese had to rely more on luck and deviousness was hardly surprising given their military weakness. And notable too is that the Portuguese were extremely fortunate that the major Eastern powers generally chose not to balance against them. Nevertheless this confirms my overall claim. For as Chaudhuri argues, there was no reason for the Asian powers to balance against the Portuguese because the latter were not considered a military threat.[34]

Much the same story applied to the Dutch experience. Thus although the Dutch relied more than any other 'coloniser' on force, nevertheless they reserved much of it for their relations with the Portuguese rather than the Asians.[35] Moreover, their successes can be easily exaggerated. Though they left Goa and Macao in Portuguese hands they succeeded in wresting control of some of the key ports from the Portuguese – Batavia, Ceylon, Melaka, Bantam – though even this had been no easy task. They had contested Melaka on various occasions (e.g. 1607), but only eventually succeeded in taking it as late as 1641. And when they sank eighty Chinese junks in 1622, the Chinese refused to trade with them until a century later in 1727 (when they were granted a mere toehold in Canton). In the intermediary period, Chinese merchants did go to Java, but 'they kept the trade in their own hands and dictated their own terms'.[36] And as we shall see later, the Dutch humiliation became complete during their stay at the Japanese island of Deshima. Even in Batavia – the so-called Dutch stronghold – Asian traders were able to resist Dutch incursion.[37]

In sum, the cold fact was that the Portuguese (and their European successors) simply did not have the military or man power to go into Asia 'all guns blazing' and force the Asians into submission in the three centuries after 1498. So militarily weak were they that they could not even plug the incessant gaps that consistently sprang up all over their fictitious empire. It was, therefore, hardly surprising that 'naval technology was seldom cited [by contemporary Europeans] as an indicator of European superiority over non-Western peoples'.[38]

The myth of the European trading monopoly in Asia

One of the prime factors that has sustained the Eurocentric belief that the Europeans dominated the Asian trading system lies in the exaggerated emphasis that has been accorded the Cape route after 1500. Indeed, the consensus is that by 1500 the Islamic heartland of the world economy had almost completely faded away as the declining Ottoman empire was displaced by the all-conquering Europeans. Thus Fernand Braudel insists that one should not 'underestimate the presence of the Portuguese who were running rings around Islam in the Indian Ocean: for this triumph of European maritime *technology* continued to prevent the Turkish monster from establishing any real presence outside the Persian Gulf and the Red Sea'.[39] An equally triumphalist conclusion suggests that:

> Central Asia was . . . isolated from the early sixteenth century . . . and therefore led an existence at the margin of world history . . . The discovery of the sea route to East Asia [via the Cape] rendered the Silk Road increasingly superfluous . . . From the threshold of modern times Central Asian history becomes provincial history. This justifies us in giving no more than a rapid sketch of the following centuries.[40]

In this Eurocentric portrayal, it is as if the European creation of a new route round the Cape had created a kind of Islamic 'ox-bow lake' in which the old Muslim trade routes increasingly dried up as the Portuguese flow via the Cape took over to become the mainstream.

There are numerous problems with this Eurocentric formulation, not the least of which is that the Portuguese were merely joining the mainstream trade that was already presided over by the Ottoman Muslims.[41] More specifically, there are five main reasons why the Portuguese Cape route failed to displace Islamic trading power. First, the new Cape route was not especially profitable because it failed to lower transport costs. Second, the fact is that considerably more trade passed into Europe via the Levant and Venice, which in turn arrived via the Red Sea, Persian Gulf, and overland caravan, routes. Indeed, even as late as 1585, over three times the amounts of pepper and spices went via the Red Sea route and overland to Europe than those that went via the Cape.[42] Moreover, only 10 per cent of the Moluccan clove trade that entered Europe went round the Cape.[43] Third, recent research reveals that before 1650 far more of Europe's bullion exports to the East went via the Ottoman and Persian empires than they did via the Cape.[44] Moreover, the amounts of silver passing through these empires increased further in the 1650–1700 period (again significantly outpacing those transported round the Cape).[45] However, it might be replied that the Portuguese surely dominated the export of silver into South Asia. Striking then is the fact that between the 1580s and 1670s the amounts of silver bullion exported by all the Europeans into East Asia stood at an average of 2240 metric tonnes, which compared with the Japanese figure of 6100 tonnes.[46] And even if the European figures were underestimated by 50 per cent, Japanese bullion exports still easily exceeded those of the Europeans combined. Fourth, clear testimony to the insignificance of the Cape route was that the Portuguese derived about 80 per cent of their trading profits within East Asia via the intra-country trade. And the myth of a Portuguese trading monopoly is perhaps nowhere more clearly revealed by the fact that much of the Portuguese profits were derived from arbitrage rather than trade. Fifth and finally, the Portuguese monopoly is falsified by the simple fact that in the sixteenth century only 6 per cent of total shipping tonnage employed in the Indian Ocean trading system was Portuguese.[47]

It might well be replied that the Portuguese did at least control the spice trade. But Portuguese control of the pepper trade was striking only for its absence. In Malabar, for example, they managed to buy and ship a mere 10 per cent of the total amount that was produced. And they handled a mere 5 per cent of the Gujarati pepper trade. Moreover, when the Portuguese took control of the Indian port of Diu in 1535, Gujaratis soon started to collect massive amounts of pepper in the Bay of Bengal, from where it was traded all over the Indian Ocean. Similarly, when the Portuguese tried to block trade from Calicut new trade routes emerged, with pepper being traded from Kanara (north of Malabar) as well as from the Bay of Bengal and Acheh. Charles Boxer calculates that in 1585 the Achinese alone were exporting to Jidda (on the Red Sea) almost the same amounts of spices that the Portuguese imported into Europe via the Cape.[48] If Portuguese control over pepper was far from impressive, their control over other spices was even more ineffective. The only spice that the Portuguese achieved a near monopoly in was cinnamon. Unfortunately for the Portuguese crown this proved to be a pyrrhic victory because, 'in actual practice the chief profits were reaped by the governors and officials who embezzled or traded in cinnamon, despite all the legislation enacted at Goa and Lisbon to prevent such malpractices'.[49]

At this point it might be claimed that there was a Portuguese trading monopoly and the proof lies in the Portuguese *cartaz* system that was enforced throughout the Indian Ocean. That is, all non-Portuguese ships had to carry a passport (*cartaz*) which required the carrier to pay money or taxes to the Portuguese. But the *cartaz* system ironically turned out to be more a tacit concession by the Portuguese that they were simply unable to establish, let alone maintain, a trading monopoly throughout Asia. What the conventional Eurocentric view misses is that the *cartaz* was, if anything, a resource that was used by the Asians to serve their own ends. Thus many Asian merchants flew the Portuguese flag not so much as a sign of submission but as a means to take advantage of the lower customs duties in the Portuguese ports (because Portuguese ships paid much lower tariff rates – 3.5 per cent as opposed to 6 per cent). And even for those not carrying a *cartaz*, 'acceptance of Portuguese control really only meant that extra customs duties of about 5 per cent had to be paid. This was all Portuguese control meant, and this comparatively trifling sum could be easily recouped by charging slightly higher prices.'[50] Moreover, many Asian ship-owners *chose* to buy a *cartaz* because it was much cheaper than arming their ships. The problem the Asian merchants faced was not so much that they were unable to match Portuguese military power, but that prior to the Portuguese arrival the Indian Ocean trading system had been conducted along peaceful lines. Accordingly for the Asians, arming ships was not only unnecessary but economically irrational. Thus 'while the Portuguese had decided to invest in arms so as to collect protection payments, the Gujarati decided to pay protection money instead [which] . . . enabled them to continue trading in their own right'.[51] In any case, this proved to be the cheaper or more 'economically rational' option. It is also notable that after the so-called 'imperial ban' in 1434 many private Chinese merchants sailed with papers purchased in Melaka or Macao. Because this made the ships officially Portuguese so they were able to successfully circumvent the ban (and cheaply at that).[52]

Thus for many Asian merchants, the Portuguese flag was in fact a 'flag of convenience' rather than inconvenience. And had the Indian Ocean been dominated by the Portuguese to the virtual exclusion of all others (which is clearly not the case), how do we explain the fact that Gujaratis and other Eastern merchant diasporas were happy to voluntarily cooperate with them and finance much of the Portuguese trade? For there were crucial trading advantages that the Asians enjoyed by forging symbiotic trading alliances with the Portuguese.[53]

Even when the Asians chose not to pay the money the Portuguese usually found that there was little that they could do. For example, if the Japanese 'Red Seal' ships were attacked by the Portuguese (or any European power for that matter) they reported the incident to the Japanese authorities at Nagasaki, who then seized and held the European ships and only released them when the required compensation was paid. This returns us to the earlier point about military inferiority. The reality was that the dreams of conquest soon subsided and the Portuguese settled down to become one of the many trading groups of the Indian Ocean. Indeed, according to Tomé Pires in his *Suma Oriental*, even at their so-called stronghold – Melaka – no fewer than eighty-four languages were spoken,[54] suggesting that the Portuguese were merely one among many other trading diasporas (and not a particularly significant one at that).

Much the same fate confronted the Dutch. Despite their very best efforts, the reality of constructing an imperial monopolistic trading system proved to be no more than a dream. In particular, attempts at monopolising trade and sending prices up often backfired. The best example here involves the Dutch attempt at creating a monopoly in cloves. Having destroyed the clove trees in the areas outside of their control, prices doubled by the 1660s. But this soon led to unrest in European markets. The solution came with the importation into Europe of Brazilian 'clove-wood'. In the end, Dutch attempts at monopoly backfired, as an oversupply of cheap cloves flooded into Europe from Brazil, the effect of which was to reduce the Dutch profits from what had been one of their most lucrative Asian operations.[55] In short, the Dutch were unable to enforce this because of global competitive pressures.

More generally though, despite its very best efforts, the VOC (the Dutch East India Company) was unable to create a monopoly market anywhere in Asia. Only in one particular product did the Dutch come anywhere near this – in cloves – though this quickly proved to be a pyrrhic victory, as was just noted. Moreover, this example turns out to be the exception that proves the 'anti-Eurocentric rule'. For in every other product market that the VOC was involved in, highly competitive global market conditions ensured that the vainglorious boast of a Dutch trading monopoly was based more on wishful thinking than fact. Many examples could be given. But two of the more illustrative concern the trade in cotton goods in the north-west Indian Ocean. Here the Dutch had to compete with the Gujarati merchants. In this trade, the Dutch managed to gain a paltry 10 per cent of market share. Moreover, the Gujaratis enjoyed higher profit margins than the Dutch. This was naturally a source of considerable irritation for the VOC, and the company enquired into the reasons for this. As Van Santen reports:

> How was a humble Gujarati merchant able to compete with the mighty VOC? The answer given by the company servants themselves sounds quite convincing. The Indian trader simply operated at far lower costs . . . Besides, as the Dutch servants admitted, he often had a much more thorough knowledge of how the market worked when he bought and sold his *baftas*, *tapechindes* or *chelas*.[56]

Van Santen goes on to point out on the same page that, 'after several decades of disappointing financial results the VOC admitted defeat, and in the 1660s it ended this trade'. The VOC also tried to enter the cotton trade in Mocha, but faced similar problems. Here the VOC exported around 70,000 pieces of cotton in the mid-seventeenth century. But this appeared paltry alongside the Gujarati figure of 990,000 pieces in 1647.[57] Thus the Dutch, like their Portuguese counterpart, found that they had little choice but to settle back and become one alongside many Eastern trading groups that plied their trade in the Asian system.

The myth of European political dominance in Asia

The final question now becomes: if military power could not secure a European trading monopoly how then did the Europeans manage to secure their, albeit modest, position or toehold in the Asian zone of trade? The Europeans – first, the Portuguese and later the Dutch and English – had no choice but to collaborate, cooperate with, and sometimes kowtow to, the stronger Asian polities and merchants. For the fact is that despite the initial vainglorious proclamation of 'death to the (Islamic) infidel', when the Portuguese arrived in the Indies 'they also entered the domain of hegemonic Islam' and had no choice but to cooperate.[58]

There were a number of aspects to this mutual collaboration or partnership. First, Asian rulers granted the Portuguese a limited form of 'extra-territoriality', which included the key settlements of Macao in China, São Tomé on the Indian Coromandel coast and Hughli in Bengal. Second, given their lack of resources, the Portuguese had no choice but to rely on local sources of finance, especially from the Indian *banians*. Third, there was considerable intermingling of Portuguese and Asian traders, to the advantage of both. Asian merchants often had more goods on a Portuguese ship than did the Portuguese traders. As Pearson notes,

> It seems that Portuguese sent goods on Gujarati ships, and vice versa, in a promiscuous and intermingled fashion quite typical of private Portuguese country trade in general. Here, rather than the grandiloquent state attempt at monopoly, was where the interest of most Portuguese was involved.[59]

And fourth, the Portuguese had no choice but to rely on local sources of knowledge. As Braudel explains:

In Kandahar . . . a Hindu merchant, taking the Spanish traveller for a Portuguese, offered his services because as he explained, 'the people of your nation do not speak the same language of these countries so you are sure to encounter difficulties unless you find someone to guide you'. Help, collaboration, collusion, coexistence, symbiosis – all these became necessary as time went by.[60]

Much the same conclusion applied to the Dutch and English right down to about 1800. As with the Portuguese, the Dutch and English intermingled with Asians in a variety of ways, not the least of which involved the mutual hiring of crews and even the hiring of whole vessels, as well as borrowing Asian capital.[61] One sign of this was that the Dutch and English soon went the same way as the Portuguese, becoming ensconced in the lucrative intra-Asian 'country' trade. Indeed, the directors of the VOC wrote in 1648 that, 'the country trade and the profit from it are the soul of the Company which must be looked after carefully because if the soul decays, the entire body would be destroyed'.[62] And as we noted in ch. 4, the Dutch relied on bullion trading for the vast majority of their income. Similarly, facing a chronic lack of products to trade with in Asia the English also ended up by ensconcing themselves in the intra-country trade:

> Unable to fill even its 10 per cent export quota, the company [EIC] had to resort to over- and under-invoicing to reduce 'total' exports, and it was under constant pressure to find financing for its Asian imports in Asia itself. Therefore, it engaged in the intra-Asian 'country trade', which was much more developed and profitable than the Asia–Europe trade.[63]

Once again, both the Dutch and English quickly found that they had little choice but to collaborate, sometimes kowtow and at all times rely on the goodwill of Asian merchants and rulers.[64] And there was no more poignant expression of the levels of humiliation that the Europeans were prepared to tolerate merely to gain a small slice of the lucrative Asian trade than in the Dutch experience in Japan. There they were confined to the tiny island of Deshima (measuring 82 paces by 236), in the port of Nagasaki. For more than two centuries:

> The Dutch were spied on by their Japanese servants and controlled by a 150-strong official interpreter corps. Just one ship a year was allowed to call and its officers were usually 'beaten with sticks as if they were dogs'. They were allowed to visit the mainland once a year in order to pay homage to the shogun.[65]

Conclusion

In sum, the greatest legacy of the Portuguese (as well as the Dutch and English) seaborne 'empire' was not how much but how little things changed in terms of Asia's dominance of the global economy between 1500 and 1750/1800. The conclusion is hard to avoid: the 'European age' or the 'Vasco da Gama epoch of Asia' turns out to be but retro-spective Eurocentric wishful thinking. This simultaneously affirms the arguments made in ch. 4: that India and South-east Asia, Japan, China as well as the Ottoman and Persian empires were economically and politically strong enough to resist the European incursion, at least until about 1800. In the light of all this it is instructive to finish by comparing the imperial boast issued by the Portuguese king, Manuel I, with that of the Ottoman emperor, Selim 'the Grim'. Manuel boasted in a letter to the pope of 28 August 1499 that he was: 'Lord of Guinea and of the Conquests, Navigations, and Commerce of Ethiopia, Arabia, Persia, and India'. While this might well have impressed the pope it proved to be an entirely fictitious claim. In this respect Selim's proud boast was far nearer the truth:

> Now all of the territories of Egypt, Malaytia, Aleppo, Syria, the city of Cairo, Upper Egypt, Ethiopia, Yemen, the lands up to the borders of Tunisia, the Hijaz, the cities of Mekka, Medina and Jerusalem, may God increase the honoring and respecting of them completely and fully, have been added to the Ottoman Empire.

Also closer to the truth were the words of the Ottoman sultan, Suley-man (whom the Europeans called 'the Magnificent'), pronounced in 1538:

> I am Suleyman, in whose name the Friday sermon is read in Mecca and Medina. In Baghdad I am the Shah, in the Byzantine realms the Caesar and in Egypt the Sultan, who sends his fleets to the seas of Europe, the Maghrib and India.[66]

In conclusion, therefore, it is necessary to correct Roberts's quotation (cited at the beginning): 'if we are merely talking about the facts, about what happened [between 1500–1800] . . . then it is quite *incorrect* to put Europe at the centre of the [Asian] story'. Much the same conclusion applies to the development of Europe in these centuries, to which I now turn.

Part III
The West as a late developer
and the advantages of
backwardness: oriental
globalisation and the
reconstruction of Western
Europe as the advanced West,
1492–1850

8 The myth of 1492 and the impossibility of America:

the Afro-Asian contribution to the catch up of the West, 1492–c. 1700

It is well to observe the force and virtue and consequences of discoveries. These are to be nowhere seen more conspicuously than in printing, gunpowder, and the magnet [compass]. For these three have changed the whole face and state of things throughout the world.

Francis Bacon, 1620

'The great age of European expansion' was no outpouring of pent-up [rational] dynamism. It was launched from the insecure edges of a contracting civilization . . . Fifteenth-century Europe will appear to [distant future historians], if they notice at all, as stagnant and introspective . . . [Its] economy as a whole still suffered a permanently adverse trading balance with Islam and could not guarantee to feed its own population.

Felipe Fernández-Armesto

[N]o equality was possible or desirable for the 'darkies'. In line with this conviction . . . Catholic and Protestant, at first damned the heathen blacks with the 'curse of Canaan', then held out hope of freedom through 'conversion', and finally acquiesced in a . . . status of human slavery.

W. E. B. Du Bois

One of the key years in the Eurocentric chronology of world history is 1492. It is taken as axiomatic that the discovery of the world would fall to the Europeans. For by then only they had developed what Max Weber called a 'rational restlessness' and 'ethic of world mastery' that enabled modern development on the one hand and the conquest of the world on the other. And the most familiar sign of this was Columbus's 'discovery' of America. By contrast, the East was governed by an irrational mind set and long-term fatalism that produced but a passive conformity to, and retreat from, the world. Thus its fate was to wallow in economic backwardness and simply wait for the Europeans to discover and emancipate it. Here I seek to critique the Eurocentric 'myth of 1492': that Europe was the architect of its own development and had arrived at the pinnacle of the world by the end of the fifteenth century.

The fact is that not only were Columbus and Da Gama pre-empted by the Afro-Asian age of discovery that began after 500 (ch. 2), but Europe was still behind much of the East in terms of economic and military power until the nineteenth century (chs. 3 and 4). This chapter claims that in the 1500–1800 period Europe was merely catching up with the East. Europe was not an early but a late developer, enjoying the 'advantages of economic backwardness'.[1] That is, it did not single-handedly pioneer its own development but continued to assimilate or emulate the superior resource portfolios pioneered by the early Eastern developers, all of which had diffused across through oriental globalisation (see below). Moreover, Europe's appropriation of American and African resources also helped it to catch up (see first section below).

The impossibility of America and the myth of Christopher Columbus
Eurocentrism celebrates Columbus's discovery as the sign of Europe's modern genius. This genius is allegedly found in Europe's advanced shipping and superior navigational techniques as well as the emergence of modern scientific and rational ideas connected to the so-called Western Renaissance. In the last chapter I discussed the 'myth of Vasco da Gama', where I claimed that virtually all of the aspects that enabled his arrival in India – his ships and navigational technologies and techniques – were in one way or another derived from either China or the Islamic Middle East. The same conclusion applies to Columbus. For without these manifold Eastern gifts, Columbus would almost certainly never have crossed the Atlantic in the first place.

The assumption that Columbus represented a set of modern rational-scientific ideas is a myth precisely because his voyages (like those of Vasco da Gama) were fundamentally entwined within a medieval Christian crusading mentality that had first emerged in the eleventh century. Because I dealt with this in detail in the last chapter I shall not belabour the point here. Suffice it to note that Christopher Columbus, like Da Gama and the Spanish monarchy, was obsessed by the idea of a crusade against Islam. And though it is indeed true that he was determined to find gold, this was necessary to finance the reconquest of the Holy Land (given Europe's backwardness relative to the Ottoman empire). On 26 December 1492 Columbus wrote in his diary that he 'hope[d] to find gold in such quantities that the [Spanish] kings will be able, within three years, to prepare for and undertake the conquest of the Holy Land'.[2] Most significantly in his 'Lettera Rarissima' in 1503 he cited Marco Polo's words: 'the Emperor of Cathay some time since sent for wise men to teach him the religion of Christ'. Is it possible that Columbus saw his mission as the return of one of the 'wise kings' back to the Orient to deliver the Word? Certainly he saw himself 'as chosen, as charged with a divine mission'.[3] It was no coincidence that the year Columbus set sail saw the official establishment of the Spanish Inquisition as well as the reconquest of Granada from the Muslims. For Columbus himself recorded the direct link between the recapture of Granada and his voyage at the beginning of his first journal.[4] Moreover, as we saw in the last chapter, various popes had prescribed the voyages through a series of papal bulls. No less importantly, Spain's 'conquest' of the Americas and Portugal's 'conquest' of Asia were granted official sanction – and thus spiritual legitimacy – by Pope Alexander VI in the 1494 Treaty of Tordesillas (though, of course, various Protestant European powers subsequently rejected its legitimacy).

To the extent that there was anything new it was that the journeys were entwined within an emerging European identity which inscribed the West as superior to 'non-Europe'. Paradoxically, this went hand in hand with Christianity (racism would only emerge much later, as I explain in ch. 10). Nevertheless it was clearly evident that the Europeans viewed the Native Indians (and subsequently the Black

Africans) as so decidedly inferior that they were axiomatically considered 'ripe for exploitation' and 'ripe for conversion'. The label 'Indian' is especially significant because it signified to Columbus the 'impossibility of America'. To his dying day he obstinately refused to accept that he had failed to discover China or the East Indies (which is why the Natives were called Indians). Indeed, he came up with all manner of bogus geographical justifications (all of which were framed within orthodox Christian conceptions of world geography) to prove that he had in fact discovered Asia. Of the many examples, two are noteworthy. He believed that Cuba was Cipangu (Marco Polo's Japan), though having landed there he properly changed his mind, but then concluded that it was instead the Chinese mainland that he had so desperately been seeking. And when the Native 'Indians' spoke about the Cariba (the inhabitants of the Caribbean) Columbus heard this as Caniba (i.e. the subjects of the Great Khan of Asia), once again 'confirming' the impossible! Hence Edmundo O'Gorman's perceptive claim that Columbus invented rather than discovered America.[5] Columbus's frame of mind was aptly captured in the words of Bartolomé de Las Casas: 'how marvellous a thing it is how whatever a man strongly desires and has firmly set in his imagination, all that he hears and sees at each step he fancies to be in its favor'.[6] Not surprisingly, naming this continent 'Columbia' proved to be an impossibility. Moreover, nowhere was the 'impossibility of America' clearer in Columbus's mind than in his perception of the peoples whom he encountered there.

When Columbus landed in the Americas he espoused two views of the Natives both of which were very much informed by his own pre-formed Christian worldview. Those who greeted him with relative friendliness were imagined as innocent 'children of nature' who would be fitting receptacles for Christianity. The hostile ones – which included those who would not accept conversion – he came to believe would have to be subdued either by force or slavery or extermination. Hence the idea of the 'noble savage', who could be assimilated, contrasted with the 'ignoble savage', whose lot was to be slavery or extermination. This was the backdrop to the famous Valladolid controversy

of 1550 in which Juan Ginés de Sepúlveda's conception of the ignoble savage faced off against Bartolomé de Las Casas's conception of
the noble savage. Las Casas won out because the Catholic Church
supported him. And it only did so precisely because to admit that
the Natives could not be Christianised would be to go against the
theory of monogenesis outlined in the Bible. Moreover, in 1537 the
pope concluded that not only were the Natives capable of receiving
Christianity but 'they desire exceedingly to receive it'.[7] Nevertheless, Columbus – alongside his fellow Spaniards – did not 'discover'
America but interpreted it (or invented it) through the selective prism
of his own pre-formed worldview. Or as Todorov put it: 'He knows in
advance what he will find; the concrete experience is there to illustrate a truth already possessed'.[8] America did not exist in and of its
own right to be 'discovered' but was understood only through imposed
or projected external Christian perceptions; hence, for Columbus, the
double impossibility of America.

Despite the ideological victory of Las Casas over Sepúlveda it
would be entirely wrong to assume that the Church's conception of
the inherent equality of all men precluded the unequal treatment of
some of them. Indeed, the two views of the Indian Natives gave rise
to an early version of the imperial discourse that would come to full
fruition in Britain mainly in the eighteenth and nineteenth centuries
(see ch. 10). The 'benign' view of Las Casas still very much gave
rise to an imperial mission in which the Natives would be 'culturally converted'; their identity and cultural practices would be transformed along Western Christian lines. And crucially Las Casas never
challenged the right of the Spanish to rule over the Natives nor did
he believe that they should be granted self-determination. Thus in
Todorov's terms, at all times the debate presupposed the inferiority
of the Natives, and was based on an ideology of enslavement versus
a colonialist/assimilationist ideology.[9] In this way these apparently
opposing ideological views of the Natives sat logically, albeit awk-
wardly, together.

Nevertheless it is worth noting that these views appeared 'relatively tolerant' compared to those of the Puritan settlers in the north,

whose paranoid antipathy towards the Natives there resulted not in 'cultural conversion' but in the 'first solution' of extermination of the Indian Other, as well as social apartheid.[10] And while the epic film, *How the West was Won*, tells us of a pioneering and freedom-loving people that built the greatest civilisation on Earth, there is a poignant silence that disrupts the celebration. For the notion that the Indians were but 'savage animals' (Timothy Dwight) or 'blood-hounds' (John Adams) who had to be weeded out 'from their dens' (Roger Williams), 'had by the 1770s become an axiom so universally accepted it was writ large on the birth certificate of the United States of America'.[11]

But to return to the narrative: the discourse of the Catholic Church bore some (though clearly not all) of the hallmarks of the British imperial discourse that would emerge during and after the eighteenth century. Indeed, the eighteenth-century European notion that 'civilisation' was the monopoly of the West was in fact 'a secularized version of the primitive Western Christian proposition: "Nemini salus . . . nisi in Ecclesia" [or "extra-Ecclesiam non est"]'.[12] That is, there could be no salvation outside of the Western Catholic Church. This was made clear right from the outset with the ritualistic Spanish reading of the 'Requirement' (*Requirimiento*), which was 'an ultimatum for Indians to acknowledge the superiority of Christianity or be warred upon'.[13] The key part of the text stated that:

> On behalf of His Majesty . . . I . . . his servant, messenger . . . beg and require you as best I can . . . [that] you recognize the church as lord and superior of the universal world . . . [If you do so] His Majesty and I in his name will receive you . . . But if you do not do it . . . with the help of God, I will enter forcefully against you and I will make war everywhere . . . I will subject you to the yoke and obedience of the Church . . . I will take your wives and children, and I will make them slaves . . . and I will do to you all the evil and damages that a lord may do to vassals who do not obey or receive him.[14]

And it was precisely this mentality that led the Church to unprob-
lematically assume that it could simply divide, or carve up the belly
of, the 'non-European' world and bequeath the spoils to the two major
Catholic countries – Spain and Portugal (via the Treaty of Tordesillas). All in all, European perceptions meant that it was simply impossible to either conceive of the American Natives in their own right
or to treat them with dignity, equality or fairness. For the effect of
all this was to render the Natives a blank page or empty vessel that
was waiting to be inscribed or filled, and thus utilised, by Western
Christianity.

The Africans were also imported into, and degraded within,
Europe's 'American experience'. Nevertheless, to search for a ready-
made and coherent ideology here would be problematic because the
degradation of the Africans was founded on a set of *ad hoc* Christian ideas. One way or another the Europeans came to believe that
African slavery was natural because it was divinely sanctioned. One
of the most important ideas was that of the biblical Curse of Ham (or
more accurately the Curse of Canaan). The Genesis story – laid out in
ch. 9, verses 18–26 – has it that Ham had seen his father Noah naked
and drunk and had mocked him. For this God cursed not Ham but
his son Canaan (even though this came to be dubbed as the 'Curse of
Ham'). (It seems that it was the medieval Arabs who initially shifted
the curse from Canaan to Ham.[15]) Nevertheless, the curse condemned
Canaan (and all of his descendants) as, 'a servant of servants shall he
be unto his brethren' (ch. 9, verse 25). Even so, it is important to note
that this religious belief did not constitute a fully worked out position.
As George Frederickson points out, the curse operated:

> on the level of popular belief and mythology rather than as formal
> ideology. In fact it was refuted by learned authorities, who merely
> had to note that the curse fell on Canaan specifically and not on
> his brother Cush, who, according to the standard biblical exegesis
> of sixteenth and seventeenth centuries, was the actual progenitor
> of the African race.[16]

It is also notable that while race as a distinct concept did not figure in the derogatory perception of the Africans, nevertheless, as George Frederickson points out, after about 1440 the Portuguese were trading Black slaves. Thus he suggests that, 'even before the discovery of America, some Iberian Christians were more likely to conceive of blacks as destined by God to be "hewers of wood and carriers of water" than to view them as exemplars of the Christian virtues'.[17] Nevertheless, the association of blackness with slavery is an idea that would take several centuries to ferment within the European mind set, even if the 'inferiority' of the Negro had already been established. Ironically too it was the ending of the slave trade that in part helped prompt the rise of scientific racism.

The key point is that it was these derogatory perceptions of the Black Africans that legitimised, or were instrumental to, the tragedy that subsequently unfolded. Because this has been so well covered in the literature, I shall simply point to a few notable features of this story. We should not fall prey to the claim made by some historians that the horrors of the 'Middle Passage' (the sea journey across from Africa) are but an exaggerated product of 'Abolitionist propaganda'. Particularly harmful was the danger of physical exhaustion brought on principally through dehydration and dysentery. The slaves often had little choice but to relieve themselves in the space in which they sat. As one contemporary ship's surgeon explained: 'The deck, that is the floor of their rooms, was so covered with blood and mucus which had proceeded from them ... that it resembled a slaughter house'.[18] Indeed, the stench of the slave ships was so bad that the American Natives knew in advance of their impending arrival even when they were still miles out to sea. As is well known, the ships' captains frequently had sick Negroes thrown overboard. As one contemporary observer informs us of the late-eighteenth century Liverpool slave trade, 'The negroes were so often thrown overboard that the course of sharks might be seen for miles watching these ships and waiting for their food'.[19] The reality of the journey was conveyed in the words of the contemporary Black slave, Olaudah Equiano, who tells us first-hand that:

> I was soon put down under the decks [of the slave ship], and there
> I received such a salutation in my nostrils as I had never
> experienced in my life: so that, with the loathsome-ness of the
> stench, and crying together, I became so sick and low that I was
> not able to eat. I now wished for the last friend, death, to relieve
> me.[20]

Indeed, for many slaves, death frequently came to the rescue. In the literature concerning the numbers transported there is a lower estimate of 12 million and an upper figure of about 20 million, though most authorities agree on about 15 million. There is also a consensus that an average of at least 10 per cent died. Thus a reasonable, if not conservative, estimate indicates that some 1.5 million Negro slaves died in the Middle Passage alone. If such rates of mortality had occurred among a young adult English population at that time, it would have been considered a tragic epidemic.[21]

Upon arrival the Africans were branded with a red-hot poker and then auctioned off like cattle to slave owners.[22] And while the treatment of the white English working classes in the eighteenth and nineteenth centuries was barely humane, they were not subjected to the same ruthless levels of exploitation and cultural degradation experienced by the Negroes in the Americas. Life expectancy in what were effectively 'forced labour camps' was no more than seven years.[23] Particularly disturbing was the institution of 'seasoning' or 'acclimatisation'. This was a three-year period in which the slave-owners attempted to 'obliterate the identities of their newly acquired slaves, to break their wills and sever any bonds with the past'.[24]

A pertinent discussion of the dehumanising aspect of slavery undertaken in the Americas is provided by Orlando Patterson in his book, *Slavery and Social Death*.[25] As he points out, the treatment of the African slave in the Americas went well beyond the concept of alienation that Marxist materialists invoke. It involved a process which sought to thoroughly strip the identity and, indeed, humanity of the slave altogether. Even so, John Thornton perceptively cautions us not to assume that the Europeans always succeeded in dehumanising the Negroes.[26] Nor is it correct to view the Africans more generally as simply 'passive victims' of superior European power. For as C. L. R. James and W. E. B. Du Bois originally pointed out, the slaves engaged in many resistance strategies ranging from suicide, to working slowly, to open revolts.[27] Indeed, the slave revolts were one factor in prompting the Abolition movement. Moreover, the slave trade would probably not have been possible without the active help provided by indigenous African elites who rounded up the slaves in Africa in the first place. And nor should we forget that the Africans played an important role in creating the global economy long before the Europeans disingenuously claimed it as their own creation.

Similarly the Spanish view of the Native Indians as inferior – especially those who resisted the Christian imperial project – led on to another of the world's great human tragedies. When trying to esti-mate the numbers of Natives who died, we immediately confront the problem of estimating the population levels of 1492 (just prior to Columbus's arrival). These range from 8 million to 113 million. A median point figure of 54 million is provided by William Denevan,[28] a statistic that many have accepted. A generally accepted figure of those who died stands at 90 per cent of the pre-1492 population. And when we 'factor in' the new births after 1492, it seems likely that some-where between 50 and 100 million died as a direct result of the Euro-pean incursion during the sixteenth century. Thus while the Native population comprised some 13 per cent of total world population in 1492, it had crashed to just over 1 per cent by 1600. The conclusion is hard to avoid. As Jan Carew noted in relation to the destruction wreaked in the Greater Antilles:

> For the [European] interlopers it was a glorious beginning, but for the unwitting and hospitable Lucayos, it was the beginning of the end. In less than forty years, Spanish conquistadores, settlers, slave-hunters, disease, hunger and despair would, like harbingers of the Apocalypse, rain death and destruction upon the innocent heads of most of the inhabitants.[29]

A further Eurocentric myth has it that the 'conquest of the Americas' was a clear sign of European military superiority (known as the 'Black legend').[30] Although this was a factor, nevertheless it cannot provide a sufficient explanation for the unfolding tragedy. Initially the major factor that promoted the European conquest was the importation or introduction of Eurasian germs and diseases.[31] Note that it was not the genetic inferiority of the Natives, but the fact that they had not developed adequate immune systems against the particular Eurasian diseases that was decisive. As Alfred Crosby points out, the conclusion is that it was the diseases that weakened the resistance of the Natives thereby easing the way for European guns to do their worst.[32] Or in Blaut's pithy formulation, 'The Americans were not conquered: they were infected'.[33] Nevertheless 'Black legend' or no legend, we should not brush over the fact that the brutal treatment of these peoples at the hands of the Spanish was a dark hour for humanity.

No less importantly, the derogatory perceptions of the Native Indians and Africans 'naturally' rendered them fit or ripe for economic exploitation at the hands of the Europeans. The paradox of the 'impossibility of America' (or the impossibility of treating the Native Indians as well as the Africans either equally or with the remotest semblance of dignity) was that it opened up the possibility of plundering their resources – not least their land, labour and bullion. As we noted in ch. 3, in 1500 Europe was unable to produce much that was of any interest to Asian consumers, and yet the Europeans were busy buying Asian goods. Indeed, the clearest sign of Europe's backwardness in 1500 was its perennial trade deficit with Asia. Even the Eurocentric scholar, John Roberts, concedes that 'without that stream [from the Americas], above all of silver, there could hardly have been a trade with Asia for there was almost nothing produced in Europe that Asia wanted'.[34] Because the Europeans could not sufficiently produce goods that the Asians wanted, they had to pay with bullion (mainly silver). But European reserves were insufficient. Accordingly, the plundered or appropriated American (and African) bullion came to the Europeans' rescue, as did the productive labour of the American Natives and African slaves that extracted the bullion.[35] Indeed, while the African slaves shared in the mining of silver with the Native Americans, they nevertheless dominated the extraction of gold.[36] It was mainly here that the African contribution to the catch up of the West was initially manifested. In the 300 years after 1500, 85 per cent of the world's silver production and 70 per cent of the world's gold output came from the Americas. The vast majority of the bullion that was shipped to Europe then went out to Asia to finance one of the most sustained continental trade deficits the world has ever seen. The majority of the bullion went to China, though significant amounts also went to India.

A further key point here – as noted in ch. 3 – is that gold and silver constituted global 'commodities' that were bought and sold in order to derive a profit from differences in bullion exchange rates (i.e. arbitrage); or what I called the 'global silver recycling process'. This was one of the main sources of profit for the European traders in Asia after 1498. Thus without the Native and African labour as well as the supply of Spanish American gold/silver (and indeed the strong demand for silver created by the Chinese as well as the Indian economies), there would have been no global arbitrage system. Nor would there have been a source of liquidity for the Europeans to pay for their perennial trade deficit with Asia. Last, and most importantly, during the eighteenth and nineteenth centuries the role of Black slavery, slave trading, American Black slave-production centres and Negro markets, all significantly contributed to Britain's agricultural and industrial 'breakthrough' (see ch. 11).

Finally, a further major benefit of the Americas to the Europeans was that they were used to shore up and reconstruct Western identity. Indeed, the critical factor in redefining Europe as the advanced West was the expansion of the frontier westward to the Americas after 1492. This entailed an expansion of the category of the Other, for now the African and American were included. Success in this imperial project was crucial in forging the notion – for the first time since the Roman empire – that Europe represented advanced civilisation. Thus the expanding western frontier enabled a shift in European identity from a peripheral status to a more elevated one as 'advanced civilisation'. This also enhanced the split between Eastern and Western Europe, as the latter came to develop commercial and naval power through its expansionism in the Far West, while the former landlocked region maintained feudalism and constituted a *cordon sanitaire* or defensive buffer to Islam in the East. Notable too is that after the fifteenth century the idea of 'Western Europe' also began to crystallise as the Ottoman Turks and the Eastern Europeans were imagined as barbarians.[37] Thus Western European identity became increasingly defined during the sixteenth and seventeenth centuries by its immediate 'pagan/barbarian' neighbours to the east and its 'savage' neighbours to the south and west.

If the Americas were important in enabling Western Europe to catch up with the East, so too was the assimilation of the more advanced Eastern ideas and technologies that diffused across through oriental globalisation. And it is this that constitutes the second major critique of the myth of 1492, which occupies the remainder of the chapter.

The 'Eastern Renaissance' and the three paradoxes of the Western Renaissance

Many Eurocentric scholars trace the origins of the 'European dynamic' to the Renaissance, which allegedly furnished the Europeans with the necessary 'scientific rationality' and 'individualism'. The Renaissance was supposedly a rediscovery of pure Ancient Greek science. One typical expression of this asserts that,

> Europe took nothing from the east without which modern science could not have been created; on the other hand, what it borrowed was valuable only because it was incorporated in the European intellectual tradition. And this, of course, was founded in [Ancient] Greece.[38]

But this obscures the point that many of the crucial ideas which under-pinned the European Renaissance and the subsequent scientific revo-lution (as well as the Enlightenment – see ch. 9) were in fact derived from the East, and diffused across the Islamic Bridge of the World through oriental globalisation. As Michael Edwardes notes:

> On the whole, this great period of gestation cared little or nothing for the East. The Renaissance, in effect, turned its back on the Orient, annexing instead a particular vision of the antique world. This did not, however, mean that the men of the Renaissance were not acutely aware of the existence of the East . . . The Renaissance, for all its Classical [Greek] face, was alive with influences from the East, often disguised, their source almost always unrecognized.[39]

Occasionally, however, Eurocentric writers concede that some of the Renaissance ideas came from the Middle East. But this con-cession is revoked by dismissing the possibility that the East could have had any independent role in all of this (i.e. the Islamic clause). This clause asserts that the Muslims were simply holders or trans-lators of the Ancient Greek texts, and that all the Muslims did was simply return them whence they originated. Thus we are typically told that '[u]ltimately the mantle of the Greeks passed to the Islamic world, where in the bosom of Allah, the Hellenic heritage was kept in custody until Western interest rekindled'.[40] In short, the Muslims are portrayed as but mere librarians rather than original thinkers. Though a neat story, it fails to square with the considerable evidence which points to the many independent Eastern ideas that permeated the European Renaissance. As William McNeill notes:

> Westerners discovered that the Muslims possessed a sophistication of mind and richness of learning far surpassing that available in Latin . . . The ease with which they [the Europeans] appropriated these alien inheritances has perhaps no equal in civilized history, unless it be the Greek assimilation of oriental [Egyptian] civilisation in the sixth century BC.[41]

Admittedly though this was hardly surprising given that 'the [intellectual] influence of the West in this period was virtually nil – perhaps for the very good reason that the West had so little to offer'.[42] Nevertheless, while the Chinese appear to have undergone a Renaissance in the eleventh century,[43] it was mainly the pioneering contribution of the Muslims that was crucial to the intellectual fortunes of Europe.

In the early ninth century CE the seventh Abbasid caliph, al-Ma'mūn, founded the 'House of Wisdom' (*Bayt al-Hikmah*) in Baghdad where *inter alia* Greek works – especially those of Ptolemy, Archimedes and Euclid – were translated into Arabic. But Arab scholars also drew heavily on Persian and Indian (as well as Chinese) texts on medicine, mathematics, philosophy, theology, literature and poetry. They then crafted a new corpus of knowledge – with the help of Jewish scientists and translators – that was not only more than simply an amalgam of Greek thought but one that was often critical of Greek ideas and simultaneously took them much further, frequently in new directions. This process was aided by the fact that Baghdad stood at the centre of the global economy and not only received new Asian ideas but, having reworked them, transmitted them across to Islamic Spain. Increasingly after 1000, Europeans translated the Islamic scientific texts into Latin. The fall of Spanish Toledo in 1085 was especially significant, for it was there that many European intellectuals gained access to Islamic technical books. Learning from Islam was continued by the Spanish King Alfonso X (1252–1284), largely through Jewish intermediaries (as did the Portuguese kings). Of the many examples on offer, notable here is that in 1266 Ibn Khalaf al-Murādī's important text, *The Book of Secrets about the Results of Thoughts*, was translated at the Toledan court. This text and many others would have furnished the Iberians with a great many of Islam's innovations. Finally, the Italians also directly learned of these ideas both through their trading links with the Middle East and during the Crusades. How then did the Muslim scholars add to the original Greek corpus of knowledge?

Islamic developments in mathematics

As Jack Goody properly notes, 'Mathematics was one of the fields in which parallel but not identical developments took place in the East and West. With geometry, the early development took place in Mesopotamia [in Ancient Iraq] and Egypt, and [was] only later taken up by the Greeks.'[44] Indeed, Ancient Iraqi schools taught algebra and geometry, knew of the theorem now called after Pythagoras as early as 1700 BCE, and knew the value of pi. They also developed the 'sexagesimal system' in which the circle is divided into 360 degrees, the hour into 60 minutes, the minute into 60 seconds, and the day 24 hours. Following on from Ancient Iraq through Ancient Egypt and then Greece (the latter benefiting from its proximity to these earlier developers), the next major developmental phase was initiated by the Muslims after about 800, who took these early developments much further. The pioneering mathematician, Muhammad ibn Musa al-Khwārizmī (780–847), produced the highly influential book, *On Calculation with Hindu Numerals* (c. 825). This book was largely responsible for the diffusion of the Indian numerical system into Islam and the West.[45] Interestingly, it was the Middle Eastern Phœnicians (though they called themselves *can'ani* – or Canaanites from Canaan, situated on the east coast of the Mediterranean) who first introduced numerals. Nevertheless, the vital breakthrough that the Indians had made was producing nine numbers and the zero (*śūnya*) in decimal place value. This system was subsequently adopted around 760 CE by Arab scholars.[46] In turn al-Khwārizmī's work was taken further by a number of tenth-century Islamic scholars, including al-Uqlidisi, Abu'l-Wafā al-Buzajānī, al-Māhānī, al-Kindī and Kushyar ibn Labban.[47] Having spread throughout the Middle East such ideas diffused to Islamic Spain by the end of the tenth century, where the backward Europeans gained access to them (especially via Córdoba and both the fall of Toledo in 1085 and the capture of Saragossa by the Aragonese in 1118).

At first the Europeans were slow to catch on, preferring to retain the old system based on the abacus. However, in 1202 the Pisan merchant Leonardo Fibonacci, living in Tunis, was persuaded by the new Eastern concepts and wrote a book rejecting the old abacus system in favour of the new Hindu–Arabic system. The new system finally emerged within the Italian merchant communes. And it is hardly controversial to note, as Charles Singer puts it, that the European adoption of this Eastern numerical system 'was a major factor in the rise of [Western] science, and was not without effect in determining the relations of science and technology in the sixteenth and seventeenth centuries'.[48]

Al-Khwārizmī's work on algebra was equally as important and was translated into Latin in 1145 by the Englishman Robert of Ketton as well as the Italian, Gerard of Cremona. Ketton's translation of al-Khwārizmī's name was 'Algorithmi' (hence the term 'algorithm'). And the term 'algebra' came from the title of one of al-Khwārizmī's books, *Al-Jabr W'almuqalah* (given that *al-jabr* was translated as algebra). Moreover, his book remained the major text on its subject in Europe right down to the sixteenth century. This was complemented by various Islamic innovations which went beyond the theory of Ptolemy. Ptolemy used chords which were based on a very clumsy theory. Al-Battānī substituted the sine for the chord. Moreover, spherical trigonometry was advanced by Abū'l-Wafā al-Buzajānī's theory of the tangent, Abū Nasr's theorem of the sines and Ibn al-Haytham's theorem of co-tangents.[49] It is no less noteworthy that by the beginning of the tenth century all six of the classical trigonometric functions had been defined and tabulated by Muslim mathematicians.[50] And Nasīr al-Dīn al-Tūsī's text on plane trigonometry in the mid-to-late thirteenth century was not matched by any European mathematician until 1533.[51]

Islamic conceptions of man as a rational agent

It was the Muslims (especially the Mutazilites) who propagated the idea that man was a free and rational agent – supposedly one of the *leitmotifs* of modern European thinking. Such an idea emerged not long after Muhammad's death signifying a move towards 'rational Islamic theology' (so that Muhammad's teachings could not be distorted by subsequent political authorities). Known as *ijtihad*, it involved the exercise of independent judgement and, above all, the notion that God could only be comprehended through unaided and individualistic human reason. This idea was incorporated into the works of scholars such as al-Kindī (800–873), al-Rāzī (865–925), al-Fārābi (873–950), Ibn Sīnā (980–1037), Ibn Rushd (1126–98) and, last but not least, al-Zahrāwī (936–1013). These ideas were also strikingly similar to those that inspired Martin Luther and the Reformation. Al-Rāzī's crucial claim was that all 'truth' (religious and scientific) can be attained directly by the individual human mind through rational contemplation or reason. In turn, this can only be achieved when the mind is set free from irrational emotions: in short, 'objectivity' is vital. Likewise, Ibn Rushd (known in the West as Averroës) insisted that scientific enquiry can only be achieved by breaking with religious dogma, and that God's existence could only be proved on rational grounds.

In short, these and other Islamic philosophers and scientists had a profound impact in changing European thinking. Their ideas, when assimilated by the West, enabled European thinkers to move beyond the extant Catholic belief in the authority of the divine towards the centrality of the individual. The Muslims also began to embrace objectivity and the process of scientific experiment, which later influenced the European scientific revolution.

Islamic scientific methods as a prelude to the European scientific revolution

One of the most radical aspects of the Islamic scientific revolution was the notion that Ancient Greek thought was by no means perfect and could, if not should, be challenged. Thus:

> While Muslim scientists did not wholly abandon Greek tradition, they reformulated it by introducing a revolutionary new concept of how knowledge ought to progress, a concept that still governs the way science is done today. Better instruments and better methods, they reasoned, would bring about more accurate results.[52]

This was something that the Greeks had not fully comprehended. And it was the paucity of Greek scientific experiments that the Islamic scholars sought to rectify. Moreover, Islamic scholars began to question the inherited traditions of many areas – of medicine, hygiene, optics, physics and so on. In this new scientific mode of thought, the Egyptian Ibn al-Haytham (965–1039) produced a book on optics that came to have an enormous impact in Europe. The Egyptian physician, Ibn al-Nafis (d. 1288), was no less important. His work on the human body, which contradicted the traditional position of the Greek physician, Galen, fully pre-empted the much heralded work of the Englishman, William Harvey, by no less than three and a half centuries.

Also important were the works of al-Rāzī, al-Fārābi and Ibn Sīnā. Their breakthroughs in medicine and hygiene were revolutionary in the European context. Al-Rāzī based his hospital on experimentation, where his patients were divided into two groups in order to prevent the spread of disease. This also enabled the rise of quarantining which was later avidly embraced in the West.[53] He also initiated knowledge on various diseases, though there is good evidence to suggest that he was significantly influenced by earlier Chinese innovations.[54] All in all, the 'medical works of al-Rāzī exercised for centuries a remarkable influence over the minds of the Latin West'.[55] Testimony to al-Rāzī's impact upon Europe lay in the fact that his translated works were reprinted some forty times between 1498–1866. Abu Nasr al-Fārābi (known in the West as Avennasar) wrote an important book, *Catalog of the Sciences*, which was translated into Latin by Gerard of Cremona and John of Seville. Notable too was Ibn Sīnā (known in the West as Avicenna) whose famous book, *Canon of Medicine*, was translated into Latin in the late twelfth century (as was his encyclopedia, *The Book of Healing*). Moreover, his *Canon of Medicine* became the founding text for European schools of medicine up to the latter part of the sixteenth century. In general, the Arabic influence on the development of the important school of Salerno after 1050 was profound.[56] Interesting too is that the Chinese also initiated many important aspects of modern medicine, including the practices of immunology, forensics and medical examinations, all of which diffused across to the West via the Islamic Bridge of the World.[57]

Islamic breakthroughs in astronomy were no less influential. Living in the fourteenth century, Ibn al-Shātir of the Marāgha school developed a series of mathematical models which were almost exactly the same as those developed about 150 years later by Copernicus in his heliocentric theory. That these models were so similar led Noel Swerdlow to suggest that it 'seems too remarkable a series of coincidences to admit the possibility of independent discovery [on the part of Copernicus]'.[58] Other experts have also argued that Copernicus borrowed al-Shātir's models.[59] Fittingly, Copernicus has been described as 'the most noted follower of the Maragha School'.[60] Moreover, the heliocentric theory was at least implicitly first discovered in the Ancient Egyptian 'Hermetic texts'.[61] Interestingly, Copernicus made explicit mention of the Ancient Egyptian, Hermes Trismegistus, in the introduction to his major book. Moreover, 'Trismegistus is not someone any scientist today would acknowledge as a forebear, yet during the Renaissance this shadowy Egyptian enjoyed an immense status'.[62] Also noteworthy was al-Khwārizmī's earlier work on astronomy. Not only did he improve on Ptolemy's text, *Geography*, but he also produced various maps that included the positions of many of the stars. These maps would prove important for oceanic commercial trade. Al-Khwārizmī also calculated the circumference of the Earth to within a margin of error of less than 0.04 per cent (i.e. he was only 41 metres out). His work was taken further by both al-Bīrūnī and al-Idrīsī.

Crucially, therefore, early Islamic thinking would have an impact that went well beyond the European Renaissance, and helped inform Europe's scientific revolution. The Baconian idea that science should be based on experimentation and that the maximum benefit could be had from the division of labour was almost word for word the same argument made by the earlier Islamic scholars. As Robert Briffault has pointed out:

Discussions as to who was the originator of the experimental
method . . . are part of the colossal [Eurocentric] misrepresentation
of the origins of European civilisation. The experimental method
of Arabs was by [Francis] Bacon's time widespread and eagerly
cultivated throughout Europe.[63]

Nevertheless, it is possible to dismiss this by positing another of the
Islamic clauses: that even if new scientific and individualistic ideas
were pioneered in Islam, they were subsequently discarded as the religious authorities sought to reassert their control. Hence this was but
an 'abortive Islamic revolution'. This is then counterposed to the
European situation where an absence of religious obstacles ensured
the unfettered development of Western science (which in turn sustained the 'European dynamic'). The immediate problem with the
Islamic clause is that it fails to detract from the simple point that
Islamic intellectual achievements were vitally important in enabling
the intellectual advance in Europe – the Renaissance and the scientific revolution in particular. And although the Europeans eventually
succeeded in taking these Eastern ideas further,[64] without the original
Eastern ideas in the first place there would have been little or nothing
to take further.

But there is a further dimension here that should be mentioned.
For it is possible that the Renaissance owes a debt not just to the
Muslims, Indians and the Chinese, but also to Black Africans.[65] As
W. E. B. Du Bois pointed out, the original Greek scientific texts not
only passed to the Middle East but also diffused to Africa, especially
Alexandria and Cairo (which, as we saw in ch. 2, economically dom-
inated the Italian traders up to and beyond 1517). Moreover, the
Black Sudan had long been a centre of culture and learning, much
of which was transmitted back to medieval Europe. However, while
Egyptians undoubtedly contributed to the development of scientific
knowledge,[66] especially via the Egyptian Hall of Wisdom (*Dār al-
Hikmah*) established in 1005, their ethnic origins are not clear. What
is clear, though, is that many of the so-called Middle Eastern Moors,

particularly those who resided in Spain, were Black African in origin (hence the medieval European term 'Blackamoor'). This hybridisation of races also allowed for an intermingling of ideas. Moreover, Black Africans visited Spain on lecture tours in the universities there, while Spaniards often travelled to North Africa to learn of their ideas. Further research might reveal that some of the famous Egyptian figures, a few of whom have already been discussed, were Black in origin (Dhu'l-Nun being an obvious example, while the North African, St Augustine – from a much earlier period, of course – was another). Interestingly, Leonardo Da Vinci's School of Athens depicts Averroës (Ibn Rushd) as dark in colour. And certainly ancient Black Egyptian – or Nubian – thought influenced the Renaissance especially via the importation of the 'Hermetic texts' (many of which were translated after 1460 by Marsilio Ficino at the court of Cosimo di Medici).[67] Either way though, Du Bois leaves us with the intriguing rhetorical questions:

> Was it possible or inherently probable that black Africa had no creative part [in the Renaissance]? That none of the science came from black brains? That the Europe which praised and lauded black folk of that day, did it in mere curiosity or charity? Or is it more probable that the cultural contributions of many Negroids have been forgotten or unrecognized because their color seemed unimportant, or was unknown or forgotten; and because to modern Europe, black civilization has been a contradiction in terms?[68]

Finally, it is important to note that this whole process was founded on three cruel paradoxes. First, at the same time that the Muslims were supplying the Europeans with new and more advanced ideas, the Christians were demonising Islam and waging war with them through the Crusades. Second, the East furnished many of the ideas of the Western Renaissance, only to find that the Europeans subsequently turned around and disingenuously claimed that they had independently come up with the ideas in the first place. Moreover, the Europeans later on pronounced the West to be the embodiment of advanced rational civilisation while the East was dismissed as an inferior civilisation that was but an irrational intellectual wasteland. The third and cruellest paradox was that it was this construct of the West-as-superior (as defined principally by 'scientific rationality') that would later on prompt the launching of the Western imperial civilising mission against the East.

The Eastern origins of printing: the myth of Johann Gutenberg

There can be no doubt that the advent of printing had massive consequences for the development of Europe. First and foremost, the impact of the Renaissance and scientific revolution would have been considerably weakened in the absence of printed books. As Marie Boas explains:

> the printing-press . . . made easier the progress of science: it became increasingly normal to publish one's discoveries, thus assuring that new ideas were not lost, but were available to provide a basis for the work of others . . . Publication enormously facilitated dissemination, and it is generally true that scientific work not printed had very little chance of influencing others.[69]

Another consequence of printing was that it helped promote the rise of nationalism,[70] as well as the consolidation of bureaucracy and the progress of the European economy more generally.[71] In short, it seems fair to say that the printing press fundamentally changed the character of Western civilisation. But what seems unfair is to credit Johann Gutenberg as the inventor of the printing press.

As Michael Clapham argues, trying to find a 'single inventor of printing, and the natural rivalry that developed between the supporters of Johann Gutenberg . . . of Mainz and Laurens Coster . . . of Haarlem, have not only led to some fabrication [but] much disingenuous interpretation of evidence'.[72] What we do know is that the origins of printing can directly be traced back to sixth-century China and early fourteenth-century Korea. Woodblock printing emerged in China during the sixth century CE. Block printing was invented at the beginning of the ninth century, with the earliest extant printed book dated 868. The printing of books then escalated after about 950.[73] As early as 953 Fêng Tao had the text of the Confucian classics printed – 'a work that did for Chinese printing almost what Gutenberg's Bible later did for that of Europe'.[74] But this is often dismissed by the claim that Gutenberg's press used the far more sophisticated movable-type letters. This obscures the simple fact that the first movable-type printing press was invented in China by Pi Shêng around 1040.[75]

Even so, Eurocentric scholars sometimes counter this by arguing that the movable-type press never caught on in China and block printing was preferred. This was not, however, due to any lack of ingenuity on the part of the Chinese but was a function of the fact that the nature of Chinese script made block printing more feasible. As the Jesuits noted, 'the Chinese method of printing was better adapted to the numerous and complex Chinese characters than was the movable-type process'.[76] Ironically, this superficially reinforces a standard Eurocentric claim: that Gutenberg's press was ultimately more effective and faster because European typography was based on only twenty-six letters of the alphabet. However, Lach and Kley point out that the Jesuits considered that the Chinese process was not only as efficient as the European, but that there were various advantages to the former over the latter.[77] Moreover, it is interesting to note that it was only in the nineteenth century that the European printing press became faster than its Asian counterparts – up until then it remained a slow and expensive form of reproducing texts.[78] Even so, David Landes insists that unlike in Europe printing never 'exploded' in China.[79] But by the end of the fifteenth century, China probably published more books than all other countries combined.[80] And even as early as 978 one of the Chinese libraries contained 80,000 volumes (though at that time this was easily exceeded by the holdings of some of the major

Islamic libraries). Nevertheless, Eurocentrism suggests that none of this can detract from the fact that it was Gutenberg who first developed the movable metal-type printing press. But the fact is that the movable metal-type printing press was invented in Korea in 1403 (a full fifty years earlier).[81]

How then, and to what extent, did these Chinese and Korean inventions spread westwards? There is strong evidence to suggest that Chinese block printing diffused across to Europe and was first used in Germany in the thirteenth century (having traversed across to Poland (1259) and Hungary (1283) under the Mongol conquests).[82] Significantly, Needham points out that,

> Robert Curzon . . . (1810–73) has said that the European and
> Chinese block books are so precisely alike, in almost every respect
> that, 'we must suppose that the process of printing them must
> have been copied from ancient Chinese specimens, brought from
> that country by some early travellers, whose names have not been
> handed down to our times'.[83]

But what of movable-metal typography?

First it must be asked whether it was just a pure coincidence that Gutenberg happened to hit upon his printing press, the general outlines of which had already been discovered in mid-eleventh century China, and the specific outlines of which had been invented in Korea some fifty years earlier. While he discerns no evidence for its direct diffusion, none the less, Thomas Carter advocates indirect diffusion. First, paper-making undoubtedly diffused westward (as we noted in ch. 6) and this was a necessary prerequisite for printing. Second, a series of printed products diffused across to Europe, including playing cards (late fourteenth century), paper money, image prints and Chinese books. And third, Carter suggests that knowledge of the actual method of typography could have been reported by any one of the numerous Europeans who had sojourned in China.[84] Either way though, Hudson's conclusion seems fair:

Since Korean typography underwent so remarkable a development just before the appearance of the process in Europe [by Gutenberg], and there were possible lines of news transmission between the Far East and Germany, the burden of proof really lies on those who assert the complete independence of the European invention.[85]

The Eastern origins of the European military revolution

The European military revolution (1550–1660), which substituted gunpowder, the gun and cannon for the sword, lance, mace and cross-bow, was undoubtedly a critical moment in Europe's development.[86] Many assume that this not only brought European military power to the fore in the world, but that it also enabled the rise of both the modern bureaucratic state and capitalism.[87] But what has been ignored in all of this is the point that all of its technological ingredients were invented during the first military revolution – in China, c. 850–1290. Because I discussed this in detail in ch. 3, I shall merely focus on the oriental global diffusion process here.

Eurocentric scholars often attribute the discovery of gunpowder to the European scientist Roger Bacon in 1267. But as we noted in ch. 3, the recipe for gunpowder stems back to China in 850 and was publicly available in print form in 1044. Joseph Needham also notes that in Bacon's published statement on gunpowder it seems clear that he was describing Chinese firecrackers.[88] Moreover, it was perfectly possible that he had gained access to the already published Chinese recipe for gunpowder. How could this knowledge have been transmitted across from China to the West? Paul Cressey and Arnold Pacey single out William of Rubrick (a personal friend of Bacon's), who returned from China in 1256/7.[89] Though he could very well have brought back the information a series of Europeans (mainly friars) had travelled to China and back ever since 1245, and any one of them could have relayed the recipe.[90]

We saw in ch. 3 that the first metal-barrelled gun emerged in China by about the mid-thirteenth century – certainly no later than

1275 – and that the first cannon (the Eruptor) was invented in China around 1288. This is significant because the first European cannon is dated to 1326 in Florence and 1327 in England (the latter is illustrated in the manuscript of Walter de Millemete).[91] As Pacey remarks:

> It is striking that the earliest illustration of a European [cannon] . . . shows a barrel of precisely [a] Chinese type, mounted on a bench and firing an arrow. It was once thought that [the cannon] was a European invention, and that Chinese weapons came later . . . This view is no longer credible.[92]

Crucially, the cannon presupposes a prior development spanning a very long time, something which is clearly missing in the European context. And in the European context no one has ever produced evidence to support this. But such a line of prior development is certainly clear in the Chinese context (stemming back some four centuries). No less significant is that the Chinese cannon delivered exploding shells, something that would only be achieved in Europe by the fifteenth century. Moreover, the Chinese cannon were sometimes made of cast iron, which was much stronger and, therefore, more effective than the wrought iron European cannon. It would only be as late as the second half of the sixteenth century that the Europeans would catch up in this respect.

The transmission of the gun and cannon to Europe is based only on circumstantial evidence. Needham and Ling suggest that this could have been achieved either by the Italian merchants who resided in Tabriz, or by the European friars (mentioned above), or by the various Muslims who were employed in the Chinese military service after 1260.[93] Certainly there was enough contact between Europe and China to enable the transmission of the idea of the cannon, perhaps through pictorial representations and/or the actual information concerning its construction. And though these claims are merely speculative it is obvious that the cannon did not simply arrive out of nowhere. Claims for an independent European invention are problematic, though not simply because the earliest extant cannon is dated almost forty years after the invention of the Chinese Eruptor. For, as noted above, the giveaway here is that no expert has ever produced any evidence for the necessary European developments that must have preceded the first European cannon of 1326/7. Without these the diffusion of Chinese knowledge of the cannon provides the only possible answer. The onus, therefore, lies with the Eurocentric scholars to prove otherwise. Notable too is the common Eurocentric assumption that the construction of large ships armed with cannon was a uniquely European innovation. But this ignores the point that cannon had long been used on the much larger Chinese ships.

Finally, we should factor in Islamic military developments, which also had an independent influence on Europe. Islamic military technologies not only developed rapidly but remained superior to those used by the Europeans for a very long time. After the eighth century, Islamic armies deployed special incendiary troops who wore fireproof clothing. They used what the European Crusaders called 'Greek fire' (petrol), which was an incendiary material. Crucially, Greek fire was a misnomer precisely because it had a Middle Eastern origin. In 673 a Syrian architect from Baalbeck known as Callinicus defected to Byzantium, taking with him the secret of the new fire.[94] Tellingly, the Byzantines did not call this Greek fire because they knew that it was Middle Eastern in origin. It was delivered through devastatingly effective flame-throwers (*zarraya*), was coated on ignited arrows and was used in grenades that were either delivered by hand and machines (trebuchets) or were shot as rockets.[95] Indeed, the counterweight trebuchet was a unique Islamic invention. By the twelfth century, the rise of Salah al-din al-Ayyubi (Saladin) marked a new and more intense phase of military technological development. Incendiary devices, for example, were used in every Muslim battle. Against this, the Crusaders had no answer – and their fate against this superior Muslim onslaught was sealed at Acre in 1291 (as was noted in ch. 2).

Later on, the Ottoman empire – which Hodgson famously called a 'gunpowder empire' – was the site of various military technological innovations, many of which diffused across to Western Europe.

Turkish guns in particular diffused rapidly across Central Asia to India in the East and Europe in the West. 'Not only was this the world's biggest export trade in guns, but some were of very high quality.'[96] In particular, the Ottomans contributed significantly to the development of the musket through the construction of steel barrels, which were stronger and less liable to burst than those made in Europe. Not surprisingly, the 'Europeans prized Turkish barrels, and the best European gun-makers sometimes used the Turkish barrels as the basis for [their] guns'.[97] Moreover, European technologists long remained baffled by the high quality of Turkish musket barrels and Indian Wootz steel (see ch. 9). The Ottomans probably also invented the trigger (known as the serpentine), though this may have been a Chinese invention.[98] Notable here is that while there was a trigger on the Roman 'proto-artillery' (e.g. catapults), and on the medieval European crossbow, nevertheless these could not have formed the basis of the later matchlock musket trigger. For the serpentine was an entirely independent invention.

In sum, just about every significant technological aspect of the European military revolution was derived from the East, and diffused across to the West through a long chain of transmissions. And while the Europeans eventually took these military technologies further – certainly by the nineteenth century – the fact remains that without the available Eastern advances there would have been nothing to have taken further.

9 The Chinese origins of British industrialisation:

Britain as a derivative late developer, 1700–1846

What is meant ... in my view, by *wu-wei* [*laissez-faire*] is that no personal prejudice [private or public will] interferes with the universal Tao [the laws of things], and that no desires and obsessions lead the true course of techniques astray. Reason must guide action in order that power may be exercised according to the intrinsic properties and natural trends of things.

Liu An, *Huai Nan Tzu*, 120 BCE

Enough of Greece and Rome. The exhausted store
Of either nation now can charm no more;
Ev'n adventitious helps in vain we try,
Our triumphs languish in the public eye. . . .
On eagle wings the poet of tonight
Soars for fresh virtues to the source of light,
To China's eastern realms; and boldly bears
Confucius' morals to Britannia's ears.

William Whitehead, 1759

The significance of labelling Britain a 'newly industrialising country' or 'late developer'

The last chapter dealt with the 1492–1700 period and argued that Europe was merely catching up with the more advanced Eastern powers. This was simultaneously enabled by the imperial appropriation of 'non-European' bullion and the assimilation of Eastern 'resource portfolios'. Here I return to the assimilationist side of the story. The next and most significant moment in the standard Eurocentric chronology of the rise of the West lies with the British industrial revolution. In fact, the British story constitutes the pivot of the Eurocentric account. For it is a universal idiom that Britain was the first industrialiser. Indeed, pick up any standard economic history textbook on industrialisation and the discussion will begin with Britain's 'early' breakthrough in the eighteenth and nineteenth centuries. This much is proclaimed even in the titles of the major texts on the subject: most notably Phyllis Deane's *The First Industrial Revolution*, and Peter Mathias's *The First Industrial Nation*.[1] Or as R. M. Hartwell succinctly proclaims, in answering his own rhetorical question 'was there an industrial revolution?' 'There *was* an industrial revolution and it *was* British.'[2]

There are two further entwined axioms that lie at the epicentre of the Eurocentric account of Britain's industrial revolution: first, that it was enabled by the positive social environment that was bequeathed by Britain's liberal *laissez-faire* state (which I critique in ch. 11). And second, the breakthrough was achieved by the unique ingenuity and individualism of the Anglo-Saxons without any external help. Typical here is Walter Rostow's claim that, 'the British case of transition was unique in the sense that it appeared to have been brought about by the internal dynamics of a single society, without external intervention'.[3] Or in a typical Marxist rendition, Perry Anderson asserts that the British 'industrial revolution . . . was a spontaneous, gigantic combustion of the forces of production, unexampled in its power and universal in its reach'.[4] The general secret to the success of the British is thought to lie in their unique characteristic of individualism or self-help. Its significance is proclaimed by David Landes, in typical Smithian fashion, as the universal cure for poverty:

> History tells us that the most successful cures for poverty come from within   [W]hat counts is work, thrift, honesty, patience, tenacity. To people haunted by misery and hunger, that may add up to selfish indifference. But at bottom, no empowerment is so effective as self-empowerment.[5]

More specifically, much emphasis is accorded to the ingeniousness of Britain's pioneering inventors. Typically, historians focus on the process by which the British industrial revolution was propelled by a purely internal 'sequence of challenge and response'. This sequence entailed a process by which, 'the speed-up of one stage of the manufacturing process placed a heavy strain on the factors of production of one or more other stages [termed "bottlenecks"] and called forth innovations to correct the imbalance'.[6] It was the cumulative solving of the numerous 'bottlenecks' by pioneering new British inventions that culminated in the final breakthrough to modern industrial capitalism. Or in Landes's terms the secret of British success lay in its ability to effect 'self-generated' change.[7]

The fundamental claim of this chapter is that although the British did have an input, nevertheless the story was significantly informed by 'other-generated' change. Marshall Hodgson once noted in passing that the Occident was, 'the unconscious heir of the . . . industrial revolution of Sung China'.[8] But for the word 'unconscious' I concur because as I argue in this chapter, the British consciously acquired and assimilated the Chinese technologies – either the actual technology or the knowledge of a particular technology. In this sense Britain was like any 'late developer' or newly industrialising country in that it enjoyed the 'advantages of backwardness' and was able to assimilate and refine the advanced technologies that had previously been pioneered by early developers. In a sense then, the British can be characterised as many Westerners like to cast the Japanese between 1868 and 1913 (or after 1945): they had a largely derivative capacity and were excellent at copying, assimilating and refining others' ideas.

While this chapter strips the Eurocentric clothing from the British industrial revolution, this is clearly a counter-intuitive task. The vast majority of us continue to believe that studying eighteenth-century Britain will furnish us with all the criteria that lead to successful economic development, otherwise known as 'modernisation'. As Eric Jones put it, '[t]he assumption is that economic historians should be looking for a unique transformation; that we have already found it; and that it was the British industrial revolution'.[9] This pervades the Western imagination. So much so that, '[e]very schoolchild knows [this], since almost any syllabus in economic history begins at this point . . . [particularly] if he or she has watched one of the television series on the rise of our species'.[10] But by locating the British story within a wider historical-global context (or the long global *durée*), we necessarily challenge the belief that the British 'great transformation' represented the most significant discontinuity in world economic history. It makes more sense to view the British industrial revolution as but a (not insignificant) moment in the ongoing cumulative story of global-economic development that links the historically distant Sung Chinese 'partners' with eighteenth-century Britain. In this sense, Eric Jones is correct to argue that Sung China's breakthrough was not like Britain's – Britain's was like China's.[11] But in another sense, this conflation obscures two crucial differences: first, that unlike China, Britain was heavily dependent on assimilating and borrowing the inventions of others, as this chapter explains. And second, again in sharp contrast to China's miracle, British industrialisation was significantly dependent on the imperial appropriation of many non-European resources – land, labour, raw materials and markets (see ch. 11). If nothing else, this should serve to invert, or at least qualify, the prevailing Eurocentric tendency to denigrate the Sung miracle in favour of Britain's 'single-handed' breakthrough.

In sum, therefore, the immediate significance of labelling Britain a late developer is twofold. First, it undermines the universal assumption that Britain was 'first'. And second, it redirects our attention both to the strategies by which the British emulated and assimilated the more advanced technologies and ideas that emanated from the early Eastern developers (most notably China) as well as the process of oriental globalisation that made this possible. This chapter advances these propositions in three stages. The first section examines the ways in which Chinese ideas affected the European Enlightenment and reveals the diffusion paths along which Chinese resource portfolios travelled across to the West. The second section examines the Chinese contributions to the British agricultural revolution, while the last section reveals the Chinese contributions to the British industrial revolution.

China: a model for British industrialisation

My central claim is that the British were not especially gifted with brilliant inventors. Their ability lay more in assimilating and refining earlier Chinese inventions and technical ideas. How then did the British gain access to these Chinese resources and how did Chinese ideas affect British culture and political economy?

The oriental enlightenment

The European age of enlightenment was essentially schizophrenic in the sense that while it was instrumental to the rise of 'implicit racism' (see ch. 10), the paradox was that many of the ideas with which the Enlightenment thinkers positively associated were directly transmitted from the East. Here I examine this positive oriental influence, before I turn in the next chapter to consider the ways in which the Europeans subsequently denigrated the East.

Chinese ideas were particularly important in stimulating the Continental European and British Enlightenment. Chinese ideas influenced European ideas on government, moral philosophy, artistic styles (e.g. rococo), clothes, furniture and wallpaper, gardens, political economy, tea-drinking and many other matters. The link between the European Enlightenment and Chinese thought was ultimately bridged by the shared faith in human reason as the centre of all things. Reason was vital because it enabled the discovery of the 'laws of motion' that were allegedly inscribed within all areas of social, political and 'natural' life. In 1687, a book on Confucius was translated (*Confucius Sinarum Philosophus*) and in the preface the author asserts that:

> One might say that the moral system of this philosopher is
> infinitely sublime, but that it is at the same time simple, sensible
> and drawn from the purest sources of natural reason . . . Never has
> Reason, deprived of divine Revelation, appeared so well developed
> nor with so much power.[12]

The book had a major impact in Europe. Indeed, on reading this text:

men discovered, to their astonishment, that more than two
thousand years ago in China, whose name was already on the
tongue of every salesman at the great fairs, Confucius had thought
the same thoughts in the same manner, and fought the same
battles . . . Thus Confucius became the patron saint of [the]
eighteenth century Enlightenment.[13]

The critical date in this story is 1700: 'the year of transition in which
the affections of the learned [European] world were turned towards
China'. For the next eighty years, many Europeans became intensely
curious about China; so much so that they formed a virtual love affair
with the world of rococo.

Many Enlightenment thinkers positively associated with China
and its ideas, including Montaigne, Malebranche, Leibniz, Voltaire,
Quesnay, Wolff, Hume and Adam Smith. One of the foremost Enlightenment thinkers was Voltaire. His book, *Essai sur les mœurs* (1756),
has been described as a 'perfect compendium of all the [positive] feel-
ings of the time about the Far East'. Moreover, in his *L'Orphelin de
la Chine* (1755), and *Zadig* (1748), Voltaire drew on Chinese conceptions of politics, religion and philosophy – all of which were
based on rational principles – in order to attack the European preference for hereditary aristocracy. Indeed, many of the major Enlightenment thinkers derived their preference for the 'rational method' from
China.

To the extent that some Eurocentric scholars concede that
China had an impact on the Enlightenment, it is usually assumed
that it only found a positive place in France (no doubt in part because
the absolutism of the French state made 'despotic China' seem attractive). But Chinese ideas also played a very important part in influenc-
ing British culture. Britons developed a strong taste for Chinoiserie,
ranging from tea-drinking to wallpaper to Anglo-Chinese gardens, as
well as to ideas about political economy.[14] In the Anglo-Saxon canon
the central European political economist was the Scotsman, Adam
Smith. But while Anglo-Saxons parochially think of Smith as the first

political economist, behind Smith lay François Quesnay, the French 'Physiocrat'. And crucially, behind Quesnay lay China.[15] Quesnay, not Smith, was the first European to critique the ideas of mercantilism. The term 'physiocracy' means the 'rule of nature'. The significance of his ideas, derived from China, was at least twofold: first, he saw in agriculture a crucial source of wealth (which became an important idea in the British agricultural revolution). Secondly, and more importantly, he believed that agriculture could only be fully exploited when producers were freed from the arbitrary interventions of the state. Only then could the 'natural laws' of the market prevail (as the Chinese had long realised). J. J. Clarke aptly notes that:

> Quesnay's revolutionary ideas amounted to a liberation from the economic orthodoxy of . . . mercantilism . . . and his influence on the free-market theories of Adam Smith was profound. What is often omitted in accounts of Quesnay's place in modern thought is his debt to China – unlike in his own day when he was widely known as 'the European Confucius'.[16]

Quesnay's debt to Chinese conceptions of political economy was found in many ideas, the most important being that of *wu-wei* – which is translated into French as *laissez-faire*. This Chinese concept had been around well before the start of the common era (see the Liu An quote posted at the beginning of the chapter). And as late as 300 CE Kuo Hsiang described *wu-wei* as that which lets 'everything be allowed to do what it naturally does, so that its nature will be satisfied'.[17] Quesnay's specific link with the Enlightenment was found in the fact that he emphasised the centrality of the scientific method, as was expressed in his (albeit bewilderingly complex) *Tableau économique*, the principles of which were substantially influenced by Chinese thinking.[18] It is also worth noting that Quesnay was followed by Nicolas-Gabriel Clerc, whose book *Yu le Grand et Confucius* (1765) explicitly urged Europeans to imitate China if they wanted to enjoy significant economic progress. Echoing Quesnay he too insisted that commerce would function best if all barriers were removed (as would Adam Smith some eleven years later). As Basil Guy put it: 'Both lawmaker and law had to recognize the principles of . . . natural order, and in so doing conform to the Chinese ideal of wu-wei [laissez-faire], which has ever inspired their theories of government'.[19]

None of this is to say that the European Enlightenment was the pure product of Chinese ideas. And clearly there were some Enlightenment thinkers who rejected China as a model for Europe – most notably Montesquieu and Fénelon. The schizophrenic aspect of the Enlightenment became apparent with the changing European perception of China. While it largely began with the perception of a wondrous Cathay, it ended after 1780 with the belief of China as the 'fallen people' of a backward, despotically smothered barbarian land. But as Martin Bernal reminds us 'no European of the 18th century [before 1780] could claim that Europe had created herself'.[20] Such was the importance that European thinkers placed on China from the late seventeenth century down to about 1780 that Voltaire even attacked Bossuet for not mentioning China in his book on world history. Sir William Temple aptly expressed the prevailing sentiment with his words: 'the kingdom of China seems to be framed and policed with the utmost force and reach of human wisdom, reason and contrivance'.[21] But by about 1780 the volte-face kicked in: the 'cycle of Cathay' had come full circle. The new view was typically represented by Oliver Goldsmith: 'Those arts which might have had their invention among other races of mankind [e.g. China] have come to their perfection there [in Europe]'.[22] Or as the eighth earl of Elgin put it (echoing Goldsmith as well as Purchas), in China's hands:

> the invention of gunpowder has exploded in crackers and harmless fireworks. The mariner's compass has produced nothing better than the coasting junk. The art of printing has stagnated in stereotyped editions of Confucius, and the most cynical representation of the grotesque have been the principal products of Chinese conceptions of the sublime and the beautiful.[23]

In the process a subtle but erroneous slip was made: for it created the illusion that the Europeans were wholly independent, original and ingenious after all. This chapter reveals this as but mere hubris. But before I demonstrate this, it is important to establish how Chinese ideas and technologies diffused across to Europe.

The transmission channels from China to Europe
Knowledge of Cathay directly transmitted to Europe began with the many Franciscan monks who first sojourned there after 1245. In turn their tales were outshone by the wondrous reports of Cathay relayed back by Marco Polo in the latter part of the century. Later on, the Jesuits were the most important conduit. Matteo Ricci wrote up a series of volumes that were translated into various European languages in 1610 which confirmed that 'his China was indisputably the same as Marco Polo's [marvellous picture of] Cathay'.[24] It was the Jesuits who persuaded the Europeans to realise that gunpowder, the compass, paper and printing were invented in China (even if these achievements were subsequently dismissed or erased from the various Eurocentric histories of the world). One contemporary European who was residing in China, Father de Magaillans, was enormously impressed by the operation of a Chinese pound-lock. Braudel rhetorically asks:

> Was Father de Magaillans, who stresses the difficulty and danger
> of such an operation, therefore right (1678) to hold up [the
> pound-lock] as an example of the Chinese custom of
> accomplishing 'all sorts of mechanical work with many fewer
> instruments than we [in the West] use'?[25]

The reports of Europeans living in, or visiting, China clearly suggested that this was so, all of which told of a uniquely impressive technological civilisation. And Westerners in general saw China (as well as Egypt) as providing 'positive examples of higher and finer civilizations. Both were seen to have had massive material achievements, profound philosophies and superior writing systems.'[26] It might, however, be replied that the Jesuits intentionally exaggerated their case and that they did so to impress the Chinese emperor in order to curry favour. But in fact most of their reports of China were surprisingly balanced and the Jesuits did not shy away from pointing to those areas in which they believed that the Europeans were superior.

Either way, though, the Jesuits constituted an important conduit for the transmission of Chinese economic ideas and above all, technologies. Examples are manifold. Louis XIV sent six Jesuits to China in 1685 with a long list of topics (drawn up by the French Academy of Science) to find out about all manner of areas ranging from science, flora and fauna to agricultural production. Interestingly, Louis was urged to do this by Colbert, who in turn had been prompted by Leibniz.[27] Leibniz himself wrote to the Jesuit mission in China and specifically asked them to relay information on the manufacture of metals, tea, paper, silk, 'true' porcelain, dyes and glass as well as Chinese agricultural, military and naval technologies. Without such knowledge, Leibniz reasoned, 'little profit will be derived from the China mission'.[28] Most significantly, Leibniz also requested that the Jesuits transport back to Europe Chinese technologies, machines and models as well as written accounts of Chinese agriculture and industry. Fortunately, the Jesuits complied. One of the most searching enquiries was made by Turgot (Louis XVI's finance minister), who sent two Christian missionaries to China with a comprehensive text of questions in 1765.[29] And numerous European writers went to China and wrote books on their findings – Captain Ekeberg's *An Account of Chinese Husbandry*, which was translated into German and English was a notable example.[30] In addition, Dutch sailors based in Batavia constituted another crucial conduit for the diffusion of Chinese ideas and technologies.

From 1600 onwards, information about China rapidly accumulated through Jesuit letters, though after 1650 books on China became prominent. Published in many European languages, they conveyed the many splendours of Cathay at a general level, and its technologies and economic ideas more specifically.[31] In addition to the writings of Matteo Ricci in 1610, Nicolas Trigault, Alvarez Semedo, Martino Martini and others provided detailed book descriptions of all aspects of China, including sections on 'fertility and products' and 'mechanical arts'. Most significantly, the many Jesuit books infused the European imagination, from the intellectual to the layperson and from the masses to some of Europe's monarchs. Thus, not only did Europe become flooded with Chinese texts, it also received numerous technologies and models which were directly copied to enable both the agricultural and industrial revolutions. One extensive summary is noteworthy:

> Hundreds of books about Asia, written by missionaries,
> merchants, sea-captains, physicians, sailors, soldiers, and
> independent travellers, appeared during the [17th] century. There
> were at least twenty-five major descriptions of South Asia alone,
> another fifteen devoted to mainland Southeast Asia, about twenty
> to the archipelagoes, and sixty or more to East Asia. Alongside
> these major independent contributions stood hundreds of Jesuit
> letterbooks, derivative accounts, travel accounts . . . pamphlets,
> newssheets, and the like. The books were published in all
> European languages, frequently reprinted and translated, collected
> into the several large compilations of travel literature published
> during the century, and regularly pilfered by later writers or
> publishers . . . Few literate Europeans could have been completely
> untouched by it, and it would be surprising indeed if its effects
> could not be seen in contemporary European literature, art,
> learning, and culture.[32]

Clearly, then, the Europeans were able to gain easy access to the more advanced Chinese (as well as other Asian) ideas and technologies. And as we shall see shortly, with this information and some of the technologies themselves, the Europeans and especially the British began to assimilate them in order to catch up and get ahead. Unfortunately virtually no Western inventor actually confessed to borrowing the ideas of other Westerners, let alone the Chinese. As Francesca Bray aptly put it,

> if we hope to find explicit acknowledgement of such influence in their works we shall be disappointed: Western writers and inventors plagiarised each other's ideas shamelessly . . . [and] we may be sure that they had no scruples in passing off as their own, ideas that had come from the other side of the world.[33]

Nevertheless, it is possible to trace the diffusion of specific Chinese ideas and technologies across to the West (even if it is a harder task for all this). Thus in the spirit of Voltaire, let us re-examine the British agricultural and industrial revolutions by resuscitating the many Chinese contributions that have been concealed by Eurocentrism.

The Chinese origins of the British agricultural revolution

The agricultural revolution is traditionally thought to represent if not one of the crucial pre-conditions then at least one of the ongoing requirements for the progress of British industrialisation. It comprised a series of allegedly ingenious and original British technological inventions. These included Jethro Tull's 'seed-drill' and the 'horse-drawn hoe' (built in 1700 but only publicised widely in the 1730s), the 'horse-powered threshing machine' (1780), the 'Rotherham plough' (patented in 1730), and the 'rotary winnowing machine'. Also stressed are new methods of land use: crop rotational techniques, fertilisers, new crops and selective breeding. Had all this been independently discovered or pioneered in Britain, then it would seem fair to concede the Eurocentric claim about British ingenuity and originality. But there is strong evidence to suggest otherwise.

The eighteenth-century iron mouldboard plough
(Rotherham plough)

Most commentators accept that the iron mouldboard plough was a vital technological innovation that boosted British agricultural productivity considerably (even if it was a long time before it came into general use). Compared to the medieval heavy turn-plough (see ch. 5), the Rotherham plough of 1730 was vastly more efficient. Crucially, the square wooden mouldboard of the medieval plough was

replaced by a twisted, curved iron mouldboard which was attached
flush to the share. This ensured a major reduction in friction (as did
the lack of wheels). This was allegedly first developed in seventeenth
century Holland (known as the Dutch 'bastard' plough). It was then
transmitted to Britain by Dutch engineers (who were involved in the
draining of the East Anglian fens). This was succeeded by the English
Rotherham plough, which incorporated many aspects of the bastard
plough. But it was a refinement with a much lighter frame, and was
refined further over the next century. Were the Dutch the original
inventors, thereby confirming the Eurocentric claim of an independent European invention?

Paul Leser originally claimed in 1931 that the modern European
plough originated in China, and that without its importation Europe
might not have undergone an agricultural revolution.[34] Indeed, all
the aspects of the Dutch bastard plough were found in China, stemming back some two millennia. But was this mere coincidence? More
recently, Francesca Bray has dismissed this possibility on the grounds
that the new European ploughs far too closely resembled the much
earlier Chinese invention. Indeed, Chinese iron mouldboard ploughs
perfectly pre-empted the model that was described as late as 1784 by
the European, James Small (a so-called pioneer of the plough). Moreover, the sudden emergence of the new European ploughs, which were
so radically different from those that had been used for about a millennium, suggests that this could not have been mere coincidence. In
any case, it is clear that the Dutch (who had resided in East Asia in
the seventeenth century) brought back the actual Chinese model and
created the Dutch or 'bastard' plough, which was then adapted into
the British Rotherham plough.[35] As Robert Temple concludes:

> There was no single more important element [than the adoption of
> the Chinese plough] in the European agricultural revolution. When
> we reflect that only two hundred years have elapsed since Europe
> suddenly began to catch up with and then surpassed Chinese
> agriculture, we can see what a thin temporal veneer overlies our
> assumed Western superiority in the production of food.[36]

The rotary winnowing machine

The invention of the rotary winnowing machine (which separated out the husks and stalks of the grain after the harvest) was a major breakthrough. But it was long preceded by the Chinese rotary winnowing machine that had been invented in the second century BCE and refined further over the ensuing centuries.[37] Like the iron mouldboard plough this was directly transmitted from China. It was first brought to France in the 1720s by the Jesuits, where it attracted much attention. Various models were brought back to Sweden, where they were adapted by Swedish scientists such as Jonas Norberg. Interestingly, Norberg broke with European convention by admitting that, 'I got the initial idea ... from three separate models brought here from China.'[38] Finally the rotary winnowing machine was also imported into Europe by Dutch sailors between 1700 and 1720 (originally discovered in use in Batavia).[39]

Seed-drills and horse-hoeing husbandry

Prior to the deployment of the seed-drill, seeds were laboriously planted by hand. This was both a slow and highly inefficient process. The result was that much of the crop was lost since some of it landed in hollows in the ground, which led to a clumping of the plants that then had to compete for light, moisture and nutrients. This contrasted with the Chinese multi-tube seed-drill first invented in the third century BCE:

> [It] could be up to thirty times more efficient in terms of harvest yield. And this was the case for seventeen or eighteen hundred years. Through all those centuries, China was so far in advance of the West in terms of agricultural productivity that the contrast, if the two halves of the world had only been able to see it, was rather like the contrast today between ... the 'developed world' and ... the 'developing world'.[40]

Europe very belatedly caught up with China once Jethro Tull had apparently discovered the seed-drill (though even so, his device was clumsy and only came into wide use many decades later). This device sowed the seed in regular rows and at a specific depth. The hoeing device was responsible for keeping the weeds down and ventilating the soil. However ingenious and revolutionary this was when it was introduced into Britain, the fact remains that it was invented in China some two millennia earlier.

Tracing the diffusion of this invention from China is not easy. Here we come across one of the dilemmas of the diffusion process. For, as in the case of the windmill, what actually diffused was the idea of the seed-drill, given that Tull's model differed in various ways from the Chinese models. This is explained by the fact that the Chinese seed-drill was confined to the northern parts, well away from the ports of South China that had been frequented by the Europeans. This meant that unlike some other Chinese inventions, this one was unlikely to have been directly carried back by European sailors. But it is extremely likely that the *idea* of the seed-drill was transmitted, most likely through the diffusion of books and manuals on this device. For example, in his book, *The History of the Great and Renowned Monarchy of China* (1655), Alvarez Semedo tells us that:

> As I passed by *Honum* [Honam], I saw one plowing with a plow of 3 irons, or plough-sheares, so that at one bout he made 3 furrowes; and because the ground was good for the seed which we here call Feazols or Kidney-beanes; this seed was put, as it were, in a bushel, or square dish fastened upon the upper part of the plough, in such manner, that with the motion thereof the Beanes were gently scattered upon the earth as some falleth upon a Milstone, at the moving of the Mill-hopper; so at the same time the land is plowed and sown with hopes of a future crop.[41]

Semedo was, of course, describing the hoe seed-drill. And note the date – 1655. This is not to say that it was this particular book that informed Europe's assimilation of the hoe seed-drill; but it is undeniably the case that published discussions of this pioneering Chinese invention were available for the Europeans to peruse at their leisure.

And it is striking to note that Tull's basic principles of the seed-drill, outlined in his book, *Horse-Hoeing Husbandry* (1733), were almost a word for word reproduction of those laid out in the original Chinese manuals dating back to the third century BCE.[42] Indeed, Bray claims that Tull's system so closely resembles 'the farming practice of Northern China that one is tempted to assume that Tull borrowed the system lock, stock and barrel from China'.[43]

Given that it was the idea that was transmitted, the Europeans had to reinvent it for themselves, and not surprisingly the final model looked different from the original Chinese version. Indeed, it was in part because the final version looked different from the Chinese model that it tended to produce the illusion of an instance of spontaneous British ingenuity. But as Bray points out:

> One might argue that the European seed-drill was a logical development from earlier horticultural techniques such as setting, yet it cannot be fortuitous that European inventors suddenly started working on machines to sow several rows of corn simultaneously in straight lines, just like the Chinese machines, precisely at the period when information about Chinese agriculture was becoming freely available.[44]

Moreover, it seems that Jethro Tull had managed successfully to keep the Eastern origins of 'his' seed-drill a secret. So successful was he in this respect that it was only as late as 1795 that the British Board of Agriculture learned that the seed-drill had in fact long been used in the East. And the Board managed to have a seed-drill (as well as a plough) sent over.[45]

So to sum up. Although the major British agricultural technologies had distinctive Chinese origins, nevertheless it took a long period of time before the techniques became widely adopted by British farmers: the mid-nineteenth century for the hoe seed-drill, the 1820s for the Rotherham plough, and about 1870 for the rotary winnowing machine. Accordingly, the story of British agricultural progress cannot begin and end with technological inventions, not least because they appeared relatively late on the scene. Though these technologies played an important role, ultimately what made the difference was the introduction of biological and ecological innovations: new land-saving crops, high-calorific foods, fertilisers and new methods of crop rotation. Indeed, it was the latter 'discovery' that had put Turnip Townshend on the map. What we are not usually told, though, is that much of this was achieved only because of the help provided by China as well as the Americas (the latter input is discussed in more detail in ch. 11).

The new crop rotation systems, which were heralded by the British as one of the crucial agricultural breakthroughs, were fully pre-empted by the Chinese. Strikingly, the Chinese had developed many such systems as early as the sixth century, all of which were reported in the *Chhi Min Yao Shu*.[46] These were not only widely used but were highly sophisticated. This was a further reason why Chinese agricultural yields had so easily outstripped British rates for so many centuries. Moreover, some of the revolutionary rotational crops used by the British in the eighteenth century were being used by the Chinese some twelve centuries earlier (e.g. broad beans, sweet potatoes, millet, wheat and barley, and turnips). It would be extremely surprising if knowledge and the details of these systems were not passed across to Europe (as discussed above). It is also important to note that the New World furnished the British with many of the crops that were vital to the agricultural revolution.[47] They included the turnip, potato, maize, guano, carrot, cabbage, buckwheat, hops, colza, clover and other fodder plants. Turnips and clover provided the basis of Britain's crop rotation system; guano was an important fertiliser and the potato greatly raised the calorific intake of the masses.[48] Finally, emphasis is usually accorded to the new horse-breeding techniques that enabled the development of larger and stronger horses. But what is usually omitted is the point that it was the early eighteenth-century introduction of 'oriental stock' – i.e. the Arab mares from the Ottoman empire (Darley Arabian, Byerley Turk and Godolphin Barb) – that significantly enabled this particular development.[49]

The Chinese origins of the British industrial revolution

Alongside cotton, the iron and steel industry constituted the major pillar of British industrialisation. The Eurocentric accounts always begin by recounting a whole series of ingenious British technological breakthroughs. The list usually includes Abraham Darby's coke-smelted cast iron (1709), Henry Cort's puddling process (1784) and especially James Watt's steam engine (1776). And as usual, Eurocentric historians recount this in terms of the 'sequence of challenge and response' (outlined in the introduction to this chapter), where pioneering British inventors were ingeniously able to solve all the bottlenecks that accompanied each invention. Thus, for example, Thomas Newcomen's atmospheric engine (1705) was refined through a long line of developments, including John Wilkinson's patented hydraulic blowing engine (1757) and James Watt's steam engine (c. 1776), before culminating with Richard Trevithick's high-pressure engine in 1802 (which led him to build the first steam locomotive in 1804). The immediate question then is, were the British as original as Eurocentrism claims? This section answers in the negative. And it makes sense to begin with the steam engine, given its pivotal role in British industrialisation.

The steam engine

Kenneth Pomeranz argues that ultimately what led to the 'great divergence' between Britain and China after 1800 was that Britain was blessed with deep and flooded mines as opposed to the shallow and arid Chinese mines. This necessitated the invention of the steam engine in Britain to pump the water out. In turn, the steam engine enabled the widespread industrialisation of Britain (given that it was widely applied not just in the mines but in the factories and railways, etc.). China's arid and shallow mines by contrast proved to be its undoing because this condition did not necessitate the invention of the steam engine – hence no industrialisation.[50]

Pomeranz's argument is rendered problematic by three main points. First, deep mining began in China as early as the Warring States period (fifth century–221 BCE). Between then and the Sung period the deepest mines averaged just under 300 feet (and during the Ming and Ching periods several mines reached to the depth of 3000 to 4800 feet and one mine even reached some 8500 feet).[51] Second, many mines were certainly below the water level and, therefore, required drainage (e.g. in the lowlands of northern Kiangsu). Robert Hartwell points out that there, 'the increase in the scale of operations during the eleventh century probably required substantial investment in drainage equipment, possibly including hydraulic bellows pumps similar to those in use at salt wells in Szechwan'.[52] And as Peter Golas explains:

> Even a little water causes a lot of trouble in coal mining but this problem was compounded in China by the fact that much of her coal lies associated with bedded limestone that frequently contains enormous amounts of water. Because of the extensive folding, these reservoirs are frequently breached in the process of mining . . . At best, it has made water removal perhaps the biggest and most widespread problem in Chinese coal mining . . . It was too much rather than too little water, however, that was by far the greater problem for Chinese miners.[53]

Third, and most ironically, it is at the very least debateable as to whether the steam engine would have been developed in Britain had it not been for many earlier pioneering Chinese innovations, most especially the hydraulic bellows pump that the Chinese deployed not least for draining flooded mines.

It is instructive to begin by noting that the essentials of the steam engine had first appeared in Chinese print form in Wang Chên's *Treatise on Agriculture* (1313). The essentials go back to the water-powered bellows (first used in 31 CE). As is usually recognised, Watt's steam engine was an advancement of Wilkinson's machine. But Wilkinson's invention was more or less identical to Wang Chên's machine. The only, albeit not insignificant, addition was the use of a crankshaft (which was one of the four genuinely independent innovations that the Europeans made in the period 500–1700). Moreover, it is no less significant to note that the Chinese box-bellows, which was a double-acting force and suction pump, at each stroke expelled the air from one side of the piston while drawing in an equal amount of air on the other side. Not only did it share a 'close formal resemblance' to Watt's engine but by the late seventeenth century, the Chinese had developed a steam turbine.[54] Interestingly, drawing from the argument made by Needham and Ling, Pomeranz notes that:

> The Chinese had long understood the basic scientific principle involved – the existence of atmospheric pressure – and had long since mastered (as part of their 'box-bellows') a double-acting piston/cylinder system much like Watt's, as well as a system for transforming rotary motion to linear motion that was as good as any known anywhere before the twentieth century. All that remained was to use the piston to turn the wheel rather than vice versa. (In a bellows, the jet of hot air moved by the piston was the goal, not a step toward powering the wheel). A Jesuit missionary who showed off working miniature models of both a steam turbine carriage and a steamboat at court in 1671 appears to have been working as much from Chinese as from western models.[55]

And moreover, Robert Temple points out:

> [The] European designs [for the steam engine] were all derived, through various intermediaries such as Agostino Ramelli (1588), from those of China. As for pistons driving wheels, rather than the other way round, Chinese stimulus was available separately there. Pistons driven by exploding gunpowder were tried in Europe on the idea, as Needham has put it, that 'the piston and piston-rod may be considered a tethered cannon-ball'. Since the Chinese invented both gunpowder and the gun, internal combustion as well as steam engines were partly inspired by the fact that a gun has a projectile which exactly fits the barrel and is expelled by force – further Chinese contributions to the ancestry of both engines.[56]

The gun and the cannon are in effect a one-cylinder internal combustion engine and, as Lynn White originally noted, 'all of our more modern motors . . . are descended from it'.[57] Indeed, one of the major challenges that had confronted James Watt when developing his steam engine was the need to bore an accurate airtight cylinder. Interestingly, he turned to John Wilkinson for help; interestingly because Wilkinson owned a boring mill that was designed for cannon production. And crucially, it was the Chinese who had invented the cannon and gun, both of which were subsequently passed on to the Europeans (as we saw in chs. 3 and 8).

None of this is to say that Pomeranz and others are wrong to emphasise the importance of the development and widespread use of the steam engine in Britain's industrialisation. But it is to say that many of the fundamental aspects of the steam engine had been pioneered in China many centuries before Europeans such as Leonardo da Vinci even dreamed of such a device. Indeed, the British steam engine did not miraculously come out of nowhere. Thus while the various British inventors did have an input, it would be remiss to discount the Chinese contribution.

Coal and blast furnaces

Eurocentrism particularly emphasises Britain's 'revolutionary' substitution of coal for charcoal (under conditions of rapid deforestation), leading to the familiar claim that Britain's Coalbrookdale was the 'first place' in the world to use coke for smelting iron ore. As Phyllis Deane puts it: 'The most important achievement of the industrial revolution was that it [i.e. coal] converted the British economy from a wood-and-water basis to a coal-and-iron basis'.[58] But as we noted in ch. 3, this obscures the fact that the Chinese had been using coal to replace charcoal back in the eleventh century. Moreover, the blast furnace originated in China in the second century BCE, and by the fifth century CE the Chinese had developed a 'co-fusion' process in which wrought and cast iron were melded together to produce steel. 'This is essentially the Martin and Siemens steel process of 1863, though carried out fourteen hundred years earlier.'[59] Nevertheless, even as late as 1850, Britain produced only relatively low levels of steel (compared to iron) because of its much higher production costs. What changed this was the invention of the Bessemer converter (1852). And here it is instructive to note that,

> Henry Bessemer's work had been anticipated in 1852 by William Kelly [even though Kelly did not get the full credit] . . . [And] Kelly had brought four Chinese steel experts to Kentucky in 1845, from whom he had learned the principles of steel production used in China for over two thousand years previously.[60]

Iron and steel production

As noted in ch. 3, even as late as 1788 British iron production levels were still lower than those achieved in China in 1078. And it would only be around the turn of the nineteenth century that the British would be able to match the low prices of the eleventh-century Chinese product. As Joseph Needham originally pointed out:

> It is an extraordinary historical paradox that . . . Western civilisation, which has so much influenced world civilisation today, is so dependent upon the working of iron and steel, [given that] the Chinese were 1300 years ahead of the West in regard to cast iron.[61]

India too was ahead of Britain. Indian Wootz steel was the finest in the world for many centuries leading up to the nineteenth century, and was especially prized in Persia where it was known as Damascus (Damask) steel. Even by the end of the eighteenth century, the British product remained inferior to that of the Damascus variety.[62] And even as late as 1842 Indian iron and steel was not only as good, if not superior to, the British product but was much cheaper than that produced in Sheffield.[63] Interesting too is that by this time, the number of Indian blast furnaces was some fifty times the number found in Britain (and was still ten times the number found in Britain in the peak year of

1873). Crucially, Western producers remained baffled by the high quality of the Indian and Persian product.

It was, therefore, not surprising that when the British belatedly became interested in steel production they looked to both Chinese and Indian production techniques. The first attempt at replicating this process was undertaken by Benjamin Huntsman in Sheffield in 1740, though other attempts were made over the next eighty years. As Arnold Pacey notes of the British system:

> [Though] the 'crucible steel' so produced was of the high quality necessary for making tools for lathes . . . [nevertheless] the pattern to be seen on some Asian blades was never obtained and this, together with its high quality, still puzzled Western steel-makers. Thus even in the 1790s Indian Wootz steel was the subject of investigation in Sheffield, where it was used to make specimen blades of a quality which could not be replicated by other means.[64]

Moreover, in the late eighteenth century a number of European scientists enquired into the origins of Indian Wootz steel, Michael Faraday being the best known.[65] As Braudel concludes: 'During the early decades of the nineteenth century, many Western scientists . . . endeavoured to discover the secrets of damask [or Wootz steel]: the results of their research marked the birth of [British] metallography'.[66] It is also important to note that British producers conducted experiments at the Corby steel works so as to reproduce the ancient Chinese steel-making techniques. These proved successful, with the production of a uniform steel being obtained.

Cotton manufacturing

The cotton industry was the other, if not the major, pillar of the British industrial revolution. By 1830 cotton manufactures became the main export. The cotton industry was, therefore, the pacemaker of British industrialisation. Once again, historians focus on a list of independent inventions that were pioneered by various British inventors including: John Kay's flying shuttle (1733), the spinning frame of John Wyatt and Lewis Paul (1738), James Hargreaves's spinning jenny (c. 1765), Richard Arkwright's water-frame (1767), Samuel Crompton's mule (1779), Edmund Cartwright's power-loom (1787) and, once more, James Watt's steam engine (1776). And again these inventions allegedly followed the internal path of a 'sequence of challenge and response', in which the sustained application of British genius invented and subsequently refined these technologies. The result was a tenfold increase in spinning, which was only met by American imports of cotton (see ch. 11).

It is usually assumed that it was from the 'grimy' northern English setting of Lancashire that the first blinding rays of modernity were supposedly emitted. But Lancashire was not actually the place where the cotton miracle began. For the cotton industry was in no way unique to eighteenth-century Britain but found strong antecedents in both India and China. Not only did China lead the way in terms of textile machines but it had invented the 'big-spinning frame' which was superior to Arkwright's machine. Moreover, in textiles the Chinese had long had machines that differed in just one crucial detail from both Hargreaves's spinning jenny and Kay's flying shuttle.[67] As Dieter Kuhn points out:

> Chinese textile technicians had invented all the essential parts of
> a spinning device [similar to these British inventions] for
> industrial use as early as the thirteenth century . . . Indeed in
> terms of mechanical structure, even the spinning jenny, which
> was never easy to operate, did not match the quality of the big
> spinning frame for ramie.[68]

The only difference was that the Chinese machine was used for silk rather than cotton production. Nevertheless, it was the diffusion of Chinese silk technologies that ultimately provided the foundation for the British cotton textile technologies.

The first diffusion of Chinese textile inventions to Europe occurred in the thirteenth century (where they enabled the rise of the Italian silk industry – as noted in ch. 6). And in turn, the Italians would pass these ideas on to the British. One of the significant moments here concerns John Lombe's silk production mills. These were significant because it was his silk mills that provided the model for cotton manufacturing that would be developed in Derby. Here we find that Lombe's machine was actually the culmination of a series of global diffusions in which China spoke indirectly to Europe and, of course, Britain. John Lombe took his ideas from Italy, where these silk machines were already being used.[69] But describing these machines as Italian inventions immediately obscures their Chinese origins. As was explained in ch. 6, the key aspect of these machines was their use of filatures (or reeling machines). These in turn had been derived from China where such machines had been in use as early as 1090.[70] Lombe's machine too was based on the use of filatures and closely resembled the Chinese machines. Moreover, as we also saw in ch. 6, almost all of the aspects of the Italian machines resembled the earlier Chinese models right down to the time when Lombe visited Italy.[71] But the main point here is that it was the Derby silk mill (which was based on Italian designs that were in turn based on the original Chinese models) which provided the model for the emergent cotton manufacturers.

Signs of British industrial superiority or just British hubris?
One of the classic signs of British industrial superiority and ingenuity, we are often told, is that the first iron bridge appeared in Britain's Coalbrookdale as early as 1779. As one text typically puts it, it was in Coalbrookdale

> that John Wilkinson and his rivals showed their ingenuity. The first Darby had used his iron for casting pots and pans, but Wilkinson and the Shropshire ironmasters were by now much more ambitious. In co-operation with the third Abraham Darby, Wilkinson constructed the first iron bridge near Coalbrookdale. It stands to this day, and so novel was the idea that the small town nearby is now called Ironbridge.[72]

This, however, entirely glosses over the fact that there were thousands of iron suspension bridges in China a millennium earlier. The *first* wrought iron suspension bridge actually appeared in China (Chingtung in Yunnan) as early as 65 CE, and iron chain suspension bridges appeared later over the Chin-sha River between 580 and 618 CE.[73] Not only were these Chinese examples 'known to have inspired Western engineers',[74] but the reports of the Jesuits on Chinese suspension bridges were discussed by various British architects such as Sir William Chambers and even attracted Thomas Telford's attention.[75] Another sign of British industrial ingenuity we are told was the 'first' appearance of a street gas-lamp system in 1798. Again, this glosses over the point that the Chinese had been utilising natural gas for lighting purposes for some two millennia before the advent of the British 'innovation'.[76]

The British drill-bit is also held up as a triumph, given that it could reach depths of some 200 feet. But these depths were dwarfed by the drill-bits that were deployed in deep Chinese mines that reached down somewhere between 3000 to 4800 feet. The Chinese were deploying long drill-bits as early as the first century BCE. It was not until as late as the nineteenth century that the West caught up. Significantly, it was Chinese drilling methods that were employed in Europe for brine (1834), as well as for oil drilling (1841). Indeed, Drake built an oil well in Pennsylvania in 1859 directly using Chinese cable methods. As Temple concludes:

> The method of 'kicking her down', as it was called, for oil drilling in America until the advent of steam power was exactly the same as the Chinese technique of bowstring drilling . . . And even the modern rotary bits seem to have partial Chinese ancestry. In short, Western deep drilling was essentially an importation from China, and the modern oil industry is founded on Oriental techniques nineteen hundred years in advance of the West.[77]

Yet another sign of British industrial supremacy, we are told, is the invention of ships with bulkheads and watertight compartments. These were attributed to the genius of Sir Samuel Bentham, who developed this great invention for the Royal Navy around 1795. But as his wife later reported (breaking with European convention), it was to the Chinese that the invention must be attributed.[78] Indeed, the bulkhead/watertight compartment was introduced into Chinese ships as early as the second century CE. Moreover, it is particularly surprising, that it was not until the end of the eighteenth century that the British navy directly emulated this Chinese invention; surprising, that is, because Marco Polo had originally reported this life-saving innovation back to the West as early as 1295. And sadly, had the British designers deployed this innovation on the *Titanic* – which was supposedly the crowning achievement of Western or British shipping design – no fewer than 1502 lives would have been saved on her maiden voyage (though the Atlantic speed record would still have been lost).

Perhaps the ultimate sign of British hubris was found in the hosting of the Great Exhibition in 1851, which proclaimed Britain's industrial supremacy to the world. This was held in Paxton's Crystal Palace, which was supposedly made of glass and supported by iron and steel structures. But what we are not usually told is that 'Paxton's longest arches, the 72-feet span transept arches, were made of laminated Memel fir. There were 205 miles of wooden sash-bars and 34 miles of wooden guttering in this ostensibly iron and glass conservatory.'[79] This reflected the now obscured point that wood rather than steel remained the base of so many things throughout much of Britain's industrialisation. Indeed, despite our imagery of iron and steel ships, the fact is that on the eve of the Great Exhibition 90 per cent of Britain's ships were made of wood. Moreover, it was only after 1852 that steel became cheap enough for the British to manufacture it in large quantities. And this was enabled by the creation of the Bessemer converter which, as we saw earlier, was influenced by Chinese expertise.

Last but by no means least, one of the classic signs of the British industrial revolution was its transport revolution, a major aspect of which was its pioneering creation of canals and especially the pound-lock. Indeed, we are typically told that it was the Briton, James Brindley, 'who was to become the greatest of the canal engineers [and whose] mechanical ingenuity . . . [was] applied to the problem of building a canal. The result was a triumph.'[80] But as we saw in ch. 3, canal construction with pound-locks was a major feature of the Sung economic miracle and was invented in 984 just under eight hundred years earlier.[81] Moreover, the 6,000 km of canal built in Britain between 1750 and 1858 paled into virtual insignificance when compared to the 50,000 km constructed during the Sung some seven hundred years earlier. And these hosted far more numerous Chinese ships that dwarfed the tiny, eccentric barges, which were propelled very slowly by horse along the narrow British canals. In the eleventh century private Chinese boats plying the Grand Canal could carry up to just over 110 tons (which exceeded the maximum displacement load of Columbus's flagship, the *Nina*). And by the late nineteenth century, Chinese canal ships could carry about 140 tons (about three times the load carried by the British barges).

Conclusion

None of this is to say that British industrialisation was erected solely on a Chinese foundation. But it is to say that British industrialisation was significantly founded on the process of 'other-generated' change that reached back to the many Chinese inventions which had been pioneered between 700 and 2300 years earlier. It would seem fair to say that the British iron/steel and cotton industries were significant not just for their lateness but also for their derivative quality. The success of the British here lay not in their originality, but in their problem-solving tenacity to work and refine the inventions of others. In this respect, Britain conforms closely to the standard view of a newly industrialising country or late developer, in which it enjoyed all the 'advantages of backwardness' and was able to assimilate and adapt others' technological discoveries. That the British very belatedly took them further seems a reasonable proposition. But denigrating China's role in all of this is entirely unreasonable, for without the earlier Chinese inventions there would have been little to take further. Moreover, without these Chinese contributions Britain would in all likelihood have remained a small, backward country floating on the periphery of an equally backward continent, that in turn had been floating on the periphery of the Afro-Asian-led global economy ever since 500 CE.

In short, my 'global-historical-cumulative' perspective of indus-trialisation suggests that the conventional emphasis on the British industrial revolution as the place where, to quote Rostow, 'it all began', can now be seen as the product of a parochial Eurocentric mind set. We could, therefore, do little better than close with the words of Eric Jones:

> Once upon a time it seemed we had a definite event to learn about. Growth began with . . . an industrial revolution in late eighteenth century Britain. Now we know quite surely that the event was really a process, smaller, far less British [and far more Eastern], infinitely less abrupt, part of a [world-historical] continuum, taking much more time to run.[82]

Constructing European racist identity and the invention of the world, 1700–1850:

the imperial civilising mission as a moral vocation

> Turkey, China and the rest would some day be prosperous. But those people will never begin to advance . . . until they enjoy the rights of man; and these they will never obtain except by means of European conquest.
>
> Winwood Reade

> It has been said that our civilizing mission alone can justify our occupation of the lands of uncivilized peoples. All our writings, lectures and broadcasts repeat *ad nauseam* our wish to civilize the African [and Eastern] peoples. No doubt there are people who delight to regard as the progress of civilization the amelioration of material conditions, increase of professional skill, improvements in housing, in hygiene and in scholastic instruction. These are, no doubt, useful and even necessary 'values'. But do they constitute 'civilization'? Is not civilization, above all else, progress in *human personality*?
>
> Father Placide

This chapter serves three main purposes. First, it advances my claim that identity formation played an important part in the rise of the West. It does this by showing that identity formation was an important factor that led on to imperialism, which in turn enabled the later phase of the rise of the West (see ch. 11). Second, it was the invention of a racist identity that lay at base of the imperial discourse. This enables me to counter the general Eurocentric assumption that progressive liberal properties underpinned the rise of the West. And third, it reinforces my general claim that the global context was vital to the rise of the West. As Gerard Delanty notes:

[t]he idea [or identity] of Europe found its most enduring
expression in the confrontation with the Orient in the age of
imperialism. It was in the encounter with other civilisations that
the identity of Europe was shaped. Europe did not derive its
identity from itself but from the formation of a set of global
contrasts. In the discourse that sustained this dichotomy of Self
and Other, Europe and the Orient [became] opposite poles in a
system of civilisational values which were defined by Europe.[1]

The claim that imperialism was founded on a racist discourse
seems implausible only if we conflate racism with its 'scientific' form
given that this emerged in Europe after the 1840s – i.e. too late for
imperialism. But following George Frederickson (as well as James
Blaut), I differentiate implicit from explicit racism.[2] First, implicit
racism was constructed in the eighteenth and first half of the nineteenth century. And while the construction of explicit racism began
in the early eighteenth century, it only forcefully emerged (especially
in Britain) after 1840. Second, implicit racism locates 'difference'
through cultural, institutional and environmental criteria rather than
genetic properties. Even so, it very much embodies a racist power
relationship that comprises Western superiority and Eastern inferiority. Accordingly, implicit racism is far more insidious than explicit
racism, since it operates at a much more subliminal level – its racist
aspect is often obscured. It was implicit racism that enabled many
Europeans to sincerely believe that they were helping the East through
imperialism when in fact they were inflicting considerable repression,
misery and unhappiness in all manner of ways – cultural, economic,
political, and military.

These ideologies have different relations to, or implications for,
imperialism. Crucially, implicit racism assumes that civilisational
inferiority can and should be remedied through the imperial 'civilising
mission'. By contrast, because explicit (or scientific) racism focuses
only on physiological/genetic properties it tends to view racial inferiority as permanent. Accordingly, explicit racism has an incoherent

relationship to imperialism. Many scientific racists were 'pessimistic' and urged against imperialism either because it was a fruitless task (given that the Eastern races were incapable of becoming civilised), or because it would lead to the degeneration of the superior race as a function of interbreeding – as in De Gobineau and Robert Knox. Moreover, some warned against imperialism on the grounds that climate would still lead to the degeneracy of the superior races. By contrast, some social Darwinists and scientific racists were less 'pessimistic'. They believed that the Anglo-Saxon race had a duty to take over the world given that the inferior races were doomed to extinction and that the progress of civilisation was safe only in the hands of the British (as in Charles Kingsley).

While this conception of racism might initially sound complex it in fact simplifies in various ways. It would be problematic to assume that explicit racism was an identical twin of implicit racism. For while there were obvious elements of continuity between them, there were also crucial discontinuities, thus implying that each phase was marked by similar as well as different qualities. At times it is almost as if the historical genealogies of implicit and explicit racism are separate. Thus the reader should keep in mind that the account I produce is necessarily a simplified version of what is in fact an exceedingly complex story. Nevertheless, two points are significant here. First, although explicit racism was an important factor, I shall place much more emphasis upon the emergence of implicit racism, given that it was this that was crucial to the construction of imperialism. And second, I am less interested in providing a genealogy that would go through the many detailed twists and turns in the construction of implicit and explicit racism. My specific focus is upon the relationship of racism and European identity formation in the construction of the discourse of imperialism.

One final point is noteworthy here. As I argue below, it was paradoxically in the age of progress/Enlightenment when implicit racism definitively emerged. But as Thierry Hentsch also notes, to view the Enlightenment as a period in which its thinkers set out to overtly construct an implicit racist worldview is far too simplistic.[3] It was above all a subconscious process. Moreover, the Enlightenment was 'schizophrenic'. For its greatest paradox was that while it borrowed and assimilated Eastern (mainly Chinese) ideas – as we saw in ch. 9 – these were then crafted into a body of knowledge that imagined the East as uncivilised and, in turn, led on to the imperial civilising mission and the repression of the East.

Reconstructing European identity: racism, the discourse of empire and the invention of the world

Implicit racism properly emerged during the Enlightenment. Above all, the Enlightenment was a defining moment in the reinvention of European identity. In effect it was based on the question who are we and what is our place in the world? Answering this question led on to the systematisation, classification and, indeed, invention, of the world, the outcome of which was the belief that the West is – and always has been – the sole carrier of civilisation and human progress in the economic, intellectual and political realms. As Samir Amin put it, this process of reimagining 'invented an eternal [progressive] West, unique since the moment of its [imagined] origins'.[4] The discourse created (largely unwittingly) a kind of intellectual apartheid regime in which the West was fundamentally segregated from the East by an imaginary borderline that stemmed back in time to Ancient Greece. While the claims that the East had long been in contact with the West and that the East had pioneered economic progress were often entertained before the eighteenth century, by the nineteenth century this idea had largely disappeared. In this way, the Europeans were able to ignore or marginalise the positive contribution that the East had made to the rise of the West. Thus the new theories of the world led on to the assertion that the rise of the West was a pure virgin birth: that it was achieved by the solo efforts of the Europeans. In this way, the Europeans delineated themselves as the progressive subject of world history both past and present, while the Eastern peoples were relegated to its passive object. As Linda Tuhiwai Smith put it:

One of the supposed characteristics of primitive peoples was that we could not use our minds or intellects. We could not invent things, we could not create institutions or history, we could not imagine, we could not produce anything of value, we did not know how to use land and other resources from the natural world, we did not practice the 'arts' of civilization. By lacking such virtues we [were] disqualified . . . not just from civilization but from humanity itself. In other words we were not 'fully human'; some of us were not even considered partially human.[5]

It was this idea that led on to the notion of the Asians as 'the people without history'. And in viewing the Eastern peoples as incapable of achieving progress, it was axiomatic that only the West could deliver the gift of civilisation to the East through imperialism.

In thinking about imperialism I begin with the claim made by John Mackenzie (following Edward Said) who views it as something 'more than a set of economic, political and military phenomena. It is also a complex ideology which had widespread cultural, intellectual and technical expressions.'[6] While economic, political and military interest groups undoubtedly benefited from imperialism, it would be wrong to assume that the discourse was created simply for them or at their behest. And equally it would be wrong to reduce imperialism to any one particular interest group (as materialist theorists often assume). Moreover, while capitalists did well out of imperialism, it is notable that they in fact had little input into the construction of the discourse. Indeed, it was mainly academics, intellectuals, teachers, scientists, travellers, novelists, journalists, Christian missionaries, politicians and bureaucrats, who were its principal architects.

If there was an essence to imperialism, it lay with the glorification of the Europeans as 'the Lords of Mankind' and a reinforcement of the European self-as-superior.[7] Thus it would constitute the vehicle by which: capitalists would spread the gift of Western capitalism; missionaries would spread the gift of the Christian message of salvation; scientists would further the development of scientific knowledge for all; teachers would spread the gift of European knowledge; bureaucrats would universalise the gift of rational bureaucracy; and politicians would deliver democracy. But as we shall see later (and in ch. 11), the 'promise' was belied by the 'practice' of imperialism, given that repression and economic exploitation became the signature tune of the British mission. One final point here is of note. My principal focus here is on the construction of the British imperial discourse. For while it shared various generic properties with other European imperial discourses, it also differed in a number of respects. I point to some of these in what follows.

The British effectively invented the world through the construction of an imaginary 'civilisational league table'. As table 10.1 shows, the British located themselves in the Premier League. The Continental Europeans were assigned to Division One (or the 'First World'); the 'Yellows' were consigned to Division Two (or the 'Second World'); and the 'Blacks' were consigned to Division Three (or the 'Third World'), teetering on the brink of relegation to Division Four (the 'Planet of the Apes'). The classificatory criteria were derived from various ideational inputs which comprised:

> The theory of oriental despotism;
> the Peter Pan theory of the East;
> classification according to climate and temperament;
> the emergence of Protestant Evangelicalism;
> the emergence of social Darwinism and scientific racism.

The theory of oriental despotism

One of the major theories of the East/West dichotomy is that of oriental despotism. This permeated the writings of European travellers in Asia as well as academic scholars ranging from Bodin, Machiavelli and especially Montesquieu to Mill, Marx and Weber among others. It asserted that Europe was the birthplace of democracy and hence the carrier of economic and political progress, while Asia was dismissed as the home of despotism and hence the victim of economic stagnation.

Table 10.1 *The British discourse of imperialism: the civilisational league table and the racist invention of the world*

Civilisational classification	'Civilised' (Premier League and Division 1) The First World	'Barbaric' (Division 2) The Second World	'Savage' (Division 3) The Third World
Corresponding countries	Britain in the Premier League; Western Europe in Division 1	E.g. Ottoman empire, China, Siam and Japan	E.g. Africa, Australia and New Zealand
Racial colour	White	Yellow	Black
Temperament	Disciplined/hard-working	Melancholic/rigid	Phlegmatic/lax
Climatic character	Cold and wet	Arid and tropical	High aridity
Human character	Christian	Pagan	Atheistic/pagan
Theory of oriental despotism	Liberal-democracy, freedom, individualism, rationality	Despotism, slavery, collectivism, irrationality	Despotism or absence of government, collectivism, irrationality
Peter Pan theory	Paternal/masculine, independent, innovative, rational	Adolescent/feminine, imitative, exotic and irrational	Child-like/feminine, dependent, indifferent, irrational
Social legitimating principles	The British as the chosen people or master-race	The fallen people	Natural man in the state of nature
Political legitimating principles	Sovereign (bordered populated space)	Non-sovereign/indirect imperial rule (borderless populated space)	*Terra nullius*/direct colonial rule (vacant or waste space)
Resulting civilisational quality	Normal	Deviant	Deviant

I have examined this theory in detail throughout this book, so it will not be necessary to repeat the argument in full. While the idea clearly emerged in the seventeenth and eighteenth centuries, by the nineteenth century it had fully percolated throughout society. The journal *The Edinburgh Review* spoke for the popular view of the age when it stated that:

> The spirit of Oriental institutions was unfriendly to the vigorous expansion of thought. In all ages of the world, Asia has been deprived of the light of freedom, and has in consequence incurred the doom of absolute sterility in the higher fruits of manual and mental culture.[8]

This was later echoed in the words of Lord Curzon (Viceroy of India, 1898–1905), whose following description of China was extended to all Asian societies:

> Distrust of private enterprise is rooted in the mind trained up to believe that government is everything and the individual nothing . . . All private enterprise is killed by official strangulation . . . The entire governing class . . . is interested in the preservation of the status quo . . . [All classes] find an equal charm in stagnation.[9]

Or as John Stuart Mill said of China and Egypt: their peoples, 'were brought to a permanent halt for want of mental liberty and individuality . . . [A]s the [despotic] institutions did not break down and give place to others, further improvements stopped.'[10]

This theory was crucially important to the process of European identity formation because it enabled the Europeans to imagine themselves as decidedly liberal and democratic if only because they were 'not-the-despotic-East'. This was necessary because – as we shall see in ch. 12 – no state in Europe was democratic or liberal before the twentieth century. Accordingly, this 'terrifying totalitarian portrait' of the Orient served to deflect attention from the European states' democratic-deficit problem.[11] Moreover, Eurocentric thinkers not only fabricated Europe-as-democratic but also sought to retrospectively draw such a notion back through time so as to (re)present Europe as the home and birthplace of democracy. We noted in ch. 5 that the identity-formation process is both simple and complex. Relevant here is the 'complex' aspect; for its complexity derives from the many intellectual acrobatics that have to be performed so as to construct a particular identity – in this case a pure and advanced Europe as permanently democratic/progressive as opposed to a permanently backward despotic/regressive East. One vital upshot of all this was the notion that European history was governed by a progressive temporal linearity, whereas the East was governed by regressive temporal cycles of stagnation.

The major intellectual acrobatic here involved the reimagining of Greece. In a comparatively short space of time (from the late eighteenth to early nineteenth century) European thinkers suddenly elevated Ancient Greece to the birthplace of European civilisation, given its alleged democratic institutions and scientific rationality.[12] Locating Greece within Europe was also crucial because of its alleged role within the all-important Renaissance (which supposedly created the 'European dynamic'). But this view of a pure European Greece was decidedly not how the Greeks saw themselves. They viewed Greece as fixed firmly within what was known as the 'Hellenic Occident'. That Europe has always been an idea as opposed to a geographical 'reality' is reflected in the fact that 'Europa' herself was in Greek mythology the daughter of Agenor, King of Tyre, situated on the coast of Lebanon.[13] Note too that Troy was in fact east of the Dardanelles. Indeed, 'Greece was linked spiritually and culturally to the East; and . . . the attempt to turn away from, or to deny, this eastern heritage has always implied for Greece a cheapening and coarsening of spiritual and cultural values'.[14] Martin Bernal labelled this the (anti-Eurocentric) 'ancient model', which asserted that Greece was heavily inspired by Ancient Egypt.

But to admit either that Ancient Greece was in part oriental, or that the Renaissance was shaped or informed by Eastern (mainly Islamic) ideas, or that Greece was not especially democratic, would have been extremely confronting. For it would have undermined the emergent claim that Europe has always been uniquely progressive and ingenious – it would have interrupted the linear line of European progress that Eurocentric scholars had now invented or imputed. Thus European intellectuals and thinkers sought to purge the oriental aspect of Greece and exaggerate its European properties as well as its scientific and democratic institutions. This was crucial given that Greek democracy was crude, to say the least, given that only Greek males participated in the political process – women were excluded – and that slavery was a fundamental institution in Ancient Greek society (naturally slaves were also excluded). Moreover, its science owed much to Ancient Egypt. Accordingly, in Bernal's terminology the 'ancient model' of Greece was now replaced by the 'Aryan model' (the modern Eurocentric construct of Greece as purely European).[15] And as Bernal and Ali Mazrui noted, the fabrication of Ancient Greece was crucial to the Eurocentric construct of democratic/scientific Europe as permanently superior to the despotic/pre-scientific East.[16]

In sum, the theory of oriental despotism was crucial not just to 'explain' Asian backwardness but, no less importantly, to cement the identity of Europe – both past and present – as the birthplace of advanced, democratic civilisation. And in this way the theory elevated the European as the permanently progressive subject or agent, while simultaneously relegating the Easterner as the permanently regressive and passive object, of world history.

The Peter Pan theory of the East

The theory of oriental despotism came to be complemented by a second idea that might be dubbed the 'Peter Pan theory of the East'. In many ways the 'findings' or the knowledge built up during the Enlightenment culminated in this theory. The basic similarity between the two theories was the invention of a rational West and an irrational East. The difference was that the Peter Pan theory conjured up a romantic image of the Other as more helpless than cruel, as well as being alluring, promiscuous and exotic. In effect, it imagined the East as an innocent child who would never grow up of his/her own accord.

Again, the upshot here was the notion that Europe was governed by a progressive temporal linearity, while the East was marked by a regressive temporal stasis.

This theory gave rise to various binary categories, which were dreamed up in order to differentiate the West from the East. Thus the West was imagined as inventive, proactive, scientific, disciplined, self-controlled, sane, sensible, practical, 'mind-oriented', independent and above all paternal. This was, indeed, an imaginary construction, for as we have already seen in previous chapters the West had been significantly dependent upon the superior Eastern technologies and ideas throughout the 500–1800 period. By contrast, the East was imagined as the West's inferior opposite: imitative, passive, superstitious, lazy, spontaneous, insane, emotional, exotic, body-oriented, dependent and above all, child-like. And for precisely the same reason, this too was no less an imaginary construct. Importantly, as was noted in ch. 1, this discourse of East and West was synonymous with patriarchal discourse. Thus we could replace the terms West and East with 'masculinity' and 'femininity' and end up with precisely the same set of binary opposites.

The Peter Pan theory of the East is synonymous with the doctrine of 'the psychic unity of mankind'. As Blaut explains, this theory was intimately related to 'rationality'.[17] The essence of the Enlightenment was that it placed all peoples along a mental continuum. Western man was privileged as fully rational in a mental and mature sense, whereas Eastern man was immature and psychically undeveloped, i.e. he had not reached the stage of full mental (rational) development. The crucial point is that:

> given the [assumption of] psychic unity of mankind,
> non-Europeans could of course be brought to adulthood, to
> rationality, to modernity, through a set of learning experiences [i.e.
> through Western imperialism]. (The phrase 'colonial tutelage' was
> a signature of the doctrine, and this conception is encountered in
> most history and geography textbooks of the time.)[18]

Indeed, the depiction of the West as a rational, independent and paternal man juxtaposed against the East as an irrational, dependent and helpless child or woman was crucial in promoting the idea of the imperial civilising mission as a moral duty. For it was axiomatic that only the paternal West could and should emancipate or redeem the child-like East, much as a father sees it as his duty to raise his child. Moreover, depicting the East as a seductive and exotic woman constituted a further drive for the patriarchal West to achieve imperial conquest, penetration, control and gratification.

Further testimony to the point that this was all constructed is provided by the fact that the Peter Pan theory and the theory of oriental despotism were in one clear sense incompatible. For while the East was being imagined as a despotic threat (an idiom of cruelty and totalitarian power), it was simultaneously imagined as a far less threatening entity that was allegedly helpless and child-like (an idiom of innocence and powerlessness). Thus the East was simultaneously tainted with a Manichean divide between 'an image of evil' and a 'romantic image of innocence'. Though these appeared to be incommensurable, the ingeniousness of Eurocentric intellectuals was revealed by their ability to successfully graft these together into one coherent and seamless imperial discourse. Representing the East as a despotic threat was as important for the discourse of imperialism as was the idea that the East was innocent, exotic and above all passive and helpless, since the latter idea was used to make imperialism appear as a 'moral vocation' (i.e. it was the Western prince's duty to emancipate his Eastern sleeping beauty). Nowhere was the link between the Peter Pan theory, the theory of oriental despotism and imperialism more clearly represented than in Rudyard Kipling's famous 1899 poem, *The White Man's Burden*. For it was there that he described the Eastern peoples as 'half-devil and half-child'. The burden constituted a moral duty to 'relieve the sickness' of Eastern depravity and deprivation. Nevertheless, it was also a burden, for the imperialists should expect no gratitude for their services to mankind. Rather, the reward, Kipling warned, would be nothing more than:

The blame of those ye better
The hate of those ye guard.

Classification according to climate and temperament
One crucial aspect of Enlightenment thinking was the importance
that was attached to the relationship between climate, temperament
and civilisation. Montesquieu, Adam Ferguson and William Falconer
were particularly important here, though they were pre-empted by the
likes of Michel Montaigne, Pierre Charron and Jean Bodin. Those living in the arid or tropical climates were deemed to be of a 'low state of
morality', while those living in temperate climates were characterised
by the 'increased activity of the brain'.[19] Indeed, it seemed entirely
natural that the Europeans were hard working given that they live in
a cold and wet climate, no less than that the Africans were phlegmatic
or lazy owing to their extremely arid environment. As Philip Curtin
put it, 'The conclusion is [that] . . . [i]n Falconer's opinion, the best
possible balance of human qualities is to be found near the northern
edge of the temperate zone – in short in Britain'.[20]

Climate and temperament were intimately tied in with the level
of civilisation. As was noted in the last chapter, the Yellow peoples
(especially the Chinese) were seen by the 1780s as a fallen people,
having slipped into moral decay and backwardness as a result of their
degenerative climate on the one hand and the crippling weight of oriental despotism on the other.[21] This, of course, was an extremely
awkward representation, that could not account for the earlier European belief that China had been an example of advanced civilisation.
Nor was it consistent with the fact that northern China is just as
'temperate' as Europe. And in any case, neither the regime nor the
climate had suddenly changed at the end of the eighteenth century
to explain this 'decline'. As Michael Edwardes explains, all this was
perhaps 'a natural reaction against [the earlier] uncritical worship of
China, but a reaction also based fundamentally on ignorance. In such
circumstances, there was no middle way between fulsome praise and
total contempt.'[22] Thus the early image of China as a noble and wise

Confucius was suddenly replaced after 1780 with the image of a sinister Fu Manchu. And Chinese temperament was deemed to be one of melancholy, given that having once been great the Chinese now had to come to terms with their 'failings'.

The Black 'savage' was imagined as, in effect, 'natural man in the state of nature' who was but one step removed from the ape. One typical example here was the view expressed by the British explorer William Dampier. Having arrived in Australia in the late seventeenth century, he was astonished at the 'natural deformity' of the Natives, who had the 'most unpleasant Looks and the worst features of any people that I ever saw, tho' I have seen a great variety of savages'.[23] The condescension of Dampier was reproduced a century later when European scientists placed the Australian Aboriginal as but one step removed from the monkey. Peter Cunningham asked if the Aborigines should be placed 'at the very zero of civilisation, constituting in a measure the connecting link between man and the monkey tribe? – for really some of the women only seem to require a tail to complete the identity'.[24]

It is here where the link between the origins of explicit (scientific) racism and implicit racism is clearly manifest. The critical moment here was the creation of the Great Chain of Being, articulated by Carl Linnaeus in his book *Systema Naturae* (1735). Through the ensuing editions of the book, he gradually laid out a rudimentary framework. Originally he described four races of man within a hierarchy: white, yellow, red and black (with the whites at the top). Then in 1758 he divided *genus homo* into two: the second group included the orang-outang and certain wild men who could not speak but none the less had emotions. Because the Blacks were placed one notch above the 'tail-less' orang-outang, and because the gradations between each member on the scale were small, it was concluded that the Negro was at the bottom of human civilisation standing only just above the orang-outang.

From there, anthropologists and biologists in particular developed a long line of 'theories' and 'classifications', which culminated in the emergence of scientific racism in Britain after 1840. In the late eighteenth century Pieter Camper began measuring the human head profile. The result was that the Europeans were endowed with the highest levels of intelligence and beauty, while the Negro resided on the lowest rung of the ladder just above the most sophisticated animals. Camper was followed by a line of thinkers who also studied the size and shape of the skull – including Cuvier, Blumenbach, and Retzius – all of whom concluded similarly, that the European was the most intelligent, the Negro the least. Comte de Buffon claimed that it was the Hottentot (the Khoi-Khoi of southern Africa) who constituted the missing link between apes and humans. And Buffon's assertion meshed neatly with Edward Long's claim that: 'Ludicrous as the opinion may seem, I do not think that an orang-outang husband would be any dishonour to a Hottentot female'.[25] While most of us today would find nothing in the first part of his statement with which to quibble, many of his contemporaries would have agreed with the second.

Another popular 'scientific' myth was initiated by Maeterlinck who 'contrasted the "eastern lobe" in the human brain, secreting intuition, religion, the subconscious, with the "western lobe" in the human brain, producing reason, science, consciousness'.[26] Moreover, Dr James Hunt claimed that, 'the arrested mental development of the Negro results from the earlier closure of the sutures of the cranium in the "lower breeds of mankind"'.[27] Interestingly, these myths were actively maintained by the British practice of wearing the pith sun-helmet. This enabled the British colonial administrators to build up a superstition, based on their greater proneness to sunstroke, that their skulls were thinner and thus by implication, that their brains were larger. As George Orwell noted, 'the thin skull was the mark of racial superiority, and the pith topi was a sort of emblem of empire'.[28]

Scientific racism was fed by the un-Christian notion of polygenesis, which asserted that the different races of man had multiple origins. In rejecting the single-blood Christian conception of man's origins (which implied that all men were potentially equal in that all could be Christianised), the way was opened up for a theory of the permanent inferiority of the Blacks as well as the Yellows. Nevertheless while this theory flourished in France, it fell on less fertile ground in England as a result of the Protestant revival.[29] Indeed, it would only be during the 1840s that explicit racism would properly emerge in Britain.

The Protestant revival

The greatest paradox of the revival of British Protestantism is that while it forestalled the proper emergence of scientific racism on account of its preference for monogenesis over polygenesis, nevertheless its contribution to implicit racism and the civilising mission was profound. The reinvoking of the Genesis story of Noah's three sons was important not least because it justified the civilising mission. The Genesis story performed this role because it proclaimed – or so it was interpreted – that the *duty* of Japheth (i.e. Europe) was to absorb Shem (the Asians) and enslave and colonise Ham or Canaan (the Black Africans). According to Genesis ch. 9, verse 27: 'God shall enlarge Japheth and he shall dwell in the tents of Shem, and Canaan shall be his servant'. The Protestant revival infused Christian missionaries with the desire to go out into the world and spread the Word among all unbelievers. As A. J. Christopher put it:

> Missionaries, possibly more than members of other branches of
> the colonial establishment, aimed at the radical transformation of
> indigenous society . . . They therefore sought, whether consciously
> or unconsciously, the destruction of pre-colonial societies and
> their replacement by new . . . societies in the image of Europe.[30]

Christian missionaries constituted one of the most powerful and influential lobbying voices for the civilising mission. Indeed, as David Abernethy points out, once they had settled in various parts of the empire the missionaries, 'pressed vigorously for government intervention to facilitate the civilizing mission'.[31]

A further important aspect of the Protestant revival was that it enabled the British to differentiate themselves not only from the Blacks and Yellows, but also various European nations. The British placed themselves at the very top of the hierarchy (in the Premier League). Below them came the Germans (at the top of Division One). They then posited a ranking within Division One. The Catholic French were placed below the Germans, with the Catholic Portuguese teetering at the bottom of Division One facing relegation. As Palmerston put it, 'The plain truth is that the Portuguese are of all European nations [bar the Irish] the lowest in the moral scale'.[32] It is also highly significant to note that the Catholic Irish were omitted from Division One, being consigned to Division Three. The British satirical magazine *Punch* characterised this view accordingly: the Irish are 'the missing link between the gorilla and the Negro'.[33] British or English upper-class pronouncements on the Irish were replete with statements to the effect that they were a particularly 'wild and savage Race' (as Samuel Marsden claimed).[34] And the English upper-class attitude of distrust and hate towards the Irish was one of the crucial factors in the policy of transporting them to the Australian colonies. This discussion is significant because it indicates that skin colour was a necessary though clearly not sufficient classificatory criterion. Ultimately what mattered most was how closely other civilisations conformed to the imaginary 'standard of civilisation' that had uniquely come to perfection in England.

As Linda Colley has so persuasively argued, the British were almost as hostile to the Catholic French (not to mention the Catholic Irish) as they were the various Eastern peoples.[35] They believed that in contrast to Catholicism, Protestantism represented civilisation. French Catholics were viewed as semi-slaves languishing under French despotism (though the Irish were denounced as but savage larrikins). And in the intensive Protestant atmosphere of eighteenth- and nineteenth-century Britain, the Britons came to imagine themselves as in God's special care – that they were truly 'God's Chosen People'. This was epitomised in William Blake's famous poem which instructed the British to never cease until they had 'built Jerusalem, in England's green and pleasant land'. As Linda Colley explains, the British Protestants knew that:

> they were bound to be regularly tested by periods of extreme sin and suffering, and they took it for granted that struggle – especially struggle with those who were not Protestants – was their birthright. But they also believed that under Providence they would secure deliverance and achieve distinction. In short, they believed, many of them, that their land was nothing less than another and better Israel.[36]

Thus from the conception of the British as God's Chosen People it was but a short step to view imperialism and the Anglicisation of the world as Britain's manifest destiny.

Social Darwinism and scientific (or explicit) racism

It was only after the 1840s that explicit (or scientific) racism emerged forcefully in Britain. There were many intellectual developments in the formation of this particular discourse (a few of which were mentioned earlier). One of the important moments lay with the publication of Charles Darwin's *On The Origin of Species*, which was quickly imported into social science theories. Nevertheless, some of the ideas in the book predated Darwin, most notably in the work of Herbert Spencer. The notions of 'natural selection' and 'survival of the fittest' (the latter phrase originally being coined by Herbert Spencer) became important in legitimising to Westerners the superiority of the white race. The importation of Darwinism into social science theory was especially important because it, 'seemed to accentuate the "scientific" validity of the division of races into advanced and backward, or European-Aryan [versus the] . . . Oriental-African'.[37] This theory found its place alongside the emerging explicit (scientific) racist treatises, which were developed by Comte Arthur de Gobineau in France, Robert Knox and Charles Kingsley in Britain, Nott and Gliddon in the USA, and a range of writers in Germany such as Karl

Vogt and the English-born Houston Stewart Chamberlain. Such theories emerged in the 1840s but proliferated after 1850 (even if their roots stemmed back into the eighteenth century).[38] In the English context, scientific racism was well characterised by one of the characters in Benjamin Disraeli's novel *Tancred* (1847), who tells us that the historical success of England is an

> affair of race. A Saxon race, protected by an insular position, has stamped its diligent and methodic character on the century. And when a superior race, with a superior idea to Work and Order, advances, its state will be progressive . . . All is race.[39]

For the first time in world history, the development of societies was assumed to be founded on permanent racial characteristics (i.e. that 'All is race'). Special emphasis was placed – again for the first time in world history – on the importance of skin colour and genetic properties as a defining criterion of civilisation. Books such as Robert Knox's *The Races of Man*, Benjamin Kidd's, *Social Evolution* or Comte de Gobineau's *The Inequality of Races*, constructed a tripartite division of races based on skin colour – white, yellow and black (corresponding with the Genesis story). This was now conceived of as a permanent hierarchy and for some, though not all, scientific racists justified the subjugation of the Other (the Yellow and Black races) by the Self (the Europeans). In its extreme form scientific racism justified the extermination of the inferior races at worst and social apartheid at best. This racist construct rapidly diffused into the popular imperial discourse, expressed in a seemingly never ending set of statements issued by Imperial bureaucrats and British politicians. Typical was Joseph Chamberlain:

> I believe in this race, the greatest governing race the world has ever seen; in this Anglo-Saxon race, so proud, so tenacious, self-confident and determined, this race which neither climate nor change can degenerate, which will infallibly be the predominant force of future history and universal civilisation.[40]

Moreover, imperialism as a civilising mission was aptly expressed in the words of Lord Curzon: 'In empire, we have found not merely the key to glory and wealth, but the call to duty, and the means of service to mankind'.[41]

Importantly, the racist discourse became imbricated within international law. James Lorrimer, for example, divided humanity into three zones: White civilized humanity, Yellow barbarous humanity and Black savage humanity.[42] M. F. Lindley asserted that, 'Backward territory includes territory inhabited by natives as low on the scale of civilisation as those of Central Africa'.[43] And John Westlake argued in his, *Chapters on the Principles of International Law* (1894), that the 'uncivilized regions of the earth ought to be annexed or occupied by advanced Western powers'.[44] Indeed, European international law actively prescribed and legitimised colonisation and imperialism in the East.[45] European international law enabled imperialism through its own classification or political construction of the different states of the world. In effect, it enabled a mental 'deterritorialisation' of the Eastern peoples. How so?

Division Three countries were branded with the concept of *terra nullius*. In essence the lands of the 'savages' were imagined as but empty or waste spaces. As Lord Carnarvon typically put it in 1874: the 'mission of England' invoked 'a spirit of adventure to fill up waste places of the earth',[46] though as Edward Said poignantly notes, 'It did not trouble [the British] that what on a map was a blank space was inhabited by natives'.[47] But, of course, it would not have troubled them precisely because the Natives were imagined as savages at best and animals at worst and were, therefore, not entitled to claim a sovereign space. This 'mental deterritorialisation' meant that full colonial take over was entirely appropriate. In contrast to the treatment of the Black savages and the conception of *terra nullius*, the 'Yellows' of the Division Two countries were conceived of as the 'fallen peoples' and their lands were imagined as 'borderless spaces'. Thus, given their so-called moral degeneration, it was only appropriate that the Europeans go in and regenerate them along civilised Western lines. Nevertheless, because their lands were not decreed *terra nullius* (but obviously fell well short of sovereignty), the Europeans administered the 'corrective' treatment through informal empire rather than outright colonial take over. Conversely, the Europeans enjoyed full sovereignty. In turn, this insulated them from the British civilising mission on the grounds that only Europe contained civilised human beings – even if in the eyes of the British some were more civilised than others.

The moral contradiction of the imperial civilising mission

Once the discourse of imperialism had been forged through the reconstruction of European identity and the racist invention of the world, so the launching of the 'civilising mission' became a moral duty. The materialist argument that Britain had reached the pinnacle of material power and, therefore, engaged in imperialism because 'it could' is too simplistic. For it misses the point that it was the new British imperial identity that inscribed its 'great power' with moral purpose. That is, their identity prompted the British to pursue imperialism not merely because 'they could' but because they believed they should (i.e. 'the White Man's Burden'). As Edward Said originally pointed out, orientals had no status other than being seen as problems that had to be solved – preferably through colonial take over. Indeed, 'the very designation of something as "Oriental" . . . contained an implicit program of action . . . Once we begin to think of Orientalism as a kind of Western projection onto and will to govern over the Orient, we will encounter few surprises'.[48] However, as I explain in ch. 13, none of this is to say that material power or material factors are unimportant. Undoubtedly material power was a vital prerequisite for British imperialism. But the critical point of note is that great power is channelled in specific directions depending on the particular identity of the 'agent' in question. How then did racist identity infuse British (or Western) great power with moral purpose to thereby lead on to imperialism?

The result of the 'civilisational league table' and the racist invention of the world was the belief that the West was normal and advanced whereas the East was imagined as deviant – as backward and either barbaric or savage (see table 10.1). Most importantly, Western identity was constructed in such a way that the East could not be tolerated for its imagined deviancy. The Europeans came to view imperialism as a 'civilising mission' whereby the 'moral duty' of Western man was to bequeath to the East the gift of civilisation. Labelling imperialism as a civilising mission is fitting for various reasons: first because it was designed to civilise and emancipate the East by eradicating Eastern identity and culture and replacing it with superior Western civilisational properties. And second, the term is useful because while imperialism was not necessarily good for the world as it actually played out, nevertheless the British imperialists sincerely believed that they were indeed 'civilising' or emancipating/redeeming the East. This belief was not paraded cynically, in order to defend their actions, as materialists assume. As Charles Dickens's Mr Podsnap famously remarked, other countries were but a 'mistake'. And in their racist imagination it fell to the British to 'correct this mistake'. The British saw nothing wrong in any of this. For what could be more noble than helping others enjoy the fruits of modernity and civilisation that only the West had created and that only the British could deliver, even if the Eastern peoples were either too ignorant or too stubborn to recognise and appreciate the gracious imperial British hand?

How then were the Eastern peoples to be treated or administered for their 'deviancy' (i.e. how could they be made to become 'civilised')? The corresponding 'civilising strategy' would be selected according to the perceived level of civilisation that the West judged each Eastern state or people to be at. Thus the more uncivilised a state or people was judged to be, the harsher the disciplinary treatment would necessarily have to be in order to cure the deviant ailment. Those residing in the Division Three countries (the Black savage races), who were gauged as barely human, would be dealt with through colonialism and, at the extreme, through genocide and social apartheid. Those residing in Division Two countries (the Yellow barbarian races), who were assessed as more civilised than the Blacks but woefully inferior to the Europeans in Division One, would be dealt with through 'informal empire'.

The British civilising mission was, however, based on a fundamental contradiction. On the one hand it was the means for imposing *cultural conversion*, which sought to 'raise the Eastern peoples up' to the level of British civilisation. This required that Eastern institutions and cultural, economic and political practices be transformed along British lines. On the other hand, cultural conversion went hand in hand with the strategy of *containment*, which sought to keep the Eastern peoples and economies down. In other words, the contradiction was manifest in the twin desire to raise them up (cultural conversion) and hold them down (containment). But this contradiction was logically coherent within the racist discourse of empire. There were two reasons for this. First, the civilising mission would convert the East along Western lines so as eradicate the identity threat that the East posed in order to make the West feel superior. But in order to remain 'superior' it was also vital that the Eastern economies be contained so as to prevent them from challenging the economic hegemony of the West. Second, cultural conversion and containment both implied the repression of the East. Cultural conversion embodied the very essence of implicit racism in which the target group's identity and culture would be eradicated and replaced by the 'superior' culture of the imperial country. Indeed, cultural conversion is equivalent to what Pierre Clastres calls 'ethnocide'. This meshed with the idea behind containment: that because the Eastern peoples were inferior at best or subhuman at worst, so they could 'naturally' be exploited, repressed and utilised to service the various needs of the 'Mother Country'.

The upshot of this discussion is that had racism not existed and had the West viewed the Eastern peoples as equal human beings, imperialism might never have occurred. Or as Edward Said put it, 'we would not have had empire itself without important philosophical and imaginative processes at work in the production as well as the acquisition, subordination and settlement of [mental] space'.[49] It now remains to enquire as to how the moral contradiction of the imperial civilising mission played out (to be discussed in the third section of ch. 11).

11 The dark side of British industrialisation and the myth of *laissez-faire*:
war, racist imperialism and the Afro-Asian origins of industrialisation

Colbert appears . . . not to have been the inventor of [the protectionist] system . . . for . . . it was fully elaborated by the English long before him.

> Friedrich List

The Pax Britannica, always an impudent falsehood, has become a grotesque monster of hypocrisy.

> John A. Hobson

The only lesson to be learnt is that East and West are no more than names . . . He who wants to will conduct himself with decency. There is no people for whom the moral life is a special mission.

> Mahatma Gandhi

[The British empire was] a magnificent superstructure of American commerce and [British] naval power on an African foundation.

> Malachy Postlethwayt

We noted in ch. 9 that British industrialisation occupies a special position within the Eurocentric discourse of world history. We also noted that the key to Britain's 'Great Leap Forward' lay with its individualistic self-help culture within which all manner of ingenious inventions were pioneered. In turn this is conventionally assumed to be a function of the minimalist *laissez-faire* (non-interventionist) posture of the state. And this in turn feeds back into the general Eurocentric proposition that British industrialisation was a purely internal affair founded on self-generated change.

In this chapter I challenge this picture by making two general arguments: first that the British state is better understood as a despotic, interventionist late developer that played a vital role in enabling industrialisation. The first and second sections elaborate on this argument as it applied to the domestic arena. And second, in contrast to the Eurocentric thesis of internally led 'self-generated' change (the 'logic of immanence'), I argue that the racist imperial appropriation of Eastern resources constituted a crucial external contribution to British industrialisation – as discussed in section 3. Thus while chapter 9 focused on the assimilation of Chinese 'resource portfolios', here I examine the imperial appropriation of Eastern resources in the story of the rise of the West; what I refer to as the Afro-Asian origins of British industrialisation. In short, the significance of labelling Britain a despotic and racist late developer is that it necessarily shifts our prime focus to the interventionist, appropriationist and repressive posture that the state deployed both at home and abroad during the industrialisation period.

War and the myth of British *laissez-faire*

Pick up any standard economic history textbook on British industrialisation and the familiar story will be told: that it was the sanctity of 'sovereign individualism' rather than 'sovereign statism' that secured Britain's 'triumph'. In its liberal incarnation the formula asserts that it is better to be governed by the invisible hand of economic competition than the visible hand of the interventionist state. Or as Dugald Stewart put it, summarising Adam Smith's position: 'Little else is required to carry a state to the highest degree of opulence from the lowest barbarism, but peace, easy taxes and a tolerable administration of justice; all the rest being brought about by the natural course of things'.[1] In essence, the British state is believed to have created the correct background conditions for the peaceful conquest of nature and 'tradition' while simultaneously refraining from directly intervening in the economy (i.e. *laissez-faire*); hence its triumphant breakthrough. Strikingly, this assumption holds universal appeal across the many theories and accounts of British industrialisation.

The crucial word that underpins the concept of *laissez-faire* is 'spontaneity'. As Peter Mathias expressed this standard view:

> Industrialization in Britain . . . is usually taken, rightly, as the classical case of spontaneous growth, responsive primarily to market influences and underlying social, institutional forms, not organized consciously by government design in the interests of promoting industrial growth. In so far as the [British] state was important, its main role was to institutionalize these underlying social and economic forces, to provide security at home and abroad within which market and economic forces . . . would [spontaneously] operate. [The state] did not aim to provide a central momentum to the process of industrial growth, to shape development . . . It was concerned more with the context than with the process; with regulating the external conditions rather than creating the actual internal forces.[2]

Eschewing 'process' (the policy of positive state intervention) and being more concerned with 'context' (i.e. *laissez-faire* and the provision of the necessary background conditions only), meant that the state secured low taxes, balanced budgets, free trade and a peaceful foreign policy. At least this is the familiar picture that we associate with the British story. But this chapter reveals this as one of the central myths of world history (Eurocentric or otherwise), given that British state interventionism was striking only for its extremely pronounced levels.

Britain's militarised industrialisation

Our conventional picture of British industrialisation is that it was secured in the absence of warfare, which enabled Britain's pioneering capitalists to get on and do what they do best. Striking then is the fact that in the important period (1688–1815), the British state was at war for no less than 52 per cent of the time. More striking still are the amounts spent on warfare. Table 11.1 produces data that represent

Table 11.1 *Real British government expenditures (spending expressed as a proportion of national income)*

	1715–1815 = 100		1715–1815 = 100		1715–1815 = 100	
	CGE	CGE	D1	D1	D2	D2
1715–1815	20	100	11	100	18	100
1760–1815	23	114	13	116	21	113
1815–1850	14	71	5	40	12	65
1715–1850	17	84	7	64	14	79
1850–1913	9	43	3	29	5	26
1914–1980	33	165	8	71	12	67

Notes: CGE = central government expenditures on all services, D1 = ordinary and extraordinary military spending, D2 = ordinary and extraordinary military spending plus interest payments on military loans.
Source: Linda Weiss and John M. Hobson, *States and Economic Development* (Cambridge: Polity, 1995), p. 130.

the real burden of defence, where the burden is calculated by taking defence spending as a proportion of national income (which simultaneously irons out the distorting effects of inflation and economic growth).

Between 1715 and 1815 defence spending (D1) was almost 300 per cent that of the 1850–1913 period and even outpaced the amounts spent between 1914–80 (which included two world wars). Most strikingly, D2 spending between 1715 and 1815 was double that spent on all services by the state between 1850 and 1913 and significantly outpaced D2 expenditures between 1914 and 1980. No less strikingly, table 11.2 reveals that the real British military burden through the main phase of industrialisation significantly outpaced all the major European powers in their respective phases. In sum, it was Britain and not autocratic Russia or authoritarian Germany that most closely conformed to a 'militarised industrialisation'.

Table 11.2 *Comparative (real) defence burdens of the major European powers during their respective industrialisation phases*[a]

	UK 1715–1850	France 1840–1913	Germany[b] 1850–1913	Italy 1860–1913	Austria 1870–1913	Russia 1860–1913
D1	7	3.7	3.8	3.4	3.1	4.7
D2	14	c. 4.5	3.8	c. 4.0	c. 3.5	c. 6.5

Notes: [a] Note that the dates of industrialisation provided here are only approximations.

[b] Prussian data from 1850–1871. Note that German D1 and D2 are the same because interest payments could not be disaggregated. Nevertheless D1 are only slightly inflated.

Source: calculated from the sources in John M. Hobson, *The Wealth of States* (Cambridge: Cambridge University Press, 1997), pp. 284–90.

The Highest national debt in the world

The popular assumption is that one of the major contributions made by the liberal British state was that it secured balanced budgets. This view is a myth, given that between 1688 and 1815 the accumulated public debt stood at a colossal 180 per cent of national income.[3] The size of the British national debt can be appreciated by comparing it with those of various countries which are conventionally thought to have been highly indebted. The Tsarist national debt in 1914 stood at 47 per cent of national income and Wilhelmine Germany's constituted 9 per cent in 1913. Another significant comparison is that in 1990 the US federal debt level was 59 per cent of national income.[4]

High and unfair taxes

The British state is supposed to have both maintained low taxes (so as to enable capitalists to save, invest and accumulate), and to have kept taxes fair so as not to penalise the masses. This is vital because we are told that late developing, despotic interventionist states tend to levy highly regressive taxes (i.e. indirect taxes) which penalise the lower income groups, in order to squeeze out a surplus which can then be used to enable industrial investment.

It is striking to note, therefore, that regressive taxes (i.e. the indirect tax burden) comprised just under 10 per cent of British national income between 1715 and 1815. This outpaced both autocratic Russia (8 per cent) in its industrialisation phase as well as Ming/Ch'ing China (see ch. 3). And for the 1715–1850 period British indirect taxes comprised as much as 66 per cent of central government revenues, whereas direct taxes comprised a mere 18 per cent. No less significant is that in Britain the growth of taxes on the lower income groups outstripped their earnings, while under Tsarist autocracy the peasantry's income growth outstripped the growth of its tax burden.[5] Moreover, indirect taxes were intimately tied in with British despotism, militarism and protectionism.

The British system of national protectionism: despotism, militarism and regressive taxation

The conventional image we hold of Britain during its industrialisation is that it was the cosmopolitan or liberal, free-trading country *par excellence*. Undoubtedly, it is the repeal of the Corn Laws in 1846 that has created this image. But the immediate problem is that of chronology: free trade came only at the end of the industrialisation process. To extrapolate this back in time to furnish a *laissez-faire* gloss to the British state during the industrialisation period is anachronistic. Table 11.3 below tells us why, revealing that British tariffs were significant both for their very high levels and for the fact that they outpaced those of all other European states during their respective industrialisation phase. In fact British rates in the high industrial phase (1800–45) were some six times higher than those levied by the supposedly protectionist German state in its industrialisation phase, and were one-and-a-half times those of Russia (usually assumed to be the arch-protectionist industrialiser of Europe).

The escalation of British tariff rates after the 1790s and especially after 1815 is highly significant for two reasons. First, this came

Table 11.3 *Average tariff rates in the industrialisation phase of selected European countries*[a]

UK 1700–1799	UK 1800–45	France 1840–1913	Germany[b] 1850–1913	Austria-Hungary 1860–1913	Italy 1860–1913	Russia 1870–1913
27	40	10	7	12	11	26

Notes: [a] Note that all figures are average tariff rates on *all* imports (rather than dutiable imports only), and are calculated by taking the proportion of customs revenue as a percentage of all imports.
[b] Prussian data for 1850–1871.

Sources: Britain: Weiss and Hobson, *States*, p. 124. Germany and Russia: Hobson, *Wealth of States*, pp. 284–90. France: J. V. Nye, 'The Myth of Free-Trade Britain and Fortress France: Tariffs and Trade in the Nineteenth Century', *Journal of Economic History* 51 (1) (1991), 26. Austria-Hungary and Italy: Brian R. Mitchell, *International Historical Statistics: Europe, 1750–1993* (London: Macmillan, 1998).

at a time when economic growth was not only increasing but 'taking off' (see next section). And second, it problematises the traditional view which asserts that after 1800 Britain led the way in tariff liberalisation to such an extent that the repeal of the Corn Laws in 1846 was inevitable. However, the raising of tariffs after 1815, 'became so much more severe in weight and effect . . . that they constituted virtually a new system'.[6] Thus between 1800 and 1809 average tariffs increased to a substantial 36 per cent; they rose to 44 per cent between 1810 and 1819 and peaked at a massive 55 per cent between 1820 and 1829. Nevertheless, even as late as 1830 to 1839 average tariff rates stood as high as 38 per cent. This latter figure is significant because at no point in time did any other European state levy such a high rate in its industrialisation phase. Moreover, by 1840 no fewer than 1146 items carried tariffs.

Significantly, in typical 'despotic' style there was a strong fiscal military rationale to tariff policy, in that the state milked the economy in general and the masses in particular in order to extract indirect trade taxes to finance British militarism. Tariff revenue comprised 2.6 per cent of national income and 37 per cent of defence spending (D1) between 1715 and 1790. Tariffs were raised further in order to finance the Napoleonic wars, comprising 3.8 per cent of national income and 25 per cent of defence spending (D1) between 1790 and 1815. They were progressively raised again after 1815 in order to help finance the massive interest payments on the national debt, which had been accrued as a function of the sustained militarism of the previous 120 years. Between 1815 and 1850 customs revenue comprised 4.6 per cent of national income and 70 per cent of average annual interest payments (while interest payments comprised just over 50 per cent of central government expenditures). Moreover, even between 1850 and 1913 regressive tariff revenues comprised as much as 2 per cent of national income and funded about 60 per cent of defence spending.

In the process of financing British militarism some 60 per cent of all raw materials were taxed through tariffs, many of which were vital inputs to British industry. This in turn increased the price of the final British export product thereby making it less competitive abroad. To appease those industrialists who were directly harmed by tariffs on manufacturing inputs, the state created a highly complex system of regulation, including bounties, drawbacks and rebates. In the end, the system of protectionist regulation was supplemented by further layers of regulation. And yet a further layer of regulation was added to this protectionist raft in the form of the Navigation Acts. In sum, it is clear that regulation rather than *laissez-faire* was the order of the day during the British industrial revolution.

Noteworthy too is that in one crucial respect 1846 did not mark the turn to British free trade. British tariffs stood at a substantial 20 per cent between 1846 and 1860, remained significant at 10 per cent between 1860 and 1879 and only dropped to a modest 6 per cent as late as the 1880–1913 period. It is true that after 1846 most of these particular tariffed imports were not produced in Britain (hence they had little protectionist rationale). But crucially, they had a highly negative impact on colonial producers (see below) as well as British working-class consumers. Moreover, revenues from progressive property and income taxation only came to exceed customs revenue on a sustained basis after 1911. Interestingly, in his classic study, *Imperialism*, my great-grandfather, John A. Hobson, properly claimed that Continental militarism and imperialism thrived upon indirect taxation and tariff protectionism.[7] What he did not quite appreciate, though, is that the same conclusion applied no less to Britain right down to 1911. Indeed, during (and after) the main industrialisation phase it was the largely unenfranchised masses who bore the brunt of the tax burden that British militarism/protectionism imposed.

The near universal assumption that the British state or the *Pax Britannica* proactively pushed Continental Europe into adopting free trade is also in need of revision. British attitudes in promoting Continental free trade were striking only for their indifference. First, European free trade was not actually achieved in the middle decades of the nineteenth century. Indeed, in 1875 (at the peak of the 'liberalisation era') average tariff rates on manufactures stood at 10 per cent for Europe and 14 per cent if we include the US (see ch. 12). The best that could be said was that this was an era of 'freer trade' (or more properly an era of moderate protectionism). And second, Europe had to await the 1860 Cobden–Chevalier treaty before it even began to move towards 'freer trade'. Indeed, it was France that took a particularly prominent role in promoting this shift.[8] Importantly, Richard Cobden initially rejected the proposal forwarded by Chevalier. And most ironically of all, Cobden:

> still shared the view that all nations should be left to adjust their fiscal [commercial] policy to their own interest unhampered by treaty arrangements with other countries, and that Britain in particular, having adopted Free Trade, should avoid any tariff arrangement with another country.[9]

It was also particularly ironic that William Gladstone did not baulk at the ending of the treaty with France in 1872. His attitude was represented by Lord Lyons, 'who told the Duc de Broglie that Britain had had enough of commercial treaties, and that he believed in the freedom of each country to set its own tariffs subject only to security for British trade'.[10] If that meant lower tariffs, this would be advantageous; if not, then too bad. Moreover, speaking of Gladstone, Sir Louis Mallet, 'observed that he had never served under a government so unsympathetic and even hostile to "the free trade policy in the largest sense" [and complained that it] had effectually demolished all his work at the Board of Trade'.[11]

Proof of this indifference, if not hostility, to promoting European free trade lay in two simple points: first that Britain did nothing to stop the Continental drift back to protectionism after 1877/9. In any case its unilateral trading posture hampered its ability to contain Continental protectionism, as did the weak institutional nature of the so-called British international trade regime. And second, the fact is that the British government had negotiated only very few treaties with other Continental powers during the so-called free trade era. Thus in the 1860s Italy negotiated twenty-four such treaties, Belgium and France nineteen each, Germany eighteen, Austria-Hungary four-teen and Great Britain eight.

In sum, the conventional characterisation of British industrial-isation as founded on *laissez-faire* is, albeit highly pervasive, a myth none the less. Britain's taxes, tariffs, budget deficits, national debt and military expenditures were striking only for their high levels. The question now becomes: was all this merely coincidental or was there a causal relationship between such pronounced levels of state intervention and industrialisation? The next section makes the case for a causal relationship.

War, late development and the despotic interventionist state

Militarism, the interventionist state and the proactive creation of finance capital

The development of finance capital rested fundamentally on the proactive policies of the British state, undertaken largely to finance British militarism. With military expenditures escalating after 1688, governments were forced to rely on loans. In order to raise the nec-essary loans the state instigated the 'financial revolution'.[12] In 1694 the Bank of England was created, specifically to organise the state's wartime loans on the London capital market. Government bonds throughout the long eighteenth century (1688–1815) provided a strong outlet for the City of London's capital. Moreover, the City's extensive capital services and invisible earnings facilitated both British indus-trialisation and secured a positive balance of payments. Indeed, these invisible earnings were vital, given that between 1796 and 1931 the balance of trade was in deficit every single year.[13] Not only did this situation contrast strikingly with China's historic trade surpluses, but it is noteworthy too that during the nineteenth century Britain never got close to matching either China's share of world manufacturing production output or the proportion of world product that the latter had achieved between 1750 and 1830.[14]

The British state also intervened in order to establish an inte-grated capital market, again largely for fiscal-military purposes.[15]

During the Napoleonic wars the state set up the London Stock Exchange in order to rationalise the selling of government bonds. This simultaneously spurred on the growth of regional banks. All in all, there can be little doubt that the British national debt was one of the main drivers of public and private finance in the eighteenth, and first half of the nineteenth, century. And nowhere was this more clearly borne out than in the implicit 'forced savings' policy.

Militarism, despotism and forced savings

Here I discuss Britain's policy of 'forced savings' (traditionally associated with autocratic or Stalinist regimes). Such a policy requires the state to levy high taxes on the lower income groups in order to squeeze out sufficient revenue to be invested in industrialisation. The obvious difference between the British and Stalinist programmes was that the Soviet state directly invested the revenues, while the British state indirectly invested them. Essentially, the British state redistributed funds from the poor consumer classes to the rich financial investors, who then used the money to invest in the economy.

We noted above that the British state financed a good deal of its military expenditures through loans raised on the London capital market. Essentially the state paid interest to rich financial investors with regressive indirect taxes that were raised mainly from the lower income groups, thereby redistributing income from the poor (consumers) to the very rich (savers and investors). I estimate that about 80 per cent of all loans were raised on the London capital market (the remaining 20 per cent being borrowed from the Amsterdam capital market).[16] This means that about 80 per cent of total interest payments made by the state went straight to the financial investors in the City of London. Given the regressivity of taxation, I assume that between 50 and 60 per cent of the interest payments were paid by the lower income groups. On this basis, I calculate that about 5 per cent of national income was transferred from the poor working class/lower-middle-class consumers to the rich financial investors in the 1715–1850 period. These are staggering figures (equivalent to almost twice the amount that Britain spent on defence between 1850 and 1913). Moreover, the amounts redistributed during the Napoleonic wars were just under 9 per cent of national income (which, according to one expert, enabled the doubling of private investment rates).[17] Not surprisingly, the eighteenth century witnessed a squeeze on consumption, while savings and investment increased considerably, thereby serving to raise the rate of economic growth.[18]

Thus it seems clear that the state in effect implemented what was a highly successful policy of forced savings. This stands the conventional assumption on its head and contradicts Peter Mathias's claim that 'the state did very little indeed to promote . . . investment, [or] to mobilize capital for productive investment . . . [either directly or] indirectly'.[19] The amounts redistributed were striking. Just under 40 per cent of all central government taxes were redistributed from the poor to the rich (which compares with the amounts redistributed by post-war Keynesian welfare states).

Tariff protectionism and late development

British protectionist policy was also tied in with the late development process. The standard assumption is that Britain was an 'early developer' and enjoyed the 'advantages of the pioneer' – i.e. that it faced no significant foreign economic competition and thus had no need to engage in state interventionism and protectionism. But Britain *did* face foreign competition, especially in the pivotal cotton textile and iron industries. Indeed, Britain was flooded with superior quality/ low-priced Indian textiles from the seventeenth century onwards.

Britain's cotton industry was developed in typical late developer style through 'import-substitution industrialisation' (and through slavery – see section 3 below).[20] The importation of printed calicoes was prohibited in two stages, 1701 and 1721. Moreover, in classic late developer style, Britons copied and refined the Indian technologies/techniques in order to cut costs and thereby enhance competitiveness.[21] Or as Braudel fittingly put it, in the face of this onslaught of Indian textiles:

> England's first step was to close her own frontiers for the greater
> part of the eighteenth century to Indian textiles . . . Then she tried
> to capture for herself this profitable market – something that
> could only be achieved by making drastic reductions in
> manpower. It is surely no coincidence that the machine
> revolution began in the cotton industry.[22]

In particular, superior Indian competition stimulated the 'invention'
of Wyatt's and Paul's spinning frame (1738), Arkwright's water-frame
(1767) and Crompton's mule (1779), which enabled the production of
yarn that could match the Indian product.[23] There was also direct diffusion, and conscious emulation, of Indian products and techniques,
particularly with respect to the process of textile dyeing.[24] Even so, it
would not be until the 1840s that the British would be able to match
the quality of Indian printing as found on their bandannas (i.e. silk
handkerchiefs). A similar story characterises the other major British
industry – iron. As noted in previous chapters, British iron and steel
remained inferior to that produced in India up to and into the nineteenth century. But by levying high tariffs on Indian iron imports and
later imposing free trade within India, the British were able to take
the lead (see below).[25] Thus protecting the two key industries was
essential if they were to have any chance of growing up in the face of
superior Eastern competition.

No less significant here is that the British state enacted a kind
of 'strategic trade policy' (usually associated with the newly industrialising countries of South Korea, Taiwan and Japan after 1945).[26]
This policy requires that the state give fiscal relief to those producers
who export their products. After 1721, the British state intentionally
promoted exports by providing rebates on imported raw materials for
those producers who exported their finished manufactured product.
Moreover, export duties were abolished and replaced by export bounties, which made British textile manufacturing exports more globally
competitive. Interesting too is that the percentage shares of British
industrial product exported abroad after 1750 were similar to those of

South Korea during its period of 'export-oriented industrialisation'.[27] Nevertheless, it would be incorrect to assume that the 1721 reform marked the inception of a purely rational economic posture mainly because tariffs were still used as a fiscal weapon in the state's arsenal.

Thus we have seen that in contrast to all the mainstream accounts, the British state deployed a highly interventionist and repressive programme which significantly enabled industrialisation on the backs of the working class (i.e. the domestic dimension of the dark side of British industrialisation). I now turn to revealing the dark side in the global context. Revealing this simultaneously falsifies the general Eurocentric proposition that British industrialisation was an internal process founded on self-generated change.

Racism, industrialisation and the moral contradiction of the British imperial civilising mission

While ch. 9 dealt with the assimilation of Chinese 'resource portfolios' in the rise of British industrialisation, this section focuses on the racist-imperial appropriation of Eastern resources that enabled Britain's breakthrough. Fernand Braudel pointed to the external – specifically imperial – origins of British industrialisation through posing a fascinating rhetorical question:

> If the little continent of Europe were to be cut loose to float among the seas and land-masses of Asia, it would vanish from sight . . . It was from all over the world . . . that [Britain] was now drawing a substantial part of her strength and substance. And it was this extra share which enabled [the British] to reach [new] heights in tackling the tasks encountered on the path to progress. Without this constant assistance, would [Britain's] industrial revolution – the key to her destiny – have been possible by the end of the eighteenth century? Whatever answer historians may propose for this question, it is one that must be asked.[28]

Here I answer Braudel's question in the negative. I also emphasise the point that imperialism was the product of the 'implicit racism' of British identity that had been constructed during the eighteenth and nineteenth centuries (see ch. 10). Moreover, my analysis views the cultural impact of imperialism upon Eastern societies as not only important, but often more important than the economic impact (though this is not to diminish the detrimental economic impact). Nevertheless this section – like the last two – stands at fundamental odds with liberal economic history which has sought to entirely discount this external input into British industrialisation. Interesting here is Patrick O'Brien's reaffirmation of Eurocentrism in response to Braudel's argument:

> Braudel delighted in big questions but the connexions from the world economy to the industrial revolution are not nearly strong enough to seriously weaken the present 'Eurocentric consensus' that its mainsprings are to be found within and not beyond the continent . . . For the history of European (and even British) industrialization the 'perspective of the world' for Europe emerges as less significant than the 'perspective of Europe' for the world.[29]

This section produces detailed empirical evidence that reveals the Afro-Asian origins of British industrialisation, thereby reaffirming Braudel's 'perspective of the world'.

The contradictions of imperial free trade: containment versus cultural conversion

In ch. 10 we noted that there was a fundamental contradiction in the imperial 'civilising mission': that cultural conversion was designed to 'raise the Eastern peoples up' to the levels of British civilisation (the civilising part of the mission), while the containment strategy entailed holding their economies down. We also noted that paradoxically, this contradiction logically flowed from the racist discourse of empire that the British had constructed. For both strands came together, insofar as they were the means by which British civilisation would be glorified. Thus cultural conversion (ethnocide or the eradication of Eastern identity/culture) served this purpose because it implied the Westernisation or Anglicisation of the world. And containment ensured that the British economy would remain unchallenged as the world's leading power. It is this story that lies at the heart of our discussion here.

Perhaps nowhere was the moral contradiction of the civilising mission more evident than in the policy of free trade. The theory asserted that free trade is a civilising force. According to Adam Smith and David Ricardo, free trade was good precisely because it rested on the notion of national 'self-help', 'specialisation' and 'comparative advantage'. It was a civilising process because free trade would force the Eastern peoples to intensively develop their economies through individualistic self-help and 'hard work' – the *leitmotif* of advanced civilisation. Interesting here is the link between individualistic self-help and Protestantism. For as Samuel Smiles told us, 'Heaven helps those who help themselves'. The ideology of free trade disseminated rapidly through British society. Richard Cobden, for example, famously proselytised the message of free commerce as, 'the grand panacea which, like a beneficent medical discovery, will serve to inoculate with the wealth and saving taste for civilisation all the nations of the world'.[30] Or as he put it in a letter to Dufour, 'Free Trade is God's diplomacy, and there is no other certain way of uniting people in bonds of peace'.[31] And then, of course, there was Dr John Bowring's epigram that, 'Jesus Christ is free trade and free trade is Jesus Christ'.[32] In short, free trade was one of the crucial means to deliver the manna of Western civilisation to the world, no less than the fruits of the East to the West. This theory was consistent with the British desire to culturally convert the East along Western lines. Nevertheless, given the presumed short-sightedness of the Eastern rulers, it was of course left to the far-sighted British to spread free trade across the world for the benefit of all; indeed, it was their 'moral duty'. But this rationale clashed with that of a more hidden 'containment' aspect of imperialism, which in turn was based upon a number of racist double standards.

Cultural conversion and containment of the East through the imperialism of free trade was manifest in a number of ways. First, there was the imposition of the unequal treaties, which constituted the vehicle through which the British would 'spread the gift of civilisation'. These were 'granted' to many 'non-Western' countries including Brazil (1810), China (1842–1858), Japan (1858), Siam (1824–1855), Persia (1836, 1857), and the Ottoman empire (1838, 1861). These treaties stripped the country of tariff autonomy and generally limited tariffs to a maximum of 5 per cent. The first racist double standard here is revealed by the fact that during the so-called free trade era of the mid-nineteenth century, European states were subject to 'reciprocity treaties' that were freely negotiated between 'contracting partners'. This clearly contrasted with the 'open door' treaties that were imposed upon the East (mainly those countries in Division Two). Moreover, British indifference to spreading free trade across Europe contrasted starkly with its forceful imposition of free trade in the 'non-European' world. And more generally, Britain's passive military posture *vis-à-vis* Continental Europe after 1815 contrasted strikingly with Britain's frequent recourse to violence in the East.[33] A second racist double standard here was that while the European economies industrialised through tariff protectionism – indeed, Britain enjoyed an average tariff of no less than 32 per cent between 1700 and 1850 – the Eastern economies were forced to move straight to free trade or near free trade. This served to contain their economies because it denied them the chance of building up their infant industries.

It is especially important to note here that the imposition of the unequal treaties was not based on a purely economic rationale but was also a more general means by which the British tried to impose cultural conversion. The harm that this caused was often more onerous than that of economic containment. Arguably the most offensive aspect of the unequal treaties lay with their general affront to Eastern sovereignty and cultural autonomy. Let us take China as an example. The Opium wars and subsequent imposed treaties proved to be a wedge to open China up to Britain's cultural assault on its identity. They were labelled 'unequal' for three main reasons. First, China did not consent to them and they were ultimately enforced by British and Western military power. Second, they were dictated solely on Western terms to the detriment of Chinese sovereignty and cultural self-determination. And third, they symbolised China's sense of humiliation and injustice.

There were three basic aspects to the negative cultural and political impact of British imperialism in China. First, through the unequal treaties Chinese sovereignty was fundamentally assaulted by the enforcement at gunpoint of 'extraterritoriality' – the notion that all foreign residents, not just foreign diplomats, might live in China but would be subject only to their own Western laws. To this end a number of 'concessions' were established (i.e. areas of land designated for foreigners who were subject to British law). And this was justified through Western international law because China was assessed as uncivilised and was, therefore, deemed to be non-sovereign. Indeed, the British steadfastly refused to treat the Chinese as equals. As the Duke of Argyll declared at the time of the Second Opium War:

> It is supreme nonsense to talk as if we were bound to the Chinese by the same rules which regulate international relations in Europe . . . It would be madness to be bound on our side by that code with a barbarous people, to whom it is unknown, and if known, would not be followed.[34]

Here it is also noteworthy that extraterritoriality was enforced against the Ottoman empire, Thailand and many other countries, on the basis that they too failed to pass the 'civilisation test'.

Second, Chinese sovereignty was assaulted through the unequal treaties by the British policy of forcing the Chinese into accepting foreign administration of key bureaucratic agencies such as the postal services, maritime customs and taxing agencies (e.g. the gabelle or salt tax). The British take over of the Imperial Maritime Customs (IMC) first occurred in 1853 when British consuls in Shanghai decided to collect customs duties. Later in 1863, Robert Hart became head of the IMC, which amounted to a full British take over. Clearly, the inability of the Chinese government to set its own foreign trade policy constituted a major affront to its sovereignty and autonomy.

The third affront to Chinese cultural autonomy through the unequal treaties lay in the British insistence upon the abolition of the kowtow. While this had no economic consequences, of all the demands that the British made this was the most humiliating and consequential. Its effect was to shatter the whole social and moral/normative structure upon which the Chinese state and society had been founded. As we saw in ch. 3, prior to the nineteenth century China had developed its own 'standard of civilisation', which was based on the kowtow. To kowtow to the emperor was to formally recognise China as the superior Middle Kingdom. But as we also noted, this was a 'defensive construct' designed to maintain the domestic legitimacy of Chinese institutions in the face of foreign invasion and 'barbarian' take over. However, after the sixteenth century this was to prove increasingly ineffective against European challenges. The challenges from Europe began with the 1645 Rites controversy, then progressed on to the Lord Macartney incident in 1793 (when he refused to kowtow) and culminated in the 1873 abolition. This constituted China's greatest humiliation as its whole international system, and along with it its domestic system of legitimacy, was effectively shattered. Moreover, cultural humiliation was effected in a whole variety of ways, perhaps the most notorious example being when the British erected signs outside the recreation ground in Shanghai (now Huangpu Park) stating: 'No dogs or Chinese allowed'. One can only imagine how the British would have reacted had the Chinese taken over St James's Park (just down the road from Buckingham Palace) only to erect signs stating: 'No dogs or Britons allowed'.

But to return to the general discussion: a second imperial containment strategy that was entwined with that of cultural conversion involved the imposition of free trade as a means to de-industrialise various colonial economies. And here we turn to the third racist double standard: for while the policy of free trade was sold as helping or civilising the colonies, its effect was to promote the British economy at the expense of the Eastern economies. One notable example here was the undermining, or the de-industrialisation, of the Indian economy. Thus having been reliant on Indian cotton manufactures in the seventeenth century, the British government responded by placing heavy tariffs on Indian imports in the early eighteenth century (as already noted). Later on, in the nineteenth century, the British ensured that the Indian market went unprotected (i.e. by imposing Indian free trade). At Lancashire's behest, duties were abandoned on cotton imports into India between 1882 and 1894 (having been lowered to 5 per cent between 1859 and 1882). The double standard and hypocritical treatment of India with respect to cotton was striking. For having held the Indian cotton manufacturing system down with one boot (through very high British tariffs), the other boot kicked British manufactures into India unimpeded. It was one of the most unfair 'free kicks' that the British awarded themselves. This takes us to what Ha-Joon Chang, following Friedrich List, refers to as the tactic of 'kicking away the ladder'.[35] As List originally put it:

> Free trade is in the interests of Britain as the means to ensure her manufacturing supremacy . . . It is a very common clever device that when [someone] has attained the summit of greatness, he kicks away the ladder by which he has climbed up, in order to deprive others of the means of climbing up after him. In this lies the secret of the cosmopolitical doctrine of Adam Smith and of the . . . British government.[36]

But *contra* List this strategy was not designed to maintain Britain's lead over other Continental countries, given that successive British governments did little to promote or maintain European free trade. It was rather designed to maintain Britain's lead over the Eastern economies since it was only outside Europe where the British imposed free trade.

Thus while in the seventeenth century the British economy was a net importer of Indian textiles, by 1815 Britain exported approximately 250 million yards of cotton worth about £40 million, while by 1874 it exported 3.5 billion yards worth about £190 million.[37] By 1873, 40–45 per cent of all British cotton textile exports went to India.[38] Thus having once exported cotton manufactures to Britain, by the mid-nineteenth century India had been transformed into a raw cotton supplier for the Lancashire industry, which in turn exported the finished product back to India. In short, the social cost of the advancement of the British textiles industry was the de-industrialisation of the Indian industry.[39] As one nineteenth-century British voice explained:

> Had not such prohibitory duties and decrees existed, the mills of Paisley and of Manchester would have been stopped . . . They were created by the sacrifice of the Indian manufacturer . . . The foreign manufacturer employed the arm of political injustice to keep down and ultimately strangle a competitor with whom he could not have contended on equal terms.[40]

Much the same story applied to the iron industry (during the nineteenth century), in which the Indian economy had been one of the world's foremost producers. As Felipe Fernández-Armesto, having noted the superiority of Indian industrial development before Britain's imperial take over, wryly notes:

> with an exactness rare in history, India's industrial debâcle [de-industrialisation] coincided with the establishment of British rule or hegemony . . . The potential competition of its [India's] economy could be stifled. No single episode was more decisive in shifting the balance of the world's resources than this shift in the sources of their [British] control.[41]

And as Friedrich List pointed out, this 'free' trading relationship between Britain and India ultimately constituted one of 'unequal exchange' in that it condemned the latter to rely on an agricultural/raw materials stage of production, thereby undermining its industrial developmental prospects.[42]

All in all, therefore, British imperial trade policy encapsulated the moral contradiction between cultural conversion and containment, which played out to the benefit of Britain and to the detriment of the economic interests, and cultural dignity, of the East. Moreover, the same problem occurred as the British sought to mobilise the Eastern peoples and economies in order to 'spread the gift of civilisation' to the whole world.

Racism and the commodification of the East: the Afro-Asian origins of British industrialisation

Convinced of their own superiority the British saw it as entirely appropriate that the East be carved up and reorganised to service their industrial needs. This was not merely a function of superior military or economic material power but emanated ultimately from a patriarchal and racist attitude towards the 'Black' and 'Yellow' races. In the British mind set it was axiomatic that they should not be treated as equals. As the scientific racist, Charles Kingsley, put it in typical social Darwinian style:

> A moral duty lies on any nation, who can produce far more sufficient than for its own wants, to supply the wants of others from its own surplus . . . [T]he human species has a right to demand . . . that each people should either develop the capabilities of their own country, or make room for those who will develop them.[43]

And as Pierre Clastres explains:

> This is why no respite could be given to [Eastern] societies who abandoned the world to its original tranquil productivity. This is why, in the eyes of the West, the wastefulness represented by the non-exploitation of immense resources was intolerable. The choice left to these societies posed a dilemma: either yield to production or else disappear, either ethnocide [i.e. cultural conversion] or genocide.[44]

Paradoxically, therefore, 'spreading the gift of civilisation' entailed the commodification of Eastern land, labour, markets and resources. For if the colonials would not contribute to civilisation, then it was axiomatic that the British should mobilise them accordingly. And it is here where we move to the centre of the appropriationist side of the story.

The ultimate expression of Britain's implicit racist attitude lay with the commodification of Black labour through slavery. Negro slavery and Africans more generally enabled British industrialisation in at least seven major ways. The first contribution lay in the profits that accrued from the slave trade. Stanley Engerman and Roger Anstey discounted this by claiming that slave trade profits were extremely small when measured as a proportion of investment or national income (known as the 'small ratios' argument).[45] However, commenting on Engerman's data, Barbara Solow argues that for 1770 the 'slave trade profits form . . . nearly 8 per cent of total investment, and 39 per cent of commercial and industrial investment. These ratios are not small; they are enormous.'[46] By way of comparison, she goes on to say that in the USA in 1980, the ratio of total corporate domestic profits to private investment stood at about 40 per cent. Moreover, no single US industry today commands as much as 8 per cent of total investment. And as William Darity argues, the profits from the slave trade in 1784–6 as a proportion of total British investment were well over three times the amount that the American car industry represented as a proportion of total American investment some two hundred years later.[47]

Nevertheless, Roger Anstey's estimates of slave trade profits are yet more parsimonious than Engerman's. His data suggest that the profits comprised a mere 0.11 per cent of national income, 'which is derisory enough for the myth of the vital importance of the slave trade in financing the British industrial revolution to be demolished'.[48] Crucially, what these figures obscure is the point that the 'small ratios' argument applied no less to the capital investment levels of the cotton and iron industries (which were the drivers of

British industrialisation). Indeed, investment levels within both these industries (running with Anstey's exaggerated guesstimate of national income to ease comparison) individually comprised some 0.22 per cent of national income in the 1780–1800 period. Recall too that Liverpool was on the doorstep of the Lancashire cotton industry, which provided a ready outlet for some of the accumulated capital. Curiously, assuming a savings rate of 7 per cent of national income, he concludes that slave trade profits would have increased total investment by an inconsequential 0.11 per cent. But this figure does not accurately reflect the relationship of profits to investment, which would be much higher than this. If we assume that 50 per cent of the profits went into the cotton industry, this would have funded somewhere between 25 and 30 per cent of the total investment of the industry – a figure that would point to a 'large ratios' thesis.

Either way, though, the immediate problem with this debate is that it evaluates the effects of Black slavery on British industrialisation only through the profits of the slave trade. Thus it is assumed that if slave trade profits were inconsequential for British industrialisation, then *ipso facto* so was slavery. However, this omits the many contributions made by Black slave labour production, the profits and proceeds from which were significant for British industrialisation in at least six further ways. All in all, these point to the need to replace the Eurocentric 'small ratios' argument by a 'large ratios' thesis.

A second African contribution lay in the reinvested profits generated by British plantation owners' exploitation of Black labour in the Americas. After 1750 many Black slave plantations were owned by absentee British landlords. This meant that the substantial profits derived from colonial trade exports found a direct outlet into British industry. Crucially, at the end of the eighteenth century income from colonial property was equivalent to about 50 per cent of British gross investment.[49] Given that much of this would have been reinvested in British industry, this alone would have provided a massive input into industrialisation. Moreover, in 1770 the profits of the export trade from the West Indies alone comprised 38 per cent of total British private investment or 2.5 per cent of national income.[50] This means that it would have taken a mere 15 per cent of this sum to finance the investment of the whole of the British cotton industry (i.e. the 'large ratios' thesis).

A third African contribution lay in the fact that in 1801, for example, net British export revenues supported about half of the non-agricultural workforce of England and Wales.[51] That about 60 per cent of this trade was with the American slave-based region and Africa at that time, means that Negro consumers and Black slaves supported about a third of the total non-agricultural English and Welsh work-force. This alone is a massive contribution. Moreover, if the Negro-supported English and Welsh workers ploughed back 8 per cent of their income (the prevailing domestic personal savings rate), this alone could have funded just under half of the total investment in the cotton industry; yet another sign of the 'large ratios' thesis.

Fourth, a special contribution of Negro slavery to British indus-trialisation lay with the Atlantic colonial supply of raw materials. Importantly, in the late eighteenth century the proportion of com-modities/raw materials produced by Africans in the Americas was as much as 83 per cent (and was still 69 per cent in 1850). Most notable here was the supply of raw cotton which was produced in the Americas almost exclusively by African Negro slaves.[52] Nevertheless, Enger-man claimed that the gross value of slave trade output comprised an inconsequential proportion of British national income (the small ratios argument). But recall that without the raw cotton produced by the slaves the British cotton industry would have been unable to play its pivotal role in industrialisation more generally. Significantly, Ken-neth Pomeranz points out that when slave-based cotton exports from the United States dried up in 1861 and 1862 (during the Civil War), British cotton consumption fell by a staggering 55 per cent and prices doubled. In just one year, the Lancashire mills halved their workforce and many firms went bankrupt.[53] Interestingly, the British responded to this by shifting to Egyptian supplies of raw cotton (in addition to

Indian raw cotton imports), thereby continuing their dependence upon Black African labour.

Fifth, the slave trade and slave-produced output contributed massively to the stimulation of British finance. Both Barclays Bank and Lloyds Bank grew up on some of the profits (as did other smaller banks).[54] British financial institutions were considerably boosted by the massive credit (as well as insurance) needs of British slavers and slave-plantation owners. According to Joseph Inikori, insurance premiums for the slave trade and the West Indian trade comprised as much as 63 per cent of the total British marine insurance market.[55] We noted earlier that the London capital market placed massive sums of money into government bonds in the industrialisation phase. Moreover, we also noted that it was only the substantial invisible earnings that enabled Britain to maintain a balance of payments surplus during the eighteenth and nineteenth centuries. Importantly, during the main industrialisation phase most of the invisible earnings were derived from the Atlantic commercial system. Strikingly, the 'large ratios' thesis is implicitly articulated by Inikori:

> As large as wartime government borrowing was [via the London capital market], it would appear that, on the average, annual dealings in mercantile instruments (bills of exchange and company bonds) in London were greater than in their dealings with government securities during the period [1700–1850] . . . The bulk of the bills of exchange that circulated in the provincial trading and manufacturing centers and in London, as well as the company bonds, originated directly and indirectly from the trans-Atlantic slave trade and the trade centered on slave produced American products.[56]

A sixth African contribution to British industrialisation was manifested in the total profits derived from British exports to the empire. For example, in 1784–6 these profits comprised as much as 55 per cent of total gross British investment or 64 per cent of total private investment (with about 80 per cent of this figure comprising trade with Africa and the Americas).[57] The significance of this is brought to light by the fact that the amounts invested in the cotton industry comprised only 4 per cent of total British gross investment. Thus it would take about 9 per cent of the profits from the triangular trade to fund the total investment of the cotton industry. Clearly the figure of 9 per cent is a gross underestimate of the amounts derived that were likely to have been invested in British industry in general. And it is no less important to note that total profits from imperial trade would have constituted much more than 55 per cent of total gross British investment. This is because many of the exports that went to Europe were in fact re-exports of imported colonial produce (originating mainly from the Black slave colonies). What this means, therefore, is that it would have taken considerably less then 9 per cent of the profits derived through the triangular trade to have financed the British cotton industry (perhaps a mere 6 per cent). Moreover, to link up with the second point made above: aggregating profits from colonial property abroad with the profits from trade with the colonies was enough to have financed the *whole* of British gross domestic investment at the end of the eighteenth century. Once again, this reinforces my 'large ratios' thesis.

Finally, a seventh African contribution lay in the fact that the triangular trading system provided not just large profits but also a huge demand for British exports in the absence of which British industrialisation would have been significantly constrained. While these markets were important for a whole range of industries, they were nevertheless essential for the rise of the all-important iron and cotton industries.[58] Here the Navigation Acts were crucial. These laws – imposed by racist government statute – created a highly protected monopolistic system that was designed to specifically privilege British merchants at the expense of the Eastern peoples. Adam Smith, to his credit, labelled these laws as but the 'impertinent badges of slavery'. In particular, the Navigation Acts were embedded in the British colonial trading system, of which the triangular trade was a vital component. Crucially the Navigation Acts and the colonial system ensured guaranteed monopoly markets for British exports precisely at a time when the levels of home demand were shrinking (i.e. when domestic aggregate demand was contracting). Thus while British industrial exports rose by over 150 per cent between 1700 and 1770, the domestic market increased by a mere 14 per cent. Moreover, European trade markets were also drying up, with Britain's share of manufacturing trade to Europe shrinking from 84 per cent (1700) to 45 per cent (1773) to 29 per cent (1855). By contrast, Britain's share of trade going to the American and African colonies rose from 12 per cent (1700) to 43 per cent (1773). And if we include all colonies, the proportion of British manufactured exports rose from 14 per cent in 1700 to 55 per cent in 1773 to 71 per cent in 1855.[59] Indeed, even some Eurocentric scholars have been forced to concede that the growth of colonial (especially American and West Indian) possessions accounted for much of the growth in English exports.[60] The major point here is that such markets absorbed much of the increment (perhaps 70 per cent) of rising British industrial production during the critical eighteenth century.[61]

Nevertheless, in a well-known article Patrick O'Brien reaffirmed Eurocentrism by dismissing the role of the colonial trading system in the rise of European industrialisation. He argued that for Europe as a whole, trade with the 'periphery' was insignificant, comprising as little as 1 or 2 per cent of European national income.[62] In this way then, such a Eurocentric argument erases or conceals the dark side of European industrialisation. But certainly in the British context, his argument is problematic. Although he recognises that this figure understates the British case he still concludes that even here the gains from trade with the 'periphery' were insignificant.[63] But according to my calculations for the 1750–1800 period alone, I estimate that British trade with the 'periphery' comprised about 15 per cent of national income. This is a colossal figure. And during the nineteenth century it rose further still, standing at a staggering 34 per cent of national income by 1855 (comprising over 900 per cent the amounts allocated to British defence between 1850 and 1913). Moreover, merely within the triangular trading system the figure stood at approximately 12 per cent of British national income between 1750 and 1800.

Paradoxically, support for this argument is provided by Patrick O'Brien and Stanley Engerman. In a 1991 piece, they concluded that:

> English shippers dominated the business of transporting slaves from Africa to the New World. Without the enforced and cheap labor of Africans, the rate of growth of transnational commerce between 1660 and the abolition of the slave trade [in 1807] would have been far slower . . . It is difficult to envisage an alternative path of development that might have carried both international and British trade to the level attained by the early nineteenth century.[64]

And moreover, rejecting the standard Ricardian counterfactual argument (see conclusion below) they go on to argue that imperial trade was a vital factor in stimulating British industrialisation more generally.

All in all, therefore, one does not have to fully subscribe to the thesis advanced by Eric Williams in his classic book, *Capitalism and Slavery*, to make the claim that African consumers/producers and Black slaves played a positive and substantial role in British industrialisation. Moreover, it is noteworthy that Negro slavery was complemented by the commodification of other Eastern peoples, not least through indentured labour, so as to service Britain's industrial needs. Chinese and especially Indian indentured labour was particularly important. The latter were assigned to various colonial production sites around the world, especially to Mauritius where they would produce sugar not least to sweeten the Indian tea that the Britons were now consummately drinking. Summarising the indentured labour system, Ronald Hyam notes that:

It was, then, a system involving large transfers of manpower, quite on a par statistically with Atlantic slavery, and reproducing many of its features. Mortality on long voyages to the West Indies was appalling, and plantation conditions were frightful. The British, however, persisted in persuading themselves . . . that it was an acceptable system – it was defended as necessary, and not 'uncivilised' like slavery. As a result, it was Indian labour which created much of the overseas wealth of the empire by exploiting the raw materials of the tropics.[65]

Similarly, many of the economies of the East were commodified and reorganised in order to produce primary products and raw materials to service the needs of British industrialisation. And again this was imagined to be a civilising process. Noteworthy here is that the British were desperate to overcome the long-held trade deficit with the Chinese which had ensured the consistent draining of bullion from Britain. One way in which this was achieved was through creating new sources of tea supply. To this end, parts of India were 'reorganised' to grow tea. While in 1850 the British had relied for all their tea supplies from China, within only fifty years they were importing 85 per cent of it from India. But the most important weapon which enabled the British to reverse their trade deficit was the exporting of opium into China. Having relied on Turkish opium since the late eighteenth century, the British then reorganised parts of India as a source of opium supply. This was especially useful, given that the Chinese consumer preferred Indian to Turkish opium. By 1828 Indian opium comprised 55 per cent of all British exports into China (even though the Chinese state had officially banned its consumption). And when Commissioner Lin understandably tried to curtail the drug trade in 1839, the British used this as a pretext for the Opium wars. In these perfidious ways the British came to reverse their historic trade deficit with China. For the fact is that only by drug-pushing in China (backed up by British military power) and drinking Indian tea in England could the draining of bullion into China be reversed.

Likewise many other parts of the world were turned into raw-material production centres for the British economy. Above all, the American colonies were reorganised to supply Britain with 'land-saving' imports. As Eric Jones notes, 'the entire expansion of the Great Frontier [i.e. the Americas] may be looked on as an extension of Europe's "Ghost Acreage"'.[66] The term 'ghost acreage' refers to the amount of land that the British would have needed to find at home in order to produce the equivalent output. On the basis of detailed calculations based on New World sugar, cotton and timber exports, Pomeranz concludes that this comprised between 25 and 30 million acres.[67] This leads on to the claim that in the absence of these land-saving imports the British would have needed to have tripled the amount of land that they were already using to produce the equivalent output. Accordingly, without these colonial contributions, the British would have been forced to redirect labour that was used for industry back into agriculture. And given the significance of this ghost acreage, it is possible that in its absence British industrialisation would have been significantly compromised.

In addition, West African agriculture was reorganised to produce palm oil, cocoa, gold and rubber so as to service the needs of the British economy. Australia was also important and was reorganised to supply a large proportion of Britain's wool. While in 1824, 2 per cent of Britain's wool imports came from Australasia, the figure rose to 40 per cent in 1860 and to 67 per cent by 1886.[68] Many other countries were also reorganised. And the final result as far as British interests were concerned was vitriolically reported by W. S. Jevons in his book, *The Coal Question* (1865):

> The plains of North America and Russia are *our* corn fields;
> Chicago and Odessa *our* granaries; Canada and the Baltic are *our*
> timber forests; Australasia contains *our* sheep farms, and in
> Argentina and on the western prairies of North America are *our*
> herds of oxen; Peru sends her silver, and the gold of South Africa
> and Australia flows to London; the Hindus . . . grow tea for us, and

our coffee, sugar and spice plantations are in all the Indies . . . and *our* cotton grounds, which for long have occupied the Southern United States, are now being extended everywhere in the warm regions of the Earth . . . [T]he several quarters of the globe [are] *our* willing tributaries.[69]

But as far as the colonies were concerned the net effect of all this was not so much the successful conversion of their economies 'up to the level' of British civilisation, but rather their containment. As Alec Hargreaves aptly noted of the European colonies, despite the rationale for cultural conversion (the 'civilising mission'):

they did not, however, produce carbon copies of Europe's industrial economies. On the contrary, the colonies remained predominantly agricultural. They were to support, but not to compete with, Europe's industrial system by supplying foodstuffs and raw materials and providing markets for manufactured goods.[70]

This once more returns us to Friedrich List. For it was this asymmetrical relationship that constituted the problem of 'unequal exchange' precisely because it condemned the colonial producers to an agricultural or primary product/raw materials stage of production that precluded a shift to industrialisation.

Finally, it is important to reiterate the point made earlier: that despite the degenerative economic impact that imperialism imposed upon the empire, the cultural impact was often far more disturbing. I touched on the dehumanising treatment of the Black African slave in ch. 8. I also briefly discussed the negative cultural impact of British imperialism in relation to China above. But a particularly poignant example lies with the Australian case, where the Aborigines faced a full cultural and existential assault after White settlement commenced in 1788. A few summary points are noteworthy.

First, after a hundred years of British settlement no fewer than 20,000 Aborigines had been killed in the frontier violence.[71] There is also compelling evidence to suggest that in Tasmania the 'final solution' was exercised.[72] Not surprisingly, the Aborigines came to view the landing of English settlers in Australia in 1788 not as a glorious settlement or pioneering discovery that should be celebrated every year on Australia Day, but as an invasion pure and simple. Nevertheless, many more lives were lost through the impact of imported European diseases. Strikingly, after one hundred years of White settlement, the Aboriginal death rate stood somewhere between 80 and 90 per cent, a figure which compares with the indigenous American death rate after one hundred years of Spanish settlement. And some Australian writers have applied the term 'holocaust' to characterise the Aboriginal experience.[73] Even so, the emergent racist ideology of the British saw this as entirely natural and appropriate. For in the words of Edward Curr, superintendent of the Van Diemen's Land Company, 'it is in the order of nature that, as civilization advances, savage nations *must* be exterminated'.[74]

Second, behind the violence lay another story that according to various Australian authors qualifies as 'peaceful' genocide.[75] This entailed the attempted destruction of Aboriginal culture, heritage and identity. Particularly noteworthy here was the story of the 'stolen generations', those Aboriginal children who were forcibly transferred to White 'guardians' with the express intent that they cease being Aboriginal. This began in the early years of colonisation and continued on into the mid-twentieth century.[76] Of course, at the time this was believed to be a civilising duty, offering such children a better future. But this was, nevertheless, a White future segregated from an Aboriginal past. Last, but not least, the Aborigines came to be segregated through social apartheid by being placed in 'settlements' that were placed on the periphery of the White towns. Conditions in these camps have been described as 'comparable to those found in prisons or mental institutions with white superintendents having extraordinary control over the day-to-day lives of Aboriginal inmates'.[77] And numerous Aboriginal testimonials described them as 'concentration camps'. Thus behind the abstract data that record the reorganisation of Australia as a wool-exporter to the mother country lay a dark story – one which points to what the civilising mission may have meant and felt like for the Aborigines in the 'left-footed' colonial outpost at the 'bottom of the world'.

Conclusion: was British state interventionism and imperialism a waste of money?

None of this is to say that such pronounced levels of domestic state interventionism on the one hand, and imperial interventionism through the appropriation of Eastern resources on the other, was the sole cause of British industrialisation. But it is to say that all this played a very important role. Nevertheless, liberal economic historians dismiss this claim by arguing that defence/colonial expenditures and state interventionist policies served only to effect a 'misallocation' of British resources thereby leading to suboptimal economic outcomes. Thus in their absence, the liberal or Ricardian counterfactual argument goes, there would have been even higher levels of domestic economic growth.[78] Such an argument effectively erases or conceals the dark side and, wittingly or unwittingly, preserves the morally sanitised picture of British industrialisation that is cherished by many Eurocentric, especially liberal, scholars. Let us take the two categories, state interventionism and colonialism, in turn to critically appraise this argument.

The first point to note is that the counterfactual approach merely tells us what might have occurred in the absence of state intervention but does not explain what actually happened. The fact is that the 'take off' of the British economy occurred at a time when military expenditures, national debt, taxes and tariffs reached staggeringly high levels. Thus even if economic growth would have been more pronounced in the absence of state intervention this does not undermine the fact that such pronounced intervention went hand in hand with the take off of the British economy. Even so there is a loophole in the liberal canon that is worth noting: that liberals would concede that state interventionism could have had a positive economic effect under conditions of low domestic aggregate demand. State interventionism is fruitful when no avenue for the absorption of higher production exists at home. This loophole is worth noting precisely because there was indeed a lack of aggregate domestic demand in the shape of a 'Keynesian depression' in the eighteenth century.[79] Perhaps then a more fitting counterfactual might be that the 'real' opportunity cost of state interventionism might have been either the non-industrialisation of the British economy at most, or at least, a much slower and more drawn out path of development.

Liberals also posit two major counterfactuals in order to discount the positive role of imperialism in British industrialisation. First, that whatever the economic benefits of the empire might have been for Britain, these were outweighed by the exorbitant military costs of imperial defence. Thus in the absence of empire, they argue, the British economy would have been even more productive since this could have raised the savings rate further (or boosted domestic aggregate demand, according to J. A. Hobson). Lance Davis and Robert Huttenback claim that between 1860 and 1912, the British taxpayer was the most burdened in Europe paying out on average £1.14 on defence (compared with £0.86 for the French and £0.75 for the German).[80] They also note that British defence spending was divided into 'home defence' and 'imperial defence'. They suggest that if Britain had given up its colonies the British taxpayer could have been relieved by an approximate 30 per cent, the results of which would have been a much enhanced savings and investment rate.

The major problem here is that measuring defence expenditures in one currency fails to reveal the real tax burden and, therefore, tells us nothing about the actual ability to pay. To do this requires estimating defence expenditures as a proportion of national income. According to my calculations, the average real defence burden of the major powers between 1870 and 1913 was as follows: Britain 3.2 per cent; Germany 3.8 per cent; France 4.0 per cent; Russia 5.1 per cent; Japan 8.2 per cent.[81] And note that a differential of 1 per cent of national income is highly significant. Clearly the British taxpayer was privileged by undertaxation rather than overtaxation. Most importantly, if the costs of empire were about 30 per cent that of total military spending, then the final real British imperial-military burden would have stood at a mere 1 per cent of national income. This was equivalent in real terms to the tiny amounts that Iceland has spent on defence in the last half-century. As even Paul Kennedy was forced to concede: 'The most remarkable feature of the post-1815 *Pax Britannica* was its cheapness'.[82] In sum then, given that the British taxpayer was in any case undertaxed relative to the Continental taxpayer, it is hard to see how in the post-1850 period the empire could have constituted a fiscal burden in any real sense. And as Avner Offer also concludes, it is hard to see how the minimal costs of imperialism could have in any way offset the significant economic benefits that the empire yielded.[83]

One obvious rejoinder here would be that in the pre-1815 period, real British defence costs were extremely high (as I pointed out in the first section above). Thus it could be replied that in the earlier period the extremely high imperial costs would have outweighed the economic benefits of empire. I offer two replies. First, Britain was at war no fewer than twelve times between 1715 and 1815. According to one expert, fewer than half of these wars were fought over the empire, and even when they were the colonies were not usually the major factor.[84] Second, as was explained above, while the costs of warfare (whether for empire or whatever) were indeed extremely high in the 1715–1815 period these would most probably have served to stimulate industrialisation, given that during this period the British economy suffered from low aggregate demand.

The second liberal counterfactual asserts that the guaranteed colonial markets served only to perpetuate the backward British industries, the opportunity cost of which was the forgone development of new and more vital industries. But given that such writers usually include the cotton textile industry in this context, this does little to explain how protectionism and colonial markets enabled its rise in the first place. Even so, Thomas and McCloskey reply by asserting that: 'at first it seems odd to argue that without foreign [colonial] markets for its output of cotton textiles . . . Britain would have been able to find markets at home'. Of course, they concede that domestic demand could not possibly have absorbed British cotton production levels. But, they claim, 'In the long run . . . the men and money used to make the excess cotton could have been turned towards making beer, roads, houses and other domestic things'.[85] Perhaps, but they were not. In any case, it is hard to see how beer-making, road-building or housing construction could have secured a more optimal outcome to the one that was actually achieved by Britain's cotton manufacturing exports. More importantly, though, none of this can discount the simple fact that the many benefits derived from the empire and state interventionism positively assisted the British economy even if all this was, in the liberal economists' favoured phrase, 'suboptimal'. Some suboptimality!

Part IV
Conclusion: the oriental West versus the Eurocentric myth of the West

12 The twin myths of the rational Western liberal-democratic state and the great divide between East and West, 1500–1900

He who knows himself and other,
Will also recognise that East and
West cannot be separated.

Goethe

As we have seen throughout this book, Eurocentrism posits a strict dividing line between the East and West. This serves to represent the East and West as not only separate but qualitatively different (in a developmental sense, that is). More importantly, as we noted in ch. 1, within the Eurocentric discourse this divide implies a kind of intellectual apartheid regime in which the superior West is quarantined off from the inferior East. The East is allegedly permeated by despotic and irrational institutions that block economic progress. The linchpin of this claim lies in the theory of oriental despotism (or what Max Weber called 'patrimonialism'). Conversely, the presence of rational and liberal states in Europe ensured that only the West was capable of progressive economic development. Part I of this book argued that the theory of oriental despotism is a fabrication and obscures both the presence of relatively rational Eastern states on the one hand, and significant economic progress in the East on the other. But the task remains to consider the degree to which the Western state was as rational as Eurocentrism has presupposed. To evaluate this claim I shall focus on three aspects of the 'rational state':

Rational state:

1 a 'rational-legal' centralised bureaucracy which operates according to impersonal (rather than arbitrary) norms and presupposes a clear separation of the public and private realms;

2 a 'minimalist' or *laissez-faire* posture in relation to the economy (i.e. where the state does not interfere in the 'natural' operation of the free market). This simultaneously goes to the heart of the claim that the economy is rational in the sense that it operates optimally in the absence of political interventions and distortions;

3 a democratic propensity where political citizenship rights are granted so as to empower individuals.

This chapter takes each of these in turn and concludes that Western states have been far less rational than has been commonly assumed (covering the whole of the 1500–1900 'breakthrough' period). And if Eastern states were far more rational than has been assumed by Eurocentrism (as was argued in chs. 2–4), then the conclusion must be that the rationality or civilisational Great Divide between East and West imputed by Eurocentrism cannot hold.[1] The implication of such a conclusion is to render moribund the explanatory Eurocentric framework of the rise of the West. This then provides the launching pad for my own anti-Eurocentric framework that is proposed in the final chapter.

The myth of the centralised and rational Western state, 1500–1900

France is generally regarded as one of the most centralised and rational states in Europe, enshrined in popular mythology by Louis XIV's famous, albeit self-deluded, proclamation that *L'état c'est moi*. This was a myth precisely because the French public realm was not divorced from the private at any point before the nineteenth century, if not the twentieth. The French state had only a weakly centralised fiscal bureaucracy with limited infrastructural reach into civil society. Even by about 1800 the ratio of bureaucrats to population stood at a paltry 1: 4100.[2] The state's weak infrastructural reach was revealed by the fact that it relied for much of its revenue on taxing collectively rather than individually. The peasants were located into collective communal settings in part for tax purposes. If one member failed to pay his share of taxation, he would face the not inconsiderable wrath of the other members.[3] In other words, members of the commune were ultimately responsible for policing the extraction of taxes, not the state. Moreover, the state was heavily dependent on the *taille* (the land tax) as opposed to taxes on commercial activity. All in all, French taxation was imposed in an arbitrary, *ad hoc* (i.e. unfair) manner and French records of taxes collected were largely invisible from the public. This only served to reinforce the general perception that the state was unfair and biased towards private interests at the expense of the public.[4]

The fusion of the public and private realms is no more clearly revealed by the fact that the state relied on venality – that is, the selling of offices to wealthy private individuals in exchange for a one-off payment. The problem here was that these individuals then used their public office to enhance their private gains along the patrimonial model (by siphoning off as much as 50 per cent of government revenues). Significantly, it was the inefficiency of the tax system that led to the fiscal crisis which in turn led on to the French Revolution in 1789.[5] Less well-known is the fact that the international bond market raised the price of the French state's loans (by raising the interest rate) owing to the lack of confidence in the French state's ability to service the debt, which in turn exacerbated the fiscal crisis.[6] In short, the French state was in no way the rational institution that Eurocentric imagination has assumed – certainly not at any point before the nineteenth, if not the twentieth, century.

While Prussia is also usually held up as one of the most rational states of Europe, it too was striking only for its pronounced degree of irrationality. The Great Elector of Prussia, Frederick William (1640–88) once proclaimed, albeit less famously than Louis XIV: 'I ruin the authority of the Junkers and build my sovereignty like a rock of bronze'. But this was yet another exercise in myth making. The fact is that the Junkers – the Prussian landed class who staffed the bureaucracy – continuously used their public office as a means to shore up their private power. Indeed, a great deal of the state's policy agenda was informed by the private interests of this class at the direct expense of the masses, ranging from tax policy to trade policy to foreign policy and many others. And the political system remained heavily distorted in favour of the Junkers through to the 1918 revolution. So, for example, although there was indeed universal suffrage in Germany in the nineteenth century, the Prussian three-class voting system ensured that Junker political interests usually won out (a point I return to below).

Strikingly, France's paltry ratio of fiscal bureaucrats per head of population (1: 4100) actually looks impressive when compared to the Prussian ratio of 1: 38,000.[7] One clear indicator of the ineffectiveness of the bureaucracy was that as late as the end of the nineteenth century, the Prussian state did not even know how many people worked for it. As Michael Mann points out, 'If a state cannot count its own officials, it cannot be remotely bureaucratic'. Accordingly he concludes that, 'it would be absurd to call the Prussian state "bureaucratic", as do most historians'.[8] Moreover, despite the post-1806 reforms introduced by Stein and Scharnhorst, the strength of the Junker class continued unabated right up to to 1918 (as already noted). The extreme irony here is that the strongest support for this claim is provided by none other than Max Weber. He argued that the failures of German foreign policy in the 1900–1918 period were a direct result of the fact that the bureaucracy was neither sufficiently rational, nor centralised, nor checked by a strong civil society. The problem was that the bureaucracy was captured by the irrational private interests of the Junker agrarian dominant class. And it was for this reason that the nation's interests were sacrificed on a militaristic Junker altar in 1914.[9]

In sum, even as late as the end of the nineteenth century the best candidates simply failed to live up to the 'rational standard of civilisation'. The major states relied to a large extent on private and local patrimonial officials, who treated their public office as their own private patrimony. This leads to the firm conclusion that Western bureaucracies were marked by arbitrary patrimonial/traditional norms rather than those associated with modern rational-legal bureaucracies.

The myth of the liberal minimalist Western state, 1500–1900

As Max Weber and especially Adam Smith argued, the rational or civilised state is thought to follow a liberal or minimalist policy stance in which intervention in the economy is avoided (i.e. the policy of *laissez-faire*).[10] This is vital because it is this which enables the economy to operate freely according to its own laws of supply and demand, thereby enabling the rational allocation of goods and service to ensure optimal outcomes. A great deal, therefore, hangs on this claim. In order to assess this, I shall focus largely on European trade policy. The question therefore is: how free trading were European states during their industrialisation phase?

European trade policy was striking only for the predominance of protectionism over free trade. This policy ran from the seventeenth century right into the second half of the twentieth century. Significantly, the British state levied average tariffs of no less than 32 per cent between 1700 and 1846. Moreover, average industrial tariffs for Europe stood at 19 per cent in 1820, 10 per cent in 1875 and 19 per cent in 1913.[11] No less importantly, the mid-nineteenth-century 'free trade era' was in fact the exception that proves the protectionist rule (as was explained in ch. 11). For there we noted that the 1860–1877/9 era was marked by moderate protectionism, not free trade. Moreover, if we take the 1846–1877/9 period as representing the European era of free trade (as do many historians), then the average tariff would be nearer 20 per cent. By way of comparison, such a figure would equate with that of the American Smoot–Hawley tariff of 1930, which is usually described in the literature as one of the most protectionist acts of legislation ever passed. It is also interesting to note that between 1600 and 1900, 'freer trade' was achieved in Europe for only 6 per cent of the time. No less interesting is that throughout this period Europe never matched the low tariff levels found in the Ottoman empire during the seventeenth and eighteenth centuries.

Also of importance is that the European great powers – especially Britain – intervened in the economy through tariff protectionism in large part to extract taxes for war purposes.[12] This precedent had been set in the age of mercantilism. Louis XIV's finance minister, Colbert, aptly summarised the general European belief that: 'trade is the source of [state] finance, and finance is the vital nerve of war'.[13] The critical point is that milking the economy for fiscal-military revenues necessarily disturbed the so-called laws of supply and demand. And this remained the case right into the second half of the twentieth century. This suggests that in various ways the key European states conformed to Weber's 'irrational patrimonial state'.

By way of a link with the previous (and next) section, it is also significant to note that one of the reasons for the resort to tariff protectionism was that European states were too weak to rely on progressive income taxation. That is, they were inadequately centralised; they had insufficient bureaucratic capacity to reach into society in order to collect the income tax; and they were insufficiently democratic. Accordingly, they relied on regressive indirect taxes – especially tariffs – which could be easily extracted and collected at specific ports, and could be levied with impunity given that the masses had no political voice (see below).[14] Indeed, even as late as the early twentieth century European tax regimes were striking only for their regressivity. Thus as of 1900 the proportion of income tax relative to overall central government revenues stood at Austria, Belgium, France, Germany and Sweden, 0 per cent; Italy, 12 per cent; UK, 13 per cent, Denmark, 15 per cent; The Netherlands, 20 per cent; Norway, 39 per cent; and Switzerland, 55 per cent.[15] As of 1900, average income tax revenues as a proportion of central government revenues across Western European governments stood at a mere 14 per cent. And even these tax data exaggerate the true progressivity of tax regimes. For in most cases, income taxation was not especially progressive because rates were either higher for the lower income groups, or the richer groups were able to substantially minimise their tax bills in all manner of ways.

No less striking is that it would be only as late as the 1960s that the West – for the first time in history – began to move towards genuine free trade (though it would still take over twenty years for this to be realised). Nevertheless, it was only during the 1960s that Western states had become sufficiently democratised and centralised to enable governments to wean their tax systems off their hitherto dependence on regressive trade taxes (i.e. protectionist tariffs) in favour of income taxation.[16] In sum, the reliance on regressive trade taxes throughout the period of the breakthrough was a function of the weakness of states' bureaucracies and the lack of democracy – the *leitmotif* of 'irrational pre-modern' patrimonial states. And as an addendum here, states also raised tariffs in order to protect various private (industrial and financial class) interests at the expense of the masses. Political economists label this process 'rent-seeking'. Once again, rent-seeking is supposedly the *leitmotif* of irrational 'patrimonial' states, because it implies that the state privileges the interests of private actors over the public interest.

Clearly, therefore, state interventionism with respect to European trade policy was striking only for its pronounced levels. More significantly, this interventionism extended to many other areas of the economy.[17] I discussed this wider context with respect to British industrialisation in ch. 11 so I will not repeat its findings here. And given that the British state is conventionally thought to be the *laissez-faire* state *par excellence* during its industrialisation phase, then turning to the European continent will necessarily fail to reveal the presence of Max Weber's or Adam Smith's *rational* 'minimalist state'. In short, then, throughout the 1500–1900 period the rational liberal state was striking in the European context only for its absence.

The myth of the democratic Western state, 1500–1900

Eurocentrism claims that in contrast to oriental despotism, Western democratic states granted powers and liberties to individuals.

Accordingly, a strong civil society is thought to have been the unique preserve of the West (which in turn constitutes the major reason why only the West broke through to modern capitalism). As we saw in ch. 10, Eurocentrism typically extrapolates backwards the modern conception of political democracy all the way to Ancient Greece. It then fabricates a permanent picture of Western democracy by tracing this conception forwards to Magna Carta in England (1215), then to England's Glorious Revolution (1688/9), and then on to the American Constitution (1787/9) and the French Revolution (1789). In this way, Europe and the West is (re)presented as democratic throughout its long rise to power. The immediate problem here is that no Western state was democratic before the twentieth century. As James Blaut argues, Eurocentric historians want 'to push back into the Middle Ages many of the positive virtues of European society that emerged after the rise of Europe, after Europe had well begun its economic modernization'.[18] That is, Eurocentric historians effectively attempt to 'push back' a twentieth-century concept that has no real application before then. If so, then the Western breakthrough could not have been a function of the liberal-democratic state. And by implication, nor could the breakthrough have been a function of a strong civil society.

A brief perusal of table 12.1 reveals that most Western states only brought in male political citizenship rights as late as the early twentieth century and, in many cases, universal suffrage was brought in only as late as the mid-twentieth century. Note that the countries are displayed in descending order, with Norway being the first to achieve universal suffrage, the USA as well as Portugal and Switzerland the last. The data are striking only for the low levels of enfranchisement that were achieved even as late as the turn of the twentieth century. Thus in 1900 only 14 per cent of the whole Austrian population (over the age of twenty) were enfranchised, while in Germany in 1912, the figure stood at 39 per cent. Surprisingly, compared to Germany, the situation was even worse for most of the European liberal states. In 1900 or later, the percentage of the adult population that was enfranchised stood at Belgium in 1900, 4 per cent; Italy in 1909,

Table 12.1 *The introduction of political citizenship rights in the major Western states*

Country	Universal male suffrage	Universal suffrage
Norway	1898	1913
Denmark	1848	1915
Austria	1907	1918
Sweden	1918	1918
Netherlands	1917	1919
UK	1918	1928
Spain	n.a	1931
France	1848	1946
Germany	1849	1946
Italy	1919	1946
Belgium	1919	1948
USA	1965 (1870)	1965
Portugal	n.a	1970
Switzerland	1879	1971

Source: Ha-Joon Chang, *Kicking Away the Ladder* (London: Anthem Press, 2002), p. 73.

15 per cent; Sweden in 1908, 16 per cent; Britain in 1910, 29 per cent; Denmark in 1913, 30 per cent; Norway in 1906, 35 per cent; Switzerland, as late as 1967, only 38 per cent; and France as late as 1940 only 40 per cent.[19] The only liberal state that outpaced Germany was The Netherlands, which by 1901 had 52 per cent of the population enfranchised. Moreover, only seven of the fourteen countries surveyed here brought in male suffrage in the nineteenth century and none brought in universal suffrage.

But even these low enfranchisement figures exaggerate the true levels of political citizenship. In Prussia (which dominated the German political system), the franchise system was rigged in favour of the richest groups. Prussia's 'three-class voting' system was unequally divided. The first group comprised the richest 3.5 per cent of the population, the second 13 per cent, and the poorest third, 83.5 per cent. But the snag was that each third had an *equal* vote: that is, the top 3.5 per cent of the population had as much say as the bottom 83.5 per cent. And the richest 16.5 per cent had a clear majority over the bottom 83.5 per cent. Moreover, when we add in the point that the German parliament had only limited powers and was subordinated to the Reich chancellor who, in turn, was responsible to the Kaiser, it is clear that the notion of political citizenship in Germany was a sham.

More generally, in all the Western countries that brought in male suffrage in the nineteenth century, a whole raft of distortions or blockages ensured that democracy remained a fiction. These included open balloting – which led to vote-buying – as well as widespread electoral fraud (note that the secret ballot only came in during the twentieth century). Although Britain introduced the Corrupt and Illegal Practices Act in 1883 this had little real impact in stemming such electoral corruption (which remained a problem well into the twentieth century). The situation was yet more bleak in the United States. As Ha-Joon Chang points out, although the Fifteenth Amendment gave Blacks the vote in 1870, it was subsequently revoked in the Southern states in 1890. Moreover, a whole raft of obstacles remained in place across the country that effectively militated against the Amendment in practice.[20] These included various formal obstacles such as problems of literacy and arbitrary 'character' requirements as well as informal obstacles, most notably the threat of violence against the Black minority who actually turned up to vote. These obstacles would only be overturned as late as 1965 when the Voting Rights Act was passed. It is also important to note that the huge cost of elections only generated further distortions that mitigated democracy in practice. As Chang concludes:

> With such 'expensive' elections, it was no big surprise that elected officials were corrupt. In the late nineteenth century, legislative corruption in the USA, especially in state assemblies, got so bad

that the future US president Theodore Roosevelt lamented that the New York assemblymen, who engaged in open selling of votes to lobbying groups, 'had the same idea about Public Life and Civil Service that a vulture has of a dead sheep'.[21]

Notable too is that the US was one of the very last of the Western countries to embrace political democracy. Thus it is clear that even as late as 1900 genuine political democracy in the West remained a fiction. As Patricia Springborg eloquently concluded:

> It is a supreme irony in the history of state legitimation theories ... that the pluralist, transactional, entrepreneurial ... East, should have been deemed 'despotic' by the pastoral, quiescent, relatively underdeveloped West, whose main concession to democracy involved parliaments, to which universal access [was] granted as late as the twentieth century of our era.[22]

Conclusion

One of the central claims of chs. 2–4 is that Eastern states were far more rational and growth-enabling than the Eurocentric theory of oriental despotism suggests. This chapter has argued that Western states have been far less rational and democratic during the period of the breakthrough than has been supposed by Eurocentrism. This necessarily falsifies the claim that the East and West have been separated by a civilisational Great Divide. And in turn, this conclusion necessarily robs Eurocentrism of its principal explanation of the rise of the West. The fundamental issue now at stake, therefore, concerns locating a more appropriate question with which to begin our analysis of the rise of the West, and which in turn requires the development of a more appropriate answer. This is the task of the final chapter.

13 **The rise of the oriental West:**

identity/agency, global structure and contingency

> If I am right in urging the overthrow of [Eurocentrism] and its replace-
> ment by [anti-Eurocentrism], it will be necessary not only to rethink the
> fundamental bases of 'Western civilization' but also to recognize the pene-
> tration of racism and 'continental chauvinism' into all our historiography,
> or philosophy of writing history.
>
> Martin Bernal

> History is marked by alternating movements across the imaginary line
> that separates East from West Eurasia.
>
> Herodotus

> The globalization of knowledge and Western culture constantly reaffirms
> the West's view of itself as the centre of legitimate knowledge, the arbiter
> of what counts as knowledge and the source of 'civilized' knowledge. This
> form of global knowledge is generally referred to as 'universal' knowl-
> edge, available to all and not really 'owned' by anyone, that is, until non-
> Western scholars make claims to it. When claims like that are made his-
> tory is revised (again) so that the story of civilization remains the story of
> the West. For this purpose, the Mediterranean world, the basin of Arabic
> culture and the lands east of Constantinople are conveniently appropri-
> ated as part of the story of Western civilization, Western philosophy and
> Western knowledge.
>
> Linda Tuhiwai Smith

We concluded the last chapter by noting that the very features that
were supposed to promote the rise of the West according to Eurocentrism – rationality and democracy – were absent in Europe during the
period of its breakthrough between 1500 and 1900. Accordingly, we
need to develop an alternative anti-Eurocentric theoretical explanation. This chapter undertakes this in four stages. The first section
suggests that the central organising question posed by Eurocentrism
needs to be reformulated before we can get a grip on understanding
either the progressive story of world history or the rise of the West.

Sections 2–4 then outline the contours of my own anti-Eurocentric explanation, emphasising the importance of global structure and the diffusion of Eastern 'resource portfolios', which were subsequently assimilated in the West, and focusing on the role of European identity and the imperial appropriation of Eastern resources after 1492 that underpinned the later phase of the rise of the West. I finally emphasise the importance of contingency, while the conclusion summarises these arguments by juxtaposing anti-Eurocentrism and Eurocentrism in order to provide an alternative sketch of world history. The upshot of my claim that the East significantly enabled the rise of Europe is that we need to replace the Eurocentric notion of the pristine West with that of the oriental West.

Looking for the answer in the wrong place – formulating a new question

Eurocentrism errs by asking the wrong questions at the outset. All Eurocentric scholars (either explicitly or implicitly) begin by asking two interrelated questions: 'What was it about the West that enabled its breakthrough to capitalist modernity?' and 'What was it about the East that prevented it from making the breakthrough?' These, of course, are the questions that informed Max Weber's research and have remained central to Eurocentrism ever since. Nevertheless, as we noted in ch. 1, many scholars do not seek to explicitly or consciously defend a body of thinking called Eurocentrism. But whether intended or not, the standard questions posed inevitably lead on to a Eurocentric story.

Ultimately, these questions are implicitly loaded against the East. First, they lead the scholar (often unwittingly) to impute an inevitability to the rise of the West. This happens because scholars begin by taking the present dominance of the modern West as a fact, but then extrapolate back in time to search for all the unique Western factors that made it so. Conversely, by taking the subordination or backwardness of the present-day East as a fact, they similarly extrapolate back in time to search for all the factors that prevented the breakthrough to modernity there. Thus they end up by imputing an inevitability to the 'present-day malaise' of the East. Most importantly, such a question requires an appraisal of the East's achievements only in terms of Western criteria – namely as to whether it made the final breakthrough. Thus because the East obviously did not make the final breakthrough, so any Eastern economic achievements that have been made are necessarily deemed to be inconsequential. In the process the East is robbed of any progressive economic capacity, thereby confirming that economic progress is and always has been the monopoly of the West.

In sum, there are three entwined consequences that follow from the standard questions: first, the imputation of an 'iron law of Western development' and an 'iron law of Eastern non-development'; second, the assumption of the 'proactive European subject', counterposed to the 'passive Eastern object', of world history. And third, the rise of the West is understood through a logic of immanence: that it can only be accounted for by factors that are strictly endogenous to Europe. The net effect of all this is that the West is selected in while the East is selected out of the progressive story of the rise of the modern capitalist world. And, whether intended or not, the upshot of this is to view the rise of the West as a triumphant and miraculous virgin birth – the very essence of the Eurocentric myth of the pristine West.

This conclusion might be objected to on the grounds that it is only reasonable to look back into the past and single out the properties that enabled the rise of the West and the 'non-rise' of the East. How else can we provide an answer to this question? But by definition the question necessarily prevents the researcher from discovering the point that not only has the East achieved significant economic progress but that this in turn significantly enabled the rise of the West. In short, this alternative point cannot logically be captured by a question that leads the researcher to treat the rise of the West and the tragedy of the East as two separate stories on the one hand, and directs analytical attention to the progressive factors that exist only within the West on the other.

To illustrate my claim that the problem lies with the initial questions posed by Eurocentrism, it is useful to engage in a simple thought experiment. Let us suppose that we were living back in say 900 CE. As ch. 2 reveals, the Islamic Middle East/North Africa was at that time the cradle of civilisation. Not only was it the most economically advanced region in the world, standing at the centre of the global economy, but it enjoyed considerable economic growth and perhaps even per capita income growth – the alleged *sine qua non* of modern capitalism (see chs. 2–4). Were we to set up a university at that time and enquire into the causes of Islamic economic progress we might come up with the following answer. The Middle East/North Africa was progressive because it enjoyed a unique set of rational and progressive institutions. First, it was a pacified region in which towns sprang up and capitalists engaged in long-distance global trade. Second, Islamic merchants were not just traders but rational capitalist investors who traded, invested and speculated in global capitalist activities for profit-maximising ends. Third, a sufficiently rational set of institutions was created including a clearing system, banks engaging in currency exchange, deposits and lending at interest, a special type of double-entry bookkeeping, partnerships and contract law, all of which presupposed a strong element of trust. Fourth, scientific thought developed rapidly after about 800. And fifth, Islam was especially important in stimulating capitalism on a global scale. Certainly no one would have entertained the prospect of writing a book entitled *The Christian Ethic and the Spirit of Capitalism*, which would dismiss Islam as 'growth-repressive'. More likely, someone would have written a book called, *The Islamic Ethic and the Spirit of Capitalism*, which would definitively demonstrate why only Islam was capable of significant economic progress and why Christian Europe would be forever mired in agrarian stagnation. Or we might subscribe to the claim made by the contemporary, Sā'id al-Andalusī (later followed by Ibn Khaldūn): that Europe's occupation of a cold temperate zone meant that its people were ignorant, lacked scientific curiosity and would remain backward.

Alternatively, we could go back to the year 1100. Were we to set up a university and an accompanying social science department, we might set out to try and answer *the* compelling question at that time. That is, how did Sung China make the breakthrough to industrial production and intensive (per capita) economic growth while Europe remained mired in a backward agrarianism and a relatively weak commercialism? We might offer the following explanation. China embodied unique properties and institutions that were absent in the West. China enjoyed a strong state, which created a stable and pacified environment and actively promoted the background conditions necessary for capitalism. By contrast, Europe was fragmented into a plethora of states, none of which was strong enough to promote a sufficiently pacified domestic environment to enable capitalism to develop. Moreover, while China had solved its internal problems as early as 221 BCE and was peaceful thereafter, Europe was in effect a realm of warring states. In addition, China enjoyed a strong work ethic contained in its uniquely rational Confucian religion. Europe, by contrast, was held back by Catholicism, which specified respect for authority and a long-term fatalism that prevented the emergence of parsimony, hard work and rational restlessness. Perhaps a book would have been written entitled, *The Confucian Ethic and the Spirit of Capitalism*, which would definitively demonstrate why Catholicism was inimical to economic progress, and why only Confucianism embodied the correct set of virtues that made significant economic progress inevitable.

The obvious problem here is that in explaining Islamic or Chinese success and European failure, we necessarily end up by ascribing permanent causes to a situation that has always been fluid. Similarly, were we to sit down say in 1900 and enquire into the West's rise to prominence, it would be no less problematic to stand the previous theory of Islamic or Chinese superiority on its head. But that is exactly what has happened. Thus we find in all mainstream Western explanations of the rise of the West a tendency to ascribe permanent attributes to the West that rendered inevitable its breakthrough to modern capitalism (i.e. the Eurocentric 'logic of immanence'), while simultaneously presupposing a backward East that was permanently incapable of progress. But given that the East had pioneered significant economic progress after 500 and that it was more advanced than the West up to 1800, it is clear that such an analysis would be entirely fruitless. And it should be clear by now that such a fruitless exercise would necessarily flow from the question that Eurocentrism begins with.

The major problem with the question – 'why Europe not China?' or, 'why the West not the East?' – is that these are absolute questions that demand absolute answers; that is, answers which attribute permanent positive characteristics to the West and permanent negative features to the East. It is this that leads to the marginalisation of the East in the progressive story of world history. What we need, therefore, is a question that is temporally relativist. It must avoid the trap of ascribing permanent features to any one region. This is important precisely because ascribing the West with unique and permanent attributes inevitably obscures the alternative Eastern story that this book has sought to uncover. In short, a temporally relativist question will allow us to bring the East back from the marginalised edge or dark ghetto that it was consigned to by Eurocentric world history.

What then might an alternative, relativist question look like? Following the analysis of Jack Goody in his pioneering book, *The East in the West*, we could ask: how and why did the leading edge of global economic power shift between the East and West between 500 and 1800 to eventually culminate with the breakthrough to capitalist modernity? As we have seen in this book, the East enjoyed the lead in both global intensive and extensive power between 500 and 1800 before the pendulum finally swung to the West in the nineteenth century.

One possible rejoinder to this is made by Michael Mann. While he accepts that China had higher levels of extensive power than Europe until at least 1500, nevertheless he claims that 'in another range of power achievements, *intensive* ones, especially in agriculture, Europe was leaping ahead by AD 1000'.[1] And this forms the basis of his rejection of what he calls the tendency of revisionist historians towards 'European self-denigration'. But in the light of the arguments made in this book, there are three reasons why this claim for Europe is problematic. First, many of the vital technologies that enabled the European medieval agricultural revolution diffused from the East. Second, Chinese agriculture remained superior to Europe's until the nineteenth century (as even various Eurocentric scholars have conceded). And a third interrelated point is that China's long-held lead was due to the fact that Chinese agricultural technologies enabled far greater levels of intensive power. This is no better represented than by the fact that the Chinese had developed the curved iron mouldboard plough, which was far superior to the clumsy medieval European square wooden mouldboard plough. And it was only during the eighteenth century that the Europeans began to catch up, in large part because they assimilated the Chinese curved iron mouldboard plough (and many other Chinese agricultural as well as industrial technologies – see below). Mann also uses the Gothic arch as another example of Europe's superior intensive power.[2] But this invention came from the Islamic Middle East via Amalfi. In sum, then, the problem as I see it is not 'European self-denigration' but the prevailing tendency among world historians towards 'European self-promotion'.

In the light of all this, we clearly cannot locate a permanent and unique set of features in one particular region. As Goody notes:

> What is clear is that the superior achievements of the West can no longer be seen as permanent or even long-standing features of those cultures but as the result of one of the swings of the pendulum . . . The merest outline of a theory must begin by accepting an alternation.[3]

The next three sections outline my own answer, which entails a multi-causal analysis that focuses on the roles of global structure, agency/identity and contingency. Let us take each in turn.

Global structure and Eastern agency: the diffusion and assimilation of Eastern resources through oriental globalisation in the rise of the oriental West

Part I of this book outlined the contours of the Afro-Asian-led global economy as it emerged after 500 (pioneered mainly, though not exclusively, by the Middle Eastern Persians and North Africans and later on by the Muslims). As we saw in ch. 2, Eurocentric historians dismiss the global origins of the rise of the West on the grounds that before and after 1500 European trade with the 'periphery' was only marginal. Even if that was true (which it is not), the crucial point is that the global economy's ultimate significance was that it provided a ready-made set of communication-arteries that linked up most of the globe, and simultaneously constituted a conveyor belt along which the major Eastern 'resource portfolios' diffused to the backward West between 500 and 1800. And particularly important was the Islamic Bridge of the World along which many of these portfolios passed on their journey from East to West.

The basic claim here is that at every major turning point of European development, the assimilation of superior Eastern ideas, institutions and technologies played a major part. This contrasts with the words of Lynn White: 'my fundamental proposition is . . . that the technological dominance of Western culture is not merely characteristic of the modern world: it begins to be evident in the early Middle Ages and is clear by the later Middle Ages'.[4] But the crucial technologies – the stirrup, the horse-collar harness, the water-mill and windmill, probably the iron horse-shoe and perhaps the medieval plough – diffused across from the East to thereby enable the European medieval economic and political revolutions. Moreover, the global flows of Eastern migrations that hit Europe in successive waves after 370 helped prompt the creation of the feudal political structure. The next phase of Europe's development concerned the various 'proto-capitalist revolutions' – commerce, production, finance and navigation – that were allegedly pioneered by the Italians after 1000. But ch. 6 reveals that the major impetus for the Italian financial revolution came from the East. For it was there (principally in the Middle East) where partnerships and contracts (e.g. *commenda*), cheques, bills of exchange, banking, money-changing, lending at interest for trade and investment, contract law and rational accounting systems were first developed, all of which were passed on to, and assimilated by, the Italians. All the major technologies that underpinned the medieval navigational revolution – the compass, maps, sternpost rudder, square hull, multiple-mast systems and perhaps the lateen sail – were pioneered, and certainly perfected in, either China or the Islamic Middle East. Moreover, advances in Indian, Chinese, perhaps African and especially Islamic, science (particularly astronomy and mathematics) as well as the Arabic refinement of the astrolabe, enabled the development of nautical techniques which then diffused across to enable the so-called European voyages of discovery. And last but not least, medieval European textile manufacturing, papermaking, sugar refinement and iron production (and probably clockmaking) were all enabled by the diffusion of Eastern technologies. While many of these diffused across the global economy, it is notable that the Crusades were also an important conduit for the diffusion of Eastern resources to Europe.

Chapter 8 reveals the major Eastern innovations that diffused across to enable Europe's 'catch up' phase after the fifteenth century. Eastern (especially Islamic though also Jewish, Indian and perhaps Black African) ideas were vital in enabling the Western Renaissance and scientific revolution. The technologies that lay at base of the so-called European military revolution (1550–1660) – gunpowder, the gun and cannon – were all pioneered during the Chinese military revolution between 850 and 1290 (though the Islamic Middle East also contributed in significant ways). Moreover, the origins of printing cannot be credited to Gutenberg, given that the first movable metal-type printing press was invented in Korea in 1403, and that many of the much earlier Chinese printing technologies or ideas diffused across to belatedly enable the 'European breakthrough'.

The next significant phase in the rise of the West that is especially prized by Eurocentrism is the triumph of the British industrial revolution. But ch. 9 reveals how some of the ideas of the Enlightenment were directly borrowed from the East – especially China. Moreover, most of the major technologies and techniques upon which the British agricultural and industrial revolutions were based were invented in China and diffused across a number of global commercial routes. These included the seed-drill and horse-drawn hoe, the curved iron mouldboard plough, the rotary winnowing machine, crop rotation methods, coal and blast furnaces, iron and steel production methods, cotton manufacturing technologies, canals and pound-locks, the idea of the steam engine and much more.

In sum, in the absence of a global economy and oriental globalisation many of the more advanced Eastern resource portfolios would have failed to diffuse across to the West. And without these, the Europeans might well have remained on the backward periphery of the Afro-Asian-led global economy. Had that been the case, of course, there would have been no need to write a book on the rise of the West. Instead, social scientists would be debating why it was that the East had been so progressive and no less, why Europe remains a backward and unchanging society that drifts on the periphery of the more advanced Asian system. No doubt the central 'Occidentalist' text would have been *Afro-Asia and the People Without History* (to paraphrase Eric Wolf's book, *Europe and the People Without History*). And no doubt someone would now be writing a book to remedy Occidentalism by showing how the West significantly shaped the East perhaps entitled, *The Western Origins of Eastern Civilisation* or *The Occidental East*.

Nevertheless, the fact is that it was Europe rather than the East that broke through to capitalist modernity (as, of course, Eurocentric scholars are so anxious to point out). But if this was not a function of superior Western rationality, ingenuity and liberal-democracy (as noted in chs. 12 and 2–4), an alternative claim might be that the West arose because of its superior adaptive capacity. Significantly, some Eurocentric scholars have indeed pursued this line, to wit:

> What made it [the West] extraordinary was less the capacity to invent than the readiness to learn from others, the willingness to imitate, the ability to take over tools or techniques discovered in other parts of the world, to raise them to a higher level of efficiency, to exploit them for different ends and with a greater degree of intensity.[5]

This adaptive argument would certainly hold some water given that the Europeans did manage to assimilate Eastern resource portfolios effectively (even if it was a very long time before they took the lead). Nevertheless, although this adaptive capacity was clearly an important factor, it could not stand as a sufficient explanation of the rise of the West. There are two main reasons for this qualification.

First, the rise of the West involved a great deal of contingency and luck (which I deal with below). Second, this adaptive argument could only occupy centre stage if we adopted a strict structuralist-materialist approach. But as the next section emphasises I also factor in the importance of European agency and identity in my explanatory framework. Here I refer to the predatory and increasingly racist identity of the Europeans that in turn gave rise to and nourished imperialism, and which in turn helped enable the later phase of the rise of the West. In other words, merely assimilating or adapting Eastern resource portfolios was a necessary though not sufficient factor in Western development.

But to sum up this section: the main ramification of the 'assimilationist' argument is that it counters the Eurocentric assumption of the radical distinction between the East and West on the one hand, and the marginalisation of the East in the progressive story of world history on the other. Thus we can see that since 500 CE the East and West have not been separate entities but have always been 'promiscuously' entwined (to borrow Michael Mann's phrase).[6] And in particular, the East cannot be represented as a passive victim or bearer of Western power not least because it not only created a global economy after 500 CE but for a very long time it led the Europeans. As Andre Gunder Frank points out:

> there was no 'European world-economy' separate from an 'Indian-Ocean world-economy'. If anything, the latter 'incorporated' the former and not the other way around . . . The only 'answer' is to understand that Europe and Asia . . . had been part and parcel of the same single world-economy since ages ago, and that it was their common participation in it that shaped their 'separate' fortunes.[7]

Above all, the origins of capitalist modernity as well as globalisation cannot be told in terms of the pioneering and independent West. Rather it needs to be retold through a long-run historical global-cumulative process (or process of 'global confluence'),[8] in which the East, conjoined with Europe through oriental globalisation since 500 CE, played a vital role in the progressive story of the rise of the West. Nevertheless, by the same token it would be wrong to view the West as but a passive beneficiary of Eastern largesse (as in Occidentalism), not least because the Europeans also had an important input in the whole process. And it is the notion of European agency that constitutes the second prong of my overall argument.

European agency/identity and the appropriation of Eastern resources in the rise of the oriental West

The second way in which the East enabled the rise of the oriental West was through Europe's imperial appropriation of Eastern resources. Critical to my argument here is the emphasis on European agency or identity. Recall that the Eurocentric accounts place special emphasis on European agency and, in particular, Europe's moral progressivity (especially liberalism and democracy) and 'rational restlessness' – all of which ensured the West's autonomous and inevitable rise. Perhaps not surprisingly, therefore, the major anti-Eurocentric scholars share a common desire to dispense entirely with European agency or identity.

Only by doing this, they believe, can they produce a theory that does not exaggerate the uniqueness of the West. And in turn, this leads them to produce theories that are essentially materialist. Janet Abu-Lughod put it thus:

> My contention is that the context – geographic, political, and demographic – in which development occurred was far more significant and determining than any internal psychological or institutional factors. Europe pulled ahead because the 'Orient' was temporarily in disarray . . . The fact that the 'West won' in the sixteenth century, whereas the earlier [Eastern] system aborted, cannot be used to argue convincingly that *only* the institutions and culture of the West could have succeeded.[9]

Eric Wolf asserts his materialist position by effectively reinvoking Marx's labour premise: 'Contrary to those who believe that Mind follows an independent course of its own, I would argue that ideology-making . . . occurs within the determinate compass of a mode of production deployed to render nature amenable to human use'.[10] But the most forceful repudiation of 'ideationalism' is made by James Blaut, who insists that European imperialism cannot be explained by a unique sense of 'cultural cupidity' on the part of the Europeans. As he put it:

> To accept this, one would have to believe that there is something absolutely fundamental in European culture . . . that makes Europeans different from other humans. This admits [or concedes] a good part of the Eurocentric claim that Europeans are unique among humans; it merely inverts the argument and claims that their uniqueness lies not in progressiveness but aggressiveness, predatoriness, and cupidity.[11]

And on the same page he goes on to claim that, 'bloodthirsty protocapitalist communities, ready and anxious to conquer, loot, and enslave wherever this brought a profit, were found in many parts of the eastern hemisphere, in all three continents'.

I begin with the assumption that we do not need to throw the 'agential baby' out with the Eurocentric bathwater when constructing an anti-Eurocentric account. There are at least three reasons why we should not dismiss European agency. First, it would at least run the risk of creating a kind of Occidentalism, where Europe appears as but a 'passive beneficiary' of global and Eastern forces or influences. Such an account might be contained within a book entitled *Afro-Asia and the People Without History* (as noted earlier). But this would merely reproduce the diffusionist discourse and its accompanying essentialism (albeit privileging the East rather than the West). Second, it is important not to reify the external or global structure. This is not the place to rehearse all the arguments made against Immanuel Wallerstein's world-systems theory. The basic point to note here is that it is important to resist the functionalist logic of a global-structural approach. Nor is this the place to revisit the 'agent–structure debate', which has become a veritable cottage industry within sociology. But as E. P. Thompson properly argued in his critique of Althusserian structuralism, agents cannot be viewed as *Träger* – that is, passive bearers of structures.[12] And third, *contra* Frank, Pomeranz and others,[13] one of the reasons why individuals are not 'passive bearers of structures' is because 'structure' (whether it be domestic or global) does not exist 'out there' independent of our understanding or perceptions. Agential perceptions that are connected to identity are important in guiding and informing the interests and actions of the agents. That is to say, agents act and respond differently within the same structural environment depending on their identity. Put simply, the way agents think of the world also informs the way that they *act* in it. To a certain (though not full) extent, therefore, structure is what agents make of it. Let us consider this a little further.

Notable in this context is that while China was the leading power for much of the second millennium, its identity led it to choose to forgo imperialism (as we saw in ch. 3). True its identity was hierarchical, with China imagined as the 'civilised Middle Kingdom' in contradistinction to all other outlier races that were perceived as 'barbarians'. But despite this superficial similarity the Chinese international tribute system was radically different from Western imperialism. As we saw in detail in ch. 3, the tribute system was more voluntary than forced and, moreover, at virtually no point did the Chinese state try and culturally convert or even exploit its so-called vassal states.[14] The tribute system was designed more to lure 'vassals' towards China not least through holding out genuinely lucrative economic gains for them. Ultimately, China's identity was more a defensive construct that was designed to both maintain Chinese cultural autonomy in the face of potential 'barbarian' invaders (e.g. the Mongols) and reproduce its domestic legitimacy in the eyes of its own population. Accordingly, the Chinese chose to eschew imperialism even though China was the leading power in the world for most of the second millennium.

The Chinese posture contrasted radically to that of Europe's. Europe's identity increasingly came to be defined in imperialist terms, beginning after 1453 but crescendoing in the eighteenth and nineteenth centuries. By the latter period the Europeans had constructed a Great Divide between West and East. Defining the East as inferior and incapable of self-development while simultaneously defining the identity of the West as independent, proactive and paternal, naturally prescribed imperialism as a moral duty (i.e. the civilising mission). It is obviously the case that by about 1800 the West had managed to take the lead in terms of material-military power. And this was no less obviously an important factor in the colonisation of the East. But there was nothing inevitable about the imperial role that the Europeans chose to undertake in the world. We have seen this in relation to the construction of China's identity. Ultimately the Europeans did not seek to remake the world simply because 'they could' (as in materialist explanations). They sought to remake the world because they believed they should. That is, their actions were significantly guided by their identity that deemed imperialism to be a morally appropriate policy (as was explained in ch. 10). In short, there is no innate relationship between imperialism and superior material power, for what ultimately made Europe imperialist, in contradistinction to China, was its specific identity.

However, none of this is to say that material power or material factors are unimportant. For they are vitally important. Indeed, the diffusion (and appropriation) of material resources from the East to the West is a vital aspect of my overall argument. And to reiterate, material power was a vital prerequisite for British imperialism. But the critical point of note is that material power in general and great power in particular, are channelled in different directions depending on the specific identity of the agent. Let us now consider the genealogy of European identity and how this informed and guided the actions that the Europeans undertook, and how these in turn enabled the rise of the oriental West. I shall discuss each row of table 13.1 in turn.

In the early medieval period the Europeans constructed their identity negatively against the Islamic Middle East. Islam was chosen as the 'Other' in part because there was nothing intrinsic to Europe which could be harnessed to create a single identity. The point here is that this negative sense of identity led to the construction of Christendom, which in turn played an important part in both consolidating and reproducing the European feudal system as well as prompting the 'first round' of Crusades (1095–1291). As was explained in ch. 5, without these Christian ideas the highly inegalitarian social structure of European feudalism would have failed to gain legitimacy and might, therefore, have imploded. Had this occurred Europe might have regressed back into the Dark Ages (though equally it is possible that the Europeans might have been rescued from such a fate by the energising impact of Eastern trade/resource portfolios that passed in principally through Italy and Spain via the Islamic Bridge of the World).

After 1453 the Catholic Europeans felt especially threatened by the so-called 'Turkish menace'. And, as we saw in chs. 7 and 8, it was this that prompted the 'second round' of Crusades after 1492/1498 (initiated by Columbus and Da Gama respectively).

Table 13.1 *The construction and consequences of Western identity*

Identity phase	Self	Other	Western appropriationist strategies in the world
(1) 500–1453	Europe constructed as Christendom	Islamic Middle East and the 'Saracens' constructed as a hostile and evil threat	Attacking Islam through the 'first round' of Crusades. No appropriationism (though the Crusades enabled the assimilation of various Middle Eastern resources)
(2) 1453–c. 1780	Europe increasingly imagined as the carrier of the Advanced West	Islam (mainly the Ottoman Turk) constructed through Christianity as a hostile and barbaric threat; Africans and indigenous Americans constructed as 'pagan' or 'savage' and thus 'ripe' for exploitation and repression	Attacking Islam through the 'second round' of Crusades, initiated by Columbus and Da Gama. Appropriation of American bullion which financed European trade deficit with Asia and enabled arbitrage profits through the global silver recycling process. Appropriation of 'non-European' resources through slave-trading and the commodification and appropriation of African and American labour, which significantly enabled Western (especially British) industrialisation
(3) c. 1780–1900	Europeans imagined as superior and the carrier of advanced civilisation	Whole of 'non-Western' world now imagined as populated by either inferior *Savages* or *Barbarians*, and is therefore, ripe for exploitation/ repression and cultural conversion along the Western model	Slave-trading (officially up to 1807 in Britain) and slave production (officially up to 1833 in Britain, 1865 in the US, 1888 in Brazil) enabled Western, especially British, industrialisation. Appropriation of Asian and African land, labour and markets through formal and informal imperialism significantly enabled European, and especially British, industrialisation

The subsequent 'American and African experience' was vital in enabling the reconstruction of European identity. Crucial here was the transmogrification of European Christendom into Europe-as-the-advanced West (see ch. 8). While under feudalism the Europeans had defined themselves negatively against Islam, it was nevertheless an identity that rested on insecurity. After the fifteenth century, Europeans began for the first time since 500 to imagine themselves as superior to the Black Africans and indigenous Americans, who were imagined as pagan savages. Eurocentrism was now beginning to emerge (even though it rested on various Christian conceptions of difference). It was this attitude that furnished the Europeans with the moral self-justification for undertaking both the imperial appropriation of American resources and the super-exploitation of indigenous Americans and, above all, the Black Africans. Initially, the major economic benefit derived from the plundered gold and silver, which enabled the Europeans both to finance their trade deficit with Asia and engage in global arbitrage. At the same time, Western Europe began to crystallise as the embodiment of advanced civilisation as the Eastern Europeans, alongside the Ottoman Turks, were imagined as 'barbarians'.

The 1500–1750/1780 'American experience' represented the transition phase from an emergent 'Christianised Eurocentrism' to a fully developed conception of Western Europe as superior to the *whole* of the world. Crucially, after 1700 European identity was now reconstructed along implicit racist grounds (down to about 1840) and explicit racist criteria after then. The upshot of this reconstruction was the prescription of imperialism as a moral duty (ch. 10). Paradoxically, conceiving of the Eastern peoples as decidedly inferior had the effect of making the exploitation and appropriation of their resources (land, labour and markets) appear as entirely natural or legitimate. In turn this significantly enabled Britain's industrialisation. As explained in ch. 11, this included first, the appropriation of land-saving agricultural products from the Americas and guaranteed raw cotton supplies through Black slave production. Second, the commodification of Black slave labour yielded profits that significantly boosted investment in the British economy (what I call the 'large ratios thesis'). Third, Black slavery also provided an enormous stimulus to British finance capital. Fourth, the Navigation Acts and the imposition of free trade in the empire enabled the increase in British exports which in turn nourished British industrial development. And fifth, the British reorganised the East as centres of industrial raw material supplies which were appropriated and exploited to service British industrial needs. Also notable was that in the process many Eastern economies were held down through 'containment', thereby maintaining Britain's economic lead. Finally, imperialism also entailed the attempted 'cultural conversion' of the East (i.e. ethnocide), given that the West felt threatened by so-called 'Eastern cultural deviancy'. And at the extreme, genocide and social apartheid were also meted out by the Europeans.

In sum, three points are noteworthy here. First, it was Europe's *racist restlessness* rather than 'rational restlessness' that enabled the later phase of the rise of the West. Second, the obvious link between my emphasis on global structure and identity lies in the fact that the latter has always been constructed within a global context. Or as Edward Said put it: 'the Orient is an integral part of European *material* civilization and culture'.[15] And third, the Eurocentric assumption of a European iron logic of immanence which made the rise of the West inevitable is rendered problematic by the fact that without the plundering and exploitation of Eastern resources – land, labour and markets – Europe would have failed to break through into industrial modernity. Moreover, the Eurocentric logic of immanence is also undermined by the fact that Europe was extremely lucky to have made the breakthrough. Or as Michael Mann put it echoing the importance of contingency: 'So world-historical development did occur, but it was not "necessary", the teleological outcome of a "world spirit", the "destiny of Man", the "triumph of the West" . . . or any of those'.[16] How then did contingency enable the rise of the oriental West?

The impact of contingency in the rise of the oriental West

The prominent anti-Eurocentric scholars, Kenneth Pomeranz and James Blaut, emphasise 'contingency' (or fortuitous accident) as the critical factor in the rise of the West.[17] In one sense the rise of the West could indeed be explained almost wholly through contingency. For the Europeans needed a great deal of luck given that they had been neither sufficiently rational, liberal-democratic nor ingenious to independently pioneer their own development. The first, and probably most fortuitous piece of luck that came their way was that the East had pioneered significant economic progress through an inventive capacity, which in turn furnished the Europeans with the many different 'resource portfolios' that underpinned the rise of the West. Second, had the Asians not also created a global economy, then many of their more advanced innovations would simply have failed to arrive in Europe in the absence of oriental globalisation.

A third piece of extremely good fortune was that the more powerful Eastern societies did not seek to colonise Europe and absorb it into their cultural orbit (as the Europeans would subsequently do to them). As we noted in ch. 2, the Mongols turned their back on conquering the heartland of Europe and turned on China instead. Paradoxically, the Europeans were extremely lucky that the Mongol empire was created. For it delivered both goods and Eastern resource portfolios to the West via the northern route of the global economy (the *Pax Mongolica*). We also noted in ch. 5 that the Muslims were not interested in conquering medieval Western Europe, even if they conducted many 'cheeky' raids across this continent. Moreover, as explained in ch. 3, Europe was ultimately blessed by China's forbearance in that it chose not to universalise its 'standard of civilisation' through imperialism. Sadly though, China's benign forbearance was later punished by Europe's imperial campaign of drug-pushing, warfare and the assault on China's very identity some four hundred years later (ch. 11).

A fourth piece of luck – as Blaut emphasises – derived from the fact that the Spanish stumbled upon the Americas where gold and silver lay in abundance (see ch. 8). This was highly fortunate in the first instance, because Columbus was supposed to have arrived in China. But he blundered. Had he not blundered he would have ended up by performing the kowtow to the Chinese emperor – a very different scenario from the one that unfolded in the Americas. Or as Fernández-Armesto aptly noted: 'Columbus, had he been able to reach Japan, would have been greeted as an exotic freak, derided for eating with his fingers; and in China he would have been received as a primitive tributary, bearing risible gifts'.[18] Moreover, had he landed in China, then the bullion resources in the Americas would have been untapped. And given that these resources were especially important in enabling the West's 'catch-up phase' after 1500, this would have been a major blow. Moreover, as James Axtell put it:

> without the immediate booty of Indian gold and silver, the
> Spanish would have [probably] dismissed Columbus after one
> voyage as a crack-brained Italian and redirected their economic
> energies eastward in the wake of the Portuguese, toward the
> certifiable wealth of Africa, India and the East Indies.[19]

Nevertheless, Axtell is perhaps wrong in one sense. For without the appropriation of American bullion, the Europeans would have been unable to maintain even their modest presence in Asia in the 1500–1800 period (since it was this money that financed their trade there – see ch. 7). Accordingly they would have been 'unable to redirect their economic energies towards Africa, India and the East Indies'. Tragically, the Europeans were also lucky that the American Natives had inadequate immune systems to counter the Eurasian diseases that were imported, which considerably eased the process of European settlement. By the same token, the Europeans were also extremely lucky to have had access to the productive labour power of the African slaves and especially that they had sufficient immune systems to resist Eurasian diseases.

A fifth generic piece of luck could be summarised under the heading, 'the Europeans often happened to be in exactly the right place at precisely the right time'. The example of the Americas springs to mind once more. But another pertinent example is that the English East India Company happened to be in India at the time when the Mughal polity began to disintegrate of its own accord into various competing factions. The fact is that the English did not initially defeat India through their 'overwhelming' military power. Robert Clive's so-called heroic victory at Plassey in 1757 was a product of good luck. What defeated the Indian army was not superior British military power but a series of internecine rifts, which led to the breakdown of the Indian army in what was effectively a 'battlefield putsch'.[20] Moreover, after 1757 the British succeeded in gaining an imperial hold only by playing off the different political factions. It was only later on that European guns succeeded in consolidating Britain's hold over India. But had the Mughal polity held up in the first instance, there might never have been an Indian jewel in the British imperial crown. More-over, had the Indians not been gracious and willing hosts to the East India Company ever since the beginning of the seventeenth century, the British would neither have enjoyed a presence there, nor would they have been able to expand their power base once the Mughal polity had begun to autonomously disintegrate. And the rest might not have been history.

To sum up these last three sections, we can now see that the story of the rise of the oriental West cannot be related in terms of the immanence of the European social structure. The leading edge of global power resided squarely within different parts of the East right down to about 1800. Between about 500 and c.1000 the leading edge of global power lay in the Middle East. By 1100 the 'pendulum' began to swing eastwards with China enjoying the leading edge of global intensive power and, by the fifteenth century, grasping the leading edge of global extensive power. After about 1500 the pendulum began very gradually to swing back westwards as the Europeans engaged in imperialism and simultaneously intensified their linkages with the East. But it was only well into the industrialisation phase that the leading edge of global intensive and extensive power shifted to Britain. Unfortunately we cannot know whether the East would have made the final transition to modern industrialism in the absence of Western imperialism. For the West's economic containment strategies stymied the growth potential of many Eastern economies (though Japan was an exception that fits the anti-Eurocentric rule given that it successfully industrialised in the absence of European colonisation). Nevertheless the best analogy for understanding the final Western breakthrough lies with the 400-metre relay race. For one thing is certain: that the British would never have crossed the finishing line first had it not been for the fact that the East had already ran the first three legs in record time. Or as Jack Goody put it:

> modernisation is a continuous process and one in which regions
> have taken part in leap-frogging fashion. No one is endowed with
> unique [inventive] features of a permanent kind that enable them
> alone to invent or adopt significant changes such as the
> Agricultural [or Industrial] Revolution.[21]

Conclusion

I can now present an alternative anti-Eurocentric vision of some of the key turning points of world history in the last fifteen hundred years – moments that I believe should constitute the main focus of our analytical attention. This simultaneously enables me to lay out in table form some of the central arguments of this book and to juxtapose them with the Eurocentric account (see table 13.2).

It is noteworthy that explicitly Eurocentric writers such as Roberts and Landes claim that unlike the anti-Eurocentric account, theirs appeal only to the 'empirical facts'. As Roberts proclaimed, 'if we are merely talking about facts . . . and not about the value we place on them, then it is quite correct to put Europe at the centre of the story in modern times [i.e. after 1500]'.[22] And no doubt David Landes would dismiss my alternative conception of world history as he did Andre Gunder Frank's: as 'bad history' or 'Europhobic',[23] or perhaps even 'Occidentalist'. In this specific context the wise words of W. E. B. Du Bois are poignant: 'we must make clear the facts with utter disregard to [our] own wish and desire and belief. What we have got to know, so far as possible, are the things that actually happened in the world.'[24] For as I have argued in this book – consciously or subconsciously – Eurocentrism does not pick out the relevant facts according to a 'scientific objectivity' but picks only those 'facts' which select in the West and select out the East of the progressive story of world history.

Thus only when we do away with Eurocentrism can we begin to produce a more inclusive, empathic and complete picture of world history. And empathy should not be translated as 'wishful thinking' (as David Landes might retort). Empathy is vital because it enables us to transcend the distorting and selective bias of Eurocentrism which mistakenly instructs us to ignore or marginalise the East. Thus empathic historical research enables us to reclaim what George James properly called the 'stolen legacy' of the East,[25] and thereby restore the Eastern peoples to the status of creative and active agents. We do this not because we wish it so but because as this book has factually demonstrated, the Easterners have undoubtedly been many 'peoples with history', who have significantly contributed and sacrificed in so many ways to enable the breakthrough to modern capitalism. And only when we recognise this can we begin to provide a satisfactory account of the rise of the oriental West.

In the light of all this it is useful to paraphrase the words of Henry Reynolds (a prominent Australian voice for Aboriginal reconciliation) taken from his book, *Black Pioneers*:

> Perhaps the strongest reason for writing a book about [Afro-Asian] pioneers was the realisation that [they] had made a significant contribution to the development of [the West], which had never been fairly or fully acknowledged. It seemed as if the legend of the [Western pioneer] . . . had been so central to the development of [Western identity and Western theories of the Rise of the West] that there was no discursive space left for [Eastern] pioneers. If

Table 13.2 *Two visions of the key world-historical moments, c. 500–1900*

	Eurocentrism		Anti-Eurocentrism
733	Charles Martel's victory over the 'Saracens' at the Battle of Tours and Poitiers	751/1453	Arab victory in the Battle of Talas establishes Islamic supremacy in West Central Asia. Ottomans take Constantinople (1453)
600–1000	Europe pioneers the medieval agricultural revolution	400 BCE–500	China pioneers many technologies which enabled the European agricultural revolution of 18th and 19th centuries
c. 1000	Italians pioneer long-distance trade/early capitalism and Italy becomes the leading global power	c. 800	Italians join the Afro-Asian-led global economy. Oriental globalisation enables the diffusion of Eastern 'resource portfolios' to enable the development of the backward West
Post-1095	European Crusaders assert control over the Islamic Middle East	1095–1517	The Italians remain dependent upon the Islamic Middle East and Egypt
c. 1400–1650	Italian Renaissance and scientific revolution	c. 800–c. 1400	Eastern or Islamic Renaissance (which subsequently enables the European Renaissance and scientific revolution)

1434	China withdraws from the world leaving a vacuum that is soon filled by the superior Europeans	1434–1800/1839	China remains pre-eminent as the foremost world trader and producer and is able to resist Western incursions as well as dictate terms to the European traders
1455	Gutenberg invents the movable metal-type printing press	1040/1403	Pi Shêng invents the movable-type printing press (1040); Koreans invent first movable metal-type printing press (1403)
1487/8	Bartholomeu Dias is the first to reach the 'Cape of Storms'	c. 200–1421	Arabs sail round the Cape (c. 1450) and into Europe. The Chinese (c. 9th century), Polynesians (c. 3rd century) and Indians sail to the Cape and East coast of Africa
Post-1492	European age of discovery and the emergence of early Western proto-globalisation	c. 500–1500/1800	Afro-Asian age of discovery: the Easterners create and maintain the global economy (and preside over oriental globalisation). Chinese choose not to initiate imperialism

(cont.)

Table 13.2 (cont.)

	Eurocentrism		Anti-Eurocentrism
Post-1492	The Spanish plunder American gold and silver bullion	c. 1450	China initiates a silver currency and, as the world's foremost producer/trader, provides a strong demand for Europe's silver plundered from the Americas
1498	Da Gama makes 'first contact' with a primitive and isolated Indian people	c. Post-800	Indians in trading contact with the rest of Eurasia; Indians are economically superior to their Portuguese 'discoverers'. Chinese, Indian and perhaps Black African and certainly Islamic, science and technologies provide the basis for Portuguese ships and navigation
1498–c. 1800	The Europeans defeat the Asians and monopolise world trade	1498–c. 1800	Europeans fail to defeat the Asians and remain dependent upon them for a slice of the lucrative Eastern trade: Afro-Asian age continues
1550–1660	European 'military revolution'	c. 850–1290	Chinese 'military revolution' – the technological ingredients of which came to underpin the European military revolution

Date		Date	
1700–1850	First industrial miracle occurs in Britain	600 BCE–1100	Chinese industrial miracle. Assimilation of Chinese technologies and ideas enables British industrial revolution
1700–1850	British industrialisation is the triumph of domestic- or self-generated change	1700–1850	'Non-Europeans' (especially Africans) significantly contribute to British industrialisation through the appropriation and exploitation of their many resources
1853	Commodore Perry 'opens up' isolated Tokugawa Japan: Meiji Japan as a 'late developer' industrialises by copying the West	1603–1868	Tokugawa Japan remains tied in with the global economy. Independent Tokugawa development provides a launching pad for the subsequent Meiji industrialisation (Japan as an 'early developer')
1820s	Britain reverses its trade deficit with China	1820s	Britain only reverses the trade deficit by pushing drugs in China
1839–1858	Opium wars and unequal treaties 'force open' and rescue China's backward economy	c. 850–1911	China remains open to world trade and achieves considerable economic progress throughout this period

> included they would complicate the story, undermine white
> heroism, dim the glory. If ['non-whites'] could be shown to have
> displayed the same [or even superior] skills and attributes as
> whites . . . then the [Western] pioneers would be diminished and
> their [brilliance] called into question. Further investigation could
> lead to the conclusion that the [West] owed much to the nameless
> 'black boy' who guided and . . . showed [the West] the finer points
> of [development].[26]

Indeed one of the major tasks of my book has been to conduct just such 'further investigation', the results of which reveal the hitherto nameless Easterners who pioneered global capitalism after 500 CE and simultaneously helped the West to develop.

Finally, the recent words of the late Edward Said in the 2003 Preface to his reprinted book, *Orientalism*, are pertinent here.

> Rather than the manufactured clash of civilizations, we need to
> concentrate on the slow working together of cultures that overlap,
> borrow from each other, and live together . . . But for [this] kind of
> wider perception we need time and patient and skeptical enquiry
> supported by faith in communities of interpretation that are
> difficult to sustain in a world demanding instant action and
> reaction.[27]

This present volume has sought to provide just such an analysis. Moreover, I fully support Said's clarion call for the further development of empathic analyses that reject the constructed bipolarism of East and West along with its oft-accompanying racist politics, not least because global humanity demands no less. For in rediscovering our global-collective past we make possible a better future for all.

Notes

Notes to ch. 1

1. Martin Bernal, *Black Athena*, I (London: Vintage, 1991).

2. Ibid.; Samir Amin, *Eurocentrism* (London: Zed Books, 1989); Janet L. Abu-Lughod, *Before European Hegemony* (Oxford: Oxford University Press, 1989); James M. Blaut, *The Colonizer's Model of the World* (London: Guilford Press, 1993); Bryan S. Turner, *Orientalism, Postmodernism and Globalism* (London: Routledge, 1993); Jack Goody, *The East in the West* (Cambridge: Cambridge University Press, 1996); Andre Gunder Frank, *ReOrient* (Berkeley: University of California Press, 1998); Kenneth Pomeranz, *The Great Divergence* (Princeton: Princeton University Press, 2000); Clive Ponting, *World History* (London: Chatto & Windus, 2000). See also the earlier works of Marshall G. S. Hodgson, *The Venture of Islam*, 3 vols. (Chicago: Chicago University Press, 1974); Eric R. Wolf, *Europe and the People Without History* (Berkeley: University of California Press, 1982).

3. David S. Landes, *The Wealth and Poverty of Nations* (London: Little, Brown, 1998).

4. John M. Roberts, *The Triumph of the West* (London: BBC Books, 1985).

5. Felipe Fernández Armesto, *Millennium* (London: Black Swan, 1996), p. 8.

6. W. E. B. Du Bois, *Africa and the World* (New York: International Publishers, 1975 [1946]), p. vii.

7. Marshall G. S. Hodgson, *Rethinking World History* (Cambridge: Cambridge University Press, 1993), p. 33.

8. Edward W. Said, *Orientalism* (London: Penguin, 1991 [1978]); Victor G. Kiernan, *The Lords of Mankind* (New York: Columbia University Press, 1986 [1969]); Hodgson, *Venture*, I; Bryan S. Turner, *Marx and the End of Orientalism* (London: Allen & Unwin, 1978).

9. Wolf, *Europe*, p. 5.

10. E.g. Joseph R. Strayer and Hans W. Gatzke, *The Mainstream of Civilization* (New York: Harcourt Brace Jovanovich, 1979); David S.

Landes, *The Unbound Prometheus* (Cambridge: Cambridge University Press, 1969).

11. Ruth Benedict, *Race: Science and Politics* (New York: Modern Age Books, 1940), pp. 25–6.

12. Du Bois, *Africa*, p. 148.

13. See especially James M. Blaut, *Eight Eurocentric Historians* (London: Guilford Press, 2000).

14. Karl Marx in Shlomo Avineri, *Karl Marx on Colonialism and Modernization* (New York: Anchor, 1969), pp. 184, 343; see also Brendan O'Leary, *The Asiatic Mode of Production* (Oxford: Blackwell, 1989), p. 69.

15. Karl Marx, 'Chinese Affairs' (1862), in Avineri, *Marx*, pp. 442–4.

16. E.g. Karl Marx, 'The Future Results of British Rule' (1853), in Avineri, *Marx*, pp. 132–3; Karl Marx, *Surveys from Exile* (London: Pelican, 1973), p. 320.

17. Karl Marx and Friedrich Engels, *The Communist Manifesto* (Harmondsworth: Penguin, 1985), p. 84.

18. Karl Marx, *Capital*, III (London: Lawrence and Wishart, 1959), pp. 791, 333–4; Marx, *Capital*, I (London: Lawrence and Wishart, 1954), pp. 140, 316, 337–9.

19. Marx, *Capital*, I, p. 338, my emphasis.

20. Karl Marx, *Capital*, III, p. 726.

21. Karl Wittfogel, *Oriental Despotism* (New Haven: Yale University Press, 1963).

22. Karl Marx, *Grundrisse* (New York: Vintage, 1973), p. 110.

23. Karl Marx, *The German Ideology* (London: Lawrence and Wishart, 1965).

24. Georg W. F. Hegel, *The Philosophy of History* (New York: Dover Publications, 1956).

25. Teshale Tibebu, 'On the Question of Feudalism, Absolutism, and the Bourgeois Revolution', *Review* 13 (1) (1990), 83–5.

26. Randall Collins, *Weberian Sociological Theory* (Cambridge: Cambridge University Press, 1986), p. 23, my emphasis.

27. See especially Weber's *The Religion of China* (New York: The Free Press, 1951); *The Religion of India* (New York: Don Martindale, 1958);

General Economic History (London: Transaction Books, 1981); *The Protestant Ethic and the Spirit of Capitalism* (New York: Charles Scribner's Sons, 1958).

28. E.g. Anthony Giddens, *The Nation-State and Violence* (Cambridge: Polity, 1985).

29. E.g. Immanuel Wallerstein, *The Modern World System*, I (London: Academic Press, 1974); Giovanni Arrighi, 'The World according to Andre Gunder Frank', *Review* 22 (3) (1999), 348–53; Jared Diamond, *Guns, Germs and Steel* (London: Vintage, 1998).

30. Max Weber, *Economy and Society*, II (Berkeley: University of California Press, 1978), pp. 1192–3.

31. Blaut, *Colonizer's Model*, ch. 2.

32. Ibid., p. 5.

33. Landes, *Wealth*, ch. 29.

34. Ibid., p. xxi.

35. Lynn White cited in Blaut, *Eight Eurocentric Historians*, p. 39 (emphasis in the original).

36. Blaut, *Colonizer's Model*, pp. 115–19.

37. Immanuel Wallerstein, 'Frank Proves the European Miracle', *Review* 22 (3) (1999), 356–7.

Notes to ch. 2

1. Michael Mann, *The Sources of Social Power*, I (Cambridge: Cambridge University Press, 1986), pp. 6–10.

2. Perry Anderson, *Lineages of the Absolutist State* (London: Verso, 1979), pp. 548–9.

3. E.g. David Held, Anthony McGrew, David Goldblatt and Jonathan Perraton, *Global Transformations* (Cambridge: Polity, 1999).

4. Janet L. Abu-Lughod, *Before European Hegemony* (Oxford: Oxford University Press, 1989), p. 8.

5. Charles Tilly, *Big Structures, Large Processes, Huge Comparisons* (New York: Russell Sage Foundation, 1984), p. 62.

6. Jane Schneider, 'Was there a Pre-Capitalist World-System?', *Peasant Studies* 6 (1977), 20–29.

7. Abu-Lughod, *Hegemony*, p. 32.

8. Robert J. Holton, *Globalization and the Nation-State* (London: Macmillan, 1998), p. 28, my emphases.

9. William H. McNeill, *The Rise of the West* (Chicago: Chicago University Press, 1963), p. 460.

10. William H. McNeill, '*The Rise of the West* after Twenty-Five Years', in Stephen K. Sanderson (ed.), *Civilizations and World Systems* (London: Altamira Press, 1995), p. 314.

11. Jerry H. Bentley, *Old World Encounters* (New York: Oxford University Press, 1993), esp. chs. 1 and 3.

12. Philip D. Curtin, *Cross-Cultural Trade in World History* (Cambridge: Cambridge University Press, 1984), p. 105.

13. Jack Goody, *The East in the West* (Cambridge: Cambridge University Press, 1996), p. 86; Nigel Harris, *The Return of Cosmopolitan Capital* (London: I. B. Tauris, 2003), pp. 15–24; André Wink, *Al-Hind: the Making of the Indo-Islamic World*, I (Leiden: E. J. Brill, 1990), ch. 2.

14. McNeill, '*Rise of the West* after Twenty-Five Years', p. 316.

15. Wink, *Al-Hind*, pp. 35–6.

16. George F. Hourani, *Arab Seafaring in the Indian Ocean in Ancient and Early Medieval Times* (Beirut: Khayats, 1963), pp. 36–8; Wink, *Al-Hind*, pp. 48–55.

17. This and the next two references are from Maxime Rodinson, *Islam and Capitalism* (London: Allen Lane, 1974), pp. 14, 16–17, 29 respectively.

18. S. D. Goitein, *Studies in Islamic History and Institutions* (Leiden: E. J. Brill, 1968), pp. 228–9.

19. Marshall G. S. Hodgson, *Rethinking World History* (Cambridge: Cambridge University Press, 1993), pp. 111–16, 141.

20. Ibid., p. 133.

21. Rodinson, *Islam*, p. 56.

22. Rita R. Di Meglio, 'Arab Trade with Indonesia and the Malay Peninsula from the 8th to the 16th Century', in D. S. Richards (ed.), *Islam and the Trade of Asia* (Oxford: Bruno Cassirer, 1970), p. 126.

23. Hourani, *Arab Seafaring*, p. 62; Abu-Lughod, *Hegemony*, p. 199; W. E. B. Du Bois, *Africa and the World* (New York: International Publishers,

1975 [1946]), pp. 174, 192; Neville Chittick, 'East African Trade with the Orient', in Richards, *Islam*, p. 98.

24. Al-Mansūr and al-Ya'qūbi cited in Hourani, *Arab Seafaring*, p. 64.
25. Marco Polo cited in Jonathan Bloom and Sheila Blair, *Islam: Empire of Faith* (London: BBC Worldwide, 2001), p. 164; cf. Ibn Battūta, *Travels in Asia and Africa, 1325–1354* (London: Routledge and Kegan Paul, 1983), p. 101.
26. Wink, *Al-Hind*, pp. 28, 47.
27. Abu-Lughod, *Hegemony*, p. 36.
28. Philip D. Curtin, 'Africa and the Wider Monetary World, 1250–1850', in J. F. Richards (ed.), *Precious Metals in the Later Medieval and Early Modern Worlds* (Durham: Carolina Academic Press, 1983), pp. 231–8.
29. Ibn Battūta cited in Du Bois, *Africa*, p. 191.
30. John Middleton, *The World of the Swahili* (New Haven: Yale University Press, 1992).
31. Du Bois, *Africa*, ch. 10; Eric R. Wolf, *Europe and the People Without History* (Berkeley: University of California Press, 1982), pp. 37–44.
32. K. P. Moseley, 'Caravel and Caravan: West Africa and the World-Economies, ca. 900–1900 AD', *Review* 15 (3) (1992), 527; E. W. Bovill, *Caravans of the Old Sahara* (London: Oxford University Press, 1933), esp. chs. 5–6.
33. Du Bois, *Africa*, ch. 7; Roland Oliver, *The African Experience* (London: Phoenix, 1999), chs. 6, 11.
34. Wink, *Al-Hind*, p. 61.
35. Jerry H. Bentley, 'Cross-Cultural Interaction and Periodization in World History', *American Historical Review* 101 (3) (1996), 764.
36. O. W. Wolters, *Early Indonesian Commerce* (Ithaca: Cornell University Press, 1967).
37. Wink, *Al-Hind*, pp. 351–5.
38. Ibid., pp. 86–104.
39. See S. D. Goitein, *Jews and Arabs* (New York: Schocken Books, 1964).
40. Eric L. Jones, *Growth Recurring* (Oxford: Clarendon Press, 1988), ch. 3.

41. Fernand Braudel, *A History of Civilizations* (London: Penguin, 1995), p. 71.

42. Bloom and Blair, *Islam*, pp. 110–11.

43. S. D. Goitein, 'The Main Industries of the Mediterranean Area as Reflected in the Records of the Cairo Geniza', *Journal of the Economic and Social History of the Orient* 4 (2) (1961), 168–97.

44. Jones, *Growth Recurring*, p. 67.

45. Felipe Fernández-Armesto, *Civilizations* (London: Pan Books, 2001), pp. 120–31.

46. Abu-Lughod, *Hegemony*, p. 159.

47. Matthew Paris cited in Michael Edwardes, *East–West Passage* (New York: Taplinger, 1971), p. 70.

48. J. B. Friedmann, *The Monstrous Races in Medieval Art and Thought* (Cambridge, Mass.: Harvard University Press, 1981).

49. Abu-Lughod, *Hegemony*, p. 149.

Notes to ch. 3

1. Tsun Ko, 'The Development of Metal Technology in Ancient China', in Cheng-Yih Chen (ed.), *Science and Technology in Chinese Civilisation* (Singapore: World Scientific, 1987), pp. 229–38.

2. Robert Hartwell, 'Markets, Technology, and the Structure of Enterprise in the Development of the Eleventh Century Chinese Iron and Steel Industries', *Journal of Economic History* 26 (1966), 29–58.

3. Donald Wagner, *Iron and Steel in Ancient China* (Leiden: E. J. Brill, 1993), p. 407 and pp. 69–71.

4. Jacques Gernet, *A History of Chinese Civilization* (Cambridge: Cambridge University Press, 1999), p. 69.

5. Joseph Needham, Wang Ling and Lu Gwei-Djen, *Science and Civilisation in China*, IV (3) (Cambridge: Cambridge University Press, 1971), pp. 300–6, 344–65.

6. Peter J. Golas, *Science and Civilisation in China*, V (13) (Cambridge: Cambridge University Press, 1999), pp. 190–7.

7. Robert Temple, *The Genius of China* (London: Prion Books, 1999), pp. 119–20.

8. Ibid., p. 119.

9. William H. McNeill, *The Pursuit of Power* (Oxford: Blackwell, 1982), p. 29.

10. Ibid., p. 30.

11. Eric L. Jones, *Growth Recurring* (Oxford: Clarendon Press, 1988), pp. 77, 81.

12. R. Bin Wong, *China Transformed* (Ithaca: Cornell University Press, 1997), p. 90.

13. Albert Feuerwerker, 'The State and the Economy in Late Imperial China', *Theory and Society* 13 (1984), 300.

14. Yoshinobu Shiba, 'Urbanization and the Development of Markets in the Lower Yangtze Valley', in John W. Haeger (ed.), *Crisis and Prosperity in Sung China* (Tuscon: University of Arizona Press, 1975), p. 43.

15. Donald F. Lach and Edwin J. Van Kley, *Asia in the Making of Europe*, III (Chicago: Chicago University Press, 1993), pp. 1606–7.

16. Shiba, 'Urbanization', pp. 20–3.

17. Francesca Bray, *Science and Civilisation in China*, VI (2) (Cambridge: Cambridge University Press, 1984), p 565

18. Temple, *Genius*, p. 20.

19. Angus Maddison, *Chinese Economic Performance in the Long Run* (Paris: OECD, 1998), p. 31.

20. Bray, *Science*, VI (2), pp. 286–8.

21. Ibid., p. 600.

22. Cited in Lach and Kley, *Asia*, p. 1614.

23. Gang Deng, *Chinese Maritime Activities and Socioeconomic Development, c. 2100 BC–1900 AD* (London: Greenwood Press, 1997), pp. 68–9.

24. Temple, *Genius*, p. 186.

25. Gernet, *History*, p. 311; Joseph Needham, Ho Ping Yü, Lu Gwei-Djen and Wang Ling, *Science and Civilisation in China*, V (7) (Cambridge: Cambridge University Press, 1986), pp. 111–17.

26. Needham *et al.*, *Science*, V (7), pp. 161–210.

27. Ibid., pp. 486–95.

28. Temple, *Genius*, p. 240; Needham *et al.*, *Science*, V (7), pp. 495–505.

29. L. Carrington Goodrich and Fêng Chia-Shêng, 'The Early Development of Firearms in China', in Nathan Sivin, *Science and Technology in East Asia* (New York: Science History Publications, 1977), pp. 128–39; Wang Ling, 'On the Invention and Use of Gunpowder and Firearms in China', in Sivin, *Science*, pp. 140–58.

30. Needham *et al.*, *Science*, V (7), p. 264.

31. Deng, *Chinese Maritime Activities*, p. 70.

32. Needham *et al.*, *Science*, IV (3), pp. 689–95.

33. Temple, *Genius*, p. 248.

34. Frederic C. Lane, 'The Economic Meaning of the Invention of the Compass', *American Historical Review* 68 (1963), 151–2.

35. Irfan Habib, 'The Technology and Economy of Mughal India', *Indian Economic and Social History Review* 17 (1) (1980), 26–8; Joseph Needham, *Science and Civilisation in China*, I (Cambridge: Cambridge University Press, 1954), p. 243.

36. See especially Perry Anderson, *Lineages of the Absolutist State* (London: Verso, 1979), pp. 541–6; Alan K. Smith, *Creating a World Economy* (Boulder: Westview Press, 1991), pp. 27–9; David S. Landes, *The Wealth and Poverty of Nations* (London: Little, Brown, 1998), pp. 55–9.

37. Takeshi Hamashita, 'The Tribute Trade System and Modern Asia', in A. J. H. Latham and Heita Kawakatsu (eds.), *Japanese Industrialization and the Asian Economy* (London: Routledge, 1994); Dennis O. Flynn and Arturo Giraldez, 'China and the Manila Galleons', in Latham and Kawakatsu, *Japanese Industrialization*, pp. 71–90; Andre Gunder Frank, *ReOrient* (Berkeley: University of California Press, 1998), pp. 111–17.

38. Landes, *Wealth*, p. 96.

39. Ibid., p. 98.

40. Witold Rodzinski, *A History of China* (Oxford: Pergamon Press, 1979), p. 197.

41. Hamashita, 'Tribute', p. 92.

42. See especially Gang Deng, 'The Foreign Staple Trade of China in the Pre-Modern Era', *International History Review* 19 (2) (1997), p. 256.

43. Anthony Reid, *Southeast Asia in the Age of Commerce 1450–1680*, I (New Haven: Yale University Press, 1993), p. 15.

44. Frank, *ReOrient*, p. 114.

45. Philip D. Curtin, *Cross-Cultural Trade in World History* (Cambridge: Cambridge University Press, 1984), p. 169.

46. Peter W. Klein, 'The China Seas and the World Economy between the Sixteenth and Nineteenth Centuries: the Changing Structures of Trade', in Carl-Ludwig Holtfrerich (ed.), *Interactions in the World Economy* (New York: New York University Press, 1989), pp. 71, 73–86.

47. Lach and Kley, *Asia*, p. 1618.

48. E.g. Jakob C. Van Leur, *Indonesian Trade and Society* (The Hague: W. van Hoeve, 1955).

49. Deng, *Chinese Maritime Activities*, p. 108.

50. P. J. Marshal, 'Private British Trade in the Indian Ocean Before 1800', in Ashin Das Gupta and M. N. Pearson (eds.), *India and the Indian Ocean 1500–1800* (Calcutta: Oxford University Press, 1987), p. 297.

51. Han-sheng Chuan, 'The Inflow of American silver into China from the late Ming to the mid-Ch'ing Period', *Journal of the Institute of Chinese Studies of the China University of Hong Kong* 2 (1969), 61–75.

52. Adam Smith, *The Wealth of Nations* (New York: The Modern Library, 1965), p. 238.

53. Clive Ponting, *World History* (London: Chatto and Windus, 2000), p. 520.

54. Richard Von Glahn, *Fountain of Fortune* (Berkeley: University of California Press, 1996); Frank, *ReOrient*, ch. 3.

55. Flynn and Giraldez, 'China', p. 75.

56. Kenneth Pomeranz, *The Great Divergence* (Princeton: Princeton University Press, 2000), p. 273.

57. Gernet, *History*, p. 420.

58. Yongjin Zhang, 'System, Empire and State in Chinese International Relations', in Michael Cox, Ken Booth and Tim Dunne (eds.), *Empires, Systems and States* (Cambridge: Cambridge University Press, 2001), pp. 43–63.

59. Joseph Fletcher, 'China and Central Asia, 1368–1884', in John K. Fairbank (ed.), *The Chinese World Order* (Cambridge, Mass.: Harvard University Press, 1968), pp. 208–9.

60. Bin Wong, *China Transformed*, p. 89.

61. Louise E. Levathes, *When China Ruled the Seas* (London: Simon and Schuster, 1994), p. 20.

62. Felipe Fernández-Armesto, *Millennium* (London: Black Swan, 1996), pp. 129, 134.

63. Fernand Braudel, *Civilization and Capitalism, 15th–18th Century*, I (London: Collins, 1981), p. 377.

64. Wang Shixin, 'Commodity Circulation and Merchant Capital', in Xu Dixin and Wu Chengming (eds.), *Chinese Capitalism, 1522–1840* (London: Macmillan, 2000), pp. 46–64.

65. Pomeranz, *Great Divergence*, pp. 62–3.

66. Fang Xing, 'The Role of Embryonic Capitalism in China', in Dixin and Chengming, *Chinese Capitalism*, p. 418.

67. Golas, *Science*, V (13), pp. 169–70.

68. Wang Shixin, 'The Iron Industry of Foshan, Guangdong', in Dixin and Chengming (eds.), *Chinese Capitalism*, pp. 93–110.

69. Robert Marks, *Tigers, Rice, Silk and Silt* (New York: Cambridge University Press, 1997).

70. E.g. Susan Naquin and Evelyn Rawski, *Chinese Society in the Eighteenth Century* (London: Yale University Press, 1987).

71. Gernet, *History*, pp. 483–9.

72. Gang Deng, *Development versus Stagnation* (London: Greenwood Press, 1993), pp. 156, 171–2.

73. Jones, *Growth Recurring*, chs. 3–4.

74. Mark Elvin, *The Pattern of the Chinese Past* (Stanford: Stanford University Press, 1973), esp. chs. 11–12.

75. See the summary discussion in Paul A. Cohen, *Discovering History in China* (New York: Columbia University Press, 1984).

Notes to ch. 4

1. Paul A. Bairoch, 'The Main Trends in National Economic Disparities since the Industrial Revolution', in P. A. Bairoch and M. Lévy-Leboyer (eds.), *Disparities in Economic Development since the Industrial Revolution* (London: Macmillan, 1981), p. 7.

2. Angus Maddison, *Monitoring the World Economy* (Paris: OECD, 1995), pp. 30, 182–90.

3. Angus Maddison, 'A Comparison of Levels of GDP per capita in Developed and Developing Countries, 1700–1980', *Journal of Economic History* 43 (1) (1983), 29–30; Maddison, *Monitoring*, pp. 23–4; David S. Landes, *The Unbound Prometheus* (Cambridge: Cambridge University Press, 1969), p. 14.

4. Bairoch, 'Main Trends', pp. 7, 12, 14.

5. Maddison, 'Comparison', 29.

6. Ibid., 32.

7. Paul A. Bairoch, *Economics and World History* (Chicago: Chicago University Press, 1995), pp. 105–6.

8. Paul A. Bairoch, 'International Industrialization Levels from 1750 to 1980', *Journal of European Economic History* 11 (2) (1982), 269–333.

9 Kenneth Pomeranz, *The Great Divergence* (Princeton: Princeton University Press, 2000), pp. 36–41.

10. Süleyman Özmucur and Şevket Pamuk, 'Real Wages and Standards of Living in the Ottoman Empire, 1489–1914', *Journal of Economic History* 62 (2) (2002), 293–321.

11. James Z. Lee and Wang Feng, *One Quarter of Humanity* (London: Harvard University Press, 1999), ch. 3.

12. Susan B. Hanley, 'A High Standard of Living in Nineteenth Century Japan: Fact or Fantasy?' *Journal of Economic History* 43 (1) (1983), 183–92.

13. Andre Gunder Frank, *ReOrient* (Berkeley: University of California Press, 1998), p. 127.

14. Om Prakash, 'The Dutch East India Company in the Trade of the Indian Ocean', in Ashin Das Gupta and M. N. Pearson (eds.), *India and the Indian Ocean 1500–1800* (Calcutta: Oxford University Press, 1987), pp. 186–7.

15. E.g. Charles P. Kindleberger, 'Spenders and Hoarders', in C. P. Kindleberger (ed.), *Historical Economics* (Berkeley: University of California Press, 1990), pp. 35–85.

16. Najaf Haider, 'Precious Metal Flows and Currency Circulation in the Mughal Empire', *Journal of the Economic and Social History of the Orient* 39 (3) (1996), 298–367; Frank, *ReOrient*, pp. 151–64.

17. E.g. W. H. Moreland, *From Akbar to Aurangzeb* (London: Macmillan, 1923); Tapan Raychaudhuri, 'The Mughal Empire', in Tapan Raychaudhuri and Irfan Habib (eds.), *The Cambridge Economic History of India*, I (Cambridge: Cambridge University Press, 1982), pp. 172–3.

18. H. Fukazawa, 'Maharashtra and the Deccan: A Note', in Raychaudhuri and Habib, *Cambridge Economic History*, p. 202.

19. B. R. Grover, 'An Integrated Pattern of Commercial Life in Rural Society of North India during the Seventeenth and Eighteenth Centuries', in S. Subrahmanyam (ed.), *Money and the Market in India 1100–1700* (Delhi: Oxford University Press, 1994), pp. 238–9.

20. Muzafar Alam, 'Trade, State Policy and Regional Change: Aspects of Mughal-Uzbeck Commercial Relations, c. 1550–1750', *Journal of the Economic and Social History of the Orient* 37 (3) (1994), 215–18, 225–6.

21. H. W. Van Santen, 'Trade between Mughal India and the Middle East, and Mughal Monetary Policy, c. 1600–1660', in Karl R. Haellquist (ed.), *Asian Trade Routes* (London: Curzon Press, 1991), pp. 94–5.

22. Ashin Das Gupta, *The World of the Indian Ocean Merchant, 1500–1800* (New Delhi: Oxford University Press, 2001), p. 124.

23. Irfan Habib, 'Banking in Mughal India', in Tapan Raychaudhuri (ed.), *Contributions to Indian Economic History*, I (Calcutta: Firma K. L. Mukhopadhyay, 1960), esp. pp. 10–12.

24. Van Santen, 'Trade', p. 92.

25. Das Gupta, *World*, p. 73.
26. Moreland, *From Akbar*.
27. E.g. Jakob Van Leur, *Indonesian Trade and Society* (The Hague: W. van Hoeve, 1955).
28. Das Gupta, *World*, pp. 66, 92.
29. Ibid., ch. 3.
30. Irfan Habib, 'Merchant Communities in Pre-Colonial India', in James D. Tracy (ed.), *The Rise of Merchant Empires* (Cambridge: Cambridge University Press, 1990), p. 384.
31. Jack Goody, *The East in the West* (Cambridge: Cambridge University Press, 1996), p. 128.
32. Das Gupta, *World*, pp. 122–33.
33. Frank, *ReOrient*, pp. 84–92.
34. Grover, 'Integrated Pattern', pp. 219–55.
35. Habib, 'Merchant Communities', pp. 376–7.
36. Braudel, *Civilization and Capitalism, 15th–18th Century*, III (Berkeley: University of California Press, 1992), p. 509.
37. Arnold Pacey, *The Maze of Ingenuity* (London: Allen Lane, 1974), pp 187–8
38. Arun Das Gupta, 'The Maritime Trade of Indonesia: 1500–1800', in Om Prakash (ed.), *European Commercial Expansion in Early Modern Asia* (Aldershot: Variorum, 1997), pp. 240–50.
39. Anthony Reid, *Southeast Asia in the Age of Commerce 1450–1680*, I (New Haven: Yale University Press, 1993), pp. 12, 15.
40. M. A. P. Meilink-Roelofsz, 'Trade and Islam in the Malay-Indonesian Archipelago Prior to the Arrival of the Europeans', in D. S. Richards (ed.), *Islam and the Trade of Asia* (Oxford: Bruno Cassirer, 1970), p. 153.
41. K. N. Chaudhuri, *Trade and Civilisation in the Indian Ocean* (Cambridge: Cambridge University Press, 1978), pp. 186–7.
42. Anthony Reid, *Southeast Asia in the Age of Commerce 1450–1680*, II (New Haven: Yale University Press, 1993), p. 2.
43. E.g. John M. Roberts, *The Triumph of the West* (London: BBC Books, 1985), ch. 1.

44. R. N. Bellah, *Tokugawa Religion* (Boston: Beacon Press, 1970); David S. Landes, *The Wealth and Poverty of Nations* (London: Little, Brown, 1998), ch. 23.

45. Walt W. Rostow, *The Stages of Economic Growth* (New York: Cambridge University Press, 1960).

46. Eric L. Jones, *Growth Recurring* (Oxford: Clarendon Press, 1988), p. 153; Christopher Howe, *The Origins of Japanese Trade Supremacy* (Bathurst, New South Wales: Crawford House Publishing, 1996), p. 49.

47. J. I. Nakamura and M. Miyamoto, 'Social Structure and Population Change: a Comparative Study of Tokugawa Japan and Ch'ing China', *Economic Development and Cultural Change* 30 (2) (1982), 263–5.

48. Susan Hanley and Kozo Yamamura, *Economic and Demographic Change in Pre-Industrial Japan, 1600–1868* (Princeton: Princeton University Press, 1977), chs. 5–7.

49. Hanley and Yamamura, *Economic and Demographic Change*, pp. 69–78.

50. Thomas C. Smith, *The Agrarian Origins of Modern Japan* (Stanford: Stanford University Press, 1959), ch. 7.

51. Norbert Elias, *The Court Society* (Oxford: Blackwell, 1983).

52. Shinzaburō Ōishi, 'The Bakuhan System', in Chie Nakane and Shinzaburō Ōishi (eds.), *Tokugawa Japan* (Tokyo: Tokyo University Press, 1990), pp. 11–36.

53. Pomeranz, *Great Divergence*, p. 35.

54. Johann P. Arnason, *Social Theory and Japanese Experience* (London: Kegan Paul International, 1997), p. 257.

55. Jones, *Growth Recurring*, pp. 152–67.

56. E. S. Crawcour, 'The Development of a Credit System in Seventeenth-Century Japan', *Journal of Economic History* 20 (3) (1961), 347, 353–4.

57. Ronald P. Toby, 'Both a Borrower and a Lender Be: from Village Moneylender to Rural Banker in the Tempō Era', in Michael Smitka (ed.), *The Japanese Economy in the Tokugawa Era 1600–1868* (New York: Garland, 1998), pp. 325–54.

58. Ulrike Schaede, 'Forwards and Futures in Tokugawa-Period Japan: a New Perspective on the Dōjima Rice Market', *Journal of Banking and Finance* 13 (1989), 487–513.

59. Hanley and Yamamura, *Economic and Demographic Change*, p. 80.

60. David L. Howell, 'Proto-Industrial Origins of Japanese Capitalism', *Journal of Asian Studies* 51 (2) (1992), 269–86.

61. Ōishi, 'Bakuhan System', pp. 26–8.

62. Frank, *ReOrient*, p. 106.

63. Dennis O. Flynn, 'Comparing the Tokugawa Shogunate with Hapsburg Spain: Two Silver-based Empires in a Global Setting', in James D. Tracy (ed.), *The Political Economy of Merchant Empires* (Cambridge: Cambridge University Press, 1991), p. 354.

64. Satoshi Ikeda, 'The History of the Capitalist World-System vs. the History of East-Southeast Asia', *Review* 19 (1) (1996), 55, my emphasis.

65. Ikeda, 'History', 55–7.

66. Maddison, *Monitoring*, pp. 182–90.

67. Ikeda, 'History', 61.

68. Norman Jacobs, *The Origins of Capitalism and Eastern Asia* (Hong Kong: Hong Kong University Press, 1958), ch. 10.

Notes to ch. 5

1. Carlo Cipolla, *Before the Industrial Revolution* (London: Routledge, 1993), p. 138.

2. Lynn White, *Medieval Technology and Social Change* (Oxford: Clarendon Press, 1962), p. 52.

3. Haudricourt cited in Joseph Needham and Wang Ling, *Science and Civilisation in China*, IV (2) (Cambridge: Cambridge University Press, 1965), p. 317.

4. James Burke, *Connections* (London: Macmillan, 1978), p. 63; Hugh Thomas, *An Unfinished History of the World* (London: Papermac, 1995), p. 90; Clive Ponting, *World History* (London: Chatto and Windus, 2000), p. 371.

5. Joseph Needham in Mansel Davies, *A Selection from the Writings of Joseph Needham* (Lewes, Sussex: The Book Guild, 1990), p. 148.

6. Needham and Ling, *Science*, IV (2), p. 313.

7. Ibid., pp. 319–28.

8. White, *Medieval Technology*, ch. 1; Marc Bloch, *Feudal Society*, I (Chicago: Chicago University Press, 1961), p. 153.

9. Joseph Needham, Ho Ping-Yü, Lu Gwei-Djen and Wang Ling, *Science and Civilisation in China*, V (7) (Cambridge: Cambridge University Press, 1986), p. 17.

10. E. M. Jope, 'Vehicles and Harness', in Charles Singer, E. J. Holmyard, A. R. Hall and T. I. Williams (eds.), *A History of Technology*, II (Oxford: Clarendon Press, 1956), pp. 556–7; White, *Medieval Technology*, pp. 14–20.

11. Ahmad Y. al-Hassan and Donald R. Hill, *Islamic Technology* (Cambridge: Cambridge University Press, 1986), pp. 95–120.

12. William H. McNeill, *The Rise of the West* (Chicago: Chicago University Press, 1963), p. 485.

13. Perry Anderson, *Lineages of the Absolutist State* (London: Verso, 1979).

14. Norbert Elias, *The Civilizing Process* (Oxford: Blackwell, 1994); Hendrik Spruyt, *The Sovereign State and its Competitors* (Princeton: Princeton University Press, 1994).

15. Maxime Rodinson, 'The Western Image and Western Studies of Islam', in Joseph Schacht and C. E. Bosworth (eds.), *The Legacy of Islam* (London: Oxford University Press, 1974), p. 9.

16. See especially R. W. Southern, *Western Views on Islam in the Middle Ages* (Cambridge: Mass.: Harvard University Press, 1962); Rana Kabbani, *Europe's Myth of the Orient* (Bloomington: Indiana University Press, 1986), ch. 1.

17. Edward W. Said, *Orientalism* (London: Penguin, 1991 [1978]), p. 68.

18. Philip K. Hitti, *History of the Arabs* (London: Macmillan, 1937), pp. 114, 459, 586, 613.

19. Kabbani, *Europe's Myth*, p. 5.

20. Said, *Orientalism*, p. 74.

21. Edward Gibbon, *The Decline and Fall of the Roman Empire*, II (New York: The Modern Library, 1931), p. 801.

22. Bernard Lewis, *The Muslim Discovery of Europe* (London: Phoenix, 1994), pp. 19–20; also McNeill, *Rise*, p. 469.

23. Bloch, *Feudal Society*, I, p. 3.

24. Ibid.

25. Maxime Rodinson, *Europe and the Mystique of Islam* (London: I. B. Tauris, 1987), p. 7.

26. Jonathan Riley-Smith, *The First Crusade and the Idea of Crusading* (London: Athlone Press, 1986), especially ch. 1.

27. V. Y. Mudimbe, *The Invention of Africa* (Indianapolis: Indiana University Press, 1988), p. 57.

28. Robert J. Holton, *Globalization and the Nation-State* (London: Macmillan, 1998), p. 32.

29. Georges Duby, *The Three Orders: Feudal Society Imagined* (Chicago: Chicago University Press, 1980).

30. Marc Bloch, *Feudal Society*, II (Chicago: Chicago University Press, 1961), pp. 412–20.

31. Gerd Tellenbach, *Church, State and Christian Society at the Time of the Investiture Conflict* (Oxford: Blackwell, 1959), p. 39.

32. Michael Mann, *The Sources of Social Power*, I (Cambridge: Cambridge University Press, 1986), pp. 381ff.

33. Thomas H. Greer and Gavin Lewis, *A Brief History of the Western World* (New York: Harcourt, Brace Jovanovich, 1992), p. 45; cf. Gerard Delanty, *Inventing Europe* (London: Macmillan, 1995), p. 26.

Notes to ch. 6

1. Armando Sapori cited in Fernand Braudel, *Civilization and Capitalism, 15th–18th Century*, III (Berkeley: University of California Press, 1992), p. 91.

2. E.g. Charles Kindleberger, *World Economic Primacy, 1500–1990* (New York: Oxford University Press, 1996).

3. Braudel, *Civilization*, III, p. 94.

4. Adam Smith, *The Wealth of Nations* (New York: The Modern Library, 1937 [1776]), p. 13.

5. Janet L. Abu-Lughod, *Before European Hegemony* (Oxford: Oxford University Press, 1989), p. 108; André Wink, *Al-Hind: the Making of the Indo-Islamic World*, I (Leiden: E. J. Brill, 1995), pp. 35–8.

6. Braudel, *Civilization*, III, pp. 128, 132.

7. Ibid., pp. 129–30; Douglass North and Robert Thomas, *The Rise of the Western World* (Cambridge: Cambridge University Press, 1973), p. 53.

8. M. J. Kister, 'Mecca and Tamīm', *Journal of the Economic and Social History of the Orient* 8 (1965), 117ff.

9. Jack Goody, *The East in the West* (Cambridge: Cambridge University Press, 1996), p. 58.

10. Abraham L. Udovitch, 'Commercial Techniques in Early Medieval Islamic Trade', in D. S. Richards (ed.), *Islam and the Trade of Asia* (Oxford: Bruno Cassirer, 1970), p. 48.

11. Abraham L. Udovitch, *Partnership and Profit in Medieval Islam* (Princeton: Princeton University Press, 1970), p. 78; S. D. Goitein, *A Mediterranean Society*, I (Berkeley: University of California Press, 1967), pp. 362–7.

12. Abu-Lughod, *Hegemony*, p. 216.

13. Goitein, *Mediterranean Society*, I, pp. 197–9; Udovitch, 'Commercial Techniques', pp. 61–2.

14. Abu-Lughod, *Hegemony*, p. 223.

15. Goody, *East*, p. 79; Abu-Lughod, *Hegemony*, p. 224.

16. Kenneth Pomeranz, *The Great Divergence* (Princeton: Princeton University Press, 2000), pp. 168–9; Goody, *East*, p. 75.

17. Goody, *East*, pp. 68, 72.

18. Emile Savage-Smith, 'Celestial Mapping', in J. Brian Harley and David Woodward (eds.), *History of Cartography*, II (1) (Chicago: Chicago University Press, 1992), pp. 12–70; Paul Kunitzsch, *The Arabs and the Stars* (Northampton: Variorum, 1989), chs. 8, 10.

19. Kunitzsch, *Arabs*, ch. 9.

20. Joseph Needham, Wang Ling and Lu Gwei-Djen, *Science and Civilisation in China*, IV (3) (Cambridge: Cambridge University Press, 1971), pp. 554–84; Hans Breuer, *Columbus was Chinese* (New York: Herder and Herder, 1972), pp. 83–102.

21. George F. Hourani, *Arab Seafaring in the Indian Ocean in Ancient and Early Medieval Times* (Beirut: Khayats, 1963), pp. 108–9.

22. Lionel Casson, *Ships and Seamanship in the Ancient World* (Princeton: Princeton University Press, 1971), pp. 243–5 and figs. 181, 182.

23. Jules Sottas, 'An Early Lateen Sail in the Mediterranean', *The Mariner's Mirror* 25 (1939), 229–30.

24. The ensuing discussion is from Lynn White, *Medieval Religion and Technology* (Berkeley: University of California Press, 1978), pp. 255–60.

25. H. H. Brindley, 'Early Pictures of Lateen Sails', *The Mariner's Mirror* 12 (1) (1926), 9–10.

26. Richard LeBaron Bowen, *Arab Dhows of Eastern Arabia* (Rehoboth, Mass.: privately published, 1949), p. 7, n. 9.

27. Brindley, 'Early Pictures', 9.

28. Needham *et al.*, *Science*, IV (3), p. 609, n. g.

29. Cecil Torr, *Ancient Ships* (Cambridge: Cambridge University Press, 1895), pp. 86–91.

30. Ibn-Shahriyā in Hourani, *Arab Seafaring*, p. 100.

31. Gerald R. Tibbetts, *Arab Navigation in the Indian Ocean before the Coming of the Portuguese* (London: The Royal Asiatic Society of Great Britain and Ireland, 1971), p. 49.

32. Needham *et al.*, *Science*, IV (3), pp. 635–54.

33. Gavin Menzies, *1421* (London: Bantam Press, 2002), p. 43.

34. Carlo Cipolla, *Before the Industrial Revolution* (London: Routledge, 1993), p. 210.

35. Arnold Pacey, *Technology in World Civilization* (Cambridge, Mass.: MIT Press, 1991), p. 43.

36. Ahmad Y. al-Hassan and Donald R. Hill, *Islamic Technology* (Cambridge: Cambridge University Press, 1986), p. 53.

37. Jonathan Bloom and Sheila Blair, *Islam: Empire of Faith* (London: BBC Worldwide, 2001), pp. 104–5.

38. Hugh Thomas, *An Unfinished History of the World* (London: Papermac, 1995), pp. 92–3.

39. Joseph Needham and Wang Ling, *Science and Civilisation in China*, IV (2) (Cambridge: Cambridge University Press, 1965), pp. 556–7.

40. R. J. Forbes, 'Power', in Charles Singer, E. J. Holmyard, A. R. Hall and T. I. Williams (eds.), *A History of Technology*, II (Oxford: Clarendon Press, 1956), pp. 614–17.

41. Dieter Kuhn, *Science and Civilisation in China*, V (9) (Cambridge: Cambridge University Press, 1988), pp. 419–33.

42. Hugh Honour, *Chinoiserie: the Vision of Cathay* (London: John Murray, 1961), p. 35.

43. Robert Temple, *The Genius of China* (London: Prion Books, 1999), p. 120.

44. Pacey, *Technology*, pp. 103–7; Temple, *Genius*, pp. 120–1.

45. Kuhn, *Science*, V (9), pp. 428–33.

46. Thomas F. Carter, *The Invention of Printing in China and its Spread Westward* (New York: The Ronald Press Company, 1955), ch. 13.

47. Jacques Gernet, *A History of Chinese Civilization* (Cambridge: Cambridge University Press, 1999), p. 288.

48. Al-Qazwini cited in al-Hassan and Hill, *Islamic Technology*, p. 191.

49. Tsien Tsuen-Hsuin, *Science and Civilisation in China*, V (1) (Cambridge: Cambridge University Press, 1985), p. 297.

50. Carter, *Invention*, ch. 13; Tsuen-Hsuin, *Science*, V (1), pp. 296–9.

51. Al-Hassan and Hill, *Islamic Technology*, p. 192.

52. Joseph Needham, *Science and Civilisation in China*, I (Cambridge: Cambridge University Press, 1954), p. 240.

53. Braudel, *Civilization*, I, p. 376.

54. David S. Landes, *The Wealth and Poverty of Nations* (London: Little, Brown, 1998), p. 49.

55. Ibid., p. 48.

56. Needham and Ling, *Science*, IV (2), p. 464, and pp. 446–63; cf. Gernet, *History*, p. 341.

57. D. S. L. Cardwell, *Technology, Science and History* (London: Heine-mann, 1972), p. 14.

58. Clive Ponting, *World History* (London: Chatto and Windus, 2000), p. 371.

59. Donald R. Hill, *Studies in Medieval Technology* (Aldershot: Ashgate, 1998), ch. 13, p. 15.

60. White, *Medieval Religion*, pp. 52–4.

61. Needham and Ling, *Science*, IV (2), pp. 543–4.

62. Bloom and Blair, *Islam*, pp. 106–7.

63. Michael Edwardes, *East–West Passage* (New York: Taplinger, 1971), p. 85.

64. Needham *et al.*, *Science*, IV (3), p. 177.

Notes to ch. 7

1. J. M. Roberts, *The Triumph of the West* (London: BBC, 1985), pp. 175, 184, 186, 188, 194.

2. Ibid., p. 201.

3. Michael Edwardes, *East–West Passage* (New York: Taplinger, 1971), p. 135.

4. Brandon H. Beck, *From the Rising of the Sun* (New York: Peter Lang, 1987), p. 17.

5. Pope Pius II cited in Robert Schwoebel, *The Shadow of the Crescent* (Nieuwkoop: B. De Graaf, 1967), p. 71.

6. Charles R. Boxer, *The Portuguese Seaborne Empire, 1415–1825* (London: Hutchinson, 1969), p. 21.

7. Ibid., pp. 22–3.

8. M. N. Pearson, *The New Cambridge History of India* (Cambridge: Cambridge University Press, 1987), p. 38.

9. See the discussion in Gerald R. Tibbetts, *Arab Navigation in the Indian Ocean before the Coming of the Portuguese* (London: The Royal Asiatic Society of Great Britain and Ireland, 1971), pp. 206–8.

10. Janet L. Abu-Lughod, *Before European Hegemony* (Oxford: Oxford University Press, 1989), p. 19; and pp. 209, 258, 363.

11. Joseph Needham, Wang Ling and Lu Gwei-Djen, *Science and Civilisation in China*, IV (3) (Cambridge: Cambridge University Press, 1971), pp. 501–2; cf. Gavin Menzies, *1421* (London: Bantam, 2002), esp. ch. 4.

12. Colin Ronan (ed.), *The Shorter Science and Civilisation in China*, III (Cambridge: Cambridge University Press, 1986), ch. 3.

13. Diogo do Couto cited in Anthony Reid, *Southeast Asia in the Age of Commerce 1450–1680*, I (New Haven: Yale University Press, 1993), p. 36.

14. André Wink, *Al-Hind: the Making of the Indo-Islamic World*, I (Leiden: E. J. Brill, 1995), pp. 27–8.

15. Pearson, *New Cambridge History*, p. 11.

16. Joseph Needham in Mansel Davies, *A Selection from the Writings of Joseph Needham* (Lewes, Sussex: The Book Guild, 1990), p. 176.

17. Joseph Desomogyi, *A Short History of Oriental Trade* (Hildesheim: Georg Olms Verlagsbuchhandlung, 1968), p. 83.

18. Michael Adas, *Machines as the Measure of Men* (Ithaca: Cornell University Press, 1989), pp. 41–5; Jack Goody, *The East in the West* (Cambridge: Cambridge University Press, 1996), p. 111.

19. This and the next two paragraphs draw from Patricia Seed, *Ceremonies of Possession in Europe's Conquest of the New World, 1492–1640* (Cambridge: Cambridge University Press, 1995), pp. 107–28.

20. Martin Elbl, 'The Caravel', in Robert Gardiner (ed.), *Cogs, Caravels and Galleons* (London: Brasseys, 1994), p. 91.

21. G. S. L. Clowes, 'Ships of Early Explorers', *Geographical Journal* 69 (1927), 216; Needham *et al.*, *Science*, IV (3), pt. 29.

22. Pedro Nunes cited in Seed, *Ceremonies*, p. 126.

23. Tibbetts, *Arab Navigation*, pp. 9–11.

24. Cited in E. G. Ravenstein (ed.), *A Journal of the First Voyage of Vasco Da Gama, 1497–1499* (London: Bedford Press, 1899), p. 87.

25. Antonio Pigafetta cited in Miriam Estensen, *Discovery* (St Leonards, New South Wales: Allen and Unwin, 1998), pp. 15–16.

26. Ahmad ibn-Mājid cited in Tibbetts, *Arab Navigation*, p. 195.
27. Ravenstein, *Journal*, p. 163; Needham *et al.*, *Science*, IV (3), pp. 480–2; Menzies, *1421*, p. 38.
28. Goody, *East*, p. 92.
29. Menzies, *1421*, p. 43.
30. Gang Deng, *Chinese Maritime Activities and Socioeconomic Development, c. 2100 BC–1900 AD* (London: Greenwood Press, 1997), pp. 70–1.
31. Reid, *Southeast Asia*, I, pp. 20–1.
32. Boxer, *Portuguese*, p. 58.
33. Jakob Van Leur, *Indonesian Trade and Society* (The Hague: W. van Hoeve, 1955), p. 159.
34. K. N. Chaudhuri, *Trade and Civilisation in the Indian Ocean* (Cambridge: Cambridge University Press, 1978), p. 79.
35. Fernand Braudel, *Civilization and Capitalism, 15th–18th Century*, III (Berkeley: University of California Press, 1992), pp. 212–13.
36. Clive Ponting, *World History* (London: Chatto and Windus, 2000), p. 525.
37. M. A. P. Meilink-Roelofsz, *Asian Trade and European Influence in the Indonesian Archipelago between 1500 and about 1630* (The Hague: Martinus Nijhoff, 1962).
38. Adas, *Machines*, p. 48.
39. Braudel, *Civilization*, III, p. 468, his emphasis.
40. P. M. Holt, Ann K. S. Lambton and Bernard Lewis, cited in Andre Gunder Frank, *ReOrient* (Berkeley: University of California Press, 1998), p. 118.
41. Marshall G. S. Hodgson, *Rethinking World History* (Cambridge: Cambridge University Press, 1993), pp. 97, 129.
42. Frederic C. Lane, 'Venetian Shipping during the Commercial Revolution', *American Historical Review* 38 (2) (1933), 228; Niels Steensgaard, *The Asian Trade Revolution of the Seventeenth Century* (Chicago: Chicago University Press, 1974), pp. 155–69.
43. Pearson, *New Cambridge History*, p. 44.

44. Najaf Haider, 'Precious Metal Flows and Currency Circulation in the Mughal Empire', *Journal of the Economic and Social History of the Orient* 39 (3) (1996), 298–367.

45. Sanjay Subrahmanyam, 'Precious Metal Flows and Prices in Western and Southern Asia, 1500–1750: some Comparative and Conjunctural Aspects', in S. Subrahmanyam (ed.), *Money and the Market in India 1100–1700* (Delhi: Oxford University Press, 1994), p. 201, also pp. 197–201.

46. Calculated from Reid, *Southeast Asia*, I, table 3, p. 27.

47. Van Leur, *Indonesian Trade*, p. 212, cf. p. 235.

48. Boxer, *Portuguese*, pp. 59, 61.

49. Ibid., p. 62.

50. Pearson, *New Cambridge History*, p. 54.

51. Philip D. Curtin, *Cross-Cultural Trade in World History* (Cambridge: Cambridge University Press, 1984), p. 145.

52. Ibid., pp. 144–8; see also pp. 159–67 and ch. 8.

53. Pearson, *New Cambridge History*, p. 55.

54. Tomé Pires, *Suma Oriental* (Glasgow: The University Press, 1944), pp. 268–9.

55. Reid, *Southeast Asia*, I, p. 23.

56. H. W. Van Santen, 'Trade between Mughal India and the Middle East, and Mughal Monetary Policy, c. 1600–1660', in Karl R. Haellquist (ed.), *Asian Trade Routes* (London: Curzon Press, 1991), p. 89.

57. Van Santen, 'Trade', p. 90.

58. Eric R. Wolf, *Europe and the People Without History* (Berkeley: University of California Press, 1982), p. 234.

59. M. N. Pearson, 'India and the Indian Ocean in the Sixteenth Century', in Ashin Das Gupta and M. N. Pearson (eds.), *India and the Indian Ocean 1500–1800* (Calcutta: Oxford University Press, 1987), p. 78.

60. Braudel, *Civilization*, III, p. 489.

61. P. J. Marshall, 'Private British Trade in the Indian Ocean before 1800', in Das Gupta and Pearson, *India*, pp. 280, 283, 287, 292–3.

62. Om Prakash, 'The Dutch East India Company in the Trade of the Indian Ocean', in J. F. Richards (ed.), *Precious Metals in the Late*

Medieval and Early Modern Worlds (Durham: Carolina Academic Press, 1983), pp. 189–90.

63. Frank, *ReOrient*, pp. 74–5.
64. Wolf, *Europe*, p. 240.
65. Ponting, *World History*, p. 525.
66. Suleyman cited in Jonathan Bloom and Sheila Blair, *Islam: Empire of Faith* (London: BBC Books, 2001), p. 158.

Notes to ch. 8

1. See also Andre Gunder Frank, *ReOrient* (Berkeley: University of California Press, 1998), pp. 318–19, 334.
2. Columbus cited in Marc Ferro, *Colonization: A Global History* (London: Routledge, 1997), p. 5.
3. Tzvetan Todorov, *The Conquest of America* (New York: Harper and Row, 1984), p. 10, and pp. 11–13.
4. See David Abernethy, *The Dynamics of Global Dominance* (London: Yale University Press, 2000), p. 184.
5. Edmundo O'Gorman, *The Invention of America* (Bloomington: Indiana University Press, 1961), esp. pt 3; also Todorov, *Conquest*, pp. 14–33.
6. Las Casas cited in O'Gorman, *Invention*, p. 79.
7. Cited in Alfred W. Crosby, *The Columbian Exchange* (Westport: Greenwood, 1972), p. 11.
8. Todorov, *Conquest*, p. 17.
9. Ibid., pp. 46–7.
10. Richard Slotkin, *Regeneration Through Violence* (Middleton: Weslyan University Press, 1973); Michael Kammen, *People of Paradox* (New York: Alfred A. Knopf, 1972); Reginald Horsman, *Race and Manifest Destiny: the Origins of American Racial Anglo-Saxonism* (Cambridge, Mass.: Harvard University Press, 1981).
11. Richard Drinnon, *Facing West: the Metaphysics of Indian-Hating and Empire-Building* (Minneapolis: University of Minnesota Press, 1980), p. 99.

12. Arnold J. Toynbee, *A Study of History*, VIII (London: Oxford University Press, 1963), p. 111, n. 2.

13. Patricia Seed, *Ceremonies of Possession in Europe's Conquest of the New World, 1492–1640* (Cambridge: Cambridge University Press, 1995), p. 70.

14. Cited in ibid., p. 69.

15. Jan Nederveen Pieterse, *White on Black* (London: Yale University Press, 1992), p. 44.

16. George M. Frederickson, *Racism: a Short History* (Melbourne: Scribe Publications, 2002), p. 45.

17. Ibid., p. 29.

18. Alexander Falconbridge cited in James Walvin, *Black Ivory* (Washington, DC: Howard University Press, 1994), pp. 49–50, and pp. 38–58.

19. 'Dicky Sam', *Liverpool and Slavery* (Liverpool: Scouse Press, 1984 [1884]), p. 34.

20. Cited in 'Transatlantic Slavery: Against Human Dignity', National Museums and Galleries on Merseyside (Liverpool, 2002), p. 12.

21. Herbert S. Klein, *The Atlantic Slave Trade* (Cambridge: Cambridge University Press, 1999), p. 150.

22. Walvin, *Black Ivory*, pp. 250–1.

23. Peter Fryer, *Black People in the British Empire* (London: Pluto Press, 1988), pp. 10–11.

24. 'Transatlantic Slavery', p. 8.

25. Orlando Patterson, *Slavery and Social Death* (Cambridge, Mass.: Harvard University Press, 1982).

26. John Thornton, *Africa and Africans in the Making of the Atlantic World, 1400–1800* (Cambridge: Cambridge University Press, 1998).

27. C. L. R. James, *The Black Jacobins* (London: Allison and Busby, 1989 [1938]); W. E. B. Du Bois, *Africa and the World* (New York: International Publishers, 1975 [1946]), pp. 60–6.

28. William Denevan, *The Native Populations of the Americas in 1492* (Madison: University of Wisconsin Press, 1992).

29. Jan Carew, 'Columbus and the Origins of Racism in the Americas: Part One', *Race and Class* 29 (4) (1988), 3.

30. David S. Landes, The *Wealth and Poverty of Nations* (London: Little, Brown, 1998), pp. 99–112.

31. See the special issue of *Annals of the Association of American Geographers* 82 (3) (1992).

32. Crosby, *Columbian Exchange*, ch. 2.

33. James M. Blaut, *The Colonizer's Model of the World* (London: Guilford Press, 1993), pp. 184, and 186.

34. J. M. Roberts, *The Penguin History of the World* (London: Penguin, 1995), p. 641.

35. Blaut, *Colonizer's Model*, ch. 4; Frank, *ReOrient*, ch. 2.

36. Joseph E. Inikori, *Africans and the Industrial Revolution in England* (Cambridge: Cambridge University Press, 2002), pp. 183–5.

37. Thierry Hentsch, *Imagining the Middle East* (Montreal, Quebec: Black Rose Books, 1992); Iver Neumann, *Uses of the Other* (Minneapolis: University of Minnesota Press, 1999).

38. A. Rupert Hall, 'General Introduction', in Marie Boas, *The Scientific Renaissance 1450 1630* (London: Collins, 1962), p. 6. For a good review of the Eurocentric position see Frank, *ReOrient*, pp. 185–93.

39. Michael Edwardes, *East–West Passage* (New York: Taplinger, 1971), p. 94.

40. Margaret Wertheim, *Pythagoras' Trousers* (London: Time Books, 1996), p. 35.

41. William H. McNeill, *The Rise of the West* (Chicago: Chicago University Press, 1963), pp. 602, 609.

42. Bernard Lewis, *The Muslim Discovery of Europe* (London: Phoenix, 1994), p. 221.

43. Jacques Gernet, *A History of Chinese Civilization* (Cambridge: Cambridge University Press, 1999), pp. 298, 337–47.

44. Jack Goody, *The East in the West* (Cambridge: Cambridge University Press, 1996), p. 234.

45. Jonathan Bloom and Sheila Blair, *Islam: Empire of Faith* (London: BBC Worldwide, 2001), p. 125.

46. Wazir Hasan Abdi, 'Glimpses of Mathematics in Medieval India', in A. Rahman (ed.), *History of Indian Science, Technology and*

Culture, AD *1000–1800* (New Delhi: Oxford University Press, 1999),
pp. 50–94.

47. Seyyed Nasr, *Science and Civilization in Islam* (Cambridge, Mass.:
Harvard University Press, 1968), ch. 5.

48. Charles Singer, 'Epilogue: East and West in Retrospect', in Charles
Singer, E. J. Holmyard, A. R. Hall and T. I. Williams (eds.), *A History
of Technology*, III (Oxford: Clarendon Press, 1956), p. 767.

49. Juan Vernet, 'Mathematics, Astronomy, Optics', in Joseph Schacht
and C. E. Bosworth (eds.), *The Legacy of Islam* (Oxford: Clarendon,
1974), p. 477.

50. E. S. Kennedy, *Studies in the Islamic Exact Sciences* (Beirut: American University of Beirut, 1983), p. 41.

51. Joseph Needham and Wang Ling, *Science and Civilisation in China*,
III (Cambridge: Cambridge University Press, 1959), p. 109.

52. Bloom and Blair, *Islam*, p. 131.

53. Lewis, *Muslim Discovery*, pp. 128–30.

54. Joseph Needham, Lu Gwei-Djen and Nathan Sivin, *Science and Civilisation in China*, VI (6) (Cambridge: Cambridge University Press,
2000), pp. 124–5.

55. Philip K. Hitti, *History of the Arabs* (London: Macmillan, 1937),
p. 367.

56. Luis Garcia Ballester, M. R. McVaugh and A. Rubio-Vela, *Practical
Medicine from Salerno to the Black Death* (Cambridge: Cambridge
University Press, 1994), pp. 13–29.

57. Needham *et al.*, *Science*, VI (6).

58. Swerdlow cited in George Saliba, *A History of Arabic Astronomy*
(London: New York University Press, 1994), p. 64.

59. Kennedy, *Studies*, pp. 50–83; Saliba, *History*, pp. 245–305.

60. N. Swerdlow and O. Neugebauer, *Mathematical Astronomy in Copernicus' De Revolutionibus* (Berlin: Springer, 1984), p. 295.

61. Martin Bernal, *Black Athena*, I (London: Vintage, 1991), pp. 155–6;
Frances Yates, *Giordano Bruno and the Hermetic Tradition* (London:
Routledge and Kegan Paul, 1964), esp. p. 154.

62. Wertheim, *Pythagoras' Trousers*, p. 81, and pp. 81–91.

63. Robert Briffault cited in Ziauddin Ahmad, 'Muslim Contribution to Scientific Progress', in Mohammad R. Mirza and Muhammad I. Siddiqi (eds.), *Muslim Contribution to Science* (Lahore: Kazi, 1986), p. 117.

64. H. Floris Cohen, *The Scientific Revolution* (Chicago: Chicago University Press, 1994), ch. 8.

65. Du Bois, *Africa*, ch. 10.

66. Hitti, *History*, pp. 628–31.

67. Cheik Anta Diop, *The African Origins of Civilization* (Westport: L. Hill, 1974); Bernal, *Black Athena*, pp. 24, 151–5, 434–7.

68. Du Bois, *Africa*, p. 223.

69. Boas, *Scientific Renaissance*, pp. 29–30.

70. Benedict Anderson, *Imagined Communities* (London: Verso, 1983).

71. Michael Mann, *The Sources of Social Power*, I (Cambridge: Cambridge University Press, 1986); Anthony Giddens, *The Nation-State and Violence* (Cambridge: Polity, 1985).

72. Michael Clapham, 'Printing', in Charles Singer, E. J. Holmyard, A. R. Hall and T. I. Williams (eds.), *A History of Technology*, II (Oxford: Clarendon Press, 1956), p. 377.

73. Gernet, *History*, pp. 332–3; Tsien Tsuen-Hsuin, *Science and Civilisation in China*, V (1) (Cambridge: Cambridge University Press, 1985), pp. 146–69; Thomas F. Carter, *The Invention of Printing in China and its Spread Westward* (New York: The Ronald Press Company, 1955), p. 41.

74. Carter, *Invention*, p. 239.

75. Tsuen-Hsuin, *Science*, V (1), p. 145.

76. Donald F. Lach and Edwin J. Van Kley, *Asia in the Making of Europe*, III (Chicago: Chicago University Press, 1993), p. 1598.

77. Ibid., p. 1595.

78. Gernet, *History*, p. 336.

79. Landes, *Wealth*, p. 51.

80. Lach and Kley, *Asia*, p. 1595, n. 209.

81. Carter, *Invention*, pp. 239–40; Sang-woon Jeon, *Science and Technology in Korea* (Cambridge, Mass.: MIT, 1974), pp. 173–84; Tsuen-Hsuin, *Science*, V (1), pp. 319–331.

82. Tsuen-Hsuin, *Science*, V (1), pp. 132–72, 303–13.

83. Robert Curzon cited in Tsuen-Hsuin, *Science*, V (1), p. 313.

84. Carter, *Invention*, p. 242.

85. G. F. Hudson, *Europe and China* (Boston: Beacon Press, 1961), p. 168; also, Clapham, 'Printing', pp. 378, 380.

86. J. M. Roberts, *Essays in Swedish History* (London: Weidenfeld and Nicolson, 1967).

87. Charles Tilly, *Coercion, Capital and European States, AD 990–1990* (Oxford: Blackwell, 1990); Giddens, *Nation-State*, pp. 103–16, 222–54; Mann, *Sources*, I, chs. 12–15.

88. Joseph Needham, Ho Ping-Yü, Lu Gwei-Djen and Wang Ling, *Science and Civilisation in China*, V (7) (Cambridge: Cambridge University Press, 1986), p. 49.

89. Paul Cressey, 'Chinese Traits in European Civilization: a Study in Diffusion', *American Sociological Review* 10 (5) (1945), 598; Arnold Pacey, *Technology in World Civilization* (Cambridge, Mass.: MIT Press, 1991), p. 45.

90. Needham *et al.*, *Science*, V (7), pp. 47–50, 570–2.

91. O. F. G. Hogg, *English Artillery 1326–1716* (London: Royal Artillery Institution, 1963), pp. 6–9, 46; William H. McNeill, *The Pursuit of Power* (Oxford: Blackwell, 1982), pp. 81, 84.

92. Pacey, *Technology*, p. 47.

93. Needham *et al.*, *Science*, V (7), pp. 572–9.

94. As even Lynn White concedes in his *Medieval Religion and Technology* (Berkeley: University of California Press, 1978), p. 285; see also Ahmad Y. al-Hassan and Donald R. Hill, *Islamic Technology* (Cambridge: Cambridge University Press, 1986), pp. 106–7; Needham *et al.*, *Science*, V (7), p. 77.

95. Al-Hassan and Hill, *Islamic Technology*, p. 108.

96. Pacey, *Technology*, p. 74.

97. Ibid., p. 80.

98. Cf. Needham *et al.*, *Science*, V (7), pp. 455–65; Pacey, *Technology*, p. 75.

Notes to ch. 9

1. Phyllis Deane, *The First Industrial Revolution* (Cambridge: Cambridge University Press, 1965); Peter Mathias, *The First Industrial Nation* (London: Methuen, 1983).
2. R. M. Hartwell, 'Was there an Industrial Revolution?', *Social Science History* 14 (1990), 575, my emphases.
3. Walt W. Rostow, *The Stages of Economic Growth* (Cambridge: Cambridge University Press, 1961), p. 157, my emphases.
4. Perry Anderson, *Lineages of the Absolutist State* (London: Verso, 1979), pp. 419–20.
5. David S. Landes, *The Wealth and Poverty of Nations* (London: Little, Brown, 1998), p. 523.
6. David S. Landes, *The Unbound Prometheus* (Cambridge: Cambridge University Press, 1969), p. 84; Charles P. Kindleberger, *World Economic Primacy* (Oxford: Oxford University Press, 1996), p. 132.
7. Landes, *Unbound Prometheus*, p. 39.
8. Marshall G. S. Hodgson, *The Venture of Islam*, III (Chicago: Chicago University Press, 1974) p. 197.
9. Eric L. Jones, *Growth Recurring* (Oxford: Clarendon Press, 1988), p. 13.
10. Ibid., p. 28.
11. Ibid., p. 80.
12. Cited in Arnold H. Rowbotham, 'The Impact of Confucianism on Seventeenth Century Europe', *The Far Eastern Quarterly* 4 (1) (1944), 227.
13. This and the next two references are from Adolf Reichwein, *China and Europe* (Taipei: Ch'eng-Wen Publishing Company, 1967), pp. 77, 78 and 79 respectively.
14. William W. Appleton, *A Cycle of Cathay* (New York: Columbia University Press, 1951), ch. 6; Reichwein, *China*, pp. 113–26; Hugh

354 NOTES TO PP. 196–201

Honour, *Chinoiserie: the Vision of Cathay* (London: John Murray, 1961), pp. 44–52, 125–74.

15. Lewis A. Maverick, *China A Model for Europe*, I (San Antonio, Texas: Paul Anderson, 1946), pp. 111–23; Martin Bernal, *Black Athena*, I (New York: Vintage, 1991), p. 172; Francesca Bray, *Science and Civilisation in China*, VI (2) (Cambridge: Cambridge University Press, 1984), p. 569.

16. J. J. Clarke, *Oriental Enlightenment* (London: Routledge, 1997), p. 49.

17. Kuo Hsiang cited in Colin A. Ronan, *The Shorter Science and Civilisation in China* (Cambridge: Cambridge University Press, 1978), p. 97.

18. Reichwein, *China*, pp. 101–9.

19. Basil Guy cited in Clarke, *Oriental Enlightenment*, p. 50.

20. Bernal, *Black Athena*, p. 198.

21. Sir William Temple cited in Michael Edwardes, *East–West Passage* (New York: Taplinger, 1971), p. 107.

22. Oliver Goldsmith cited in Bernal, *Black Athena*, p. 198.

23. The eighth earl of Elgin cited in Ronald Hyam, *Britain's Imperial Century 1815–1914* (London: Batsford, 1976), p. 37.

24. Jonathan Spence, *To Change China* (Boston: Little, Brown, 1969), p. 6.

25. Fernand Braudel, *Civilization and Capitalism, 15th–18th Century*, I (London: Collins, 1981), pp. 338–9.

26. Bernal, *Black Athena*, p. 172.

27. Maverick, *China*, pp. 13–14.

28. Leibniz cited in Bray, *Science*, VI (2), p. 569.

29. Maverick, *China*, pp. 41–59; Bernal, *Black Athena*, p. 199.

30. Bray, *Science*, VI (2), p. 570.

31. Maverick, *China*; Wolfgang Franke, *China and the West* (Oxford: Blackwell, 1967), ch. 4.

32. Donald F. Lach and Edwin J. Van Kley, *Asia in the Making of Europe*, III (Chicago: Chicago University Press, 1993), p. 1890; see also Clarke, *Oriental Enlightenment*, p. 40.

33. Bray, *Science* VI (2), p. 571.

34. See ibid., pp. 553–5, 558–9.

35. Ibid., pp. 581–3.

36. Robert Temple, *The Genius of China* (London: Prion Books, 1999), p. 20.

37. Bray, *Science*, VI (2), pp. 366–75; Joseph Needham and Wang Ling, *Science and Civilisation in China*, IV (2) (Cambridge: Cambridge University Press, 1965), p. 154.

38. Cited in Bray, *Science*, VI (2), p. 377.

39. Temple, *Genius*, pp. 23–5.

40. Ibid., p. 27.

41. Alvarez Semedo cited in Lach and Kley, *Asia*, p. 1595.

42. Tull's principles and the Chinese formula are reproduced in Bray, *Science*, VI (2), pp. 559, 560.

43. Bray, *Science*, VI (2), p. 571.

44. Ibid., p. 582.

45. Arnold Pacey, *The Maze of Ingenuity* (London: Allen Lane, 1974), p. 191.

46. Bray, *Science*, VI (2), pp. 429–33.

47. Alfred W. Crosby, *The Columbian Exchange* (Westport: Greenwood, 1972), ch. 5; Braudel, *Civilization*, I, pp. 158–71.

48. Kenneth Pomeranz, *The Great Divergence* (Princeton: Princeton University Press, 2000), pp. 57–8.

49. Stuart Piggott, *Ruins in a Land Scape* (Edinburgh: Edinburgh University Press, 1976), pp. 115, 124.

50. Pomeranz, *Great Divergence*, pp. 59–68.

51. Peter J. Golas, *Science and Civilisation in China*, V (13) (Cambridge: Cambridge University Press, 1999), pp. 285–7.

52. Robert Hartwell, 'Markets, Technology, and the Structure of Enterprise in the Development of the Eleventh-Century Chinese Iron and Steel Industry', *Journal of Economic History* 26 (1) (1966), 48.

53. Golas, *Science*, V (13), pp. 186, 336.

54. Needham and Ling, *Science*, IV (2), pp. 135–6, 225–8, 369–70, 387, 407–8, 411.

55. Pomeranz, *Great Divergence*, pp. 61–2.

56. Temple, *Genius*, pp. 65–6; Joseph Needham, Ho Ping-Yü, Lu Gwei-Djen and Wang Ling, *Science and Civilisation in China*, V (7) (Cambridge: Cambridge University Press, 1986), pp. 544–68.

57. Lynn White, *Medieval Technology and Social Change* (Oxford: Clarendon Press, 1962), p. 100.

58. Deane, *First Industrial Revolution*, p. 129.

59. Temple, *Genius*, p. 68.

60. Ibid., p. 49.

61. Needham in Mansel Davies, *A Selection from the Writings of Joseph Needham* (Lewes, Sussex: The Book Guild, 1990), p. 144.

62. Ahmad Y. al-Hassan and Donald R. Hill, *Islamic Technology* (Cambridge: Cambridge University Press, 1986), pp. 256–7.

63. Dharampal, *Indian Science and Technology in the Eighteenth Century* (Delhi: Impex, 1971), pp. 220–63.

64. Arnold Pacey, *Technology in World Civilization* (Cambridge, Mass.: MIT Press, 1991), p. 81.

65. Arun Kumar Biswas, 'Mineral and Metals in Medieval India', in A. Rahman (ed.), *History of Indian Science, Technology and Culture, AD 1000–1800* (New Delhi: Oxford University Press, 1999), p. 312, nn. 78–83.

66. Braudel, *Civilization*, I, p. 377.

67. Joel Mokyr, *The Lever of Riches* (New York: Oxford University Press, 1990), p. 221.

68. Dieter Kuhn, *Science and Civilisation in China*, V (9) (Cambridge: Cambridge University Press, 1988), p. 224.

69. A. P. Wadsworth and J. Mann, *The Cotton Trade and Industrial Lancashire 1600–1780* (Manchester: Manchester University Press, 1931), p. 106.

70. Pacey, *Technology*, pp. 103–7; Temple, *Genius*, pp. 120–1.

71. Kuhn, *Science*, V (9), pp. 428–33.

72. Denis Richards and Anthony Quick, *Britain 1714–1851* (London: Longmans, 1961), pp. 132–3.

73. Davies, *Selection*, p. 151.

74. Jones, *Growth Recurring*, p. 36.

75. Pacey, *Maze*, p. 190.
76. Braudel, *Civilization*, I, pp. 368, 370.
77. Temple, *Genius*, p. 54.
78. Joseph Needham, Wang Ling and Lu Gwei-Djen, *Science and Civilisation in China*, IV (3) (Cambridge: Cambridge University Press, 1971), pp. 420–2.
79. F. T. Evans summarised in Jones, *Growth Recurring*, pp. 18–19.
80. Richards and Quick, *Britain*, pp. 149–50.
81. Needham *et al.*, *Science*, IV (3), pp. 300–6, 359; Pacey, *Technology*, p. 6.
82. Jones, *Growth Recurring*, pp. 26, 27.

Notes to ch. 10

1. Gerard Delanty, *Inventing Europe* (London: Macmillan, 1995), p. 84.
2. George M. Frederickson, *Racism: a Short History* (Melbourne: Scribe Publications, 2002); James M. Blaut, *The Colonizer's Model of the World* (London: Guilford Press, 1993), p. 65.
3. Thierry Hentsch, *Imagining the Middle East* (Montreal, Quebec: Black Rose Books, 1992), pp. 112–13.
4. Samir Amin, *Eurocentrism* (London: Zed Books, 1989), p. 89.
5. Linda Tuhiwai Smith, *Decolonizing Methodologies* (London: Zed Books, 1999), p. 25.
6. John R. Mackenzie cited in Smith, *Decolonizing Methodologies*, p. 22.
7. See Victor G. Kiernan, *The Lords of Mankind* (New York: Columbia University Press, 1986 [1969]).
8. *The Edinburgh Review*, cited in C. Northcote Parkinson, *East and West* (London: John Murray, 1963), p. 196.
9. Lord Curzon cited in Parkinson, *East*, pp. 221–2.
10. John Stuart Mill cited in Ronald Hyam, *Britain's Imperial Century, 1815–1914* (London: Batsford, 1976), p. 55.
11. Hentsch, *Imagining*, pp. 107ff.
12. Martin Bernal, *Black Athena*, I (London: Vintage, 1991).

13. Denys Hay, *Europe: the Emergence of an Idea* (Edinburgh: Edinburgh University Press, 1957), p. 1.

14. John Campbell and Philip Sherrard, 'The Greeks and the West', in Raghavan Iyer (ed.), *The Glass Curtain Between Asia and Europe* (London: Oxford University Press, 1965), p. 71.

15. Bernal, *Black Athena*, chs. 4–8.

16. Ali Mazrui, *World Culture and the Black Experience* (Seattle: University of Washington Press, 1974), esp. pp. 38–81.

17. Blaut, *Colonizer's Model*, pp. 95–102.

18. Ibid., p. 96.

19. D. N. Livingstone, 'Climate's Moral Economy: Science, Race and Place in Post-Darwinian British and American Geography', in A. Godlewski and N. Smith (eds.), *Geography and Empire* (Oxford: Blackwell, 1994).

20. Philip D. Curtin, *The Image of Africa* (Madison: University of Wisconsin Press, 1964), pp. 65–6.

21. Hyam, *Britain's Imperial Century*, p. 37.

22. Michael Edwardes, *East–West Passage* (New York: Taplinger, 1971), p. 109.

23. William Dampier cited in Richard White, *Inventing Australia* (Sydney: Allen and Unwin, 1981), p. 3; see also Robert Hughes, *The Fatal Shore* (London: Harvill, 1996), p. 48.

24. Peter Cunningham cited in White, *Inventing*, p. 8.

25. Edward Long, *History of Jamaica*, cited in Homi K. Bhaba, *The Location of Culture* (London: Routledge, 1994), p. 91.

26. Raghavan Iyer, 'The Glass Curtain Between Asia and Europe', in R. Iyer (ed.), *The Glass Curtain Between Asia and Europe* (London: Oxford University Press, 1965), p. 20.

27. Dr James Hunt cited in Hyam, *Britain's Imperial Century*, p. 81.

28. George Orwell cited in Hyam, *Britain's Imperial Century*, p. 158.

29. Frederickson, *Racism*, ch. 2.

30. A. J. Christopher, *Colonial Africa* (Totowa: Barnes and Noble, 1984), p. 83.

31. David B. Abernethy, *The Dynamics of Global Dominance* (London: Yale University Press, 2000), p. 222.

32. Lord Palmerston cited in Hyam, *Britain's Imperial Century*, p. 39.

33. *Punch* (1849) cited in Richard Ned Lebow, *White Britain and Black Ireland* (Philadelphia: Institute for the Study of Human Issues, 1976), p. 40.

34. Marsden cited in Hughes, *Fatal Shore*, p. 188.

35. Linda Colley, *Britons: Forging the Nation 1707–1837* (New Haven: Yale University Press, 1992).

36. Colley, *Britons*, pp. 29–30.

37. Edward W. Said, *Orientalism* (London: Penguin, 1991 [1978]), p. 206, also p. 227.

38. See the summary discussion in: Curtin, *Image of Africa*; Ivan Hannaford, *Race: The History of an Idea in the West* (Baltimore: Johns Hopkins University Press, 1996); Michael Banton, *The Idea of Race* (London: Tavistock, 1977); Frederickson, *Racism*.

39. Benjamin Disraeli cited in Banton, *Idea of Race*, p. 25.

40. Joseph Chamberlain cited in White, *Inventing*, p. 71.

41. Lord Curzon cited in A. P. Thornton, *The Imperial Idea and its Enemies* (New York: St Martin's Press, 1966), p. 72.

42. James Lorrimer, *Institutes of the Law of Nations*, I (Edinburgh: Blackwood and Sons, 1883), pp. 10–12.

43. M. F. Lindley, *The Acquisition and Government of Backward Territory in International Law* (London: Longmans, Green, 1926), p. v.

44. John Westlake summarised in Said, *Orientalism*, pp. 206–7.

45. Mohammed Bedjaoui, 'Poverty of the International Order', in Richard Falk, Friedrich Kratochwil and Saul Mendlovitz (eds.), *International Law* (Boulder: Westview Press, 1985), p. 153.

46. Lord Carnarvon cited in Hyam, *Britain's Imperial Century*, p. 105.

47. Said, *Orientalism*, p. 216.

48. Ibid., pp. 207, 95.

49. Edward W. Said, 'Representing the Colonized: Anthropology's Interlocutors', *Critical Inquiry* 15 (1989), 216.

Notes to ch. 11

1. Dugald Stewart cited in Friedrich List, *The National System of Political Economy* (London: Longmans, Green, 1885), p. 120.

2. Peter Mathias, *The First Industrial Nation* (London: Methuen, 1983), p. 31.

3. Linda Weiss and John M. Hobson, *States and Economic Development* (Cambridge: Polity, 1995), p. 115.

4. *Economic Report of the President* (Washington, DC: United States Government Printing Office, 1996), p. 367.

5. J. V. Beckett and Michael Turner, 'Taxation and Economic Growth in Eighteenth Century England', *Economic History Review*, 43 (3) (1990), 377–403; Paul Gregory, *Russian National Income, 1885–1913* (Cambridge: Cambridge University Press, 1982), pp. 130–2, 193.

6. Albert H. Imlah, *Economic Elements in the Pax Britannica* (Cambridge, Mass.: Harvard University Press, 1958), p. 115.

7. John A. Hobson, *Imperialism* (London: George Allen and Unwin, 1968 [1902]), pp. 98–109.

8. J. V. Nye, 'The Myth of Free Trade Britain and Fortress France: Tariffs and Trade in the Nineteenth Century', *Journal of Economic History* 51 (1) (1991), 23–46.

9. D. C. M. Platt, *Finance, Trade, and Politics in British Foreign Policy 1815–1914* (Oxford: Clarendon Press, 1968), p. 87.

10. Platt, *Finance*, p. 89.

11. Sir Louis Mallet cited in Platt, *Finance*, p. 89.

12. P. G. M. Dickson, *The Financial Revolution in England* (London: St Martin's Press, 1967).

13. Imlah, *Economic Elements*, pp. 70–5; Phyllis Deane and W. A. Cole, *British Economic Growth 1688–1959* (Cambridge: Cambridge University Press, 1969), p. 37.

14. Paul A. Bairoch, 'International Industrialization Levels from 1750 to 1980', *Journal of European Economic History* 11 (2) (1982), 296; Angus Maddison, *Monitoring the World Economy* (Paris: OECD, 1995), pp. 30, 182–90.

15. Weiss and Hobson, *States*, pp. 118–19; P. K. O'Brien, 'The Impact of the Revolutionary and Napoleonic Wars, 1793–1815, on the Long-Run Growth of the British Economy', *Review* 12 (3) (1989), 349–50.

16. Calculated from Stefan Oppers, 'The Interest Rate Effect of Dutch Money in Eighteenth Century Britain', *Journal of Economic History* 53 (1) (1993), 25–43.

17. O'Brien, 'Impact', 346 and 345–57.

18. N. F. R. Crafts, *British Economic Growth during the Industrial Revolution* (Oxford: Clarendon Press, 1985), pp. 62–3; Weiss and Hobson, *States*, pp. 120–1.

19. Mathias, *First Industrial Nation*, pp. 32–3.

20. Joseph Inikori, 'Slavery and the Revolution in Cotton Textile Production in England', in J. E. Inikori and S. Engerman (eds.), *The Atlantic Slave Trade* (London: Duke University Press, 1992), ch. 6.

21. Kenneth Pomeranz, *The Great Divergence* (Princeton: Princeton University Press, 2000), p. 53.

22. Fernand Braudel, *Civilization and Capitalism, 15th–18th Century*, III (Berkeley: University of California Press, 1992), p. 522.

23. K. N. Chaudhuri, *The Trading World of Asia and the English East India Company 1660–1760* (Cambridge: Cambridge University Press, 1978), pp. 273ff.; Braudel, *Civilization*, III, pp. 566–7, 572.

24. A. P. Wadsworth and J. Mann, *The Cotton Trade and Industrial Lancashire, 1600–1780* (Manchester: Manchester University Press, 1931), pp. 124–8.

25. Arnold Pacey, *The Maze of Ingenuity* (London: Allen Lane, 1974), pp. 278–82.

26. Ha-Joon Chang, *Kicking Away the Ladder* (London: Anthem, 2002), p. 22.

27. Joseph E. Inikori, *Africans and the Industrial Revolution in England* (Cambridge: Cambridge University Press, 2002), pp. 151–5.

28. Braudel, *Civilization*, III, pp. 386–7.

29. P. K. O'Brien, 'The Foundations of European Industrialization: from the Perspective of the World', *Journal of Historical Sociology* 4 (3) (1991), 305, 311.

30. Richard Cobden cited in Ronald Hyam, *Britain's Imperial Century, 1815–1914* (London: Batsford, 1976), p. 56.

31. Cobden cited in Platt, *Finance*, p. 88.

32. Bowring cited in Eric Williams, *Capitalism and Slavery* (London: Andre Deutsch, 1944), p. 136.

33. John M. Hobson, 'Two Hegemonies or One? A Historical-Sociological Critique of Hegemonic Stability Theory', in P. K. O'Brien and A. Clesse (eds.), *Two Hegemonies* (Aldershot: Ashgate, 2002), esp. pp. 307–14.

34. Duke of Argyll cited in Hyam, *Britain's Imperial Century*, p. 66.

35. Chang, *Kicking Away the Ladder*.

36. Friedrich List, *National System*, pp. 189, 368.

37. Hyam, *Britain's Imperial Century*, p. 25.

38. Werner Schlote, *British Overseas Trade from 1700 to the 1930s* (Westport: Greenwood Press, 1952), pp. 172–3.

39. R. P. Dutt, *The Problem of India* (New York: International Publishers, 1943).

40. Horace Wilson (1845), cited in Peter Fryer, *Black People in the British Empire* (London: Pluto Press, 1988), p. 12.

41. Felipe Fernández-Armesto, *Millennium* (London: Black Swan, 1996), pp. 361, 367.

42. List, *National System*, chs. 8, 13.

43. Charles Kingsley cited in Hyam, *Britain's Imperial Century*, p. 106.

44. Pierre Clastres, 'On Ethnocide', *Art and Text* 28 (1988), 57.

45. Stanley Engerman, 'The Slave Trade and British Capital Formation in the Eighteenth Century: a Comment on the Williams Thesis', *Business History Review* 46 (1972), 430–43; Roger Anstey, 'The Volume and Profitability of the British Slave Trade, 1761–1807', in Stanley Engerman and Eugene Genovese (eds.), *Race and Slavery in the Western Hemisphere* (Princeton: Princeton University Press, 1975), pp. 3–31.

46. Barbara Solow, 'Caribbean Slavery and British Growth: the Eric Williams Hypothesis', *Journal of Development Economics* 17 (1985), 105.

47. William Darity, 'British Industry and the West Indies Plantations', in Inikori and Engerman, *Atlantic Slave Trade*, p. 256.

48. Anstey, 'Volume', p. 24. Note that he reckons slave trade profits at £200,000 pa and national income at £180 million.

49. Calculated from Deane and Cole, *British Economic Growth*, p. 34.

50. Calculated from Ronald Bailey, 'Africa, the Slave Trade, and the Rise of Industrial Capitalism in Europe and the United States', *American History: a Bibliographic Review* 2 (1986), 32.

51. P. K. O'Brien and S. L. Engerman, 'Exports and the Growth of the British Economy from the Glorious Revolution to the Peace of Amiens', in Barbara Solow (ed.), *Slavery and the Rise of the Atlantic System* (Cambridge: Cambridge University Press, 1991), p. 189.

52. Wadsworth and Mann, *Cotton Trade*, pp. 183–92; Inikori, *Africans*, pp. 372, 482.

53. Pomeranz, *Great Divergence*, p. 278.

54. Williams, *Capitalism*, pp. 98–102; Darity, 'British Industry', p. 257.

55. Inikori, *Africans*, p. 356.

56. Ibid., p. 361.

57. Darity, 'British Industry', p. 255.

58. Inikori, *Africans*, pp. 427–72.

59. Crafts, *British Economic Growth*, p. 145.

60. R. P. Thomas and D. N. McCloskey, 'Overseas Trade and Empire 1700–1860', in Roderick Floud and Donald McCloskey (eds.), *The Economic History of Britain Since 1700*, I (Cambridge: Cambridge University Press, 1981), p. 92.

61. O'Brien and Engerman, 'Exports', p. 189.

62. P. K. O'Brien, 'European Economic Development: the Contribution of the Periphery', *Economic History Review* 35 (1982), 1–18; O'Brien, 'Foundations', 303–6.

63. O'Brien, 'Foundations', 310–11.

64. O'Brien and Engerman, 'Exports', pp. 181–2.

65. Hyam, *Britain's Imperial Century*, p. 209.

66. Eric L. Jones, *The European Miracle* (Cambridge: Cambridge University Press, 1981), p. 83.

364 NOTES TO PP. 274–8

67. Pomeranz, *Great Divergence*, pp. 274–8.
68. Calculated from Hyam, *Britain's Imperial Century*, p. 322.
69. W. S. Jevons cited in Hyam, *Britain's Imperial Century*, pp. 47–8, my emphases.
70. Alec Hargreaves, 'European Identity and the Colonial Frontier', *Journal of European Studies* 12 (1982), 167.
71. Richard Broome, *Aboriginal Australians* (St Leonards, New South Wales: Allen and Unwin, 1982), p. 51; Henry Reynolds, *The Other Side of the Frontier* (Ringwood, Victoria: Penguin, 1982), pp. 122–3.
72. Henry Reynolds, *An Indelible Stain?* (Harmondsworth: Penguin, 2001), ch. 4.
73. See T. Barta, 'After the Holocaust: Consciousness of Genocide in Australia', *Australian Journal of Politics and History* 31 (1) (1984), 154–61.
74. E. Deas Thomson (1842) cited in Robert Hughes, *The Fatal Shore* (London: Harvill, 1996), p. 278.
75. Barta, 'After the Holocaust'; Colin Tatz, *Genocide in Australia* (Canberra: Aboriginal Studies Press, 1999); Reynolds, *Indelible Stain?*
76. Reynolds, *Indelible Stain?*, pp. 155–79.
77. Anne-Marie Willis, *Illusions of Identity* (Sydney, New South Wales: Hale and Iremonger, 1993), pp. 96–7.
78. Jeffrey G. Williamson, 'Why was British Growth so Slow during the Industrial Revolution?', *Journal of Economic History* 44 (1984), 687–712.
79. Weiss and Hobson, *States*, pp. 119–23; O'Brien and Engerman, 'Exports', pp. 193–209.
80. Lance Davis and Robert Huttenback, *Mammon and the Pursuit of Empire* (Cambridge: Cambridge University Press, 1988).
81. John M. Hobson, 'The Military Extraction Gap and the Wary Titan: The Fiscal Sociology of British Defence Policy, 1870–1913', *Journal of European Economic History* 22 (3) (1993), 463–73, 478–93. See also Niall Ferguson, 'Public Finance and National Security: the Domestic Origins of the First World War Revisited', *Past and Present* 142 (1994), 148–53.

82. Paul M. Kennedy, *The Realities Behind Diplomacy* (London: Fontana, 1989), p. 32, his emphasis.
83. Avner Offer, 'The British Empire, 1870–1914: a Waste of Money?', *Economic History Review* 46 (2) (1993), 215–38.
84. K. J. Holsti, *Peace and War* (Cambridge: Cambridge University Press, 1991), ch. 5.
85. Thomas and McCloskey, 'Overseas Trade', p. 100.

Notes to ch. 12

1. Cf. Graeme Gill, *The Nature and Development of the Modern State* (Basingstoke: Palgrave Macmillan, 2003), pp. 172–91.
2. Linda Weiss and John M. Hobson, *States and Economic Development* (Cambridge: Polity, 1995), p. 45.
3. Margaret Levi, *Of Rule and Revenue* (London: University of California Press, 1988), pp. 112, 115.
4. John D. Brewer, *The Sinews of Power* (London: Unwin Hyman, 1989), pp. 129–32.
5. C. B. A. Behrens, *The Ancien Régime* (London: Thames and Hudson, 1967), pp. 138–43.
6. J. C. Riley, *International Government Finance and the Amsterdam Capital Market 1740–1815* (Cambridge: Cambridge University Press, 1980).
7. Weiss and Hobson, *States*, p. 45.
8. Michael Mann, *The Sources of Social Power*, II (Cambridge: Cambridge University Press, 1993), p. 390, also pp. 450–2.
9. Max Weber, *Gessamelte Politische Schriften* (Tübingen: J. C. B. Mohr, 1988), pp. 126–7, 180–1, 230, 282, 377, 410. See also John M. Hobson and Leonard Seabrooke, 'Reimagining Weber: Constructing international society and the social balance of power', *European Journal of International Relations*, 7 (2) (2001), 239–74.
10. Adam Smith, *The Wealth of Nations* (New York: The Modern Library, 1937 [1776]).
11. Paul A. Bairoch, *Economics and World History* (Chicago: University of Chicago Press, 1993), p. 40.

12. Weiss and Hobson, *States*, ch. 4.

13. Colbert cited in E. H. Carr, *Nationalism and After* (London: Macmillan, 1945), p. 5.

14. John M. Hobson, *The Wealth of States* (Cambridge: Cambridge University Press, 1997); cf. John A. Hobson, *Imperialism: a Study* (London: George Allen and Unwin, 1968 [1902]), pp. 94–109.

15. Peter Flora, *State, Economy, and Society in Western Europe 1815–1975*, I (London: Macmillan, 1983), pp. 281–339. I have corrected his figures for Germany.

16. Hobson, *Wealth*, esp. pp. 19–20, 210–11.

17. E.g. Clive Trebilcock, *The Industrialization of the Continental Powers 1870–1914* (London: Longman, 1981); Alexander Gerschenkron, *Economic Backwardness in Historical Perspective* (Cambridge, Mass.: Harvard University Press, 1962).

18. James M. Blaut, *Eight Eurocentric Historians* (London: Guilford Press, 2000), p. 144.

19. Flora, *State*, pp. 96–151.

20. Ha-Joon Chang, *Kicking Away the Ladder* (London: Anthem, 2002), pp. 74–5.

21. Ibid., pp. 75–6.

22. Patricia Springborg, *Western Republicanism and the Oriental Prince* (Austin: University of Texas Press, 1992), p. 19.

Notes to ch. 13

1. Michael Mann, *The Sources of Social Power*, I (Cambridge: Cambridge University Press, 1986), p. 378.

2. Ibid., p. 404.

3. Jack Goody, *The East in the West* (Cambridge: Cambridge University Press, 1996), p. 8.

4. Lynn White, *Medieval Religion and Technology* (Berkeley: University of California Press, 1978), p. 80.

5. F. Oakley cited in Goody, *East*, p. 8.

6. Mann, *Sources*, I, ch. 1.

7. Andre Gunder Frank, *ReOrient* (Berkeley: University of California Press, 1998), pp. 335–6.

8. The phrase that Nathan Sivin attributes to the framework deployed by Joseph Needham; see Sivin, editor's introduction, in Joseph Needham and Lu Gwei-Djen, *Science and Civilisation in China*, VI (6) (Cambridge: Cambridge University Press, 2000), pp. 13–14. Pacey's term 'global dialogue' is also useful; Arnold Pacey, *Technology in World Civilization* (Cambridge, Mass.: MIT Press, 1991); cf. Jerry H. Bentley, *Old World Encounters* (New York: Oxford University Press, 1993).

9. Janet L. Abu-Lughod, *Before European Hegemony* (Oxford: Oxford University Press, 1989), pp. 18, 354.

10. Eric R. Wolf, *Europe and the People Without History* (Berkeley: University of California Press, 1982), p. 388, and pp. 385–91.

11. James M. Blaut, The *Colonizer's Model of the World* (London: Guilford Press, 1993), p. 208, n. 2.

12. E. P. Thompson, *The Poverty of Theory and Other Essays* (London: Merlin Press, 1978).

13. Frank, *ReOrient*, pp. xvi, xxvi; Kenneth Pomeranz, *The Great Divergence* (Princeton: Princeton University Press, 2000); Marshall G. S. Hodgson, *Rethinking World History* (Cambridge: Cambridge University Press, 1993).

14. Cf. David Abernethy, *The Dynamics of Global Dominance* (New Haven: Yale University Press, 2000), esp. ch. 10.

15. Edward W. Said, *Orientalism* (London: Penguin, 1991 [1978]), p. 2, his emphasis.

16. Mann, *Sources*, I, p. 531.

17. Pomeranz, *Great Divergence*; Blaut, *Colonizer's Model*.

18. Felipe Fernández-Armesto, *Millennium* (London: Black Swan, 1996), p. 345.

19. James Axtell, 'Colonial America without the Indians: Counterfactual Reflections', *Journal of American History* 73 (4) (1987), 984.

20. Fernández-Armesto, *Millennium*, pp. 365–7.

21. Goody, *East*, p. 7.

22. John M. Roberts, *The Triumph of the West* (London: BBC Books, 1985), p. 201.

23. David S. Landes, *The Wealth and Poverty of Nations* (London: Little, Brown, 1998), p. 514.

24. W. E. B. Du Bois, *Black Reconstruction in America* (New York: Russell & Russell, 1935), p. 722.

25. George G. M. James, *Stolen Legacy* (New York: Philosophical Library, 1954).

26. Henry Reynolds, *Black Pioneers* (London: Penguin, 2000), pp. 9–10.

27. Edward W. Said, Preface (2003), in *Orientalism* (London: Penguin, [1978] 2003), p. xxii.

Index